On Class, Race, and
Educational Reform

Also Available from Bloomsbury

Teacher Agency, Mark Priestley, Gert Biesta and Sarah Robinson
Peace Education, edited by Monisha Bajaj and Maria Hantzopoulos
Pedagogy of Resistance, Henry A. Giroux
Education for Critical Consciousness, Paulo Freire
Capitalism, Pedagogy, and the Politics of Being, Noah De Lissovoy
On Critical Pedagogy, 2nd edition, Henry A. Giroux
Critical Human Rights, Citizenship, and Democracy Education, edited by Michalinos Zembylas and André Keet
The Student Guide to Freire's "Pedagogy of the Oppressed," Antonia Darder
Pedagogy of the Oppressed, Paulo Freire

On Class, Race, and Educational Reform

Contested Perspectives

Edited by
Antonia Darder, Cleveland Hayes II, and Howard Ryan

BLOOMSBURY ACADEMIC
LONDON • NEW YORK • OXFORD • NEW DELHI • SYDNEY

BLOOMSBURY ACADEMIC

Bloomsbury Publishing Plc

50 Bedford Square, London, WC1B 3DP, UK

1385 Broadway, New York, NY 10018, USA

29 Earlsfort Terrace, Dublin 2, Ireland

BLOOMSBURY, BLOOMSBURY ACADEMIC and the Diana logo are trademarks of Bloomsbury Publishing Plc

First published in Great Britain 2023

Copyright © Antonia Darder, Cleveland Hayes II and Howard Ryan and contributors, 2023

Antonia Darder, Cleveland Hayes II, and Howard Ryan have asserted their right under the Copyright, Designs and Patents Act, 1988, to be identified as Editors of this work.

Cover design: Grace Ridge
Cover image © Bettmann / Getty Images

All rights reserved. No part of this publication may be reproduced or transmitted in any form or by any means, electronic or mechanical, including photocopying, recording, or any information storage or retrieval system, without prior permission in writing from the publishers.

Bloomsbury Publishing Plc does not have any control over, or responsibility for, any third-party websites referred to or in this book. All internet addresses given in this book were correct at the time of going to press. The author and publisher regret any inconvenience caused if addresses have changed or sites have ceased to exist, but can accept no responsibility for any such changes.

A catalogue record for this book is available from the British Library.

A catalog record for this book is available from the Library of Congress.

ISBN: HB: 978-1-3502-1238-1
PB: 978-1-3502-1237-4
ePDF: 978-1-3502-1239-8
eBook: 978-1-3502-1240-4

Typeset by Deanta Global Publishing Services, Chennai, India

To find out more about our authors and books visit www.bloomsbury.com and sign up for our newsletters.

Contents

List of Illustrations		vii
Editors' Preface *Antonia Darder, Cleveland Hayes, and Howard Ryan*		viii
Foreword *Stephen Brookfield*		xvii

Part I The Race-Class Debate in Education

1	Race, Class, and the Hidden Aims of School Reform *Howard Ryan*	3
2	Doing Class in Critical Race Analysis of Education *Michael J. Dumas*	54

Part II Responses from Marxist Perspectives

3	Centering the Oppressed: Marxism and the Question of Race and Class *Pranav Jani*	69
4	"Race," Class, and Education in South Africa *Salim Vally*	82
5	A Marxist Challenge to the Concept of "Race" *Antonia Darder and Rodolfo D. Torres*	91
6	Race, Class, and Accumulation in Education: A Decolonial Marxist Perspective *Noah De Lissovoy and Adam Martinez*	104
7	A Marxist Critical Realist Perspective on Social Class and "Race" *Alpesh Maisuria*	112
8	The Exigency of Radical Class Politics: A Personal Journey *Kevin D. Lam*	123

Part III Responses from Critical Race Theory and Allied Perspectives

9	Significance of a Race-Based Approach to Teacher Mobilization *Margarita Berta-Ávila*	135
10	Empire, Class, and the Struggle for Value in English Educational Reform *Christy Kulz*	147

11	The Wall of Whiteness and White Supremacy Persists: A Critical Race Response *Cleveland Hayes II*	159
12	Academic Laboring with Critical Social Theories in a Torus of Education Reform *Vonzell Agosto and Ericka Roland*	169
13	Capitalism and Caste *Christine Sleeter*	178
14	Critical Race Theory, Materialism, and Class *Ali Meghji and Tiger Chan*	186
15	Engaging Islamophobic Racism in the Classroom *Shirin Housee*	195
16	An Intersectional Reflection on Race, Class, and Education Reform *Nicholas D. Hartlep and Nicholas C. Ozment*	206

Afterword *Cheryl E. Matias*	217
Bibliography	222
List of Contributors	265
Index	269

Illustrations

Figures

12.1	A Static Image of a Torus	170
16.1	Schematic for Understanding Importance of Intersectionality	207

Tables

1.1	California Statewide Test Results, 2018	15

Editors' Preface

Antonia Darder, Cleveland Hayes, and Howard Ryan

When you have a conflict, that means that there are truths that have to be addressed on each side of the conflict. And when you have a conflict, then it's an educational process to try to resolve the conflict. And to resolve that, you have to get people on both sides of the conflict involved so that they can dialogue.

—Dolores Huerta (qtd. in Dawson 2017)

For more than a century, radical and progressive scholars and activists have grappled with making sense of questions linked to class, race, and educational reform, both in the United States and in other parts of the world. In the process of doing so, the battles between Marxists and critical race theorists, in particular, have resulted in positions that remain stubbornly inflexible, leaving little opportunity for substantive dialogue across perspectives. Consequently, differences and disagreements between these schools of thought and their contributions to what is, in fact, a shared political vision—to end racism and advocate for a genuinely democratic society—can seldom be discussed openly, in ways that might enhance our capacities to work, with respect and solidarity, across our divergent viewpoints. In fact, a recent article in *The Atlantic*, focused on the idea that "democracies don't try to make everyone agree," admonished scholars from both Marxist and critical race traditions as having one thing in common: "a tendency to see their own view of the world as the only valid one" (Applebaum 2021). Similarly, within educational circles, people seem to be "increasingly retreating into informational silos, rather than being able to be present with another point of view, hear it, weigh it against a personal perspective, and draw a conclusion" (Durvasula 2022). Bearing these concerns in mind, this book aims to engage scholars, students, and activists in the very necessary but contentious arenas of left thought and practice, particularly with respect to questions of class and race.

What most would agree with is that race and class both have profound implications across education and the society at large, as many of the contributors to this book confirm. The pertinent inequalities and exclusions bear upon all fields and institutions across society, while interacting with a myriad of other categories by which people define themselves, create hierarchies, and struggle for social justice (e.g., ethnicity, nationality, caste, gender, sexuality, faith). Our particular concern, as social justice practitioners, activists, and educators, is how our competing ideas about race and class seem to perpetually foment contestations on the left, rendering us less politically effective and, thus, making it more difficult to find the common direction and solidarity that is fundamental to social transformation. A unifying framework or, as Paulo Freire (1997) advocated, *unity within diversity*, will perhaps not come easily—given that even the three co-editors here have divergent views. However, as Dolores Huerta's words, above, suggest, we wholeheartedly agree that dialogue is a political necessity in our struggle to advance social justice and radical possibilities for democratic life.

The Book's Origin

On Class, Race, and Educational Reform: Contested Perspectives has its genesis in a paper written by a graduate student and long-time community and labor organizer Howard Ryan. Ryan, like many others, was shocked by the US presidential election of Donald Trump in 2016. How could such a fierce bigot win such hefty voter support? In search of answers and with a sense of deep urgency, Ryan initiated a study of race and racial theory, relying on the large race collection of the library at Philadelphia's Temple University. If America has hardly progressed on race since the rightward turn of the Reagan years, some insights and answers as to why might be found in the left/progressive scholarship. And perhaps from there, those on the left could fashion better strategies in the future.

Ryan did find many insights in the literature. But what struck him most was the extent to which many scholars adopted positions founded on a belief in race primacy—that is, made race their central category for explaining the nature of society and power relations within it. As a Marxist, Ryan had his own assumption, embracing the primacy of class. Nevertheless, he appreciated those scholars who tangled with the tensions between race-based and class-based thought, as in the works of critical race theorist Zeus Leonardo (2012, 2013). One takeaway was that the contestation between race and class may, in fact, constitute the *central* historic challenge for the left in the United States, and similarly in other countries. He further reasoned that the left's capacity to find answers for Trumpism had to be grounded in a critical engagement with the race-class nexus, and one that was undertaken in a more comprehensive and dialogic way than has been typical in the left's long history of relevant debate.

Ryan's intent, similar to the purpose of this book, has been to open up a scholarly conversation on the left, with his paper as a step in that process. The paper does not attempt a comprehensive or unified theory of race and class, which would be too ambitious a task. Rather, it focuses on a specific policy arena in which race and class come to bear—that of school reform. Notably since the 1980s, school reform has become synonymous with the corporate-led regime of high-stakes testing and privatization that dominates K-12 education in the United States, as well as globally (Saltman and Means 2019). One of the reform's major impacts has been to exacerbate educational inequities, partly because test-based schooling does not address the wider societal inequities that affect school performance and test scores (Au 2009). In the United States, these inequities are sharply racial. Thus, white students have been passing state tests in California at roughly double the rate of Black and Latino students (Cano and

Hong 2020). A common thesis among progressive education scholars influenced by critical race theory (CRT), in the United States and the United Kingdom, posits white supremacy as the primary driver of school reform (Gillborn 2013; Au 2015). Ryan (2016), however, drawing on his previous investigation into school reform, challenges this race-based interpretation and proposes instead a class-based interpretation that sees such reform primarily as a capitalist project. His hope was that a concrete focus on school reform, while pitting his own Marxist interpretation of the phenomenon against that of critical race scholars, might help facilitate a more wide-ranging dialogue on race and class.

After drafting the paper, Ryan reached out in search of collaborators. He found his first working partner in Antonia Darder, an international Freirean scholar and Marxist, who years earlier had co-authored a seminal critique of CRT in the book *After Race: Racism after Multiculturalism* (Darder and Torres 2004). In considering how to move forward, Darder and Ryan envisioned an anthology that would launch with Ryan's paper—Chapter 1 of this volume—followed by responses from theorists aligned with critical race, Marxist, and allied perspectives. They identified many interested contributors, including those from the UK, South Africa, and Germany. One of the contributors was education professor and critical race scholar Cleveland Hayes, who had co-edited *Unhooking from Whiteness: The Key to Dismantling Racism in the United States* (Hayes and Hartlep 2013). Hayes agreed to become the third co-editor for the book. Despite the conceptual differences at work in our readings of class, race, and school reform, the three editors brought two important points of agreement to the table. First, there is a dire need to find ways to promote and enact critical dialogues across various perspectives on the left; and second, there is a need for a book that provides a vehicle for stimulating dialogues within the classroom, communities, and movement organizations.

Race and Class Debates within Movement and Political Contexts

While often the subject of scholarly exchange—as with the Marxism/CRT discussions in the education field—the race-class debate has a significant presence and impact across a wide range of movements and political contexts. One significant historic context is that of the US Black movement of the 1960s and early 1970s. In the mid-1960s that movement saw a split between traditional civil rights groups, such as the NAACP and Martin Luther King Jr.'s Southern Christian Leadership Conference, and a younger generation of activists that comprised the Student Nonviolent Coordinating Committee (SNCC). SNCC, led by Stokely Carmichael in 1966–7, broke from the civil rights emphasis on integration, nonviolence, and partnerships within the Democratic Party, and instead called for Black power, Black political independence, and a fundamental challenge to the "colonial white power structure" (Carmichael and Hamilton 1967: 22). During that same era, in 1966, the Black Panther Party for Self-Defense was founded in Oakland, California, by Huey P. Newton and Bobby Seale. As a revolutionary organization with an ideology of Black nationalism, socialism, and armed self-defense, particularly against police brutality, the Black Panthers were most fundamentally engaged in radical national and international political projects that kept issues of race and class central to Black liberation.

The Black movement's divisions were more complicated than simply one of race versus class (Carson 1992; Ransby 2003), despite the importance of that dimension. It is interesting to note that when Bayard Rustin (1966: 40), an ally of King, denounced Black power for its alleged isolationism, he did so in class terms, highlighting the need for a "liberal-labor-civil rights coalition" fighting for a proposed Freedom Budget that would end poverty for all, regardless of race. Political scientist Charles Hamilton, who co-authored *Black Power* with Carmichael in 1967, answered Black power's critics in an afterword to the book's 1992 edition. Historically, Blacks have always understood the class dimension of the political struggle, he writes, but all too often their coalition efforts were thwarted. In the Populist era of the 1890s, for example, "it was not blacks . . . who disdained class alliances; it was whites, leaders and followers" (Hamilton 1992: 206). While Blacks supported organized labor, Hamilton adds, racist union locals denied membership to Blacks and excluded them from apprenticeships.

Race/class divisions hindered one of the Black movement's most promising projects—the League of Revolutionary Black Workers, which was active in the Detroit auto industry and beyond from 1968 to 1973. The league grappled with internal struggles between a cohort of Marxist-Leninists, who favored collaboration with white workers and supporters, and the majority of league activists and contacts, who gravitated to Black nationalism. The nationalists rejected a strategy of alliance with white workers and declined to study Marxism, saying that "Marx and Lenin were white and not relevant" (qtd. in Geschwender 1977: 178).

The race-class debate has since remained front and center in US left politics. In 2016, during Senator Bernie Sanders's first presidential bid, an Iowa Black and Brown Forum asked the candidate if he supported Black reparations for slavery. He replied that he did not, contending that the chances of getting reparations through Congress were "nil," and that it would be "very divisive." He offered instead an economic program reflecting his class politics—investment in cities, decent-paying jobs, free higher education (cited in Coates 2016a). Respected author and reparations advocate Ta-Nehisi Coates promptly countered that Sanders was embracing class at the expense of race:

> Raising the minimum wage doesn't really address the fact that black men without criminal records have about the same shot at low-wage work as white men with them; nor can making college free address the wage gap between black and white graduates. Housing discrimination, historical and present, may well be the fulcrum of white supremacy. Affirmative action is one of the most disputed issues of the day. Neither are addressed in the "racial justice" section of Sanders's platform. (Coates 2016a)
>
> If class-based policy alone is insufficient to banish racism in Europe, why would it prove to be sufficient in a country founded on white supremacy? (2016b)

Sanders would soften his reparations stance during his second presidential bid four years later: if Congress passed a bill commissioning a study of reparations, he would of course sign it, he said (Crowe 2019). The class and race tensions, as woven in the remarks of Coates, however—uplifting Blacks versus uplifting all—have never been adequately explored by the left.

A similar issue confronts the US left amidst the Covid-19 pandemic. In April 2020, after Senator Elizabeth Warren and other progressives called for special focus on the particular pandemic risks in low-income communities of color (Morrison 2020), Adolph Reed (2020), one of America's foremost Marxist scholars, criticized such calls as an expression of "disparity ideology" that overlooks the systemic flaws in capitalist health care. If our concern is to combat health-care inequalities, he reasoned, "it is not at all clear that the 'blacks have it worse' trope does us much good. The problem lies in the irrationality and injustice of a for-profit healthcare system and its market-driven rationing of access to care." The AfroSocialist Caucus in Democratic Socialists of America took objection: "In Reed's opinion, are we ever allowed to talk about race?" Reed's posture, minimizing the effects of racism, "only hurts our ability to build a multiracial movement that takes class politics as seriously as it does race politics," the caucus argued (DSA AfroSocialist 2020).

In some circumstances, the left's posture on the race-class debate can bear profoundly on a nation's future. Such was the case in South Africa during the height of the anti-apartheid movement in the 1980s, a period that also witnessed an active labor movement. Some labor leaders and leftists wanted the anti-apartheid movement to incorporate socialist, along with racial equality, goals. Anti-apartheid's lead organization, the African National Congress, declined. Socialism would be pursued at a later stage, it was proposed; the task in the present was overturning the white regime and winning constitutional democracy and protections for human rights through the Black vote. As both Ryan and Salim Vally assert in this volume (in Chapters 1 and 4, respectively), putting questions of socialism and class on hold did not bode well for the country's majority-Black working class in the post-apartheid era.

The global left still struggles to find a theorization or practice that effectively integrates issues of class and capitalism with race and grapples equally with multiple other identities and social structures that define our lives. Three decades after Kimberlé Crenshaw (1989) introduced intersectionality, a framework now widely employed by scholars and activists, the left remains far from having an agreed way of making sense of the world or guiding us forward. Two Canadian authors ask, "What is to become of us after our gender, race, class, sexuality, disability, and more intersect? What is being socially constituted by these identity lines crisscrossing and intersecting each other?" (Mojab and Carpenter 2019: 277). Our hope is that this volume's inquiry into race and class, as well as the policy terrain of school reform, can support those engaged in the larger struggle for social justice, both in theory and practice.

Scope and Structure of the Book

The volume begins with Ryan's feature chapter, "Race, Class, and the Hidden Aims of School Reform." The chapter poses the question: Who is ultimately driving reform and toward what ends? It investigates two competing answers—white supremacy and capitalism—and argues for the latter by tracing the genesis of US and then global school reform, connecting both to a corporate-led rightward turn that began in the 1970s. The chapter theorizes about the relationship between capitalism and racism in the context of school reform. It urges us all to articulate our grand theories of the world that inform how we think about education. A final section reflects on race and class more generally, including an inquiry into South Africa's anti-apartheid movement and post-apartheid challenges that are also relevant in other contexts.

In Chapter 2, critical race educator Michael J. Dumas makes a case for CRT becoming as critical about class as it is about race. Originally published in the *Handbook of Critical Race Theory in Education* (Lynn and Dixson 2013)—and we thank Routledge for permission to reprint it—the chapter was specifically written for an audience of critical race scholars. Dumas's chapter is situated immediately after Ryan's because it best speaks to many of the issues raised in the volume. His exploration of the tensions between Marxism and CRT, and past debates between them, is one of the most nuanced and outstanding treatments in print, suggesting strengths and weaknesses in both frameworks. With respect to Marxism, Dumas writes, "To say that Marxian theory addresses race is not to say that it addresses it in a manner or to the extent that critical race scholars believe necessary."

The next fourteen chapters, across the two sections that follow, are responses to Ryan's chapter. Contributors in Part II provide responses from Marxist readings of Ryan's work. In Part III, contributor responses bring to bear critical race, intersectionality, and critical social theory, as well as critical ethnic studies perspectives. The volume's main "conversation"—Ryan's argument and fourteen responses—generates a rich range of themes and points to the many further conversations that deserve attention as part of any political project on the left.

One familiar theme is that of competing primacies where, for example, Margarita Berta-Ávila (Chapter 9) considers Ryan's class primacy "troublesome" and offers that centering race is essential in teacher preparation, teacher/faculty unionism, and mobilizing with communities of color. Cleveland Hayes II (Chapter 11), Ali Meghji and Tiger Chan (Chapter 14), Shirin Housee (Chapter 15), and Nicholas Hartlep and Nicholas Ozment (Chapter 16) all contend that race and class are both important but argue the salience of beginning firstly with issues of racial equality, strategically speaking. Pranav Jani (Chapter 3) brings a unique angle through contesting Ryan's class primacy but doing so as a Marxist and describing how a rigid class primacy led to the subordination of members of color in the socialist organization he belonged to for many years. Another thesis—advanced by Christy Kulz (Chapter 10), Vonzell Agosto and Ericka Roland (Chapter 12), and Christine Sleeter (Chapter 13)—not only rejects the primacy of class or capitalism but also rejects all primacies. Here, primacy between categories is viewed as lacking nuance or sensitivity to specific locales and circumstances, or as producing new forms of hierarchy that undermine progressive and democratic goals.

Questions about primacy spill over into wider questions about how we think and theorize generally. Agosto and Roland, Kulz, and Sleeter all take objection to Ryan's call for grand theory, partly for its alleged Eurocentricity. In this regard, Sleeter calls Marxism to task: "Marxists (who in my experience are overwhelmingly white) tend to position their analysis as a totalizing framework, even while traditional Marxism does not speak to racism, caste, patriarchy, colonialism." Agosto and Roland challenge Marxism in similar terms, as do Meghji and Chan, with all citing Cedric Robinson's influential *Black Marxism: The Making of the Black Radical Tradition* (2000). Robinson's work, it should be noted, has been quite central to race/class and primacy discussions across the left (see Kelley 2016), although interpretation of his work itself remains in dispute. In this volume, for example, Ryan problematizes Robinson's apparent dismissal of class struggle.

For the contributors who object to grand theory, the alternative is to engage multiple theories. Agosto and Roland believe such an approach was implied in the Combahee River Collective's 1977 Black feminist statement:

> Similar to how the Combahee River Collective's liberation praxis extended from and merged Black feminist and Marxist analysis to address issues pertaining to race, class, gender, and sexual orientation simultaneously, we consider addressing the compoundness of race and class by the way of multiply integrated theories. Instead of solely relying on a grand theory to understand race and class, we advocate that educators, researchers, and activists collaborate and cycle through multiple theories across various traditions.

Kulz connects these theoretical disputes to interpretations of school reform, where she believes that Ryan, through his application of grand theory, has misconstrued and oversimplified the underlying forces in England's reform:

> Ryan seems determined to designate class, rather than race, as the primary driver of the hidden aims of educational reforms. I will question the usefulness of this task by using this chapter to trace the mutual formation of race and class through empire and capitalism, and connect this to the historical specificities of the English educational landscape.

One final theme, raised by several of the Marxist contributors, concerns the left's engagement of race. Salim Vally (Chapter 4), Antonia Darder and Rodolfo Torres (Chapter 5), and Kevin Lam (Chapter 8) contest the left's unproblematic acceptance of "race," a social invention, which may ultimately impede our capacity to challenge and transform racisms. As such, Darder and Torres grapple with Ryan's chapter through offering a Marxist challenge to the analytical category of "race," calling for an incisive examination of racism within a larger anti-capitalist project for socialist reform. Moreover, they argue for the importance of an analysis that focuses "on the manner in which the logic of capital and the primacy of class fuel racism, in contrast to an analysis that focuses on the socially constructed and fictitious phenotypical category of 'race,' an idea grounded in an oppressive dualistic epistemology that ultimately bolsters conditions of racialized oppression." With similar concerns, Alpesh Maisuria (Chapter 7) calls for a critical realist perspective on social class and "race," while Noah De Lissovoy and Adam Martinez (Chapter 6) argue for a decolonizing Marxist perspective in analyses of race, class, and accumulation in education.

Toward Living the Book's Purpose

We see the primary audience for this book as those readers who seek to move toward more meaningful, actionable, and transformative dialogues about issues of class inequalities, racism, and educational reform. This is to say, there is a need to move toward a praxis of critical dialogue that can drive social justice agendas with the political power necessary to eliminate educational inequities. For undergraduate and graduate students whose studies engage questions of race, class, and education, we hope this book will move them away from the tendency toward siloed conversations, in ways that can help them appreciate more deeply the differences and contributions of different discourses of scholars who are uncompromisingly committed to a vision of economic democracy and social equality across all communities.

Toward that end, the different response chapters speak to important issues and concerns spurred on by their reading of Ryan's chapter. Some chapters argue for a class-centered analysis of the issues, while others argue for a race-centered approach, and still others argue for the equal importance of a combined race and class intersectional approach in educational debates. In this way, the responses of contributors move widely across the class-to-race spectrum, which permits readers to consider fundamental differences at work in the analyses offered and the urgencies that compel particular responses. This opens the way for dialogues that allow researchers, students, and activists to engage important questions about various conditions of racialized and class inequalities—past, present, and future—with respect to both the potential contributions to and limitations of each of these perspectives in our ongoing struggles for liberation. This seems a truly worthy undertaking; for if we are to achieve genuine conditions of social justice in education, we must begin to examine together the impact of our differing perspectives in our scholarship and how we live our politics out in the world. Another important aim of this book, then, is to provide readers with a starting place for authentic and courageous conversations across our multidimensional understandings of the inequalities and oppressions that exist within schools and societies.

Building Political Solidarity across Differences

Most importantly, this volume seeks to speak to a dire need for activists, educators, and scholars on the left to build genuine solidarity—first and foremost, built upon our diversely collective and unapologetic political commitments to a radically democratic vision of the world, where educational justice is the lived experience of all students and others engaged in their education. We also hope that the contributions in this volume, which daringly cut across epistemological boundaries tied to race, class, and intersectionality, can serve as an example for coalition building across our many differences. Such coalitions can provide significant avenues for cultivating much-needed political solidarity in the realm of educational reform efforts, as well as for deepening our creative responses to many of the recalcitrant conditions of racism we face in the world today.

Moreover, Davidson, Fielden, and Omar (2010) posit that the social support such solidarity building can offer must be understood as a multidimensional construct with a number of key facets. Two facets are particularly necessary in these difficult times. First is emotional (or affective) support, which involves intangible caring, acceptance, and respect for each of us committed to this long-standing struggle for justice. Second is instrumental (or behavioral) support which involves tangible assistance, in the form of financial support, sharing of information, knowledge, and providing mentorship and advice. What all this suggests is that only through a willingness to extend genuine support to one another (rather than demonizing one another for our different points of view) can we begin to consciously, respectfully, and deliberately labor together for change—moving beyond an academic culture of competition and rewards and punishment that stifles radical movements for change. It is, as Freire (1971) so often reminded us, only through open and coherent dialogue, grounded in a deep sense of love for the world and one another, that we may come to challenge and dismantle together the true culprit of the oppressive divisions manufactured in our societies—a racializing global economic system that strips us all of our dignity and unmercifully erodes the preciousness of life in the world.

Foreword

Stephen Brookfield

I came of age as a white man in the UK in the 1960s and, though not considered smart enough to go to university, I eventually enrolled at a newly created college of technology. Like so many of my friends, I assumed a socialist stance politically and thought a lot about the possibilities for the much-vaunted student-worker alliance. When not a student, I worked on the shop floor, on various assembly lines in auto parts or food manufacturing companies, where the primacy of class analysis was accepted as truth.

In 1982 I moved to the United States and, even though I lived and worked in New York, I was surprised at the ideological absence of that analysis, even at Teachers College, Columbia University, where I was a junior professor. I had imagined Columbia as a hotbed of student radicalism; but, even though John Dewey's bust and presence were all over the halls of academe, it was clear that the ideological myth of the United States as a classless meritocracy was firmly embedded in what I had thought of as a progressive institution.

Interestingly, however, my students asked a lot of questions about race. I had grown up with a pretty standard analysis of the effects of British (or, more accurately, English) imperialism, was familiar with Marx on the Irish question, and viewed racial oppression as a by-product of the capitalist need to search for raw materials, develop new markets, and secure free or cheap labor. Materialist determinism appeared to account neatly for my world and, although the feminist theorizing I had been exposed to had challenged the singularity of class analysis, I still nested patriarchy within Marxism.

But in my classes at Teachers College, Black, Indigenous, People of Color (BIPOC) students would ask me questions about how I responded to their contributions—or rather, why I *didn't* respond to them. I was in that stage of white racial identity development where I felt that demonstrating racial solidarity meant I should self-censor my voice as a white person. I was very much the self-satisfied white man congratulating himself on his supposed racial sensitivity, on creating spaces for previously suppressed voices. That lasted until students pointed out to me that my lack of teacher response signified to them that either I didn't think their contributions were good enough to warrant a response or that I had simply not been listening.

In the 1990s and 2000s I team-taught several courses in Chicago with two African American women—Scipio Colin Jr. III and Elizabeth Peterson—who considered themselves, respectively, an Afrocentric theorist and a critical race theorist. During that time, it became very clear that the majority of our African American students saw life overwhelmingly, sometimes exclusively, in racial terms. I vividly remember one African American woman stressing to me, "Stephen, you have to know that I see *everything* through the lens of race." This created a new problem for me as both a scholar and a teacher which, in an uncritical way, I posed as: "How do I get these students to understand that racial oppression is a by-product of capitalism and that class analysis remains the central point of analysis?" It was a response that showed I had *not* learned the lesson Marcuse had tried to teach regarding the slavish, repetitive, and ultimately uncritical invocation of Marxist concepts and slogans that he witnessed leftist activists and educators slipping into. He railed against "the distortion and falsification of Marxian theory through its *ritualization*" (1972: 33). By mechanically repeating a basic vocabulary—*proletariat*, *exploitation*, and *impoverishment* were some examples he gave—critically inclined activists only ensured "a petrification of Marxian theory into a rhetoric with hardly any relation to reality" (p. 34). Not only does this jargon petrify Marxism, it also ensures that educators and activists actually undercut the possibility of their reaching many of those they are trying to teach, whether in the workplace, classroom, or social movements.

This book explores the intersections and sometimes contradictions of class and racial analysis and their impacts of practice. As someone who has worked in predominantly white communities, workplaces, classrooms, and organizations attempting to help white people understand that being white constitutes a racial identity, I have become all too aware of these issues. One of the most frequent and predictable responses around racial analysis that emerges from white working-class students is to resent the idea that racial oppression exists as a separate category of analysis. There is a particular repugnance evident when the presence of white supremacy as a dominant ideology is introduced into the discussion. White students, especially white working-class students, are often highly resistant to the notion that their racial identity gives them any kind of advantage, power, or privilege, saying things like "no one gave me anything"; "people have always looked down on dirt-poor families like mine"; "I have to work three jobs, get no benefits, my car don't work, we have to go hungry and decide between food or heat—how the fuck can you say I have White privilege or unearned advantage?" It often feels like my identifying white supremacy as a dominant American ideology (along with capitalism, patriarchy, democracy as majority vote, and militarism) only serves to impede the development of alliances based on a perception of common interests.

In an analogous manner, when I try to introduce intersectionality with students and colleagues of color, there is often the sense that they believe that I'm delegitimizing the significance of racial identity by viewing it as only one factor among many important axes of oppression. The sentiment, "I see *everything* through the lens of race," cannot be wished away. Colleagues of color will frequently tell me that their class position has *nothing* to do with racism; or rather, that it's not a necessary correlate of oppression. They can be solidly middle or even upper class, firmly located within the bourgeoisie, in the top 10 percent of earners in the United States, yet their racial identity trumps all economic and class indicators. They will be stopped while driving their own car. If they are tenured professors with fine academic reputations, they will be assumed to occupy their positions because of unjustifiable affirmative action policies. If they are seen fumbling with locks while entering their own houses, they will be seen as burglars.

In December 2015 the eminent philosopher George Yancy wrote a letter, published in the *New York Times* philosophy column, "The Stone." Titled "Dear White America," the piece was framed as a gift inviting whites to consider their often-unacknowledged collusion in a white supremacist system. But for George it was the start of a vicious and sustained assault unleashed on him that continues to this day. Death threats were among the consequences and being called "a fucking racist . . . a piece of shit destroying the youth of this country . . . a fucking smug nigger . . . a fucking animal" (Yancy 2018: 36–7) (all from one voicemail) became his new normal. His endowed chair, his academic titles, his reputation as a nationally known public intellectual all mean nothing when he dares to point out racial realities in the contemporary United States.

How, then, do we respond to these dual analytical frameworks when the need for social movements, new political parties, and multiracial, multigender, and class alliances is so important in the face of right-wing attempts to manipulate the political system? A precondition of any alliance building and development of movements is a commitment to political interests that unite particular identities and sectional interests in the pursuit of a shared project. This is one reason why whites need to realize that it is in their own self-interest to challenge white supremacy. Paradoxically, however, for a movement to endure beyond the pursuit of specific tactical and strategic goals, and to become a project of societal, economic, and political transformation, an acknowledgment and appreciation of differences, divergence, and dissent within its own community is crucial.

So any activist, leader, organizer, or educator is sooner or later faced with the choice of whether or not to acknowledge the normality of white supremacy and view race as a singular component of identity that sometimes outweighs the significance of class in an intersectional understanding. CRT posits the importance of narratives and counter stories in challenging white supremacy, and there is no doubt that many BIPOC see race as an identifier that transcends class. How, then, do we build a broad coalition that encompasses this variety of perspective?

One response, of course, is to initiate the kind of continuous dialogue this book is encouraging. Another is to acknowledge the fact that we cannot talk of "race" as if racial identity confers a particular worldview. Talking in broad terms about the African or Asian diasporas, Latinx interests, or an Indigenous perspective runs the risk of distorting the incredible complexity of positionality, culture, and viewpoint present among those groups. Racism and its ideological handmaiden of white supremacy legitimizes structural inequities around poverty, so at some point the building of a working-class movement across racial differences requires that the destructive potential of racist divisions be addressed.

Yet we also need to take white working-class perspectives seriously and not reflexively dismiss white complaints that view affirmative action policies as the practice of a reverse racism designed to disempower white people. To tell someone straight off the bat that such a viewpoint is evidence of how successfully they have been politically duped and ideologically manipulated means they will likely view you as one of the "elites" that the corporate leaders funding Trumpism have warned them against. The European American Collaborative Challenging Whiteness (2010) has done an excellent job of laying out the missteps made by overzealous white anti-racist educators, with respect to their habits of preaching and disdaining. Preaching occurs when those running anti-racist training give voice to a wish for white sinners to confess their anti-racist sins and request absolution. Disdaining happens when white educators become obsessed with displaying their enlightened racial cognizance and persistently seek to point out the errors of their less enlightened colleagues' ways. The ECCW warns that communicating any hint of smugness or greater racial sophistication is likely to lead to the rejection of anti-racist efforts.

From the perspective of a white educator trying to work in an anti-racist way in a multitude of different, predominantly white, contexts (higher and adult education, hospitals, churches, the military, community groups, etc.), a few critical presumptions are always at the forefront of my mind. Together, these constitute a heuristic that guides how we plan and conduct at least the initial stages of anti-racist work, particularly within a predominantly white space. First, anyone leading such efforts must model their own ongoing struggles with "race" and not hold themselves out as a fully formed, idealized, anti-racist educator. Before you ask others to examine the ways they have internalized, and continue to support, white supremacy, you need to talk about how you continue to struggle with your own learned racism, how you enact microaggressions, and how you (often unwittingly) support the white supremacist structures you move through every day.

Second, it's important to work, as early as possible, on clarifying what you mean by racism and white supremacy as *systemic* phenomena. Pedagogically this is one of the hardest tasks to negotiate, given the determinedly individualist culture of both higher education and American society. Moving from an understanding of racism as acts of individual meanness that can be eradicated through the application of moral will to a structural analysis takes time and is usually resisted. As Kendi (2019) points out, talking about racism as structural or systemic should be redundant; after all, that's its nature. However, the idea of racism as an individual moral failing is so strong that constantly emphasizing its structural nature becomes crucial. As Sullivan (2014) describes, a common way for whites to avoid dealing with race is to revert to a color-blind perspective and proclaim their personal moral innocence.

Third, narrative—both digital or textual (Hess 2019), and in the form of vocalized personal testimony (Solomon and Rankin 2019)—is a more accessible point of initial entry into class and racial analysis for many than beginning with theory, structural analysis, or the presentation of statistical data illustrating structural inequity. A personal story dramatizes and concretizes the structural contradictions of capitalism in a way that can serve to illustrate difficult theoretical understandings. This is, of course, a central tenet of CRT (Delgado and Stefancic 2017). Begin with a story, featuring a strong voice and a powerful counternarrative, and you'll draw people in at a visceral, emotional, somatic level.

Finally, conversations around race can stall very quickly as people become defensive, try to close some perspectives down, and perceive emotions to be running high. But righteous anger, tears, raised voices—as well as so-called "awkward" silences—are all part and parcel of talking about race and intersectional oppression. So people need to lose their preconceptions of "good" conversations as being those where things stay on an emotional even keel and everyone leaves feeling good about what was shared. Real conversations about racial identity are rarely calm or cool. Rather, they are animated, yet also feature long silences.

They are also best facilitated in teams that are comprised of activists and educators with and informed by different racial and other identities and positionalities. In many ways this book is an example of exactly that type of process in action, featuring authors and perspectives of varying standpoints united by a common concern to clarify the nature of oppression. A necessary element in developing a racialized view on the world is the awareness that one's consciousness is always particular. This requires you to stop universalizing your own experience and appreciate that others move through the world in a fundamentally different way based on how their racial identity is perceived. As you move through the pages ahead you will be inspired and challenged to question your experiences by the vigorous exchanges you encounter.

Part I

The Race-Class Debate in Education

1

Race, Class, and the Hidden Aims of School Reform

Howard Ryan

I begin this examination of race, class, and school reform with several purposes. One is to make a certain argument, challenging the "retreat from class" (Wood 1998) that has characterized much of the global left in the neoliberal era. Another is to grow politically as I study issues of race, class, and education. And a third is to invite a progressive dialogue on the questions raised herein.

My particular line of inquiry draws on previous research conducted for my book, *Educational Justice: Teaching and Organizing against the Corporate Juggernaut* (Ryan 2016). That book's opening chapter investigated the forces behind the corporate assault on schools, or what some critics call the Global Education Reform Movement (GERM) (Sahlberg 2012). Here I'll extend that work into new territories, of race and class.

Among the varied progressive analyses of school reform can be found a race-based one that sees current reform, with its high-stakes testing and privatization, as "essentially a white phenomenon" (Howard 2016: 123) and "an act of white supremacy" (Gillborn 2005). There is a case to be made for such interpretation, and strongly so in the United States, where school reform has been highly racialized, reinforcing and deepening historic inequities. This interpretation of reform is, in turn, grounded in a larger race-based worldview. One of its respected proponents is critical race theorist Charles Mills, who sees race, not class, as society's "primary contradiction" (1999: 141–2). The race-based argument is certainly a challenge to me, as a long-time Marxist with attendant embrace of class politics. One task of this chapter is to grapple with those issues.

This chapter challenges what I call *race-based theory* and argues for the validity and importance of class analysis—in the study of education and politics and in the pursuit of racial and social justice. The chapter does not attempt to provide a comprehensive theory on race and class, or on related topics, such as the primacy of one category over the other or the pursuit of race/class fusion. The aim, rather, is to foster discussion toward the building of such theory; and it assumes that how we address these theoretical matters, and how we imagine the world is constructed, bears considerably on how we strategize and organize for social change.

My case for class is pursued primarily through a practical application: an inquiry into the driving forces behind school reform. Here I contrast the race-based interpretation, which ties reform to a whiteness or white supremacist agenda, to a class-based/Marxist one that sees reform as "part of the grander project of capitalism" (Maisuria 2010: 187). In this regard, there is no dispute that the reform regime is racist in character. The disagreement concerns the underlying purposes of reform and whether and how class and capitalism come into play. An argument about education policy and its drivers certainly does not, by itself, answer the big questions on race, class, or how society operates. Rather, I have come to see education policy as one window for examining these larger issues.[1]

The first section frames the chapter with some initial theoretical remarks. The second, third, and fourth sections then investigate the aims of school reform, the forces that drive it, and competing progressive interpretations of it. The fifth section reflects more broadly on race and class as pertain to social change theory and strategy, concluding with a relevant treatment of the anti-apartheid movement in South Africa and the role of the African National Congress in the post-apartheid era.[2]

Race Primacy, Intersectionality, and the Retreat from Class

Current debates on race and class revolve around three divergent interpretations of the world: (1) Marxism, which sees class (and capitalism, a class-based system) as the overarching structure driving the social order; (2) race-based theory, which sees race, or white supremacy, as the driving structure; and (3) intersectionality, which rejects the notion of a primary category, and sees race, class, gender, and other social divisions as more or less co-equal and interlocking. We could also cite a fourth posture that gives primacy to gender, or patriarchy, but this stance has waned, with much of feminist theorizing adopting an intersectional stance over recent decades.[3]

Race-based theory is reflected in several frameworks. Given particular attention in this chapter is *critical race theory* (CRT), a body of thought originating in US legal studies in the 1980s and which today is "the dominant framework for a critical study of race" in US education (Leonardo 2013: 11). Two pertinent frameworks in the field of sociology are the *systemic racism theory* of Joe Feagin (2006, 2014) and the *racial formation theory* of Michael Omi and Howard Winant (2015). More broadly, Black nationalism and Pan-Africanism are both major expressions of race-based theory.[4]

Although race-based theory and intersectionality differ on the question of primacy, the two postures share an important feature in common: both reject Marxism's centering of class. My concern about race-based theory and intersectionality, however, is not their failure to embrace class primacy as such but rather their tendency to overlook or diminish class. Antonia Darder and Rodolfo Torres observe in CRT a "conspicuous absence of a systematic discussion of class" or "substantive critique of capitalism" (2004: 99). Law scholar Devon Carbado adds that "the CRT literature on race and class is decidedly thin." For the most part, he says, "scholars outside of the field of CRT are framing the debate about race and class" (2011: 1633).

The neglect of class is not exclusive to these frameworks but fits a broad pattern in progressive politics that has been in motion for perhaps four decades. The 1960s and 1970s were a time of progressive advance, not only in terms of mass action but also for political thought. The "new social movements"—addressing race, gender, sexuality, ecology, peace, democracy in the university—stretched left and Marxist theory in new ways and beyond an historic tendency to focus narrowly on workplace organizing. Yet, when mass action receded and corporate power reasserted itself, the new bodies of thought generated by the social movements lost their radical edge and, in particular, their connection to Marxism and class politics. Delia Aguilar (2012) traces these changes through the evolution of feminist theory and the rise of intersectionality. Intersectionality's antecedents in 1970s Black feminism included a sharp anti-capitalism and anti-imperialism focus, observes Aguilar. As such, Jennifer Beal's groundbreaking essay, "Double Jeopardy: To Be Black and Female" (1970), argued that the labor movement's failure to fight the super-exploitation of Black workers and women "impeded the advancement of the real struggle against the ruling class" (p. 346). The Third World Women's Alliance in New York City aligned itself with national liberation struggles, such as in Vietnam (Aguilar 2012: 421). The Combahee River Collective, in a 1977 Black feminist statement, declared themselves socialists who aimed to destroy "the political-economic systems of capitalism and imperialism as well as patriarchy" (Combahee River 2017: 19). By the 1990s, however, most intersectionality theorists regarded the "trinity" of race, class, and gender apart from any grounding in capitalism, claims Aguilar. For such theorists, the fundamental problem was not an exploitative economic system driven by a ruling class but a hazier "matrix of domination" (Aguilar 2012: 426; citing Collins 1991). The term *class* itself was stripped of its Marxian class-conflict meaning, replaced by the mainstream sociology definition based on a person's occupation, income, and lifestyle, thus failing to address systemic power relations.

Aguilar's historic tracing of intersectionality through a class lens may be equally applied to the broader Black movement. In the 1960s, this movement had shown potentials of fusing of anti-racism with class analysis—as with the later years of Malcolm X and Martin Luther King Jr.'s work; the Black Panthers' conjoining of Black power with a Maoist-influenced Marxism; and the role of the League of Revolutionary Black Workers, based in the Detroit auto industry (Breitman 1970; Shawki 2006: 170–221; Georgakas and Surkin 2012). Opportunities for such fusion were fewer from the 1980s onwards, as Black politics shifted from mass movement building to a conservatizing electoral focus. The distancing of Black politics from class politics could also be witnessed in the scholarly arena, for example, in Cedric Robinson's influential *Black Marxism: The Making of the Black Radical Tradition* (1983/2000). The late Robinson was anti-capitalist but with a race-based Pan-African orientation rather than a class-based orientation. He saw in the African diaspora a "single historical identity" which stood "in opposition to the systemic privations of racial capitalism." At the same time, he held that "the experiment with Western political inventories of change, specifically nationalism and class struggle, is coming to a close" (317). What Robinson did not indicate was how racial capitalism—the subject of his book's first chapter—might be overturned without class struggle or what his alternative to racial capitalism would look like. His book nevertheless remains foundational among race-based scholars.[5]

On Grand Theory

The aim here, as noted above, is not so much to construct a theory as to offer a series of arguments and questions that I hope will foster conversation, and perhaps, beyond that, collaborative theory building. In this regard, it may be an achievement for us, as scholars and activists from divergent perspectives, to merely agree on the importance of theory, especially theory of a grand or totalizing nature—that is, which attempts to fathom the nature of the world order, the roots of oppression, the possibilities for transformation. The historic retreat from class has, according to Aguilar (2012) and Ellen Meiksins Wood (1998), been accompanied by a more general retreat from grand theorizing. This trend is suggested by the remarks of CRT co-founder Kimberlé Crenshaw at an intersectionality conference in 2009 (Crenshaw 2011). While she coined the term *intersectionality* (1989), Crenshaw differs from those who frame it as an overarching theory of oppression. She views intersectionality as "a heuristic or hermeneutic tool" for analyzing problems but regards "grand theory" as "itself a dubious enterprise" (2011: 232). If we are, as Crenshaw is, doubtful about grand theory, then we must also be doubtful about systemic change, since the latter requires, at the minimum, theorizing expansively about social systems.

Progressive discussions of grand theory inevitably engage the matter of primacy. Marx set the pattern with his notion of capital accumulation as a pivotal force shaping all corners of life. His class primacy has come under challenge from race and gender perspectives—and, since the 1990s, from an influential version of intersectionality, co-developed by Patricia Hill Collins (1991, 1993), which has brought all primacies into question. Intersectionality, though not the focus of the present work, is today a vital part of any progressive dialogue across frameworks. Claims of primacy are unproductive, in Collins's view. They degenerate into "internecine battles of whose oppression is more fundamental," and lock us in "a dangerous dance of competing for attention, resources, and theoretical supremacy" (1997: 74, 1993: 26). She proposes instead "a working hypothesis of equivalency between oppressions" that allows us to explore the interconnections between oppressive systems (1997: 74). With co-author Sirma Bilge, Collins presents intersectionality as a robust, multi-axis alternative to Marxism and other "single-axis" models: "When it comes to social inequality, people's lives and the organization of power in a given society are better understood as being shaped not by a single axis of social division, be it race or gender or class, but by many axes that work together and influence each other" (Collins and Bilge 2016: 2). Collins and Bilge oversimplify Marxism as a "class-only" framework (15) and do not allow that a class-based perspective can also be intersectional, integrating the various social divisions (Mojab 2015). Still, one merit of their work, for purposes here, is that the authors do propose an overarching framework and, in this sense, contribute productively to conversations on grand theory and primacy.

Race-based frameworks are uneven when it comes to grand theorizing. Black nationalism and Pan-Africanism tend to be vigorous both with grand theory and assertions of race primacy. In the early 1970s, when some Black organizations were turning to Marxism and sought an eventual unity between Black and white workers, Pan-Africanist Haki Madhubuti countered: "There is one central thread connecting all the problems we face which is the creator of the problems—the white man. . . . 'The whites are the implacable foe, the traditional and everlasting enemy of the blacks'" (1974: 45; quoting Williams 1974: 205). Furthermore, "As far as we are concerned communism and capitalism are the left and the right arms in the same white body" (54).

CRT, on the other hand, rarely delves into grand theory or matters of primacy. Although there exist straightforward stances, such as that of Mills, who identifies race as the primary contradiction (1999), and Ricky Lee Allen, who calls for inverting Marxism's race-class order by "standing class on its head and placing race at the top" (2001: 476), such declarations are exceptional. The CRT anthologies (e.g., Crenshaw et al. 1995; Delgado and Stefancic 2000; Dixson, Anderson and Donnor 2017) do not generally situate racism within an expressed overarching theory, be it race primacist or other perspectives. The same is true for summary descriptions of CRT such as the following from Mari Matsuda et al. (1993: 6), which is geared to the legal studies field and presented here in shortened form:

- CRT recognizes that racism is endemic to American life.
- It expresses skepticism toward dominant legal claims of neutrality, objectivity, color blindness, and meritocracy.
- It insists on a contextual/historical analysis of the law.
- It recognizes the experiential knowledge of people of color and their communities of origin.
- It is interdisciplinary and eclectic.
- It works to eliminate racial oppression as part of the broader goal of ending all forms of oppression.

Identifying racism as "endemic"—a claim that would find wide agreement among US progressives—is certainly not the same as identifying race as the primary contradiction. In this sense, Mills and Allen go further in asserting a grand theory—a broad notion of how the world works—than does the CRT consensus as outlined by Matsuda et al.

CRT's somewhat muted posture on the most significant global questions does not mean that the field lacks a grand theory. Rather, the field appears to be guided by a widespread *implied* belief in race primacy. In fact, in CRT and beyond, I believe that race primacy has a following and influence that is much greater than meets the eye, though its detection often requires reading between the lines. Again, the matter of class comes to bear. When we encounter scholarship on systemic racism, but which leaves the class system unexamined, then a race-primacist principle may well be in play.

Such is evident in the work of David Gillborn, the UK's leading CRT proponent. Gillborn identifies English education policy—that is, test-driven school reform—as "an act of white supremacy." By this, he means that the policy ties to a larger racial system, supporting "the very structure of racist domination and oppression" (2005: 497; quoting hooks 1989: 113). He explores the matter further in *Racism and Education:*

Coincidence or Conspiracy? (2008). England's educational inequities "are shaped and legitimated by the assumptions, interests and actions of white people," he writes (36). Education policymakers are "pandering to the feelings and fears of White people" (86). Gillborn draws on powerful truths about systemic racism and yet leaves large gaps, because his racial analysis does not incorporate class analysis. English school reform is rooted in a broader neoliberal/conservative regime, launched in 1979 under Margaret Thatcher (Jones 2016). That regime was effectively a ruling-class initiative against the working class—with slashed corporate taxes, reduced public services, and attacks on organized labor.[6] Such important context is not explored by Gillborn. When the author describes elected officials as beholden to white priorities, he fails to also consider the role of corporate priorities in government. The corporate elite's "stranglehold on British democracy," with a "revolving door between the civil service and big business" (Jones 2015: 77, 216), receives no attention in Gillborn's work. Although Gillborn doesn't set forth a theory of race primacy per se, his examination of racism and education, with class politics notable for its absence, suggests white supremacy as the pivotal driver in education and society.

Kimberlé Crenshaw and her co-editors echo Gillborn's approach in their CRT-guided volume, *Seeing Race Again: Countering Colorblindness across the Disciplines*. The authors describe how "not seeing race" becomes a strategy for perpetuating racism in academe and social policy. The book evokes race primacy, though not expressly articulating this theory. Thus, Crenshaw et al. (2019: 5) observe that "every established discipline in the academy has an origin that entails engagement and complicity with white supremacy." Scholars are urged to "use race as a central analytic and framework" to reimagine their disciplines, research, teaching, and public engagement (15). And co-editor/contributor George Lipsitz scrutinizes "key mechanisms of white racial rule in U.S. history" (Lipsitz 2019: 26). While providing analyses of color-blind racism that are rich and instructive, the volume nevertheless neglects class and does not situate white racial rule in the context of capitalist class rule—hence implying race primacy.

To make our implicit beliefs explicit would be a helpful starting point for beginning the race/class dialogue and left theory-building project proposed in this chapter.

While my own framework is Marxist, I do not regard it as providing all the answers. A number of Marxists have pointed out the racial shortcomings within the Marxist tradition (Bannerji 2005; Camfield 2016; Roediger 2017; Virdee 2010, 2014). Others, on the other hand, note historic commitments to issues of race and gender within that tradition (Anderson 2010; Eagleton 2011: chap. 10). One of my hopes, through this writing, is to connect with others who are interested in integrating class, race, and anti-capitalism—in theory and practice.

School Reform and Hidden Aims

School systems around the world have, since the early 1980s, come increasingly under the grip of a global education reform movement whose chief calling cards are high-stakes testing and privatization. Who is driving this movement? And what are their ultimate aims?

The school reform movement presents itself as a collaboration among grassroots groups, business leaders, and private donors in pursuit of high-minded goals—improving education, fostering a better economy, and helping poor children escape poverty. Barack Obama, who expanded US schools' high-stakes testing and privatization during his two terms in the White House, sought to "prepare America's children for success in college and careers" (White House Office of the Press 2010). Microsoft founder and top edu-philanthropist Bill Gates (2009) wants to "give low-income and minority students a world-class education."

Yet, the prevailing practice of reform—test-driven curriculum in under-resourced schools—would not be considered "world-class education" by most educators. A large body of research challenges the chief elements of the reform package (Gorski and Zenkov 2014; Mathis and Trujillo 2016). Indeed, the reformers' interest in public school improvement often appears to be less than genuine. They prescribe models for mass education that they do not consider suitable for their own children.[7] They sponsor think tanks to produce "junk research" praising their models, while ignoring studies that contradict their models (Welner, Hinchey and Molnar 2010).

For these and other reasons, the critics of this reform movement widely suspect a hidden agenda, even if they have reached no consensus as to its nature. The most familiar progressive interpretation depicts reform as a scheme to turn schooling into yet one more source of private profit. David Sirota (2013) describes the charter school phenomenon as the work of "cutthroat businesspeople making shrewd financial investments" and wealthy CEOs "getting rich off of schoolchildren." In a similar vein, Michelle Fine and Michael Fabricant (2013) argue that, with the US empire losing ground to global competitors, ruling elites have "opened a fire sale" on the public sector, including schools: "We may be witnessing the cannibalization of our children's future as their public assets are being sold to private sector bidders" (27).

This "edu-profits" thesis certainly explains why education and technology companies would rally behind reform. But it cannot account for the pro-reform enthusiasm of non-education companies, such as Boeing or Exxon Mobil, which, along with many other major corporations, support the Common Core—the US English and math standards devised by reformers and adopted by most states.[8] Nor does it account for the diversity of philanthropists who back reform. Some arguably have a financial stake in reform, among them a cohort of pro-charter school hedge fund managers (Vasquez Heilig 2012; Gonzalez 2012) and technology-linked foundations, such as Dell and Hewlett. However, other big donors, such as real estate/insurance magnate Eli Broad, the Walton family (owners of Walmart), and former US education secretary Betsy DeVos, have little apparent direct financial stake in high-stakes testing or school privatization.

A second interpretation sees reform as primarily an expression of neoliberal ideology. Rich corporate donors "are motivated by neoliberal political and economic ideology that favors marketing virtually all aspects of public life," theorizes Elizabeth Bloom: "These people believe that public education is bad, and in fact the whole public sector is bad, and it needs to be privatized and marketized in order to save it" (2015: 7).

Bloom's ideological reading may well account for school reform philanthropists such as Gates, who has declared that "we can make market forces work better for the poor if we can develop a more creative capitalism" (2007), or DeVos, who comes to reform as a Christian rightist (Rizga 2017). But a focus on ideology overlooks the many reformers whose motivation is primarily financial. Also, the nature of the reform movement—its urgent and deliberate character; the powerful consensus it has built in elite circles and major political parties in country after country—suggests a driving agenda stronger than ideology alone: something material appears to be at stake.

A third progressive approach interprets reform by asking, Who benefits? Italian Marxist Antonio Gramsci considered this the essential question to pose with respect to social actions, explains Ellen Brantlinger (2004), who then produces an extensive list of reform's beneficiaries, among them test producers, trans-global capitalists, media moguls, politicians, enterprising school superintendents, and the educated middle class (84–91). While Brantlinger's propositions are largely reasonable (though some are challengeable), the question only takes us so far. At minimum, the list of beneficiaries needs sorting; a trans-global capitalist would likely be a far more powerful reform player than would a school superintendent. A policy history would also help as we attempt to determine who is driving policy and toward what end.

Race-Based Interpretation of School Reform

A fourth progressive interpretation sees reform, first and foremost, in racial terms, as part of a white supremacist system. The reforms "oppress communities of Color while at the same time rewarding whites," claim Bree Picower and Edwin Mayorga, editors of the anthology, *What's Race Got to Do with It?* (2015b: 10). The race-based interpretation holds particular power in the United States and England, where reform's role in exacerbating historic educational inequities has been well documented. In the US case, reform has meant students of color facing higher failure rates on standardized tests, and higher rates of drop-out, suspension, and expulsion, in comparison to white students. This is joined with increased segregation and funding inequities, and suppression of multicultural and bilingual education (Orfield et al. 2016; Au 2009; Picower and Mayorga 2015a.). Many of these trends are mirrored in England (Gillborn 2008; Tomlinson 2008). One reform practice that is sharper in the United States is the racial targeting associated with school closures and privatization. In 2013–14, Black students comprised 27 percent of enrollment in US charter schools,[9] nearly double the 15 percent Black enrollment in regular public schools (NCES 2016: 214). School closures are even more racially skewed (Tilsley 2017), which Chicago witnessed in 2013. Among fifty-five schools targeted by the Chicago education board that year, majority-Black schools were ten times more likely than majority-white schools to be closed or "turned around" (i.e., through the mass dismissal of staff) (Chicago Teachers Union 2014: 3). Furthermore, schooling's "savage inequalities" of race (Kozol 2012) echo across virtually every other arena of social policy—employment, housing, immigration, policing and incarceration (Bonilla-Silva 2017; Murakawa 2014; Kundnani 2007).

The racial interpretation of school reform ties to a larger body of race-based theory, as discussed earlier. I'll touch on this theory a bit further, before examining how it has been applied to the analysis of school reform. Race-based scholars identify white supremacy as "the basic political system that has shaped the world for the past several hundred years" (Mills 1997: 1). Government is viewed as "the racial state" (Goldberg 2002; Omi and Winant 2015), not "the capitalist state," as in Marxism. Systemic racism theorists Sean Elias and Joe Feagin (2016: 117) regard racism, not capitalism, as the appropriate starting point for social analysis: "Rather than begin by asking how . . . racism develops within a capitalistic society, we ask how does capitalism develop in white-racist societies."

As already noted, not all race-based scholars subscribe to race primacy in express terms. An intersectionalist sensibility may come into play—that is, shouldn't race be situated as *a* central driver, co-equally with class and gender, rather than *the* central driver? In this vein, I have noticed some scholars vacillating between a position of race primacy and that of race/class or race/class/gender equivalence. Illustrative is the work of Picower and Mayorga in their introduction to *What's Race* (2015a). On the one hand, they describe their book's analytic framework in terms of race/class equivalence: the framework "seeks not to privilege one analysis (class or race) over the other" but to "work in both" in order to better examine "the connections between capitalism and structural racism, or racial capitalism" (2015b: 8). On the other hand, elsewhere in the introduction, the authors seem to drop equivalence and privilege race. Thus, they describe racism as encompassing "a web of economic, political, social, and cultural structures" that unequally distributes "privilege, resources and power in favor of the dominant racial group" (p. 6; quoting Derman-Sparks and Phillips 1997: 10); but they do not offer a similar description of capitalism's class system. Likewise, the authors identify race as "the driving force" behind school reform but do not cite class or capitalism as also driving reform (8).

While race-based theory and Marxism lie in opposition—giving primacy to race and to class, respectively—there are certainly theorists who productively integrate race and class, as seen in Virdee (2014), Marable (2015), Roediger (2007, 2017), the journal *Race and Class* and other works from the London-based Institute of Race Relations, and sometimes in Marxist-feminist writings (see Holmstrom 2002; Mojab 2015). A grouping called ClassCrits, which is active in the milieu of CRT legal scholars, also pursues this line of inquiry.[10] The predominant trends in race-based theory, however, diminish class. Race-based theorists sometimes short-change class even as they mindfully seek a race-class synthesis. Revisiting the work of Picower and Mayorga: the authors propose to engage the "raceclass perspective" of Zeus Leonardo (Picower and Mayorga 2015b: 8; citing Leonardo 2012b). Yet, at the same time, their conception of white supremacy—as "the way in which our society was founded and remains organized so that white people are at the top of the hierarchy of power" (6)—neglects class. Their conception draws upon a major truth: a racist society does allocate to whites innumerable small and large privileges (McIntosh 1997). Yet, most whites are far from "the top of the hierarchy of power" in a class society ruled by corporate elites. Moreover, some Blacks, such as billionaire media mogul Oprah Winfrey, enjoy class power far beyond that of working-class whites. Class is similarly underexamined by

Gillborn. In a response to Darder and Torres's criticism, he insists that "the best CRT scholarship tries to work through the interrelations between racism and other forms of structural and ideological exclusion, including class" (2008: 37). When Gillborn writes, however, that "the emphasis in CRT is on the shared power and dominance of White interests" (p. 34), he does not examine how that very thrust can diminish a class understanding of power.

No one has been a stronger advocate for a "union between race and class analysis in education" than Berkeley critical race theorist Zeus Leonardo (2009: 45). While CRT "has developed race and class insights alongside each other," Leonardo believes that the field "ultimately superimposes a racial discourse over class issues" and "does not incorporate Marxism's problematic, such as a fundamental analysis of capital" (2013: 35).

Yet, despite his promising calls for a "raceclass perspective" and an "historical and conceptual integration of race and Marxist discourse" (2009: 46), Leonardo himself does not quite transcend the constraints of race-based theory. Consider his *Race, Whiteness, and Education* (2009). In one chapter, he proposes that Marxism's "material, objective analysis" be productively joined with "an analysis of subjectivity" found in racial theory (46). In a later chapter on the No Child Left Behind Act of 2001 (NCLB)—which made high-stakes testing the chief engine of US schooling on a national scale—Leonardo has a fine opportunity to demonstrate how his proposed integration of Marxism and racial theory might be applied in an analysis of policy, but the opportunity is largely missed.

On the one hand, the chapter aptly sets NCLB in the context of color-blind racism. Color blindness is a dominant perspective which assumes racism to have declining significance in the US post-civil-rights era, and that, with discrimination allegedly a thing of the past, all are now equally free to pursue their individual success. Incorporating color-blind racism, NCLB avoided any commitment to remedy the socioeconomic and educational inequities that continue to affect student achievement; rather, Leonardo (2009: 136) points out, the law allows students of color to be declared failures under "a presumed-to-be fair system."

On the other hand, the chapter does not mention a second crucial part of NCLB's context: the leading role of big business. Corporate engagement in shaping and passing the law, through a coalition of fifty business groups (Hoff 2006), is well known among NCLB's critics (Metcalf 2002; Altwerger 2005a). With respect to the study of NCLB, Leonardo remarks that policy analysis "is poor without a sense of causality" (137). Given this acknowledged need, it is quite unexpected that his inquiry into NCLB's causality never asks *who* drove this historically pivotal measure. Instead, Leonardo attributes NCLB to an ideology—a legislative "act of whiteness" (127). *Whiteness* has been defined as "the ideology and way of being in the world that is used to maintain White supremacy" (Picower and Mayorga 2015b: 7).

Policy is made by people, not by ideology per se. Addressing the *who* of policymaking helps us inquire into the *why* of policy—for example, what was business's stake in NCLB? How do business interests connect with color-blind racism? While Marxists may offer varied answers to such questions, they do bring a predilection for asking about capitalist interests with respect to policy. "The executive of the modern state,"

Marx and Engels (2008: 36) asserted, "is but a committee for managing the common affairs of the whole bourgeoisie."

Does Reform Benefit Whites?

If race-based theorists are at times vague about the *who* behind reform, they are certainly much clearer about the *why*: the purpose of reform is to advance white supremacy. Integral to this interpretation is the claim that reform benefits white people.

Without doubt, reform benefits *some* white people—for example, the mainly white investors tapping the edu-business[11] profits generated by reform; and the predominantly white professionals who make their careers in the reform movement as education leaders, think tank staff, and lobbyists. But race-based theorists indict a much larger population: pretty much all whites are held to be beneficiaries of reform. Picower and Mayorga (2015b:10), as noted, argue that the reforms "oppress communities of Color while at the same time rewarding whites." Leonardo (2009: 138) considers it tempting to dub NCLB "No Caucasian Left Behind," because of the "whiteness" and color-blind racism behind the law. Gillborn (2009: 34), who calls current education policy an act of white supremacy, further argues that white supremacy benefits all whites—even if they "are *not* all active in identical ways" and "do *not* all draw similar benefits" (emphases in original).

These are complex issues to sort through, extending well beyond the education field and engaging matters of class as much as race. The question, Does reform benefit whites?, is nonetheless a helpful entry point. Let's consider Wayne Au's handling of the question in "High-Stakes Testing: A Tool for White Supremacy for over 100 Years," a chapter in the Picower/Mayorga volume (2015). Au's racial analysis certainly aids a critical discussion of reform. He addresses the racial gap in test scores, a widely recognized marker of educational inequity. But he also points to multiple other inequities of the testing regime, including a narrowed curriculum, with losses in non-tested subjects (the sciences, the arts) and in multicultural, anti-racist perspectives; school closures; the feeding of a school-to-prison pipeline; and differential life chances in terms of high school graduation/college access/job success. Au shows how white students are favored over non-white students in each area.

The advantages afforded white students, vis-à-vis students of color, under reform and its testing mandates are many and indisputable, and sharply so in the United States. This does not, however, demonstrate that reform actually makes things better for whites. That is, reform can have unequal results while still affecting all negatively. An alternative to the race-based formulation—with reform rewarding whites and oppressing non-whites—is that reform oppresses working-class whites, oppresses working-class people of color more so, and with the major rewards accruing to a tiny capitalist class. Reform's harm across race shows itself most clearly if we engage a class perspective and if we situate current education policy in the context of political, economic, and historic trends of neoliberal capitalism.

In that vein, and before delving into the educational evidence, it will be helpful to touch on some matters of class theory and economic history. Prevailing usage in education and many other fields of study treats class as a matter of one's income or socioeconomic status (SES). The "middle class" is relatively affluent, compared to a non-affluent "working class." An alternative Marxian usage defines class in terms of one's relationship to capitalist production, with the capitalist class as owners of production and a working class selling its labor power to the capitalists and to the capitalist state. With respect to industrialized countries, such as the United States and England, my own Marxist interpretation (drawing on Callinicos 1983 and Domhoff 2013) identifies a working class comprising roughly 90 percent of the population and a capitalist class constituting perhaps 1 percent. What remains is a middle class of small business owners, self-employed individuals, and independent farmers.

Some theorists have carved away from the working class a *professional/managerial class*, or PMC—teachers, social workers, writers, mid-level managers, engineers, and technical workers—claiming that this group's relationship to the working class is "objectively antagonistic" (Ehrenreich and Ehrenreich 1979: 9; see also Apple 2006; Au 2008). Thus, Barbara and John Ehrenreich (1979) argued in an influential article that engineers strip skills from workers as they redesign production, teachers convey official knowledge and capitalist ideology to their students, and social workers wield control over their working-class clients. More recently, the Ehrenreichs substantially retracted the PMC theory that they had advanced many years before. They noted that three decades of free-market neoliberalism had downsized and proletarianized the PMC, with many doctors and lawyers absorbed into corporate structures—and managers, technology workers, and social service professionals losing their positions to outsourcing and government austerity. "In this setting," observe the Ehrenreichs (2013), "we have to ask whether the notion of a PMC, with its own distinct aspirations and class interests, still makes any sense, if it did in the first place."

The argument here applies class in its traditional Marxist usage; it also selectively employs the more common socioeconomic usage, making the latter clear with the terms *working class-SES* and *middle class-SES*. The concept of a broad Marxian working class, one that includes college-educated and professional workers under a changing capitalism, sheds new light on our immediate question—Does reform benefit whites? If we apply Marxist understandings of these concepts, while acknowledging that whites disproportionately constitute the middle and capitalist classes, whites are still mainly working class. An inquiry that incorporates class would therefore ask whether reform benefits *working-class* whites. By the same token, our inquiry must bear in mind how the working class, across race, has endured a decades-long corporate assault, which includes not only the fall of the so-called PMC but also a broad degradation of working conditions, labor rights, and social programs, all aiding a massive shift of wealth and income toward the top 1 percent (Lafer 2017).

Who Benefits from Testing?

Central to the whiteness thesis of Au, Leonardo, and others is an assumed correlation between passing tests, gaining college access, and securing economic success and upward mobility. The higher test scores of whites purportedly translate into economic power. Who benefits from testing? Au (2015: 34) asks. The short answer, he proposes, is "Whiteness," and, "by extension, White people," since "high-stakes, standardized testing selectively supports the upward mobility of affluent White folks over others." Yet, the linkage between education and economic success has been eroding for decades (Marsh 2011). Young adults, even after passing the big tests and going on to graduate college, encounter a "humbling" job market, as the *New York Times* reports:

> The individual stories are familiar. The chemistry major tending bar. The classics major answering phones. The Italian studies major sweeping aisles at WalMart. Now evidence is emerging that the damage wrought by the sour economy is more widespread than just a few careers led astray or postponed. Even for college graduates—the people who were most protected from the slings and arrows of recession—the outlook is rather bleak. (Rampell 2011)

The *Times* story, citing not only a forbidding job market but also rising student debt, ran in 2011, addressing the recessionary conditions following the 2008 financial crash. But such a story could well have appeared in the 1970s, when Harvard economist Richard Freeman wrote *The Overeducated American* (1976).

Au's (2015: 33) picture of high-stakes testing, as "part of a system that supports affluent, White success," must be placed in the context of historic trends—job market decline, erasure of the living wage, concentration of wealth at the top—that undermine working-class opportunity across race. Such trends do not forestall the continuing racial advantage that reform allocates to white students. But they do make problematic the equation of reform with "White success."

Let's consider some evidence from the schools, first with a glance at test results and then with a look at test-driven curriculum. The "racial achievement gap," well established in the United States, is exemplified in Table 1.1, based on the 2018 results of California's Assessment of Student Performance and Progress, a high-stakes English and math exam administered in grades 3 through 8 and 11. To aid discussion, I've added a "composite" column by averaging the English and math results.

California's white students produced a composite pass rate of 59.5 percent, roughly double that of Blacks (26 percent) and Latinos (33 percent). The higher Asian pass rate of 75 percent, partly attributable to the immigration of highly educated, higher-income families such as from China, Taiwan, and Korea (National Commission on Asian American 2008), does not alter the huge and nationally familiar gap between

Table 1.1 California Statewide Test Results, 2018

Race/Ethnicity	English: % Meeting or Exceeding Standards	Math: % Meeting or Exceeding Standards	Composite: % Meeting or Exceeding Standards
Asian	76	74	75
Black	32	20	26
Latino	39	27	33
White	65	54	59.5
All students	50	39	44.5

Source: English and math data from California Department of Education (2018).

whites and Blacks/Latinos. For the race-based theorist, the California data provides further evidence of whiteness in practice, as white students gain a substantial edge in the race for educational credentials and good jobs.

But alternative readings are possible. First, the corollary of white students' 59.5 percent pass rate is a 40.5 percent *failure* rate. In effect, the state's reformed school system is marking four of ten white students as academic failures, just as it does for the majority of Black and Latino students. Second, even those who do pass the tests are likely to encounter tough life chances; upward mobility will not be forthcoming for the vast majority of working-class students. Third, the overall performance of California's public school students—with a 44.5 percent composite pass rate bearing a 55.5 percent majority failure—should be placed next to that of a student group not appearing in the data: the children of the capitalist elite, whose private schooling is generally free of high-stakes testing and who are virtually all guaranteed educational and economic success. The narrative of the race-based literature points to white winners and Black/brown losers in the race for success. An alternative class-based narrative points to capitalist winners and working-class losers, with racial and other differentiations (e.g., by language, immigration status, national origin) among the losers.

Test-Driven Curriculum

A critical impact of high-stakes testing lies in the narrow kinds of curriculum produced. Again, Au (2015) underscores the continuing white advantage. For example, regarding NCLB's impact, he cites a 2006 study which found that 97 percent of high-poverty school districts, enrolling disproportionately non-white students, have instituted policies aimed at increasing time spent on reading. This compared to only 55 to 59 percent of wealthier, whiter districts instituting such policies. Thus, Au (2015: 31–2; citing Center on Education Policy 2006) observes, high-stakes testing produces "more restrictive, less rich educational environments for non-White students"—that is, with less time spent on science, social studies, and the arts. Again, the data showing a white advantage is indisputable. What needs acknowledgment is that a majority of the whiter districts (55–59 percent) did impose the restrictions. With such acknowledgment, testing's racial differential becomes not one of white benefit versus non-white harm, as Au asserts, but of harm versus greater harm.

That testing bears down in shared ways across the working class deserves at least as much as attention as do the differential impacts, and these shared impacts may help us uncover reform's systemic aims. Consider the intensely test-focused writing instruction at two schools. One, Tyler Heights Elementary in Annapolis, Maryland, enrolls primarily low-income Latino and Black students; the other, a fictitiously named Pontiac High School, is a "working-class" school in a deindustrializing area of New York with a 95 percent white student population.

At Tyler Heights, as Linda Perlstein (2007) describes, the test-obsessed instruction owed much to a looming threat of NCLB sanctions, similar to that faced by virtually all high-poverty, low-scoring schools in the United States. Especially in the state-tested grades (grades 3, 4, and 5), writing at Tyler Heights consisted overwhelmingly of producing "brief constructed responses" (BCRs), a paragraph-sized answer that follows a certain format geared to the state test. The first day of school will be the last day that students won't write a BCR, explains one third-grade teacher, adding: "Later, you'll be doing five BCRs a day" (qtd. in Perlstein: 18, 87). A BCR formula was spelled out in posters hung in every classroom: borrow from the question, answer the question, use text support, and "stretch," meaning to include a "so I think" or "so I know" sentence. Students were taught to fill their paragraphs with "hundred-dollar words" and underline them for emphasis. These included transition words and terms such as "character trait," "graphic ads," and "dialogue" that appear on the state's content standards.

Perlstein found that the BCRs and other test-prep forms of instruction frequently deprived Tyler Heights students of the joy of learning. In reference to the third graders, she observes that reading seemed "merely a prelude to a BCR." Students were given very little time to read for fun in school, and "teachers despaired of ever getting their students to love books the way they did" (82, 83). Perlstein also notes the school's lack of experiential learning. The students repeatedly wrote BCRs that begin, "I know this is a play because . . ." but, Perlstein points out, they "never got to take the parts of characters and act a play out loud." They wrote, "I know this is a fairy tale because" and "I know this is a fable because" but "never tried their hand at creating either" (127).

As at Tyler Heights, high-stakes testing was by far the most significant factor affecting writing instruction at Pontiac High School. Julie Gorlewski (2011: 90–1, 86–7) asks a Pontiac English teacher whether the New York state Regents exams influenced her writing instruction. "Yeah. That's all we do," the teacher replies. "All of our assessments have to look like the [state] exam, so even if you wanted to have kids write a poem for an end of the unit assessment, we're technically not supposed to because it has to parallel what's on the exam." A science teacher sums up how writing fits into her own curriculum: "I think that we're getting them [the students] used to the exam."

"Chloe," a Pontiac student, describes the formulaic approach to literary analysis that had been "drilled in my head since September." Students are asked to prove a literary quote to be "true," following a model used in the Regents English language arts exam. The first sentence in response to the quote, Chloe explains, is supposed to identify the book, the author and a literary element such as a character or a conflict. Chloe continues: "Then the second sentence would be like, 'For example, in *Macbeth*, Lady Macbeth was persuasive,' and you would say how it proves the quote true." In the past, Chloe had thought she was a good writer. But she doesn't feel that way anymore. The prospect of failing the state exam is scary, she says, "so you want to do exactly what they tell you to do" (qtd. on p. 52, 53). Not surprisingly, Gorlewski (2011: 9) concludes that the state Regents exams had a "powerful reductive effect on writing" at Pontiac, and that "the expression and development of original or critical thought is discouraged."

A comparison of Tyler Heights and Pontiac does have limitations, since neither school has a middle class-SES student body—that is, from the more affluent part of the working class. Catherine Luna and Cara Livingstone Turner (2001) help fill the gap with their comparison of two high schools grappling with the introduction of the high-stakes Massachusetts Comprehensive Assessment System (MCAS). One school, "Urban High," enrolls a diverse, high-poverty student population that is nearly 50 percent Latino; the other, "Suburban High," enrolls students who are majority-white and middle class-SES. At Urban High, teachers saw MCAS as a "wrecking ball," with tightening administrative control, intense pressures to teach to the test, and a threatened state takeover of the school. At Suburban High, MCAS caused less panic. Administrators approached the test "as if it were some sort of puzzle—like a Rubik's cube," while teachers were asked to take much of the responsibility for figuring out how best to respond to it (84). Still, even at Suburban, MCAS and attendant test-prep activity meant losses in such areas as in-depth teaching and learning; student curiosity, creativity, and inventiveness; and field trips and special projects (86). Teachers also worried about the impact on the more academically struggling students at the school.

Abundant studies reiterate the findings at Tyler Heights, Pontiac, and the two Massachusetts schools. The greatest harm of high-stakes curriculum falls on the high-poverty schools, found disproportionately in communities of color (Amrein and Berliner 2002; Valenzuela 2005). At the same time, negative effects—such as narrowing of curriculum, teaching to the test, decreased teacher and school morale, and greater stress on students—are reported from a broad spectrum of high-scoring and low-scoring schools (Abrams, Pedulla and Madaus 2003; Taylor et al. 2003; Mertler 2011).

Even when accounting for racial and socioeconomic inequities, including comparative advantages allotted to white students, what is arguably reform's centerpiece is a "hidden curriculum" (Anyon 1980; Hill 2001) that extends across the working class. Students are learning to "do exactly what they tell you to do," as Chloe puts it. Their original or critical thoughts are discouraged. Reform's meritocratic ideology—in which one's success or failure in life is a matter of individual ability and effort—leaves students ill equipped to grapple with an unjust world and disappearing economic opportunity.[12] As the next discussion contends, such educational outcomes are fully intended and tied to capitalist class purposes.

Class-Based Interpretation of School Reform

Critical scholarship about the current reform movement tends toward fragmentary perspectives. Networks are mapped; various philanthropies, think tanks, and edu-businesses are put to scrutiny (Ball 2012; Au and Ferrare 2015; Schneider 2014). Such fragmenting is exemplified in the post-structuralism of Stephen Ball (2012: 90), who sees the global reform movement in terms of "messy hybridities," "diverse partnerships," and "new spaces of entangled possibilities." It is also observable in race-based theories insofar as they divorce race from class. Recall the example of Gillborn, who analyzes England's school reform in racial terms but without reference to the corporate/conservative attack on the working class stretching back to Thatcher.

This section of the chapter pushes in the opposite direction by attempting to create order from the pieces, even if tentatively and speculatively so. I'll begin by sorting the reform movement's complex terrain into certain classifications. The movement's *drivers* are its major funders, along with key institutions they control. Its *implementers* are the politicians, think tank directors, school superintendents, and others who carry out the drivers' wishes and may also provide them with strategic advice. The implementers are the less consequential of the two in terms of the present inquiry, since their role in reform typically depends on the preferences and decisions of the drivers.

Next, the drivers are sorted into three sectors. One sector, *edu-business*, encompasses large companies and investors with a direct financial stake in reform; among these are publishing and testing companies, technology firms, and real estate and banking interests that feed off charter school expansion. A second group, the *philanthropic sector*, consists primarily of charitable foundations. A third group, the *organized business sector*, represents business interests as a class. This sector's clearest expression is business federations, such as the Business Roundtable, US Chamber of Commerce, Confederation of British Industry, and Confederation of European Business. It is also expressed through policy planning groups and think tanks that have a class-wide character. One such planning group, the American Legislative Exchange Council, represents capitalist class interests on a state and national level. Other planning groups, such as the World Bank and the Organization for Economic Cooperation and Development (OECD), gear globally on behalf of a "transnational capitalist class" (Robinson 2014).

School reform serves distinct, if overlapping, aims for each of these sectors. For edu-business, the goal is school-related profits. For philanthropists, the chief aim appears to be ideological, as reflecting their free-market world vision. Some philanthropists, however, stand to profit directly from reform, and in such cases, they may be better placed in the edu-business sector. For organized business, the aim is to bolster corporate hegemony through education.

Is one of these sectors more pivotal than the other two in terms of leading the reform movement? For many observers of reform in the United States, the philanthropic sector appears to be running the show, headed up by a new breed of "venture philanthropists" such as Gates, Broad, and the Waltons. The new breed—more politically aggressive than are the traditional foundations such as Carnegie, Rockefeller, and Ford—borrows its methods from the field of venture capitalism (Saltman 2009; Tompkins-Stange 2016). Gates in particular has been viewed as a self-appointed education czar, given his driving role behind the Common Core (Layton 2014); the power wielded by his foundation in the US Department of Education during Obama's tenure (Tompkins-Stange 2016; Strauss 2016); along with the endless number of school reform projects and organizations funded by the foundation.

Yet, when we consider the history of the current reform movement, the philanthropists appear less pivotal. Venture philanthropy's major interventions into reform didn't begin until the early 2000s. Gates made his own entry with a national initiative to break up high schools into smaller schools; this began in 2000, the same year that his foundation was established (Ravitch 2010). The reform movement, however, has been going strong since the early 1980s. In fact, when the reform movement is considered historically and globally, as pursued below, the organized business sector becomes the project's clearest ringleader. I also suggest what such leadership implies regarding the hidden aims of school reform.

Organized Business and the Origins of the School Reform Movement

In tracing the origins of current US school reform, historians widely cite the 1983 report, *A Nation at Risk: The Imperative for Educational Reform* (Guthrie and Springer 2004; Mehta 2015). The product of a National Commission on Excellence in Education (NCEE) convened by Reagan education secretary Terrel Bell, the report attributed America's faltering global economic competitiveness to mediocre teachers and schools and recommended that schools and colleges "adopt more rigorous and measurable standards" (National Commission on Excellence 1983: 27). The report had enormous impact. Within a year of its release, over six million copies had been distributed, and more than 250 state task forces had come together to study education and make recommendations (Mehta 2015: 87).

While some critics (Berliner and Biddle 1995) would accuse the NCEE and the subsequent reform movement of manufacturing a crisis to advance a conservative political agenda, Harvard professor Jal Mehta challenges that interpretation and sees the commission as politically unbiased. The NCEE's composition did not support claims of an ideological, partisan, or corporate agenda, he writes. Chaired by University of Utah president David Gardner, the commission included only one business leader and one politician, alongside "some very distinguished educators who presumably would not be easily swayed by political concerns, including Gardner, Chemistry Nobel Prize winner Glenn Seaborg, Harvard physics professor Gerald Holton, and Yale President A. Bartlett Giamatti" (Mehta 2015: 88). Furthermore, Mehta points out, Reagan's educational priorities—such as abolishing the federal Department of Education, bringing God into the classroom, and promoting school vouchers—were shared neither by Secretary Bell nor by the NCEE. Mehta notes too that Bell's proposal for a presidential commission received little support from Reagan's office, leaving Bell to appoint a commission himself.

Several pieces of evidence, however, would support the critics' suspicions. Even if we cannot document that corporate actors gathered in a room to plot out the school reform movement, with invented crises and with designs on using schools to boost the expansion of corporate power, we can reasonably hypothesize that such occurred. The evidence lies not so much in the composition of the NCEE as in the historic context—in corporate political activity in the preceding decade, in events surrounding the release of *A Nation at Risk* itself, and in the continuing corporate role in school reform from the 1980s forward.

Revolt of the Bosses

The school reform movement grows out of a broader reassertion of power initiated in the early 1970s by major corporations in the United States and that would later spread globally. What one writer calls the "revolt of the bosses" (Nace 2003) came in response to two developments: first, falling rates of profit, as Japan and West Germany came to challenge US dominance in global markets from the mid-1960s on (Brenner 2006); and second, the threat of democratic and anti-capitalist movements springing up around the world in the 1960s and into the early 1970s.

The bosses' revolt was outlined in an August 1971 memo sent by corporate lawyer Lewis Powell to a friend at the US Chamber of Commerce. Powell, who would soon be appointed to the US Supreme Court, warned that an attack on the "American free enterprise system" is "gaining momentum and converts." He singled out leftist college professors and especially consumer advocate Ralph Nader, who had become "a legend in his own time and an idol of millions" and, in the words of *Fortune* magazine, "aimed at smashing utterly the target of his hatred, which is corporate power." Powell's (1971) remedy was clear and urgent: "Independent and uncoordinated activity by individual corporations, as important as this is, will not be sufficient. Strength lies in organization, in careful long-range planning and implementation, in consistency of action over an indefinite period of years, in the scale of financing available only through joint effort."

Powell's friend, Eugene Sydnor, the president of a department store chain and a director of the Chamber of Commerce, had asked Powell to write the memo, which Sydnor then shared with Chamber leaders and with friends, including the general counsel of General Motors. Sydnor, according to Kim Phillips-Fein (2009: 157–8), wanted to transform the Chamber from "a quiet business organization, into a powerful force capable of defending business in the new and uncertain political world." After the memo was leaked to the *Washington Post*, the Chamber distributed it to the Chamber membership and released it publicly.

Business leaders answered Powell's call. In 1972, the heads of General Electric, US Steel, and aluminum manufacturer Alcoa led a merger of three organizations to form the Business Roundtable (BRT), an organization of two hundred big-company CEOs. The following years saw the formation of new right-wing think tanks, such as the American Legislative Exchange Council and the Heritage Foundation, along with battalions of corporate political action committees and lobby groups. By the end of President Reagan's first term, the corporate-conservative movement was setting the terms of national politics, promoting deregulation, regressive tax reforms, and steep cuts to social provision. This, combined with new savings on labor costs—whether through union-busting, technological advances, or offshoring of jobs—all helped the richest Americans amass wealth with unprecedented speed and rapacity.

The bosses' revolt was accompanied by a global shift in economic philosophy. The previously long-dominant Keynesian model, which in its progressive versions emphasized full employment and a strong welfare state, fell to the free-market neoliberalism of Friedrich Hayek and Milton Friedman. Marxist geographer David Harvey notes, however, that neoliberalism was less a philosophical project than "a political project carried out by the corporate capitalist class." Harvey (2016) elaborates: "I don't think they started out by reading Hayek or anything. I think they just intuitively said, 'We gotta crush labor, how do we do it?' And they found that there was a legitimizing theory out there which would support that."

The "corporate capitalist class" that Harvey identifies finds a lead US voice in national business federations. The three that were most pivotal in the neoliberal turn of the 1970s were the Chamber of Commerce, the BRT, and the National Association of Manufacturers (NAM) (Phillips-Fein 2009). The new neoliberal corporate offensive saw each of these federations engaged in educational initiatives in the years preceding *A Nation at Risk*. Much came in the form of "economics education" which, says

Benjamin Waterhouse, "provided little more than philosophical propaganda" aimed at shoring up the low public opinion of big business (2014: 71). One such program, produced by the Chamber in the mid-1970s and targeting high school students, was "Freedom 2000," which included a teacher's manual, comprehension and discussion questions, and an animated motion picture. In the movie, aliens visit Earth to learn why some societies are wealthier than others. The wealthier societies, we learn, feature "an economic system in which the rights and choices of the individual are of paramount importance" (qtd. in Waterhouse 2014: 69).

Waterhouse notes that Freedom 2000, and a similar program produced by NAM, generally avoided specific issues and aimed instead for a more visceral reaction, "hoping to boost students' appreciation of the free enterprise system and of corporations" (69). Another program, Students in Free Enterprise (SIFE), launched in 1975, enjoyed generous backing from the BRT and Walmart. SIFE recruited college students to become public advocates for free enterprise, which included making presentations to schoolchildren and rallying support for business-backed political causes, such as reducing the federal deficit and limiting corporate liability in lawsuits. SIFE's economic concepts, Bethany Moreton (2009: 211) observes, were extremely basic: "profits are beneficial; government is wasteful; unions are illegitimate; corporations are natural persons," and "free markets abhor environmental regulation."

The federations' educational focus would later shift from pro-free enterprise curriculum toward subtler forms of social engineering through the imposition of standards and testing. But the economics education projects of the 1970s and 1980s did indicate that organized business was intervening in the schools, and doing so with political purposes, in the period leading up to *A Nation at Risk*.

Task Force on Education for Economic Growth

The Task Force on Education for Economic Growth was a corporate initiative temporally situated much closer to *A Nation at Risk*, being established in December 1982 under auspices of the Education Commission of the States, a corporate-funded think tank. The body's major report, *Action for Excellence: A Comprehensive Plan to Improve Our Nation's Schools*, was approved at a task force meeting of May 4, 1983—just one week after the April 26 release of *A Nation at Risk*—and was published the following month (Task Force 1983; Fiske 1983b). The task force report coincides with *A Nation at Risk* not only by way of timing but also in content. Both reports framed education reform in terms of an urgent call focused on the nation's economic survival:

> Our nation is at risk. Our once unchallenged preeminence in commerce, industry, science, and technological innovation is being overtaken by competitors throughout the world.
> —*A Nation at Risk* (National Commission on Excellence 1983: 5)

> Our faith in change—and our faith in ourselves as the world's supreme innovators—is being shaken. Japan, West Germany and other relatively new industrial powers

have challenged America's position on the leading edge of change and technical invention.

—Action for Excellence (Task Force 1983; reprinted as Education Commission of the States 1984: 15)

The two reports also made strikingly similar recommendations, calling for greater rigor for students (more homework, a longer school day, higher standards); tougher certification and higher salaries for teachers; and standardized testing. Though less known than the federally appointed NCEE, the task force was actually the more high-powered body, with top officers from a dozen major corporations, including AT&T, Dow Chemical, and Ford Motor Company; eleven state governors; and the presidents of the National School Boards Association, National Association of State Boards of Education, and National Academy of Sciences. The major business federations also had a presence on the task force, with three task force members listing such affiliation. Thus, one task force member, the president of MISSCO, a school supply company, also chaired the Chamber's Education Employment and Training Committee; a second member, the CEO of EG and G, Inc., a defense contractor, was also the chairman of NAM; and a third member, the CEO of Xerox, was also a BRT member (Education Commission 1984: 14).

Role of the Media

One further corporate initiative surrounding *A Nation at Risk* deserves our attention—that being coverage of the report by the major media, which consistently echoed the report's argument that our schools were putting our nation at risk and that it was time to "return to excellence." The *Washington Post*'s lead line is representative:

> American education has deteriorated so drastically in the past two decades that "our very future as a nation and a people" is threatened, an education commission warned yesterday in a study released by the White House. (Feinberg 1983)

The *Post*, *Time*, *Newsweek,* and the *New York Times* all repeated the report's ominous statement: "If an unfriendly foreign power had attempted to impose on America the mediocre educational performance that exists today, we might well have viewed it as an act of war" (Feinberg 1983; McGrath, Constable and Stanley 1983; Williams 1983; Fiske 1983a). *Newsweek* opined: "Education rarely commands broad national attention for very long—only, it seems, when the country is in trouble. The country is in trouble" (Williams 1983). Coverage of the report was both abundant and sustained over time. The *Washington Post*, for example, published nearly two articles per week on *A Nation at Risk* in the year following the report's release (Guthrie and Springer 2004: 11–12).

The media certainly played a prominent role in helping catapult *A Nation at Risk* into a school reform movement. Major media may also be considered a de facto voice of organized business, given boards of directors that include numerous interlocks with the boards of other major corporations. Ben Bagdikian (1983: 25) observed in 1983 that Time, Inc. "has so many interlocks"—such as with Mobil Oil, American Express,

General Dynamics, and "most of the major international banks"—that "they almost constitute the leadership of American business and finance." Noteworthy too is that Time president and CEO Richard Munro served on the Task Force on Education for Economic Growth. Munro and other media owners were almost certainly part of the national business leadership's conversation on school reform, on what business would like schooling to be, and on how to organize to make it so.

It is not hard to imagine organized business, in the early 1980s, coming to school reform with a strategic plan. The Task Force on Education for Economic Growth would seek to align education policymakers—notably the governors and state and local school boards—behind business's reform message: "Mediocre schools are putting the nation's economy at risk, and something needs to be done." At the same time, the NCEE would deliver this message to the general public under the newsworthy auspices of a federal commission. The media would then spread the message far and wide.

The particular recommendations of the two reports were perhaps not so important, as the legislative details would be hammered out in the proper venues. It was sufficient that the reports called for rigor, high standards, and similar positive-sounding concepts with which few people could disagree. In many ways, the reports sought simply to build a consensus for change, and to do so with business leaders in the driver's seat. Conservative demands for school prayer or vouchers were avoided as too controversial. Higher teacher salaries were recommended as a gesture toward professionalism but would not be a reform priority. Only minor mention is made of standardized testing, this being a potentially divisive topic. In practice, of course, high-stakes testing would become the centerpiece of school reform.

In all, there is good reason to believe that the corporate sector, and its politically organized element in particular, was instrumental in the reform movement's origins. Identifying its role, during that period of the movement's birth, does require some speculation. In the 1990s, on the other hand, the driving role of the organized business sector becomes indisputable.

Business Roundtable

At their 1989 annual summer meeting, the BRT's two hundred CEOs launched a very ambitious school reform organizing project. The group's ten-year initiative, well documented in a 2002 dissertation by Kathy Emery, lobbied every state to commit to education standards—especially those approved by business leaders—together with high-stakes tests aligned to the standards. Furthermore, the BRT connected this state-level work to demands for action at the federal level; toward the latter, it spearheaded a larger business coalition that helped pass NCLB, with its imposition of corporate, test-driven schooling on a national scale.

In the BRT campaign, each CEO took responsibility to promote the cause in one or more states. Emery (2002: 50) describes the group's work in Maryland:

> The Maryland BRT [MBRT] surveyed candidates during election years and testified in state legislatures. They also reviewed the state test in order to correlate student ability on it to the ability to perform well in the workplace. When MBRT sponsored focus groups of parents, teachers, and principals and discovered widespread concern about the tests, MBRT had the state delay the introduction of

the new exams and then used funds from the Anne Casey Foundation to create a 45-member speakers bureau to begin to change the public opposition to the test.

In Washington state, Emery continues, the BRT pushed education reform through Partners for Leadership in Education, a body funded by Boeing, Microsoft, Washington Mutual Bank, and the timber company Weyerhaeuser.

One BRT initiative in Washington, a push to revise the state's reading standards, suggests how the organization geared curriculum toward the subordination of working-class students. The state's original policy held that "the student reads to construct meaning from a variety of texts for a variety of purposes." After the BRT's intervention, this was changed to read: "The student understands the meaning of what is read." By omitting the phrase "construct meaning," the revised standard uses "clearer language" and avoids "education jargon," explained the BRT's *Business Leader's Guide to Setting Academic Standards* (Business Roundtable 1996: 22). Yet, the children of BRT members have wide access to pedagogies that invite them to construct meaning. As a statement by the elite University of Chicago Laboratory Schools (2013:10) explains to kindergarten parents: "Our program builds on young children's curiosity and enthusiasm and is based on the understanding that young children learn best when they can construct meaning in a context-rich environment."

Under corporate schooling, public school students do not enjoy the same privilege, are not asked to make their own interpretations and discoveries, but instead are told that there is only one "correct" interpretation of a text, to be found and marked on their worksheet. Such curriculum conveys the lesson to working-class students that they are not empowered, do not have a say-so about the meaning of things, and that the written word represents an authority to which they are subordinate. Today, Common Core, backed by both the BRT and the Chamber (Elkind 2015), carries the same message: its central concept of "close reading" requires students to focus on "what lies within the four corners of the text," and to avoid connecting the text to oneself, or to the world at large (Ferguson 2013–14).

In 1999, State Farm Insurance CEO Edward Rust assessed the progress of the BRT's education campaign in an internal report. In the state of Washington, he noted, Boeing CEO Frank Shrontz "worked with Governor Booth Gardner to draft comprehensive reform legislation that passed in 1993." In Kentucky, the CEOs of United Parcel Service, oil refiner Ashland, and health insurance giant Humana each "personally intervened to save school-improvement legislation" (Rust 1999; qtd. in Emery: 48). The BRT worked closely with the National Governors Association, a collaboration that involved several national education summits and the founding of a think tank, Achieve, that would later lead development of the Common Core.[13]

Rust further reports that the BRT took the lead in establishing a Business Coalition for Education Reform (BCER) in the late 1990s (Rust 1999; cited in Emery: 45). Composed of the BRT, the Chamber, NAM, the National Alliance of Business, and several other national business federations, the BCER sought to intensify "standards, testing, and accountability reforms" at the federal level (Rhodes 2012: 136). Giving congressional testimony on behalf of the BCER in 1999, Rust spoke in terms that foreshadowed NCLB. "Federal aid should be used to encourage continuous improvements in state academic standards and assessments," he said. "Accountability should be measured by student performance results," and "those results should be disclosed publicly. Parents and the community at large should know how well their schools are doing and how they compare with schools elsewhere" (Business Coalition 1999; qtd. in Rhodes: 136). BCER's successor organization, the Business Coalition for Excellence in Education, would lobby hard for passage of NCLB, which was signed by President Bush in January 2002 (Rhodes: 152–3).

Today, while the BRT still maintains an Education and Workforce Committee, headed by General Motors CEO Mary Barra, it has clearly adopted a lower profile on education following the passage of NCLB. Assumably, with national education policy now aligned with high-stakes testing, and the shift toward private management of public schools well underway, the organization considered its campaign successful and turned to other priorities. Nowadays, in terms of the organized business sector, reform's leading US driver is the American Legislative Exchange Council (ALEC). The most important national organization advancing the corporate agenda at the state level, ALEC joins some three hundred corporate members in an "exchange" with two-thousand-member state legislators, or one quarter of the country's state lawmakers. The organization estimates that two hundred of its sponsored bills, covering a broad range of issues, are passed each year. Legislators who support the ALEC bills are often repaid with corporate political contributions toward their reelection (Lafer 2017: 13). On education, ALEC's priorities include the expansion of charter schools and vouchers, expansion of digital instruction, and promotion of "teacher quality" (American Legislative Exchange Council 2016). Its criteria for teacher quality are guided by the corporate-backed National Council on Teacher Quality, which gives high ratings to states that link teacher job security and pay to student test scores, that reduce teacher job security generally, and that test teachers for their subject knowledge (National Council on Teacher Quality 2015).

Neoliberal School Reform as a Global Movement

The neoliberal/rightward turn in the United States was mirrored by the same political turn in England, with both launching school reform movements in the 1980s (Jones 2016). At the same time, reform took on a global character—first, through the World Bank, with a focus on the developing world; later, through the OECD, which focused on the advanced economies of the North. With these two agencies giving lead, the contemporary global reform movement is headed up by an organized business sector aligned behind a neoliberal agenda, just as in the United States. The sector's global expression manifests less through business federations, however, than through pro-business planning institutions such as the World Bank, OECD, International Monetary Fund (IMF), World Trade Organization, and the G7 (comprised of seven of the wealthiest industrialized countries). Also distinguishing the sector at the global level is its particular dominance by banking interests, operating as government appointees—whether as agency directors or as representatives of the US Treasury, the US Federal Reserve Board, and the central banks and finance ministries of the other participating countries (Panitch and Gindin 2012; Peet 2007). Let's glance at the school reform work of the World Bank and OECD.

World Bank

The World Bank and its sister institution, the IMF, were created in 1944 with a view to promoting world economic stability following a period of two world wars and a major depression. Subsequently their primary role became that of extending low-interest loans to developing countries, ostensibly to aid economic growth and reduce poverty. Since the early 1950s, however, both agencies have attached conditions to their loans affecting the borrowing countries' economic policies. The required policies gear to the interests of global capital, critics assert, widely exacerbating poverty rather than reducing it (Bond 2003; Peet 2009). Patrick Bond (2003: 23) outlines the economic reforms or "structural adjustments" that the IMF and World Bank regularly require in Africa, and which are similarly imposed across the developing world:

- Government budget cuts, increases in user fees for public services, and privatization of state enterprises;
- Lifting of price controls, subsidies, and any other "distortions of market forces";
- Liberalization of currency controls and currency devaluation;
- Higher interest rates and deregulation of local finance;
- Removal of import barriers (trade tariffs and quotas); and
- Emphasis on the promotion of exports, above all other economic priorities.

As US and English school reform gathered steam in the 1980s, the Washington-based World Bank began prescribing a version for the Global South. Consistent with its general demands for austerity, the bank issued education reports in 1986 (Psacharopoulos et al.) and 1988 (World Bank) that emphasized cost cutting by lowering teacher salaries, reducing teacher qualifications, containing teachers unions, and shifting school and college costs to students and their families. The bank continued in this vein in a 2011 report, *Making Schools Work*, whose recommendations included "school-based management," which allocates decision-making power to local communities and school-site bodies (Bruns, Filmer, and Patrinos 2011: 218–23). School-based management is a subtle reform strategy that shifts school costs to parents and local entities under an aura of grassroots democratization (on its practice in Honduras, see Levy 2014). While the demand for austerity has led to the deterioration of public education in many developing countries (Reimers and Tiburcio 1993: 5), the bank insists that cost cutting need not mean a loss in education quality: "Researchers have documented the weak correlation between spending and results in education," explains *Making Schools Work*. Quality, it is claimed, is ensured through accountability measures such as applying sanctions against schools with low test scores and linking teacher pay and job security to performance. Here, the bank's commitment to the US school reform model is quite clear. Studies of the US experience, according to the bank, "have typically found that the impact of accountability on test scores has been positive" (Reimers and Tiburcio 1993: 13).

The World Bank is also an avid supporter of school privatization. In 2014, the International Finance Corporation—the World Bank's private investment arm—invested $10 million toward the expansion of Bridge International Academies, the world's largest private school chain (International Finance 2014). With over five hundred schools in Kenya, Nigeria, Uganda, Liberia, and India, and plans to reach 10 million students by 2025, Bridge claims to offer education to poor students that is both affordable and world class. "Even those living in extreme poverty on less than $1.25 a day can afford to send at least two children," asserts company co-founder Shannon May (qtd. in Benson 2016). Moreover, the Bridge website reads: "Our pre-prepared lessons include step-by-step instructions explaining what teachers should do and say during any given moment of a class. This allows us to bring best-in-class instruction expertise and academic experts into every single Bridge classroom no matter where it is" (Bridge, n.d.). In contrast, Curtis Riep and Mark Machacek (2016: 2, 24, 33), who investigated the company's operations in Uganda, contend that its school facilities, and reliance on predominantly unlicensed and underpaid teachers reading out lessons from tablet computers, neglect the Ugandan government's educational standards. The authors also find that, based on average household income in the Uganda communities served by Bridge, a typical family would need to spend 15–27 percent of its income to send just one child to Bridge for a year. The authors conclude that the Bridge model involves "serious deprivations for teachers and learners alike," representing "a form of neocolonialism."

World Bank backing of a project like Bridge—whose other investors include Bill Gates, Facebook's Mark Zuckerberg, and Pearson Education—has broad implications. It certainly involves edu-business aims, tapping profitable opportunities among the world's poor. James Stanfield writes of the "fortune at the bottom of the pyramid in education": as much as $11 billion in profits can be accessed within ten years, according to JP Morgan, by investing in the primary education market among the 4 billion people who live on less than two dollars a day (Stanfield 2012). But the project also represents a larger social vision—in which the extremely rich package curriculum for the very poor, transferred through the medium of tablet technology; in which education and economic uplift become the private responsibility of the individual family, rather than public social responsibility of the state. We'll return to this topic shortly as pertains more broadly to the organized business sector.

OECD

School reform's lead promoter in the Global North is the Paris-based OECD (Meyer and Benavot 2013). The OECD is a think tank and policy center funded by its thirty-eight-member countries. Its top contributor is the United States, which supplied 21 percent of the agency's 2017 central budget. Established in 1961 with a broad mission to promote economic and social well-being, the OECD has developed a high profile on education issues over the past two decades. Its centerpiece educational initiative is the Program for International Student Assessment (PISA), a triennial math, science, and reading test for fifteen-year-olds, in which over seventy countries now participate. First administered in 2000, PISA promptly became the world's gold standard for measuring and ranking national school systems. But the OECD does more than test students and rank countries; it also produces education policy papers and recommends reforms to help individual countries improve their PISA scores. As with the World Bank, the OECD's educational prescriptions accord with the US reform model: promoting standards, testing, and privatization, with a notable emphasis on "competencies" designed to meet the demands of the "21st century job market."

The competency education upon which PISA is modeled—now widely marketed as "personalized learning"—breaks instruction into sharply defined and standardized learning modules; once students master one module, they move on to the next. Critics charge that competency education narrows curriculum to that which is measurable, while diminishing learning as a process of discovery (Hyland 1994; Singer 2015). Terry Hyland (1994: 67) explains:

> Instead of an experiential holistic approach, CBET [competency-based education and training] atomises and fragments learning into assessable chunks, rather than valuing process and experience, CBET is concerned only with performance outcomes, and most significantly, instead of fostering critical reflection and alternative perspectives, CBET offers a mono-cultural view based on the satisfaction of restricted performance criteria directed towards fixed and pre-determined ends.

A computer-driven approach to competency education is the current rage among US school reformers (National Governors Association 2015; Sturgis 2015), and the Every Student Succeeds Act of 2015, in section 1204, offers federal grants for the model's further development.

PISA serves, in effect, as a global marketing tool for corporate education policy. A 2006-7 Education International survey of teachers' unions showed that many countries had reoriented their education systems toward reform after receiving unhappy PISA results. Germany, which was gripped by "PISA shock" after a disappointing ranking in 2000, instituted a new regime of national standards and "testing testing testing." Irish respondents to the survey affirmed that PISA "has been and still is a catalyst for change in favor of more testing and evaluation." In Australia, a government report on *The Future of Schooling* made "considerable use of the PISA data" to show a "long tail of underachievement." This document became the basis for setting national goals shaped by "testing accountability regimes" (Figazzolo 2009: 14–16; citing Dawkins 2007). While OECD policy generally gears toward the advanced capitalist economies, the agency also markets policy to developing countries: the OECD consulted closely with Mexico on its recent education reforms, provoking fierce resistance from teachers (OECD 2010; Slaughter 2015).

Beyond education, the OECD's economic perspective is squarely neoliberal and consistent with the broad aims of transnational corporate and financial interests, as seen in the agency's 2006 "jobs strategy" report. The document favors unrestricted global flows of capital and investment; privatization and deregulation; dismantling worker protections against layoffs; keeping a lid on minimum wage protections; and curbing unemployment, welfare, and retirement benefits (OECD 2006: 21–2). While the OECD assumes a public posture of class neutrality, political economist Richard Woodward (2009: 91, 94) describes the OECD's annual forum as a business-sponsored affair where "speakers representing pro-capitalist, corporate interests" outnumber those from "more socially or charitably orientated organizations," and where "choirs of neoliberal prophets congregate to eulogize about the benefits of capitalist globalization."

Theorizing the Organized Business Sector

The forgoing sought primarily to establish the "who" of school reform, proposing three driving sectors—edu-business, philanthropy, and organized business—with the last being the pivotal player. Let's now take a closer look at the "why" of school reform, from the standpoint of organized business. The sector's public rationale, stressing the need for a more skilled workforce, doesn't match up with the economy's decades-long trend toward deskilled jobs (Marsh 2011). "The consensus among top economists is that the skills gap is a myth," urban policy specialist Marc Levine (2013: 4) finds in a research review. The particular claim of an urgent shortage of science, technology, engineering and math (STEM) graduates has also been challenged. "Nearly all of the independent scholars and analysts who have examined the claims of widespread shortages" in science and engineering "have found little or no evidence to support them," finds Michael Teitelbaum of Harvard Law School's Labor and Worklife Program (2014). Ron Hira of the Rochester Institute of Technology adds that companies such as Microsoft advocate for more federal STEM education money and more visas for foreign information technology workers—even as they lay off thousands of American employees with comparable skills (cited in Anft 2013).

A second motive that might be attributed to organized business is that federations such as the BRT back school reform in order to aid those of its members engaged in edu-business. Bess Altwerger (2005b: 37–8), for example, points out that the Roundtable roster included Harold McGraw III of the McGraw-Hill publishing company. The BRT-backed No Child Left Behind Act boosted the sales of McGraw-Hill reading programs and standardized tests. No doubt, such rewards informed the BRT's embrace of school reform. On the other hand, the federation would not likely devote itself to an ambitious ten-year reform campaign in order to benefit only a certain segment of its members. Rather, we would be on sounder footing to look for aims that benefit the entire membership—in effect, aims that benefit a broad capitalist class.

One such broad class aim would be austerity. In a great many locales, school reform is co-joined with education budget cuts and public service cuts generally— these helping to expedite tax cuts for corporations and the wealthy. Or, in the case of the Global South, austerity is prescribed by international lending agencies partly as an assurance to investors for repayment of loans. School reform, however, cannot be understood simply as an austerity strategy. First, it is not unusual for school reform to coincide with *increased* education spending. For example, the UK's public education spending—for all education levels combined, as a percentage of gross domestic product—grew from 4.4 percent in 1990 to 6.2 percent in 2010. This was during a period of intensive school reform. US education spending increased marginally in the same period, from 4.8 to 5.4 percent.[14] Second, an austerity aim doesn't account for the specific kinds of curriculum and mechanisms of control that are integral to the reform package.

This leads to a further broad class aim, and to my central thesis, which is that the organized business sector seeks reform primarily for curricular purposes: it wants curriculum that fosters a subordinate working class and that, in other ways, advances capitalist hegemony. Just as Harvey identifies neoliberalism as "a political project carried out by the corporate capitalist class," school reform is a front line in that same project. Dave Hill (2001) writes of such aim in England, where Prime Minister Thatcher's landmark Education Reform Act of 1988 included a new national curriculum. The curriculum, Hill (2001: 96) contends, sought to create "a Conservative hegemony in ideas" and "to remove liberal, progressive and socialist ideas from schools and from the minds of future citizens." This change came in the context of growing numbers of teachers and local school councils who, since the 1970s, had been practicing progressive pedagogies—child-centered models, Black and working-class studies. The 1988 curriculum, with its conservative "national culture" and intensified testing, reduced the space for progressive classroom practice. Hill quotes Richard Hatcher in this regard: "Once we had equal opportunities working groups in schools, now we have National Curriculum or SATs [Standardized Assessment Tests] working groups, or none" (98; quoting Hatcher 1995).

In the US case, reform brought no national curriculum per se; but the standards, tests, and commercial curricular packages accomplished much the same. A promising movement of "whole language" teachers had come to fore in the 1980s, shifting power to students in reading and writing workshops; this would be beaten back in the following decade by a coalition of conservatives and textbook publishers touting "systematic phonics" and scripted reading programs (Goodman 2016). Teachers committed to incorporating multicultural and anti-racist perspectives found less space or support for such innovation, as school districts increasingly demanded test-prep instruction (Agee 2004; Sleeter 2012). Today, the corporate curriculum is epitomized by the Knowledge Is Power Program (KIPP) charter schools' widely emulated "no-excuses" model, which imposes a militaristic discipline: "sit up," "nod," "track the speaker with your eyes." Obedient students are rewarded with privileges and "scholar dollars," while students who break the rules face demerits, humiliations such as facing the wall, and, in many cases, suspension or expulsion (Horn 2016).

One concrete way to capture the school reform aims of the organized business sector is to examine the policy platforms of the sector's various organizations. The OECD platform includes the policies forwarded in the above-cited jobs strategy paper (OECD 2006), such as unrestricted global flows of capital, privatization and deregulation, and minimizing labor costs. ALEC's platform includes eliminating minimum wage laws, reintroducing child labor, weakening unions, removing limits on corporate political spending, and passing laws that make it harder for college students, seniors, and low-income citizens to vote (Lafer 2017; Nichols 2011). School reform hopes to facilitate the winning of these and more. Of course, policy platforms change, and we must also talk about corporate hegemony in general. Ultimately, the capitalist class wants the freedom to do as it wishes, without democratic interference.

Growth Coalitions

The organized business sector is comprised primarily of corporations that operate nationally or globally, and whose main objective in school reform lies in shaping the curriculum, a kind of pro-corporate social engineering. Yet, one segment of organized business, which we'll call *growth coalitions*, operates locally and with a school reform objective that is more akin to that of edu-business. Sociologist William Domhoff (n.d.) distinguishes between two sectors of capital: one, made up of "national-level corporate capitalists," derives its income from the production and sale of goods and services; the other, made up of "land-based elites," earns from rents and mortgages. The land-based sector tends to organize as local growth coalitions, aimed at maximizing members' profits through the intensification of land use.

In some US cities, growth coalitions have been intimately involved in school reform, promoting school privatization in particular, and with such privatization linked to a larger land development and gentrification strategy. A sharp example is the Commercial Club of Chicago, made up of the city's business power hitters. In 2004, together with then mayor Richard Daley, the club began its reform/privatization trajectory with Renaissance 2010, a plan to close sixty to seventy schools and open one hundred new schools, most of which would be charter schools or contract schools (district schools run by private contractors). Renaissance was linked to a larger plan for elite urban restructuring. As Pauline Lipman (2009, 2011) describes, public school dismantling took place after years of public housing demolition in majority low-income Black neighborhoods. Real estate developers and city leaders then marketed new housing, together with new charter schools, to more white and affluent populations in these same areas. This gentrification would, in turn, aide the rise of a downtown envisioned as a world-class corporate and tourist center.

Variations of the Chicago model, fusing school privatization with gentrification and elite land development, can be found in New Orleans, Philadelphia, and elsewhere (Buras 2015; Cucchiara 2013; Martin 2011). The extent to which such fusion defines the school reform movement as a whole has not been studied. Such research would likely find wide variation, with land development a central element of the reform movement in Chicago and New Orleans, while barely visible, say, in Los Angeles. The latter city's charter school push has been led not by a growth coalition but by philanthropists, such as the late Eli Broad (Blume 2015; Blume and Phillips 2017).

Race, School Reform, and Capitalist Aims

The forgoing has argued, along with Maisuria (2010), that school reform is less a "white phenomenon" than a capitalist one, integrally linked to capital's systemic aims. But, as noted earlier, school reform is deeply racialized and notably so in the United States. Establishing reform's capitalist character does not, in itself, explain why race and racial inequity have been so central to the school reform project. This subsection offers some ideas on the matter, while framing the discussion within the race/class debate that is central to this chapter. If, as proposed here, school reform is ultimately a social engineering project of big capital, and such engineering includes the advancement of racism—for example, sharpened inequality, increased school segregation, suppression of anti-racist teaching—then the apropos question becomes: Why does capital support and promote racism? This, in turn, raises questions about the core aims of capital.

The Marxist answers here are rather well known: capitalists want to gain profits and accumulate capital; they seek to advance their political interests as a class; and they use racism to divide and weaken the working class. Race-based theory has no comparable consensus about capitalists and their aims, such being rarely theorized in the literature. One pertinent treatment, focused on globalization, is that of critical race scholar Ricky Lee Allen (2001: 476). The core aim of globalizing capitalists is racial, Allen believes. "Globalization is *primarily* about white supremacy and the construction of a global white polity" (emphasis in original). He elaborates with an historic perspective: "It is difficult to believe that the rise of European imperialism was rooted mainly in capitalistic greed since access to equity was distributed along racial group lines." Here, Europe's working- and middle-class whites were "paid off in the currencies of white skin privilege and the psychological wages of whiteness, not to mention land and natural resources" (478; citing Du Bois 1935: 18–21). In modern times, Allen continues, the IMF and World Bank "dictate policy to indebted nation-states rather than organizing a redistribution of wealth from white nations back to the people from whom it was stolen." While such agencies are often viewed as acting in the service of capitalism, Allen sees them as acting "under pressure from the white polity" (480). He also applies this perspective to IMF/World Bank education policy for the Global South: "These prominent institutions do the bidding of the global white polity through blaming the educational conditions of these countries on the lack of competition rather than the globalization of white supremacy" (483).

Allen, however, doesn't look very closely at the corporate actors who brought forth neoliberalism and globalization and to whom he attributes an overarching white supremacist agenda. He does observe their white skin: "In essence, global capital is white capital in that the bodies of most capitalists are seen as white" (474; quoting McLaren, Leonardo and Allen 2000: 110). But he also misses a lot. As the Lewis Powell memo suggests, the 1970s bosses' revolt came substantially in response to the mass movements of the 1960s. Those movements addressed racism and much more—war, democracy, women's and gay rights, the environment. Much evidence, including the Powell memo, indicates that the CEOs were pursuing *corporate* power, not *white* power per se. In the US case, numerous studies observe how corporate leaders operated with greater *class* consciousness through the 1970s and 1980s (Phillips-Fein 2009; Useem 1984; Clawson and Neustadtl 1989; Reuss 2013). Whereas before, corporate leaders had often focused on the narrower interests of an individual company or industry, they were now taking class-wide action through the BRT, a rejuvenated Chamber of Commerce, revved-up lobbying and political action committees, and new think tanks.

It is true that the neoliberal/conservative movement encompasses a resurgent racism. A "wage of whiteness" would continue to be paid, one indicator being the Black-white poverty gap: US Black poverty in 2016, as federally defined, was double that of white poverty—22 percent versus 11 percent.[15] But neoliberalism meant tougher times for working people across race, with wages, job security, and the social safety net all under attack (Greenhouse 2009). Two signal events of the neoliberal turn were Reagan's firing of striking air traffic controllers in 1981 and Thatcher's crushing of the British miners' strike of 1984–5. Both of these historic blows to organized labor targeted primarily white workforces.[16] Neoliberalism may have boosted a white identity, and discouraged class identity, among the white working class; but capitalists themselves acted along class lines, extending solidarity toward other capitalists, not toward white workers.

Racism is best understood as a mechanism of ruling-class social control, albeit one which enjoys substantial traction within the white working class. Theodore Allen makes the case for such interpretation in *The Invention of the White Race* (2012). He shows how a plantation-owning elite in colonial Virginia fashioned the idea of a superior white race in the late seventeenth and early eighteenth centuries. This racial concept, promulgated through churches and public meetings, was bolstered by a series of new laws extending privileges and freedoms to European Americans but denied to African Americans. These included the right to vote and hold office, to marry by choice, to carry a gun, to move about freely, to acquire property, and to be given corn and money at the end of one's indentured labor. This racial regime was created as a divide-and-rule strategy, responding to trends toward collective revolt among white and Black indentured and free laborers, accentuated during Bacon's Rebellion of 1676–77.[17]

The capitalist response to the radical 1960s bears comparison to the events traced by Theodore Allen, where both periods saw elites use race as a tool for quelling and diverting upsurge from below. Although the modern neoliberal/conservative movement encompasses a wide range of issues and components, I think it fair to say that racial politics have been pivotal—both in the progressive upsurge and its conservative suppression. That is, anti-racism was a driving force in the 1960s New Left, where civil rights and Black power organizing gave inspiration to the student movement (Sale 1973: 23–4), women's movement (Gordon 2014: 100–4) and Chicano movement (Mantler 2011). Anti-racism played a similar role in galvanizing British progressivism in the 1970s and 1980s (Virdee 2014: chaps. 7 and 8). Conversely, regressive racial and anti-immigrant politics have been vital in the resurgence of corporate power, both in the United States and in England and Europe more broadly (Panitch and Albo 2015).

Conservative Ideological Web

Pivotal as race may be, we should not regard it in isolation. The modern capitalist offensive merges race with what I call a *conservative ideological web*—comprised of hierarchies of race, class, gender, national origin, sexuality, and physical ability—along with other elements such as individualism, meritocracy, patriotism, and "free enterprise." Any element in the web may be applied as a wedge issue in order to advance other elements, with race and national origin giving lead in this respect across much of the world. While advancing conservative ideology, capital also seeks to suppress a counter-web of ideas—equality, anti-racism, solidarity, socialism—that comprises progressive or leftist ideology. And, of course, education is a major terrain where capital and its challengers (such as progressive teachers) conduct battle for hearts and minds.

My suspicion is that the capitalist class (or its politically organized segment) is very mindful of these connections, and of using race or ethnicity to advance its own class objectives. By that token, I would propose that the reform curriculum's suppression of anti-racist teaching is as much about capital advancing broad rightist objectives as it is about race.[18] To give a flavor of the conservative ideological web in action, I'll offer two case illustrations, both involving education policy in the 1980s.

Illustration #1: An Education Policy Paper: In 1981, the Heritage Foundation published *Mandate for Leadership*, a federal policy manual that was embraced by Reagan and which would become a landmark document of the modern right. A *Mandate* chapter on the Department of Education (DOE) gives particular scrutiny to the department's civil rights and diversity programs. Author Ronald Docksai ties these programs to a larger leftist agenda, as he knits together an alternative rightist platform. Thus, the DOE Office for Civil Rights is dismissed as a "vocational haven of class action advocates" perpetuating "the federal government's legal harassment of schools and colleges" (Docksai 1981: 165, 166). The DOE Women's Education Equity program is accused of awarding grants that are "more in keeping with extreme feminist ideology than concern for the quality of education," while DOE regulations on bilingual education are chastised for usurping the decision-making authority of state and local school administrators (179, 185). Docksai calls for the narrowing or drastic reduction of such programs. He also proposes that Title I federal moneys—which aid high-poverty schools that heavily serve students of color—be redirected to private school vouchers. This, he argues, would rescue "the public-school monopoly's most helpless victims, the inner-city Blacks and Hispanics, at a single stroke" (177). The corporate-backed Heritage Foundation stands opposed not only to these various equity programs but also to the left-influenced movements from which they emerged. "During the past 15 years," Docksai remarks, "there has been a concerted nationwide effort by professional educationists to turn elementary and secondary school classrooms into vehicles for liberal-left social and political change in the United States" (187).

Illustration #2: A Disinformation Campaign: In 1986, a local education authority in Brent, a borough in the northwest of London, designed and prepared to launch a program "to enable schools to develop methodologies, structures and curricula which will improve the attainment and life chances of Black pupils, and thereby create greater race equality" (qtd. in Richardson 1992: 134). Aided by central government funding, fifty-five positions, primarily for teachers, were established to implement the program. Robin Richardson, who co-designed the Brent program, recalls the day when the world began to hear about it. "RACE SPIES SHOCK," blared a headline from London's *Mail on Sunday*, which reported:

> Race commissars in a Left-wing borough are recruiting 180 Thought Police to patrol schools for prejudice.... Brent plans to put a race adviser in every school from January. They will be backed by project teams who will move in at the first hint of prejudice. The 180 advisers will have the power to interfere in every aspect of school life, from discipline to the curriculum. (qtd. on 136)

The project involved no "race advisers" and was not centrally concerned with "prejudice," according to Richardson. But other newspapers promptly pitched in with further falsehoods, distortions, and disapprovals. The *Daily Telegraph* editorialized the next day:

> It is unpleasant, and potentially dangerous for central government to override democratically elected authorities. But as the Government watches the race relations policies of Brent Council proceeding from the absurd to the evil, it may feel that it has no choice but to act. . . . This action by Brent, which will lead to the indoctrination of children, the loss of good teachers, the lowering of standards and the subversion of the British educational ethos throughout an entire London borough, signals that enough is enough. . . . Mr. Baker, the Education Secretary, cannot allow this to go on. (qtd. on 137)

In the wake of the media assault, the Brent program was "virtually strangled at its birth," and its source of government funding was frozen. Meanwhile, Richardson (1992: 142–3) recounts: "No other authority dared to introduce a scheme remotely similar to Brent's," and "several considered abrogating the policy commitments to race equality which they had made earlier in the decade." The national scorning of a school racial equality program also fed into a political environment that aided passing of the 1988 Education Reform Act, with its conservative national curriculum.

As with the policy paper from Heritage, the English media's disinformation campaign engaged race to stir up a broader anti-left politics. The *Mail* apparently hoped to reverse not only the school racial initiative but also the political orientation prevailing in Brent, which the paper identified as a "Left-wing borough." The *Mail* called the school program staff "race commissars" and "Thought Police," evoking images of Soviet-style socialist bureaucracy and repressive government.

Race and Capitalist Differences

We should also acknowledge political differences within the capitalist class, including different racial postures and different strategies for advancing the conservative ideological web. In the United States, centrist capital is represented through the Democratic Party, and rightist capital through the Republican Party. The centrists prefer to rule through cooptation, granting concessions such as in labor rights, social programs, and racial and gender equity. Rightists, on the other hand, apply a more iron hand. While the neoliberal turn has narrowed the degree of difference between right and center, with the capitalist class as a whole granting fewer concessions, differences do remain important and pertinent.

The split can be illustrated through comparing education civil rights enforcement under Obama to that under Trump. The DOE's Office for Civil Rights reported resolving over sixty-six thousand cases during Obama's two terms, including those related to racial and sexual harassment, accessible technology for students with disabilities, and equitable access to courses and educational opportunities (Black 2016). Under Trump, that same office scaled back investigations (Green 2017), while weakening the rights of transgender students, disabled students, and women attending college (Balingit 2017; Peters, Becker, and Davis 2017; Saul and Taylor 2017). A similar split can be found in ethnic studies, with Arizona Republican governor Jan Brewer signing a 2010 ban that targeted a Mexican-American studies program in the Tucson schools (Cruz 2010). Democratic governors, on the other hand, have signed bills moving California and Oregon schools toward ethnic studies programs (Planas 2016; June 2017).

A close reading, however, shows that even the Democrats are aiding the rollback of education civil rights and the suppression of multicultural teaching, notably through their support of the charter school movement. Obama was aggressively pro-charter—for example, urging states to lift caps on the number of charters allowed, as part of his Race to the Top federal grants program. Former California governor Jerry Brown, who signed a bill to create a model ethnic studies curriculum, was nonetheless pro-charter; for example, he vetoed a state bill that would have barred conflicts of interest in charter schools (Ravitch 2016). With charter schools come a deregulated environment that makes it hard to enforce civil rights—such as for race, gender, disability, or language diversity (Fabricant and Fine 2012). The charter chains, which politically dominate the charter movement, are widely hostile to ethnic or multicultural studies, offering instead a relentlessly test-driven pedagogy with no-excuses cultural conservatism.[19]

Insights from England

Education reform being a global movement, global studies and comparisons can certainly shed light on the race and class issues raised in this chapter. Let's take a glance at England, whose school reform regime bears many similarities to that in the United States, but where privatization is far more advanced. In 2016, England's Department for Education issued a white paper calling for a fully privatized, but publicly funded, schooling system by 2022 (Department for Education 2016a). The government later backed down in the face of strong opposition (Kulz 2017: 14). But the proposal wasn't an outlandish reach in the English context.

England's primary vehicle for privatization, called *academies*, roughly mirrors the US charter model, with public funding, private management, and a growing trend toward chain operations. Academy conditions are also similar to those of charters, with frequent use of no-excuses curriculum; cronyism and conflicts of interests; and the pushout of students who struggle academically (Trades Union Congress 2014; Kulz 2017). As in the United States, England uses schools' low test scores as justification for forced privatization—and the government keeps raising the bar for acceptable performance (Bloom 2017). Academy conversions may be imposed against the will of communities and despite concerted protest (Baynes 2013; Tweedie 2012). Pursuant to the 2010 Academies Act, the country added the option of voluntary conversion; and, as of January 2016, 73 percent of students attending academies at the secondary level were in schools that had been voluntarily converted (Department for Education 2016b). The government offers school budget increases as an enticement to convert, and school decisions to convert may often be linked to budgetary pressures associated with the country's ongoing austerity (West and Bailey 2013: 153).

England's school privatization has advanced much more rapidly than in the United States, however. Sixty-six percent of students in state-funded secondary schools were attending academies as of January 2016; the figure for primary schools was 20 percent (Department for Education 2016b). By comparison, US charter schools had captured only 5 percent of public school enrollment as of fall 2014 (NCES 2017). Also, the academy enrollment figures do not suggest racial targeting, as discussed earlier with respect to US privatization. A 77 percent white enrollment in the secondary academies in January 2016 was comparable to the white enrollment in all state-funded secondary schools, which was 76 percent (Department for Education 2016b).

Another distinction between the two countries involves use of the prison-like no-excuses model. While its US application is best known in schools serving predominantly students of color (Horn 2016; White 2015), the model extends across race in England. Among the secondary academies established through a forced conversion is Magna Academy, enrolling seven hundred students in the city of Poole on England's south coast. In June 2017, Magna advertised for a "director of isolations and detentions" for its "Behaviour Correction Unit." The advertisement explained, "If you believe in a strong 'tough love' approach to discipline, no excuses and that children should be respectful and obedient at all times then this may be the role for you" (qtd. in Tingle 2017). The academy, which was praised by former prime minister David Cameron, has shocked parents when they learn that their children are sent into isolation for such infractions as coming to school with pencil cases that are the wrong length ("Dorset School Praised" 2015). Magna's student population is 91 percent white British and relatively high income, with only 9 percent eligible for free student meals (SchoolDash, n.d.).

The distinct state of privatization in England is attributable to that country's unique conditions. Its greater central government control over education, versus significant state and local control in the United States, has no doubt facilitated England's broad privatization.[20] England's more even spread of privatization in racial terms may owe partly to the country's more dispersed Black, Asian, and minority ethnic population, as compared to extreme residential segregation in many US cities.[21] Despite such contextual differences, the English experience—and other country or global studies of the school reform movement (Saltman and Means 2019)—can help us make sense of reform and its class/race significance.

Race, Class, and Social Change Strategy

When school reform is viewed as a project of capital's most powerful players, and who are using schools to advance their own class hegemony, then the task of resisters does become daunting. The struggle for a democratic and just schooling system may not prevail apart from winning wider social change and redistribution of wealth and power—a transformation not likely achievable in the short term. Public schools nevertheless remain a pivotal arena where educators, parents, and youth can collaborate to build grassroots capacity and community power (Ryan 2016; Bradbury et al. 2014).

The final section of this chapter offers a series of reflections on race and class, tending to topics that deserve attention as part of a political dialogue on the left. I make a particular call for class politics in Marxian terms while, at the same time, acknowledging that the Marxist tradition itself needs development in its engagement of racism. As Manning Marable remarked in 1983:

> There is not, at the moment, a body of knowledge which could be described as a Marxian theory of racism which can be directly applied to our understanding of American social reality. (1983a: 107)

> To insist, as some dogmatic Marxists often do, that the transfer of the ownership of the means of production to the working class will create the material conditions for immediate biracial cooperation and social harmony, is to greatly underestimate the power of an idea: racism. (1983b: 142)

There has been, in the intervening years, a growing body of Marxian work around race, including Marable's own *How Capitalism Underdeveloped Black America* (2015); Gerald Horne, *Fire This Time: The Watts Uprising and the 1960s* (1997); Antonia Darder and Rodolfo Torres, *After Race: Racism after Multiculturalism* (2004); Satnam Virdee, *Racism, Class and the Racialized Outsider* (2014); Neville Alexander, *An Ordinary Country: Issues in the Transition from Apartheid to Democracy in South Africa* (2003); John Saul and Patrick Bond, *South Africa—The Present as History* (2014); Robert Miles and Malcolm Brown, *Racism* (2003); and Elizabeth Esch, *The Color Line and the Assembly Line: Managing Race in the Ford Empire* (2018). As David Roediger (2017) makes clear in *Class, Race, and Marxism*, however, there is no Marxian consensus on these issues.

Marable (1983b: 142) didn't throw the baby out with the bathwater: "Personally, I became a Marxist because I am convinced that Black people cannot obtain freedom or self-determination under capitalism." He did fashion his own approach, drawing from a left Black nationalism. In a contribution to the anthology, *Socialist Visions*, Marable (1983a: 110) proposed a system of dual power after the revolution to "protect blacks from the inevitable attacks of racist whites," including social/political institutions to "erase any privileges that whites formerly received simply for being white." The point here is that Marxism isn't set in stone as a body of thought, and it isn't necessary to reject class struggle in order to embrace the racial struggle. To the contrary, says Virdee (2017a), "If we are to ever forge a sustainable solidarity between the ethnically diverse proletariat in the imperialist core (as well as with those beyond), it is more than likely we will have to go through race, rather than around it."

Toward Vision and Strategy

As the first section noted with respect to Cedric Robinson's work, race-based scholars have developed a critique of racial capitalism but haven't offered a clear sense of how it might be challenged or what its alternative would be. Marxism, by contrast, identifies a particular vision of socialism, defined in terms of workers' democracy, as suggested in

Marx's admiring account of the 1871 Paris Commune (Marx 1989). The forementioned *Socialist Visions* (Shalom 1983) explores potential contours of a workers' democracy and proposes other dimensions of a socialist society in such areas as race, family sex roles, economy, and the environment. While this visionary conversation is not finished, any viable political theory ought to include a concept of the world we wish to build, giving flesh to such terms as "equity," "justice," and "ending oppression."

With respect to strategy: one major question deserving discussion concerns the relationship between anti-racist struggles and other struggles, including that against capitalism. Should our movement seek to address all the oppressions at the same time? Or is anti-racism a better focus, where the obtaining of racial equality could then lay foundation for wider victories? The latter approach is implied in Joe Feagin's (2006) *Systemic Racism: A Theory of Oppression*. An epilogue suggests various ways to reduce or eliminate racism, such as through "large-scale antiracist organization and action" (314); a "constitutional convention at which all groups of Americans are fairly represented" (317); and exerting international pressure through the United Nations Convention on the Elimination of All Forms of Racial Discrimination. Although Feagin also acknowledges issues beyond race, including class, gender, imperialism, and multinational capitalism, he makes no organizing suggestions pertaining to these other forms of oppression. Readable in Feagin, though not expressly asserted, is that progress must be made around racism before adopting a wider focus.

There are problems and challenges in a "race first" approach. Most manifestations of racism, especially of the institutional kind, are not separable from other forms of oppression. And the most significant anti-racist demands—related to jobs and housing, or education, or policing and incarceration—will require movements of enormous multi-issue and multiracial breadth. Few movements, though, come ready-made with complete and comprehensive political platforms. Moreover, the multiracial movements themselves cannot be built without consciously creating organizing models that are anti-racist, anti-sexist, pro-LGBT, and pro-youth. Marx (1998) saw the revolution as the means by which the working class could rid itself of "the muck of ages" and "become fitted to found society anew." I would add that the muck must also be addressed as part of the organizing process and as a foundation for revolution.

Without proposing a specific strategy, I would suggest that a productive dialogue around race and class theory must incorporate ample discussion of organizing strategy, allowing us to entertain the strategic implications of this or that theory and the theoretical implications of strategy.

Toward Class

I've identified my outlook in this chapter as class-primacist. This means that, with Marx, I consider the economy—that is, the means by which humanity sustains itself—to be society's central motor; undemocratic control of that motor constitutes our most fundamental social problem. The economy's private ownership, and its increasing concentration into a few hands, has enabled the owning class to dominate government, schools, media, and most other of society's institutions. Another part of my class understanding is that those of us who, as a matter of survival, must sell our labor to capital, and under terms largely determined by capital, have the capacity to unite, win power, and effect democratic transformation. I see class as a lens for political analysis, which I've attempted to apply to the phenomenon of school reform. And I see it as a foundation for social change strategy. Here I align with a liberatory view of class that David McNally (2006: 351) expresses in *Another World Is Possible*:

> Genuine liberation cannot be provided by a narrow "class" politics that evades these issues [of gender and racial domination]; it requires the self-emancipation of women, sexual minorities, and racially-oppressed peoples. Yet, class politics are crucial if capitalism is to be challenged. Consequently, we need an anti-racist, feminist class politics, i.e., one that makes feminism and anti-racism central building blocks of its struggle for full human emancipation.

Part of the divide separating race-based theory and Marxism owes to competing definitions of class, which can interfere with productive conversations between the two traditions. Race-based scholars predominantly employ the stratification model of class that prevails in academe and in society generally, rather than a Marxian class-conflict model. Under stratification, class is viewed as a marker of income or socioeconomic status—with upper, middle, and lower classes; and the working class situated vaguely across the lower-middle and lower strata. By contrast, the class-conflict model defines class as a relationship to capitalist production (Gimenez 2007). Categorizing people by income certainly has many scholarly uses. Its drawback, when applied to political analysis and organizing, is it tends to hide economic relationships and interests. That the bulk of low and middle earners share a common interest, as members of an exploited working class, is made invisible in the stratification scheme. The approach thus tends to reinforce the prevailing low levels of class consciousness and anti-capitalist awareness, an historic problem in the United States.[22]

Let's consider these issues in reference to multicultural teacher education, this being a large area of race-based scholarly practice. Stratification is the class model of choice within the field. Note that a great majority of students attending multicultural education courses, primarily preservice and practicing teachers, are white and female.[23] Multicultural teacher educators regard this cohort as predominantly middle class, not working class. "Typically, white middle-class prospective teachers have little or no understanding of their own culture," says Gloria Ladson-Billings (2001). "Most students were from middle-class backgrounds with a few from low-income families," explain Sandra Lawrence and Beverly Daniel Tatum (1998:46) in describing two of their multicultural courses. This includes the identification of *practicing teachers* as middle class, as seen in the work of Christine Sleeter (1995: 118):

> A large proportion of teachers are women, and a large proportion have also worked their way up from lower or working-class origins. In that regard, they are members of oppressed groups, and their experiences with social class and gender provide teachers with a perspective about how they believe social stratification works.... Historically, teaching has provided members of the lower- and working-class

entrée into middle-class status; many teachers have experienced working their way up by attaining education.

In Sleeter's stratification-based perspective, teachers may be class-oppressed because of their low-income origins, but they are not class-oppressed as teachers. That is, teachers are not part of the working class. The working class, in turn, is not a group with a certain relationship to production or to the capitalist state; rather, it is an income group.[24]

Today's teachers vitally need a class-conscious framework to help them understand and challenge the capitalist assault on the working conditions and learning conditions in schools. A recent study of Vermont teachers found that the predominantly female workforce is "feeling the strain": "They are working long hours at school, stretching themselves to support student educational and economic needs, and struggling to support their own families" (Givan and Whitefield 2018: 11). Teaching conditions are worse in the charter school world. A former KIPP teacher recalls: "It felt like sprinting a marathon for two years. I probably worked somewhere between 80 and 100 hours every single week" (qtd. in Horn 2016: 8). The long hours often include intense managerial scrutiny and intimidation. An academy manager in England describes how he supervises the teachers under his watch:

> So if I am not happy with something I will meet with the teacher and I will pick out individual students and I will say: "Why has this student done worse in your class? Please explain. Why have you not picked this up? Why did you say they were going to get one grade and they got something completely different? Please explain this to me." (qtd. in Kulz 2017: 52)

A class-conscious and union-conscious framework is especially valuable for female teachers who may have imbibed societal messages that encourage women's self-sacrifice or subordination. These issues were palpable in my case study of the mostly female teachers who rallied to challenge a scripted reading program and build an enriching "balanced literacy" alternative, at their elementary school in a low-income Latino neighborhood in East Los Angeles (Ryan 2016: chap. 7). At one point in the campaign, pursuant to the union contract, the teachers held a formal vote on whether to confirm the principal's preferred candidate for a newly created coordinator position that would bear large impact on the school's literacy program. Activist teachers were calling for a strong no vote, mindful that their balanced literacy campaign would either advance or be set back based on the vote's outcome. The teachers did indeed turn down the principal's choice and subsequently voted to install their campaign leader into the new coordinator slot, affirming their new culture of solidarity in the process. But "it took a lot for them to vote no," recalls the campaign leader. "A couple of the teachers said, 'I don't know if that's disrespectful to the principal'" (qtd. on 199). In the East L.A. organizing project, the teachers' ability to recognize themselves as workers, and with the daring to stand together against management—that is, an emergent form of class consciousness—tied integrally to educational justice issues in this low-income community of color.

Teachers do need multicultural education, and with an anti-racist edge rather than "heroes and holidays" (Lee, Menkart, and Okazawa-Rey 2008). Multicultural teacher educators are fighting the good fight when they encourage their predominantly white students to reflect upon their racial privileges and assumptions and to become better attuned to the needs of diverse communities. Such teacher educators can be even more effective by revisiting class and developing frameworks that properly place class and race in a capitalist context. Teachers who incorporate both class and anti-racist sensibilities are best equipped to help build the kind of resistant cultures and transformed unions required in neoliberal times. With respect to anti-racism as classroom practice: school reformers are aggressively narrowing the space for such. Here too, teachers need class *and* anti-racist consciousness in order to fashion the kinds of teachers' unions and community alliances that can sustain and grow such curriculum (Ryan 2016; Bradbury et al. 2014).

Racism and White Interests

Within these competing class models lies a theoretical dispute with many practical implications for anti-racist teaching and organizing. This concerns the matter of where white interests—especially *working-class* white interests—ultimately lie with respect to racism. A prevalent assumption in race-based theory is that racism benefits whites, *all* whites, giving them an attendant material interest in racism's continuation. As Elias and Feagin (2016: 258) explain, systemic racism "unjustly enriches, materially and socially, the oppressor racial group (whites) and thereby unjustly impoverishes, materially and socially, subordinated racial groups (people of color)." Feagin (2006: 21), in a separate work, adds that "white Americans have political-economic interests that are quite different from those of African Americans and other Americans of color."

Marxists have a different reading. While racism does extend advantage to whites over non-whites within the working class, we argue that racism is ultimately contrary to all working class interests, in that it helps keep class exploitation in place. Marable (1983b: 140) articulated this stance in 1983:

> My research from the late seventies convinces me that (1) the white bourgeoisie benefits decisively from racist propaganda, primarily because it divides workers; (2) the white middle stratum and working classes benefit from racism in relative, but not in absolute terms. . . . Overall, racism allows the capitalists to perpetuate the exploitation of white workers, in such a manner that whites are collectively worse off than if racism in socioeconomic relations did not exist. Racism gives many whites a false sense of security under capitalism, and obscures the essential dynamics of their own brutal suppression.

Gerald Horne (1990: 173–4) similarly argues: "It would be a mistake to suggest that Euro-American workers have benefited as a class from white supremacy. If that were the case, white Mississippians would be the most affluent and successful of any people in the union. But actually, they are at the bottom of the heap."

The contrasting assumptions of race-based and class-based thinkers with respect to white interests can lead to strategic differences. Since Marxism assumes shared working-class interests, its strategic emphasis lies in helping working people discover those shared interests, especially by engaging in common struggle. The best in Marxism sees anti-racist organizing as pivotal to such efforts. Virdee (2014), for example, hails the independent self-organization of Blacks and Asians—both in community and labor organizing—which aided the growth of anti-racist consciousness in sectors of the British working class in the 1970s. In the contemporary United States: labor organizer Gabriel Kristal (2017) talks about how the pursuit of shared goals, joined with racial and related discussions, helped break down divisions among health-care union members while preparing for contract campaigns in California:

> My job was to explicitly talk about racism, sexism, ethnocentrism, homophobia and religious intolerance as specific barriers to a strong union. A good union member can't complain about Mexicans "taking jobs" while also asking Latino colleagues to make common cause with him. My experience was that union members took this seriously.

Race-based theorists, however, tend to regard class unity strategies with skepticism. "Historically speaking," say Omi and Winant, "the call for class unity across racial lines has amounted in practice to an argument that non-whites give up their racially based demands in favor of 'class unity' on white terms" (1994: 31). Historical patterns of racism in the US labor movement would certainly justify Omi and Winant's caution (Kelley 1999). On the other hand, the potential of bridging Black and white interests along class lines—and with an authentic anti-racist orientation—is rarely explored in the race-based literature.[25] CRT offers an "interest convergence" principle, which holds that "the interest of Blacks in achieving racial equality will be accommodated only when it converges with the interests of whites," and where the applicable remedy does not threaten "the superior societal status of middle and upper class whites" (Bell 1980: 523; a similar posture from a Latino perspective is that of Alemán and Alemán 2010).

If class-based strategies *are* dismissed, how then might whites be rallied en masse to anti-racism? Feagin's approach relies heavily on morality. Whites, Feagin (2014: 314) asserts, have a "moral obligation" to "overturn the oppressive and systematic racism they and their ancestors have created." And furthermore, "the moral and ethical costs of racism lie deep in the white psych" (Feagin, Vera and Batur 2001: 226). Feagin's strategy isn't based *solely* on moral appeals: he also believes in mass anti-racist action. But we must still tackle the question of how deep or broad will be white engagement in a movement that demands material betterment for people of color but only ethical betterment for whites. This concern is not to minimize the power of anti-racism—or the specific pursuit of Black or Latino demands—as an organizing focus but rather to call on ourselves to address matters of strategic vision across the social and material suffering of all working people. This, in turn, will require a viable theoretical framework, including the sorting out of working-class interests and how we imagine winning a solid majority to our vision of fundamental change.

Race and Class in South Africa

This closing subsection shines further light on race/class discussions through the case of South Africa—addressing the anti-apartheid movement and the post-apartheid government under the African National Congress (ANC). To help frame my treatment, I'll draw upon an observation of Canadian political economist John Saul (2002), in regard to the tension between Marxism and those rejecting it in favor of what has been called identity politics. Saul advises his fellow Marxists to continue to "emphasize the production process as our chosen entry-point into social analysis and political practice" while also "taking seriously the concerns of those who wish to highlight, alternatively or simultaneously, the claims to our attention of other nodes of oppression and resistance." This done, he continues, all that Marxists need ask of those whose political focus lies in struggles around race or gender or sexual orientation is that they "take seriously the goal of overthrowing, sooner or later (but preferably sooner rather than later), the capitalist system" (354).

If we apply Saul's thesis, then one part of a dialogue between these frameworks might explore what it means to take anti-racism and anti-capitalism with equal seriousness. After all, the longstanding contention of race-based theorists and intersectionalists has been that Marxism is class reductive, that it falls short around race and other non-class categories. Conversely, the Marxists, myself included, contend that the non-Marxist traditions give too little attention to capitalism. I believe that the South African experience can enrich such dialogue and debate: the anti-apartheid movement and its aftermath demonstrate with clarity why anti-racist struggle can and must be co-joined with class struggle.

The anti-apartheid movement, stretching from the 1950s to the early 1990s, targeted South Africa's white supremacist system but gave less attention to the capitalist system that birthed apartheid.[26] What kind of society did the movement leadership envision? Had it an agenda to truly empower the country's majority-Black working class politically and economically? Or, alternatively, would it pursue a narrower program of constitutional equality but where capitalism's racialized legacy of mass poverty and inequity remains intact and where new access to wealth and power extends mainly to a small Black elite? My reading is that the movement leadership held hope and vision far beyond what was finally achieved. At the same time, the movement's lead trajectory—the pursuit of racial equality within an ultimately pro-capitalist framework—would limit the potential for social transformation.

Socialist and socialistic aims were actually an important part of the discourse within the ANC and the larger Congress Alliance that comprised the main anti-apartheid leadership. This could be seen in the early writings of the African National Congress Youth League (CYL), founded in 1944 and which would lead the senior ANC away from its traditional posture of quiet advocacy and toward that of mass resistance. The first crop of CYL leaders included Nelson Mandela, Oliver Tambo, and Walter Sisulu, who would later become core leaders of the ANC. CYL was guided by a philosophy of African nationalism. "*Africans are one*," explained the group's first president and influential thinker, Anton Lembede. "Out of the heterogeneous tribes, there must emerge a homogeneous nation. The basis of national unity is the nationalistic feeling of the Africans, the feeling of being Africans irrespective of tribal connection, social status, educational attainment or economic class" (emphasis in original; qtd. in Karis and Carter 1973: 317). But this nationalism also had a socialist character, as Lembede explained:

> The fundamental structure of Bantu Society is socialistic. There was for instance no individual ownership of land in ancient Bantu society. There were no landlords or the so-called "absentee" landlords. Land belonged virtually to the whole tribe and nominally to the King or Chief. Socialism then is our valuable legacy from our ancestors. Our task is to develop this socialism by the infusion of new and modern socialistic ideas. (qtd. in Karis and Carter: 314)

A socialist or social-democratic influence could again be seen in the Freedom Charter, adopted in 1955 and the anti-apartheid movement's most honored document:

> The national wealth of our country, the heritage of all South Africans, shall be restored to the people;
> The mineral wealth beneath the soil, the Banks and monopoly industry shall be transferred to the ownership of the people as a whole;
> All other industry and trade shall be controlled to assist the well-being of the people. (South African Congress Alliance 1955)

The charter also called for decent housing, free medical care, freedom from hunger, and basic workers' rights.

The movement's socialist ideas were addressed only vaguely, however, and were often contradictory. Neither the CYL nor ANC favored the Marxist concept of socialism realized through class struggle. In a 1948 manifesto, the CYL national executive committee dismissed class analysis as irrelevant to South Africa:

> There are certain groups which seek to impose on our struggle cut-and-dried formulae, which so far from clarifying the issues of our struggle, only serve to obscure the fundamental fact that we are oppressed not as a class, but as a people, as a Nation. Such whole-sale importation of methods and tactics which might have succeeded in other countries, like Europe, where conditions were different, might harm the cause of our people's freedom, unless we are quick in building a militant mass liberation movement. (qtd. in Karis and Carter 1973: 329)

Shortly after the Freedom Charter's adoption, Nelson Mandela denied any socialist implications:

> Whilst the Charter proclaims changes of a far-reaching nature, it is by no means a blueprint for a socialist state but a programme for the unification of various classes and groupings amongst the people on a democratic basis. Under socialism the workers hold state power. They and the peasants own the means of production, the land, the factories, and the mills. All production is for use and

not for profit. The Charter does not contemplate such profound economic and political changes (qtd in Meridith 2010: 135).

Rather, in Mandela's elite vision, democratizing the monopolies would open "fresh fields for the development of a prosperous non-European bourgeois class" (qtd. in Meredith 2010: 135). Mandela's mixed relationship to socialism was further in evidence during the 1964 trial that led to his long imprisonment. In response to charges of treason, he spelled out his political views. On the one hand, he and other nationalist leaders (Gandhi, Nehru, Nkrumah, Nasser) "all accept the need for some form of socialism to enable our people to catch up with the advanced countries of this world and to overcome their legacy of extreme poverty" (Mandela 1965: 182). On the other hand, the organization he led had no anti-capitalist intentions: "The ANC has never at any period of its history advocated a revolutionary change in the economic structure of the country, nor has it, to the best of my recollection, ever condemned capitalist society" (179).

Helping to manage tension between the movement's nationalist and socialist aspirations was a two-stage theory espoused by the South African Communist Party (SACP), the party being a close ally of the ANC from the 1950s forward. The two-stage concept, advanced by the Third Communist International under Joseph Stalin's supervision, has influenced many national liberation movements (Legassick 2007: chap. 5). In the South African case, the first stage would be the defeat of apartheid and the second would be socialism. "For many within the Congress Alliance," explained one contributor in a 1985 ANC anthology, "the existence of colonialism of a special type necessarily entails a political strategy of 'two-stage revolution'":

> The reality is that the chief content of the present phase of our revolution is the national liberation of the black people. It is actually impossible for South Africa to advance to socialism before the national liberation of the black oppressed nation. . . . To proceed and say that the same nationalist struggle is also socialist in content is to make real confusion. (Mzala 1985; qtd. in Saul 1986: 11)

Not all within the anti-apartheid movement favored socialism's postponement to a distant second stage. Jay Naidoo, who served as general secretary of the Congress of South African Trade Unions (COSATU), the country's largest labor federation, describes his meeting with the ANC and its labor arm, the South African Congress of Trade Unions (SACTU), in Zimbabwe shortly after the COSATU's founding in 1985:

> I told the ANC and SACTU delegations we did not want superficial changes or black bosses to replace white bosses, while the repressive machinery of state and capital remained intact. I expressed very clearly to them our commitment to see a society which was not only free of apartheid but also free of the exploitative, degrading and brutalizing system under which black workers suffered. This meant a restructuring of society so that the wealth of the country would be shared among the people. ("COSATU Spells Out Its Aims," 1985; qtd. in Saul 1986: 17)

COSATU gave pivotal leadership in the final years of anti-apartheid resistance. In 1990, it joined with the ANC and SACP in a new Tripartite Alliance. COSATU's position within that alliance, however, "drifted into one of subordinacy" in the post-apartheid era (Southall and Webster 2010: 140).

Post-Apartheid Era

Unfortunately, during over two decades of ANC government, socialism has clearly been off the table. On May 1, 1994, days after the ANC swept to power in the country's first election under majority-Black rule, soon-to-be president Mandela assured nervous capitalists: "In our economic policies . . . there is not a single reference to things like nationalization, and this is not accidental. There is not a single slogan that will connect us with any Marxist ideology" (qtd. in Marais 2011: 97). Nor has economic/social uplift such as in jobs, housing, and water and electricity services been implemented beyond "tokenistic" levels (Saul and Bond 2014: chap. 5). "We need to disabuse people of the notion that we will have a mighty powerful developmental state capable of planning and creating all manner of employment," Finance Minister Trevor Manuel remarked in 2008 (qtd. in Lapper and Burgis 2008).

Rather, the new South Africa was promptly delivered into the hands of neoliberal corporate interests led by the IMF and World Bank. Long-time ANC/SACP leader Ronnie Kasrils (2013) calls an $850 million IMF loan, secured by South Africa's transitional government in December 1993, "our Faustian moment." The loan, with strings attached, would augur an ANC policy agenda of austerity, privatization, and liberalization of trade and finance. From 1991 to 1996, Kasrils recalls, "the battle for the ANC's soul got under way, and was eventually lost to corporate power: we were entrapped by the neoliberal economy—or, as some today cry out, we 'sold our people down the river.'"

The late educator/activist Neville Alexander (2003: 67) stressed the "continuities between the apartheid and the post-apartheid capitalist state." "Ownership and control of the commanding heights of the economy, the repressive apparatuses of the state," and "top echelons of the civil service" have "remained substantially in the same hands as during the heyday of apartheid" (64). The most fundamental difference, Alexander observed, is that all adult South Africans now have the right to vote. "We should not underestimate the psychological and political significance of the vote to an oppressed people, especially to a people discriminated against on the basis of colour for more than three centuries." Yet, he noted, as with other constitutional democracies, "the underlying capitalist production relations" afford the individual voter little leverage, leaving most South Africans voiceless in fact (68).

Mass poverty has remained entrenched in the post-apartheid era; inequality has increased (Marais 2011: chap. 7; Bhorat 2009). The majority-Black working class has, in the meanwhile, not endured the new order's shortcomings quietly but has sustained an outpouring of protest around issues of wages; housing; electrical, water, and sanitation services; and political cronyism. Post-apartheid South Africa has been dubbed the "protest capital of the world" (Runciman 2017). In some cases, the ANC government responds to protesters with local improvements. But in at least one instance, the new regime behaved much like the one it had replaced. In 2012, at a platinum mine outside the town of Marikana in the North West province, striking miners were slaughtered by police, with thirty-four killed. The event has been compared to apartheid-era massacres such as in Sharpeville, 1960; and Soweto, 1976. Kasrils (2013) comments:

> The Sharpeville massacre in 1960 prompted me to join the ANC. I found Marikana even more distressing: a democratic South Africa was meant to bring an end to such barbarity. And yet the president and his ministers, locked into a culture of cover-up. Incredibly, the South African Communist Party, my party of over 50 years, did not condemn the police either.

Conflicting Interpretations

There is no progressive consensus on South Africa and the political course taken. Some leftists (Alexander 2003; Legassick 2007; Saul and Bond 2014) suggest that South Africa had, and still has, socialist potential, and that a working-class-led movement could have made that course possible. Others, however, defend the ANC's general course, proposing that a "compromise" with neoliberal capital was the only viable option, given national and global economic realities. "The South African government cannot repudiate capitalism, domestic or multinational," argue Howard Winant and Gay Seidman (2001: 208) in a co-authored chapter in Winant's book, *The World Is a Ghetto*.

> To do so would be both to depart from economic logic and responsibility, and to incur the wrath and discipline of global financial markets. The national crackup that would ensue would not mean "merely" the end of the masses' hopes for a better life; it would mean the destruction of a multiracial society, the occasion for white flight, and the descent of the black majority into a regime of scarcity and autarky. Where would the "miracle" be then?

The ANC government must therefore walk a tightrope between competing agendas, the authors explain: "To accede systematically to the demands of capital would be to fall back into the status quo ante of apartheid. Yet to concede too much to the Black masses who furnish the ANC base would be to plunge the country into economic chaos" (211). Winant and Seidman praise the new government for wisely navigating a difficult situation:

> If the credibility of the ANC remains intact despite inability to deliver the economic goods either to transnational capital or to the black masses, this can best be attributed to the striking creativity with which the organization has tackled the enormous tasks of the transition. (210)

Winant and Seidman's perspective has echoes of Thatcher's famous claim about neoliberalism: "there is no alternative." Some economists have challenged that dictum specifically with respect to the Global South and its developmental options (Chang and Grabel 2014). A good many countries have contradicted IMF/World Bank consensus, such as by implementing capital controls—that is, restricting a country's financial inflows or outflows—and have done so effectively (Bond 2003: chap. 12). But beyond specific policy and technical questions are matters of political belief, class orientation, and social vision. A large swath of the global left has concluded, with Winant and Seidman, that global capital cannot be defeated. Several left-of-center governments in Latin America have, like the ANC, surrendered to neoliberalism in recent years.[27] However, the neoliberal turn has also met with mass resistance across Africa, Latin America, and elsewhere.[28]

The Winant and Seidman piece situates within the broader race-based theory that drives Winant's book, seeking to "reclaim the centrality of race" (Winant 2001: 6).[29] As often seen in such scholarship, Winant's centralizing of race does not lead to an effective race/class fusion but instead to a diminishing of class. A class outlook, with respect to the post-apartheid ANC, is offered by Alexander (2003: 152), who contends that the party is "placing its faith in the international capitalist class rather than in the social movements of the common people." Saul and Bond (2014: 123) similarly find that the ANC has become the representative of an elite Black layer, the "well-rewarded junior partners of global capital" (2014: 123). None demonstrates that elite role better than current South African president Cyril Ramaphosa. The former union leader was elected ANC general secretary in 1991 and served as the ANC's chief negotiator during the transition to a new order. Post-apartheid business opportunities have since helped Ramaphosa become the country's second richest Black man (Faku and Bloomberg 2015). His name was also prominent in the official inquiry over the 2012 Marikana massacre. As shareholder and board member of Lonmin, the struck mining company, Ramaphosa had pressed for government action to suppress the wildcat strike. In a trail of emails sent to company and state officials, Ramaphosa described the strike as "dastardly criminal" and urged "concomitant action to address this situation" (qtd. in Smith 2012).

In Winant and Seidman (2001: 212–13), however, the ANC government seems to be free of any class allegiance and becomes more of a wise facilitator helping to resolve conflict between capital and labor. The ANC's "sophisticated progressives and technocrats" have been developing an economic policy approach based on "the principle of class compromise," explain the authors. The model would balance "measured redistribution and the deepening of social security programs" with "a measure of economic streamlining and labor discipline." The state's role would be to "enforce the compromise, disciplining both labor and capital while acting in a neo-Keynesian fashion to invest in the country's infrastructure."

The South African masses expect more from their government, Winant and Seidman acknowledge: "These millions of newly enfranchised citizens not only elected and reelected the ANC, but also expect great reforms from their party: housing, jobs, education, services, land." While those expectations have yet to be met, owing to circumstances purportedly beyond the government's control, the masses "have not lost hope in democracy or in the ANC. So far, they have been patient" (207). What Winant and Seidman do not propose is a mass strategy other than being patient. If the authors see a way to move beyond "labor discipline," austerity, and the IMF, they do not articulate it, nor even urge discussion along these lines.

The bowing to global capital, in the ANC's South Africa and elsewhere, is further justified by the authors in separate works. If the South African people have been patient so far, says Winant (2004: 120) in *The New Politics of Race* (2004), "this may be because they recognize the challenges that redistribution poses for the democratic state, or it may be because a viable and more progressive political alternative to the ANC simply has not emerged and probably cannot be created." Seidman (1993: 179) too sees "narrowed options": "Even if a government sympathetic to popular demands took power, how much could it do?" Socialist experiments in Nicaragua and Mozambique faced bloody destabilization campaigns in the 1980s, she points out. "The dominant powers of the new international order seemed unwilling to tolerate attempts to use the state to redistribute wealth or services. Monetarist ideologies, which insist that growth requires unlimited freedom for capital, seemed to have become internationally hegemonic."

The questions raised by Seidman, of how socialist or social-democratic experiments can survive in a hostile world, are important and complex. One topic this involves is an historic debate on whether socialism can survive in one country. Another is how we assess particular country experiences where socialist goals have been lost (e.g., Russia, China, Venezuela) or where left-leaning governments have opted for neoliberalism (e.g., South Africa, Brazil).[30] I'll not delve here beyond my short treatment of South Africa. But all bear upon matters raised in this chapter—of class, capitalism, and connecting anti-racism to anti-capitalism. Also, all are impacted by our underlying theoretical frameworks. That Winant and Seidman assess post-apartheid South Africa—its status quo, its possibilities—quite differently than do others cited above is, I suspect, a reflection of differing worldviews, even among those of us who have broad progressive values in common.

While taking issue with race-based theory in a number of ways, I do agree that anti-racist struggles are pivotal to the success of any progressive program or endeavor. David Roediger (2017: 12) describes struggles for racial justice as "sites of learning for white workers, of self-activity by workers of color, and of placing limits on capital's ability to divide workers." Race-based theorists and critical race education scholars have rightfully kept racial justice issues in the forefront of scholarship and practice. My hope is that the discussion set forth here can contribute to our analyses of school reform and help us to forge much needed dialogues on the race-class nexus.

Notes

1 An extended theoretical approach to these issues is Mike Cole, *Critical Race Theory and Education: A Marxist Response* (2017). Other Marxist treatments are Cole (2009), Darder and Torres (2004: chap. 5) and Maisuria (2010, 2012). Responding to Marxist critics and in defense of critical race theory are Stovall (2006), Gillborn (2008: 37–8, 2009), Dumas (2013) and Warmington (2020).
2 I want to thank Joel Jordan—a retired California teacher, now a teachers' union consultant as well as political theorist and strategist—for his kind feedback on earlier drafts of this paper.

3 For a glimpse of this shift, see Patricia Hill Collins, "Toward a New Vision: Race, Class, and Gender as Categories of Analysis and Connection" (1993), and the early issues of the journal in which it is published, *Race, Sex and Class*. See also the special issue on intersectionality in the feminist journal, *Signs: Journal of Women in Culture and Society*, 2013, vol. 38, no. 4.
4 Past voices for Black nationalism and Pan-Africanism—with no sharp line of distinction being drawn between the two strands—include Marcus Garvey (Martin 1976); W. E. B. Du Bois (Kendhammer 2007; Ratcliff 2013); and Malcolm X (Breitman 1965). Current proponents include Molefi Kete Asante, with an "Afrocentric" cultural perspective (2003), and Omali Yeshitela, with a socialist perspective (2014).
5 On the influence of *Black Marxism* and Robinson's other scholarship, see Kelley (2016).
6 The fourth section discusses this process in the United States.
7 Barack Obama's two daughters have attended the Quaker-run Sidwell Friends school in Maryland. Sidwell has no high-stakes testing, emphasizing instead a "constructivist" curriculum, wherein students learn academic skills and make sense of the world by pursuing their own curiosities and interests (McHenry 2008; Strauss 2010). Bill Gates's son, Rory, attended Lakeside School, a private school serving grades 5–12 in Seattle, and where instruction is clearly not test-driven. Lakeside's Middle School English department strives to "unleash the authentic voice of each adolescent writer" and to "create a community of readers and writers who inspire each other to experiment with different written forms and support and learn from one another." https://www.lakesideschool.org.
8 See the list of financial contributors to Achieve, the main Common Core think tank, at http://achieve.org/contributors.
9 US charter schools are publicly funded but privately operated.
10 At http://classcrits.org. An exemplary exploration of race and class in the civil rights arena is that of ClassCrit affiliate faculty member Frances Lee Ansley (1989).
11 Edu-business refers to businesses that seek to profit from the marketization of educational programs and institutions.
12 On meritocracy and education, see Bowles and Gintis (1976), chapters 2 and 4.
13 Several of these national summits are documented at http://achieve.org/summits.
14 Based on figures from the World Bank database at http://data.worldbank.org.
15 Author's calculation based on data from the US Bureau of the Census (2017).
16 Among some two hundred thousand British miners at the time, the number of Blacks has been estimated at one thousand and three thousand (Kelliher 2017: 159, note 8). Regarding the predominance of whites among the striking air traffic controllers: I rely here on my own memory from attending an air traffic controllers' strike support march at the Oakland, California, international airport in 1981.
17 The book's argument is helpfully summarized in Allen (1998).
18 I detect this in Hill's account of the reform process in England (2001). On current suppression of anti-racist teaching in the United States, see Agee (2004) and Sleeter (2012).
19 The cultural conservatism is seen in Whitman (2008); a critical study is White (2015); for a similar effect in England, see Kulz (2017).
20 My thanks to Ken Jones of England's National Union of Teachers for his insight about this.
21 Alpesh Maisuria of the University of East London offered me this insight.

22 As applied in this chapter and in the Marxist tradition, *class consciousness* refers not to an awareness of one's income level relative to that of others but to an awareness of one's economic/political *interests* in connection to a larger group.
23 The US teacher workforce in 2011 was 84 percent white and 84 percent female (Feistritzer 2011: 12, 15).
24 Chapters on class in multicultural education books consistently embrace the stratification model. "In crude positional terms," one explains, "teachers are considered middle-class, occupying a rung in the middle of the occupational status hierarchy, and large numbers of them come from middle-class families" (Knapp and Woolverton 2004: 660). Another informs us that "labor movements had a significant role in creating the kind of organized workforce that became the middle class" (Adams, Hopkins, and Shlasko 2016: 222).
25 One exception is the work of legal scholar and ClassCrit member Martha Mahoney (2000, 2003, 2009).
26 On the emergence of South Africa's racist system in the context of capitalism and Dutch/British colonialism, see Saul and Bond (2014: chap. 1).
27 For entrée into the Latin American debate on these matters, see Ellner (2004) and Webber (2010).
28 On resistance to neoliberalism in Africa, see Prempeh (2008). For the same in Latin America, see the special issue of *Socialism and Democracy*, 2009, vol. 23, no. 3.
29 The theoretical orientation of his co-author, Gay Seidman, is unclear; her various writings (e.g., 1993, 1994, 2007) do not identify a broad worldview to which she aligns. She is, however, a labor sociologist whose scholarship often carries a left labor sensibility.
30 Helpful on Brazil is Saad-Filho and Boito (2015).

2

Doing Class in Critical Race Analysis of Education

Michael J. Dumas

Village Voice columnist Greg Tate, in his commentary on the lack of Black involvement in the Occupy Wall Street (OWS) movement, quotes one of the young Black men he spoke to, who told him, "I ain't about to go get arrested with some muhfuhkuhs who just figured out yesterday that this shit ain't right" (Tate 2011). For Tate, this young man's reluctance to participate in the nascent movement reflects a broader wariness among African Americans about social analyses and political action which seemingly have little to say—at least explicitly—about race and racism. Implicit in this critique is a sense that white people are just beginning to resist state policies, corporate interests, and hegemonic cultural-ideological logics that have long wreaked havoc in Black communities. The problem, as these skeptical observers see it, is that, in reframing the debate solely in terms of class, in which the so-called 99 percent stand in solidarity against the abuses of the economically elite 1 percent, supporters of the OWS movement collapse the 99 percent in ways that ignore differential access to economic and political resources, delegitimize race-based appeals for social redress, privilege the interests and voices of those (middle-class whites) most recently hurt by inequitable policies and practices and problematically posit class dominance as more disastrous, more explanatory, and more material than racial dominance.[1]

Historically, Black people have understood their oppression—including their economic oppression—through the lens of race. Thus, race and racism are situated at the center of Black popular analyses of the social policies and everyday institutional and cultural practices that so heavily inform Black life and Black life chances (Cohen 1999; Dawson 1994, 2001; Gordon 2000; Marable and Mullings 1994). As the young man quoted by Tate points out, "shit ain't [never been] right" for Black people in the United States. Black unemployment has consistently been double that of white US citizens. Housing and employment discrimination on the basis of race has long been codified in a number of federal, state, and local policies (Massey and Denton 1993; Wilson 1997, 2009). Access to well-resourced schools has been a struggle since the end of slavery, with stark differences between the educational opportunities available to Black and white children and young adults (Anderson 1988; Walker 1996; Watkins 2001). For most African Americans, the latest economic downturn may have exacerbated but did not mark the beginning of their social and financial woes or serve as their first awareness of how powerful corporate and state interests collude in social policy. For this young man, that so many of the 99 percent appear in the streets only now, and with such new-found surprise and dismay, only highlights their whiteness, and all the privilege and naiveté that that connotes (Leonardo and Porter 2010). As Greg Tate (2011) notes in his piece, "Black folk got wise to the game back in 1865 when we realized neither 40 acres nor a mule would be forthcoming."

Critical race theory (CRT), consistent with this popular-cultural imagination, situates race at the center of social analysis. Differences such as social class, gender, ethnicity, and language are acknowledged and understood as dimensions of intersectionality that impact how race shapes policy and everyday life; however, race is the primary object of analysis, and explanations of social phenomena are primarily offered through a racial lens. That is to say, in CRT, inquiry revolves around understanding how race and racism work in the formation and implementation of social policy and how racist (or white supremacist) ideologies act to establish and continually justify the political and moral "rightness" of these policies.

As we have witnessed an increase in CRT scholarship in education, it has become subject to critique from Marxian[2] scholars, who argue that CRT problematically prioritizes race over class, fails to account for the political-economic foundations of racial inequities and racialized processes, and focuses on white supremacy as the explanation for the persistent oppression of people of color, without due attention to the impact of capitalism and market forces. Some of these critics have argued that, in their advancement of the notion of race, CRT scholars only lend credence to a discredited construct and reinforce essentialist understandings of racial identity that misstate and perhaps romanticize racial collective identification. Further, they would contend, such investment in viewing the world through the lens of race undermines efforts to imagine a politics that transcends the "false" boundaries of race and moves toward a more material, and therefore "real," politics that brings *all* poor and working people together in solidarity to struggle for more equitable social and economic conditions. Ultimately, for Marxian scholars, CRT may usefully highlight racial dimensions of social inequality, but its race-based analyses and solutions miss the (material) point (Cole 2009, 2011; Darder and Torres 2009).

Critical race theorists have responded to these critiques in a number of ways, challenging what they contend are a number of reductionist misrepresentations of CRT and reasserting the need to interrogate white supremacy as a "totalizing" frame for understanding racism, akin to the scrutiny of capitalism in critical class analyses.

In this chapter, rather than attempting to resolve this contentious debate, or somehow pick a "winner" between race and class, I highlight the primary tensions between Marxian and critical race approaches. Drawing on this discussion, I offer some persistent and emerging challenges for critical race theorists who wish to richly and incisively take up and explain class within decidedly *racial* policy analyses that— and this is important—are situated within and aim to inform a broader leftist project. In short, how do we sustain a CRT that speaks in radical ways about class in policy discussions of what "ain't right" in the lives of people of color in general and, more specifically here, in the lives of Black people?

The Marxian Critique of Critical Race Theory

The Marxian critique of CRT, it must be said at the outset, is not a denial of the political and economic significance of race and racism or an attempt to dismiss the validity of anti- racist theorizing and activism. In fact, as I will explain below, Marxian scholars account for race as a social construct, and racism as an oppressive practice, within the framework of their critique of capitalism. However, this is not to say that their analysis of race and racism is necessarily satisfactory or adequate. To be sure, as we shall see in the response from critical race scholars, there may be reason to doubt the capacity of Marxian theory to fully explain or even acknowledge certain dimensions of racism; at very least, to say that Marxian theory addresses race is not to say that it addresses it in a manner or to the extent that critical race scholars believe necessary. Indeed, many Black Marxists have contended that Marxism must address racism as an integral part of its project and have critiqued the racism of white workers as an impediment to socialist revolution (Du Bois 1935/1999; Kelley 2002; Robinson 1983/2000). My point here is that the contention between Marxian and critical race scholars is not a matter of choosing between race and class but of how to best explain the relationship between race and class and how to situate and engage race and racism within a critical social critique and political praxis.

The Marxian critique in education has been expressed most prominently in the United States by Antonio Darder and Rodolfo Torres (2004, 2009) and in the UK by Mike Cole (2009, 2011) and Dave Hill (2009). Here, I use their writings to enumerate the primary Marxian contentions with CRT, fully cognizant that there may be other critics and critiques that might be mentioned. However, these are Marxian critiques from within the education, so it makes sense to highlight them in this chapter. Also, the texts discussed here are the ones referred to most often in responses from critical race scholars.

First, Marxian scholars argue that CRT erroneously assumes that race provides a totalizing explanation for persistent social inequities equal to or in place of class. For Marxian scholars, the foundation of social inequities is rooted in capitalism, in the political economy, and in class exploitation. Class is central, global, and pervasive in ways that make it exceptional and exceptionally capable of explaining the human condition, oppression, and the very idea of freedom. Darder and Torres (2009: 152) see "power as unrelentingly anchored in external material conditions." For them, race (or gender or sexuality) simply does not "have the same meaning or constitutive power" (161). As they explain, "It is the *material* domination and exploitation of populations, in the interest of perpetuating a deeply entrenched capitalist system of world dominion, which serves as the impetus for the construction of social formations of inequality" (160). In the view of Darder and Torres, a theory which helps us understand systems of power and their material effects in the world on human populations must be regarded as transcending, as "more total" than, a theory which revolves around a social construction, a fiction that is not, in the end, real.

For Mike Cole (2009: 119), although CRT offers important social insights, it cannot provide the kind of comprehensive analysis or program of political action needed to combat capital. CRT is not, in his estimation, "up to such a gargantuan task," because it is not situated in a class analysis but instead seeks to offer a project of anti-racism as if race is its own totalizing system. For Marxists, Cole contends, "the debate between class *or* racism becomes redundant, in that . . . the struggle is against racialized (and gendered) capitalism" (37). In this sense, class becomes the broader framework within which race means or effects anything.

Second, and proceeding from this point, Marxian scholars critique CRT because it fails to theorize capitalism as a force in the construction of race and operationalization of racism. Two points need to be made here, one about race and racism and the other related to theorizing capitalism. Marxian scholars suggest that, once we acknowledge that race is a social construction, we need to understand that racism is intended to exploit and dominate those marked as "Other" for the benefit of capitalists. As Darder and Torres (2004: 101) note, "Racism is one of the primary ideologies by which material conditions in society are organized and perpetuated in the service of capitalist accumulation."

Marxian theorists would emphasize that this stands in contrast to class, which unlike race "is more than a constructed category. It refers to real, historical, material relations. The social mechanisms that give rise to the various historical expressions of 'racism' lie deep in class relations" (Banfield; quoted in Hill 2009: 25). If indeed racism is founded in class relations, and in the logics and institutions of capital, then any analysis of the construct of race or institutional and cultural practices of racism must be based in a class critique. Put another way, in Marxian analysis, discussion of race is only critical and only makes sense when racism is understood as a powerful instantiation of capitalism.

Given the relationship between racism and capitalism in a Marxian framework, it becomes imperative to theorize how capital works in processes of racialization and racial exploitation and violence. For Marxian scholars, such theorizing is absent in CRT, and this limits the ability of CRT to effectively and fully explain just what is happening racially in the world. While they acknowledge that CRT scholarship makes some mention of social class, these references are "generally vague and undertheorized." Thus, CRT has "done little to further our understanding of the political economy of racism and racialization" (Darder and Torres 2004: 99).

Rather—and this brings us to the third critique—in CRT, class is most often presented as a dimension of intersectionality, in which class (alongside such categories as nationality, gender, and ability) is a social identity and descriptor of personal life experience, rather than a pervasive and structural exercise of the power of capital. Intersectionality has been advanced within CRT as a way to capture the dynamic relationships between race and other "differences," including gender, sexual identity, disability, and, of course, social class (Crenshaw 1995). However, as should be clear by now, Marxian scholars reject the idea that class is an identity akin to a range of countless others which might be put forth. Not only does this deny the powerful structural dimensions of class, but it also dangerously mischaracterizes the relationship of social class to other differences, which, for Marxian scholars, are all constituted and serve their oppressive functions within (and not aside from or in addition to) capitalism. As Darder and Torres (2004: 106) explain, intersectionality "ignores the fact that notions of identity result from a process of identification with a particular configuration of historically lived or transferred social arrangements and practices tied to material conditions of actual or imagined survival." In shifting our focus to race, they argue, CRT furthers an identity-based politics that "glosses over class differences and/or ignores class contradictions, in an effort to build a political base" (106). The problem for Marxian scholars is that this serves to separate the political and economic into two separate and independently operational spheres, which only obscures and deemphasizes class relations in capitalist societies.

Fourth, Marxian scholars are concerned that CRT's focus on white supremacy reifies racial identities in ways that legitimize broad generalizations about whites that fail to account for the ethnic and economic diversity within this population and ignore the significance of class differences among people of color. Mike Cole argues that the concept of white supremacy, as employed in CRT, conflates the differences among white people. For Cole, "white supremacy" suggests that all white people wield the power of being white, regardless of class or ethnicity, which positions whites differently in relation to the modes of production. Further, Cole (2009: 113) maintains, while Marxists fully acknowledge racism across hundreds of years, white supremacy "does not in itself *explain* this continuity [of racism], since it does not need to connect to modes of production and developments in capitalism." CRT scholars thus fall short in their analysis of the trajectory of racism, because white supremacy alone cannot account for its reproduction. Cole laments that, while Marxian analysis includes interrogation of racialization, there is no corresponding attention to class within CRT. Although some CRT scholars may indeed note the significance of class relations in their discussion of race, "there is no *a priori* need in CRT formulations [e.g., white supremacy] to connect with capitalist modes of production" (2009: 113).

Darder and Torres (2004) contend that "White supremacy," in addition to naturalizing the "black–white binary" of race discourse, advances the flawed and (over)psychologized race relations paradigm, in which racism is seen as an ideological or attitudinal problem that needs to be addressed through appeals to whites. Their fear is that CRT, in its conceptualization of white supremacy, locates racism primarily in the ideological-discursive realm, as a matter primarily of combating ignorance and building multicultural understanding.[3] Instead, they argue, we need an analysis of racism that acknowledges the fictive nature of race and the power of racial(ized) discourse but keeps our attention on "the complex nature of historically constituted social relations of power and their material consequences" (Darder and Torres 2004: 112). Racial inequities, then, are not a result of white supremacy pursued for its own sake—that is, for the advantage of whites as a social group. Rather, they can be explained as a result of racism employed to foment agitation among working people and maintain the advantage of class elites.

Fifth, Marxian scholars argue, CRT counterproductively advances a racial-political project that undermines the possibilities of a truly multiracial mass solidarity movement among poor and working people. As noted above, Marxian critics of CRT worry that an emphasis on (racial) identity politics, and specifically a critique of white supremacy, serves to alienate working-class whites who should be part of the alliance pushing back against the forces of capital. Indeed, Darder and Torres (2004: 23) call for a new "cultural citizenship" which, contrary to a politics centered on race, "seeks not only to establish a collectivity in which no one is left outside the system, but [is extended] the rights of first-class citizenship."

Although CRT includes similar aims related to opportunity and justice, Cole (2009: 117) contends, most of its proponents are far too vague about what the "struggle" or "transformation" is really about, or how to get there from here. He states, "no indication is given of what they are struggling towards, what liberation means to them, or what is envisioned by social transformation and the end of all forms of oppression." Ultimately, for Cole, CRT, despite its consideration of class oppression, falls short of presenting a pathway toward realization of a radical vision because it has no inherent critique of class relations themselves. "While challenging the *oppression* of people that is based on their social class (classism) is extremely important, and is championed by Marxists," he notes, "the fundamental point is to also challenge the *exploitation* of workers at the point of production, for therein lies the economic relationship that sustains and nurtures the capitalist system" (118).

The Response from Critical Race Theorists

The essence of the critical race response to Marxian critics is perhaps foretold in CRT's emergence years ago as a critique of critical legal studies (CLS) (Matsuda 1995). Although CRT shares with CLS a radical commitment to challenging normative explanations of power, rights, and justice, early writings in the field of CRT lament the marginalization and erasure of the voices of people of color in CLS and detail CLS's failure to account for how racism heavily informs the public imagination of whom policy is for and whom laws are meant to protect. CRT scholars have also raised serious concerns about the tendency within CLS to engage questions of law only in the abstract and not in solidarity (or even in dialogue) with oppressed communities at the center of the storm.

These same tensions re-emerge in the more recent CRT response to Marxian critiques. First, CRT scholars insist that, just as capitalism is regarded as totalizing in analysis of class relations, white supremacy should be regarded as equally totalizing in the sphere of racial analysis and lived experience. As David Stovall (2006: 248) argues, while social critique might emphasize, for example, that the majority of members of the US Senate are among the wealthiest individuals in the nation, "a CRT critique would remind us that this ruling class continues to be White." Stovall acknowledges that there are certainly individual people of color among this ruling elite, but "their actions as people of color in serving the interests of the conservative right reifies current racialized power structures in that those who control the resources and social status to which they emulate remain White" (248–9).

In his introduction to David Gillborn's (2008: xv) book, which offers a critical race analysis of education in the UK, Richard Delgado notes that white supremacy has all the "structure of a conspiracy." Indeed, Gillborn spends the greater part of the book detailing how white supremacy in education is, ultimately, a set of "concerted actions" for a common purpose "always to the benefit of the racist status quo. It's a web of actions by teachers, policymakers, right-wing commentators, uncritical academics and the media—all working in one direction, day after day and to incredibly powerful effect" (192). In this sense, then, white supremacy is, like capitalism, pervasive, invasive, expansive, and devastating in its ideological and material destruction—or, in a word, totalizing.

It follows from this that, second, racism is not entirely dependent on capitalism. It has its own logics, its own hegemonic frames, and its own material effects. Stovall (2006: 251) notes that critics of CRT such as Darder and Torres insist that we need to focus on the material conditions of poor people of color but do not acknowledge that these material conditions are just as much a result of white supremacy as they are of class domination. And, as Ladson-Billings and Tate (1995: 50, 52) explain, the problem with relying solely on a class-based (or gender-based) approach is that race is likely to be left untheorized:

> By arguing that race remains untheorized, we are not suggesting that other scholars have not looked carefully at race as a powerful tool for explaining social inequity, but that the intellectual salience of this theorizing has not been systematically employed in the analysis of educational inequality . . . Class- and gender-based explanations are not powerful enough to explain all the difference (or variance) in school experience and performance.

Although Marxian scholars would likely respond by pointing to their own analysis of race and racism, CRT scholars would contend that a Marxian approach is limited from the beginning in its theoretical denial of racism as a system of its own and not simply an ideological dimension of capitalist modes of production.

Third, CRT scholars push back against the assumption by Marxian critics that CRT situates all white people as equally positioned in relation to power. Gillborn (2010: 4), in his own work on the white working class in the UK, insists that critics are flatly wrong on this count:

> CRT does not imagine that all White people are uniformly racist and privileged. However, CRT *does* view all White-identified people as implicated in relations of racial domination: White people do not all behave in identical ways and they do not all draw similar benefits—but they *do* all benefit to some degree, whether they like it or not.

Because they do benefit, even as they may be exploited for their labor, it becomes important to investigate how they become complicit, however unwittingly, in the system of domination. In turn, this racial analysis helps us understand more complexly how ruling-class elites employ race to legitimize and maintain their economic dominance.

Fourth, CRT scholars insist that, despite the claims of Marxian critics, CRT does offer a meaningful class analysis. Stovall (2006) points to Cheryl Harris's (1993) explication of whiteness as property as a prime example of CRT's engagement of social class. In her seminal piece, Harris offers a detailed historical account of whiteness as one of the most significant foundations of the US economy. Whiteness, she explains, accorded (white) citizens an important set of privileges in the market and in civil society, including the right to own (i.e., to accumulate) Black people as one's property and, beyond that, to claim superiority over all other racialized groups in legal proceedings and everyday social interactions. Taking the *Brown* decision as one exemplar, Harris points to the Court's refusal to acknowledge whiteness as a form of material property that not only subjected Black citizens to (past) subordination but also ensured that whites would maintain and actually strengthen their hold on educational resources long after desegregation was declared unconstitutional. As Stovall (2006: 249) explains:

> "Property" in Harris' sense operates on material and social levels, expressed in common assumptions on race. Contrary to Darder and Torres's point on CRT as divorcing itself from the "realities of class struggle," it makes room for the realities of class while discussing them in the context of what race means historically and what it has come to mean in contemporary analysis.

Within CRT, Stovall contends, Marxian class analysis is credited for its contribution but is complicated by interrogating how racial myths of white entitlement, including the entitlement to exclude, facilitate the reproduction of class inequities. In this way, then, racism is not merely a function of class domination; we must also acknowledge that class domination serves to maintain and legitimize systems of white racial supremacy. (For a detailed explanation of the concept of whiteness as property, see Harris 1993.)

Fifth, CRT pushes back against the Marxian tendency to view the politics of identity as merely an obsession with fictive notions of affiliation. In CRT, validating and nurturing racial identities are a meaningful and valid response to the experience of everyday life in racialized bodies and enduring the material effects of racism in racialized communities. Also, importantly, identity is a crucial frame through which people of color give voice to their lived experiences and make sense of resistance against the forces acting against them individually and collectively. "To critique CRT simply as 'identity politics,'" David Stovall (2006: 251) states, "ignores the necessity of narrative in developing coalitions across racial and class boundaries."

In CRT, of course, counter stories are the primary way of articulating and developing a coherent (and ultimately collective) narrative. As Dixson and Rousseau (2006: 35) note, "This, then, is the essence of 'voice'—the assertion and acknowledgement of the importance of the personal and community experiences of people of color as sources of knowledge . . . Thus, voice scholarship provides a 'counterstory' to counteract or challenge the dominant story." If the only "dominant story" were offered by class elites (and not also racial elites), Marxian analysis might suffice. However, from the perspective of CRT, white supremacy (again, as an equally impactful totalizing frame) necessitates a decidedly racial politics that, while eschewing crude racial essentialisms, embraces "the common experience of racism that structures the stories of people of color" (35) and provides a way to organize their words into communities of resistance.

Finally, following from this, CRT rejects the assertion by Marxian scholars that CRT has no concrete or transformative praxis. Precisely because CRT places such a strong emphasis on voice, critical race theorists maintain, it is able to connect theory with everyday experience and politics at the community level. Stovall (2006: 253) explains,

"Through counter story we are able to discover the relationships between nuanced experience, individual responses and macro-policy." In fact, Stovall offers a case example in which critical race scholars, informed by both CRT and socialist critique, have been able to work with a specific school community to initiate political resistance to educational inequities. In this case and others, CRT did not serve as an impediment to praxis, as some Marxian scholars have maintained; rather, it was a crucial piece in creating a theoretical synergy (of race and class) that facilitated action in racialized communities.

Gillborn (2008), writing about his own responsibilities as a white anti-racist scholar, notes that he uses CRT to help influence policy in the UK at the governmental level and in strategizing for action with community-based and advocacy organizations. While CRT offers a cogent intellectual analysis of racism, Gillborn (2008: 202) points to the extensive work on critical race praxis (McKay 2010; Stovall et al. 2009; Yamamoto 1997) to stress that CRT scholars "do not imagine for a second that an analysis of racism alone is a sufficient contribution to the struggle for racial equality."

In calling for a "ceasefire" between class-based analyses and CRT, Stovall (2006: 257) concludes that what is ultimately needed is for each side to acknowledge and incorporate the strengths of the other, not to win some academic argument but to effectively respond to social and educational inequality. He states:

> The social justice project in education will require the recognition of the interplay of race and class ... Doing so will require those of the side of CRT to recognize that there may be intra-racial issues that need class analysis, while not separating them from the larger construct of White supremacy. Those who engage class analysis will have to recognize the dynamics of racialization in discussions of the ruling classes, in under-standing that racism is not the sole byproduct of capitalism.

However, Stovall (2006: 257) does point to what may be irreconcilable differences when he insists that "the dynamics of race inextricably identify a system of shifting hierarchies that are not married to a stringent interpretation of class analysis." And indeed Mike Cole (2009: 33), in his critique of CRT, suggests that ultimately "Marxist conceptions of racialization . . . [have] the *best purchase* in explaining manifestations of racism, Islamophobia and xenoracism in contemporary Britain" (emphasis added). Surely, much has been written and will continue to be written about the (in)compatibility of Marxian and critical race analyses. What I wish to do in the final section of this chapter is bypass that theoretical wrangling, largely because I believe there may indeed be—if not clear contradictions—what we might call *necessary tensions* between the two camps. Mindful of those tensions, which I have detailed throughout this chapter, I want to identify some persistent and emergent priorities facing critical race scholars as we move forward, both in our development of CRT and in pursuit of a transformative critical race praxis.

Class-Related Priorities for Critical Race Theory and Praxis

In an article in the *Iowa Law Review*, Richard Delgado (2011: 1288) worries that critical race scholars may have "failed to expand analytically or even to keep up with the times." Here, he cautions that CRT, in an effort to attend ever so carefully to the diverse voices of people of color, has pursued intersectionality at the expense of analysis of the material effects of racism and the broader exercise of power. He explains: "By itself, intersectionality does not mount a challenge to anything important. Moreover, in focusing on smaller and smaller units of analysis, you can easily overlook large-scale processes that are working to the disadvantage of large classes, say, workers vis-à-vis management or women vis-à-vis men" (1264–5). I do not mean to engage this complex critique of intersectionality here. However, for the purpose of this discussion, I am taken with two ideas underlying his argument. First, strategies or analyses that may have made sense ten or fifteen years ago may be inadequate or even counterproductive today, given the shifting terrain of racial identities and affiliations and, importantly, changes in how ruling elites engage the politics of race for their own purposes, and in ways that have real ramifications for the life chances of people in racialized communities. In other words, there can be no CRT that is not also critical of its own historicity—that is not, in Delgado's words, keeping up with the times.

Second, Delgado (2011: 1287) points us toward the need to recommit to an analysis and politics that is as concerned about economic justice as it is about combating white racism. He insists, "Unless one dismantles both systems, white privilege and outright oppression of minorities, workers, and the poor, *class and racial lines will remain the way they are forever*" (emphasis added). CRT must, at its core, also offer a critical class analysis or it is, in the end, useless. This reinforces a point he made some years before, in the *Texas Law Review* (Delgado 2003: 144). Noting improving racial attitudes in the United States over the past several years, he notes, "Yet the black–white gap in income, family wealth, educational attainment, and health and longevity is as great as ever." Lamenting a sharp turn toward discursive analysis of the social construction of race, Delgado (2003: 151) calls on critical race theorists to "examine the relationship between class and race more carefully than they have done," with a focus on issues that "span race, class, and the profit motive."

CRT was envisioned as a leftist, activist intellectual project. This should mean that it is critical not only about race but about class as well. Although this is certainly open to debate, I would argue that a CRT that has an inadequate critique of capitalism is not worthy of the name: Not only is it *not* critical, but it cannot even offer us a meaningfully transformative analysis of race. Even so, I believe we need a robust conversation about the meaning of "critical" in CRT, in which we consider the possibility of whether one can advocate radical action against white supremacy while keeping the foundations of capitalism intact. Or, put another way, how do we theorize—not merely acknowledge or address—class in CRT? What are our responsibilities here, if we understand that the lives of people of color are (also) governed by class relations, which are materially imbricated with race, largely through the (mal)distribution of economic and human resources (Dumas 2009, 2011)?

CRT may also need to move toward greater sophistication in its analysis of middle-class people of color vis-à-vis poor and working-class people of color. This is not merely a matter of intersectionality, in which we readily acknowledge the diversity of racialized experiences. Instead, we also need to theorize what it means for a small number of people of color—including most critical race theorists!—to have a different relationship to the modes of production than the masses of people of color. Again, this is not simply about being culturally different but also about being starkly different in power, in access to resources and importantly in our (class) interests.

I am not denying what political scientist Michael Dawson (1994a, 2001) has called "linked fate," in which Black people—and this may be true for other peoples of color as well—see their own well-being as connected to that of the racial group as a whole. I part ways with many, but not all, Marxists in embracing collective politics informed by notions of racial communality, even as I understand this communality to be fluid, indeterminate, and fictive (Dumas 2010). Following Stuart Hall, I have called for a Black cultural politics of education without guarantees, in which we are constantly re-examining "our representation(s) of 'Black' in education to ensure that Black people have the freedom to imagine all that we now need (and need to *do*) at this historical moment in our struggle" (2010: 404). So I do in fact believe there are some ways in which Black people reasonably and necessarily see their fates as linked across social class.

However, I also fully agree with Cathy Cohen's (1999: 19) assessment that certain Black political interests are more likely to be regarded as more valid than others:

> While there is a history of contestation around the definition of a broad and expansive black political agenda, one that includes issues affecting all segments of the community . . . the political issues that continue most often to be pursued and embraced publicly by community institutions and leaders are those thought to be linked to, or to conform to, middle-class/dominant constructions of moral, normative, patriarchal citizenship.

Thus, it becomes that much more important for critical race theorists to understand how Black class elites can shape and determine what counts as racial injustice, on the one hand, and, on the other, what issues are deemed to be—in Cohen's term—"cross-cutting issues," those that only affect certain, and usually marginalized, segments of the racial group. Cohen contends that the further we get from the Civil Rights Movement, the more our racial concerns become local and specific, and the more our experiences become less likely to be shared broadly over the entire group. I have a sinking suspicion that access to public education may become, if it isn't already in some places, one of these cross-cutting issues, in which the class interests of affluent and middle-class people of color lead them to very different analyses and engagement of the problem, and that, since they are more likely to hold the economic and political purse strings in communities of color, critical race theorists and activists may increasingly be called upon to highlight and address these divisions, and speak (class) truth to (racial) power even in the face of calls by these elites for loyalty to their self-serving notions of racial solidarity (Carbado and Gulati 2004; Cohen 1999; Dawson 2011; Dyson 2006; Marable and Mullings 1994).

Finally, returning to Delgado's concern about connecting racial analysis to economic justice, we may be seeing a resurgence of critical race research that directly takes on persistent racialized economic inequities in specific spaces—a kind of convergence of CRT and (urban) political economy. Legal scholar Elizabeth Iglesias (2000), most notably, proposes the concept of "racial spaces" to explain how neoliberal economics reimagines communities as "networks of markets" to be primed for the flow of capital. Such racial spaces are both created by, and simultaneously the result (at least in part) of, white supremacy, which not only constricts where people of color can live but also privileges white racial spaces for advantage in the "free" marketplace. Thus, neoliberal formations, while on the surface racially disinterested, attribute value to certain spaces, and lack of value to others, and ultimately contribute to patterns of development, marginalization, and exploitation aligned with the racial composition of different communities.

"Racial spaces," Iglesias (2000: 1040) explains, "are visible artifacts of both racial segregation and the relations of investment, production and exchange that are reflected in the export of capital; monopolies of political and economic power; and the restricted circulation of goods, services and capital within racially subordinated communities." With this conceptualization of the relationship between race and class—as both cultural and political-economic constructs—critical race theorists can offer a more incisive intervention at the point of analysis and then again at the point of policy intervention.

One exemplar in educational research is a study by Janet Smith and David Stovall (2008) of the intersection of housing and education policies in the Kenwood-Oakland area of Chicago and how race plays a central role in determining the allocation of resources in ways that are ultimately detrimental to people of color, across lines of social class. Through their analysis, they emphasize how racism acts to powerfully inform policies and sense-making in the interest of whites as a group, in ways that simultaneously, and by design, benefit ruling elites. "The argument is not that thee developers in Kenwood-Oakland are racist," the authors conclude, "but rather that their contribution to a system of displacement contributes to a larger racist system, centered in making the city 'safe again' for its returning white residents" (Smith and Stovall 2008: 149). Importantly, in Smith and Stovall's study, the focus is not so much on the individual racial attitudes of whites and doesn't stop at deconstruction of racial discourses. Rather, they aim to impact how researchers, policymakers, and youth and community activists might improve the material well-being of people of color. The article ends with a series of concrete questions, informed by a critical race analysis, intended to push back against policies of containment that deprive working-class communities of color of educational resources.

Here, and in the best critical race research, we see an approach to the intersectionality of race and class that is far more than a passing nod to the significance of class. Rather, these critical race scholars incorporate class into their theorizing about race and racism and explicate what their findings mean for critical race praxis. As Gillborn (2010: 5) states, "Serious critical work on intersectionality requires us to do more than merely *cite* the difficulties and complexities of intersecting identities and oppressions, it challenges us to *detail* these complexities and account for *how* categories and inequalities intersect, through what processes, and with what impacts." This is the work we need, to enrich an ongoing dialogue among critical scholars from varying traditions and, more importantly, to develop the knowledge needed to help our folks where they live.

Notes

1. This chapter was originally published in Handbook From: *Handbook of Critical Race Theory in Education*, edited by Marvin Lynn and Adrienne D. Dixson, Copyright 2022, Routledge. Reproduced by permission of Taylor & Francis Group.
2. I use the term "Marxian" here to denote a sociopolitical theoretical orientation that emphasizes the inherent destructive material and cultural impacts of capitalism, views the relationships between individuals and modes of production as the most significant social (group identity) differentiation, and foregrounds a politics of struggle in which working people (i.e., those who make their living through their own labor, rather than the labor of others) must collectively unite to demand concessions from the ruling class, who employ physical force and/or ideological formations in order to justify their own class dominance, and exploit the labor of working people for their own economic gain. I fully acknowledge various forms of, and conflicts among, Marxisms and that many who agree with these basic Marxian ideas may themselves not choose to identify as Marxists, for a variety of reasons. For the purpose of this chapter, I chose the term "Marxian" because most of the critics of CRT have identified as Marxists and/or have acknowledged being most heavily influenced by Marxian thought.
3. This claim that CRT does not engage the materiality of race is certainly refuted by critical race theorists. I will elucidate this later, in my discussion of CRT responses to Marxian critics.

Part II

Responses from Marxist Perspectives

3

Centering the Oppressed

Marxism and the Question of Race and Class

Pranav Jani

If Black women were free, it would mean that everyone else would have to be free since our freedom would necessitate the destruction of all the systems of oppression.
—Combahee River Collective Statement, 1977

For a long time, I believed that it would only be possible to overthrow the Irish [colonial] regime by English working-class ascendancy. . . . . Deeper study has now convinced me of the opposite. The English working class will never accomplish anything before it has got rid of Ireland. The lever must be applied in Ireland. That is why the Irish question is so important for the social movement in general.
—Karl Marx to Frederick Engels, 1869

Howard Ryan's "Race, Class, and the Hidden Aims of School Reform" analyzes the neoliberal roots of the decades-long assault on public education, pointing to its anti-working class and racist implications. But the essay has a broader project as well: to argue that a Marxist understanding of the relationship between race and class allows a better grasp of school reform than do "race-based" approaches derived from critical race theory (CRT), Black feminism, and related fields. Writing from a critical Marxist position that is informed by intersectionality, I find that Ryan's assertion of a "class primacy" approach threatens to reproduce the very dichotomy between race and class that the article seeks to avoid.

Rather than asserting the importance of CRT and Black feminism, as I regularly do, my contribution to this collection is to complicate and historicize our understanding of the race/class question in Marxism itself. I outline an alternative genealogy of Marxist thought around race, class, colonialism, and identity, showing that debating "class primacy" has, in fact, been central to Marxist thought on racism, colonialism, nationalism, and revolution for over a century. Furthermore, I link relevant historical and political questions with the practical challenges of contemporary multiracial socialist organizing. Indeed, as I can attest from my long experience in the International Socialist Organization (ISO), which dissolved in 2019, such political debates about race and racism have real-life implications. I am interested, then, in the relationship between two broad questions:

1. Why is Marxism, despite a long record of fighting racism and imperialism, constantly battling the critique that it is Eurocentric and class reductionist?
2. Why do white-majority Marxist organizations, even those with a record of solid anti-racist work, seem to have trouble recruiting, retaining, and following the leadership of Black/Indigenous/People of Color (BIPOC) members?[1]

Resolving such questions is crucial if socialists are going to play a role in building the forces on the ground necessary to challenge school "reform" and other atrocious policies. I suggest that the contemporary demand of social justice movements to always "center the oppressed" can, in fact, be compatible with the best practices of Marxism—but only if and when Marxists are open to comprehensive, intersectional understandings of the project of liberation.

The Scope of the Argument

Certainly, Ryan's position is more nuanced than some of the blatant renditions of "class primacy" that have gained currency across much of the socialist movement today. I value Satnam Virdee's insight, cited by Ryan, that proletarian solidarity requires us to "go through race, rather than around it" (Virdee 2017a)—emphasizing that confronting racism is essential for the struggle against capitalism. This perspective more or less reverses the position that Vivek Chibber, a leading theorist of the Democratic Socialists of America (DSA), expressed in a recent interview with *Neues Deutschland*, a German socialist publication:

> The problem of the black population in the US is essentially an economic one. Anti-discrimination laws only help the top third of the black population—the ones who compete for the better jobs. The fight for equality is therefore a struggle of the black upper class for better conditions... Anti-racist struggle is only possible with class struggle, otherwise it is a lost cause. (Chibber 2020)

Perhaps Chibber is echoing the idea, uncontroversial among socialists, that Black oppression is intertwined with capitalist society and uprooting racism requires tying anti-racism to the class struggle. But the passage above amounts to class reductionism. Not only are struggles against legal discrimination quite significant to Black workers, who have participated in them in mass numbers, but every fight against racism and for expanding democracy, whoever it benefits, ought to matter to socialists. Adolph Reed, Jr. goes even further than Chibber does: for him, the concepts "racism" and "white supremacy" themselves are said to be constructs of middle-class academics that are incapable of addressing class inequality. Even the #BlackLivesMatter protests against police brutality are misguided, according to Reed, since police brutalize and kill many white people too (Reed 2016).

Movements against racism and white supremacy on the ground, thankfully, have regularly offered a clearer picture of the dynamic relationship between race and class. Often led by working-class activists, they have constantly linked white supremacy and police brutality to the capitalist state. Some unions, too, have been inspired to fight in support of anti-racist movements. After the murder of George Floyd on May 25, 2020, for example, the Amalgamated Transit Union defended its Minneapolis local when they stood by city bus drivers who refused to transport arrested protesters to the jails (Amalgamated Transit Union 2020). National Nurses United issued a statement about the "horrific effects of racism in our hospitals and community every day" (National Nurses United 2020), while Chicago Teachers Union president Jesse Sharkey explained why educators needed to oppose racist policing (Sharkey 2020).

Beyond the "color-blind" socialists, there exists a more sophisticated strain of class reductionism in which racism is mainly seen as an *ideological* tool to divide and conquer the working class—a false consciousness that, if addressed, would allow the proletariat to recognize its true unity. Akin to the liberal models of anti-racism, in which a good dose of multicultural education is seen as adequate to remove centuries of material inequality, such perspectives grant importance to the fight against racism primarily because they believe it contributes to a more powerful struggle against capital. As Cornell West argued in an educational article for DSA activists, such positions produce "a 'color-blind' strategy for resisting racism in which all workers [are] viewed simply as workers with no specific identity or problems. Complex racist practices within and outside the workplace [are] reduced to mere strategies of the ruling class" (West 2018: 2). Such thinking has a cost. Entire aspects of racism and white supremacy are ignored by the US left when race is primarily considered to be a function of class—as evidenced by the US left's difficulty in grappling with racism against Asian Americans (Jani 2021).

Virdee's formulation of class solidarity as moving "through race," while compelling, falls short of the truly intersectional approach necessary for combating class reductionism. Issues surrounding race are not something that Marxists can just take up along the way to achieve workers' unity. In capitalist society, there exists no prior moment of class without race and given this, there are aspects of racial oppression that Marxists should seek to explain that cannot be reduced to class, and there is a complexity to US (and global) racialization that cannot be reduced to a Black/white dichotomy.

Race and Class in the ISO

The ISO always viewed racism and capitalism as intertwined, a far cry from the positions of Chibber and Reed. Our problem was different: even though we engaged in a great deal of effective anti-racist work, we failed to recruit BIPOC members in sufficient numbers, to retain those we recruited and to bring them into leadership. We were unable to create spaces in which comrades of color could support one another and strategize together, in which white comrades' attitudes and behavior could be challenged without defensiveness, and in which the plethora of studies about race and racism could be discussed in an honest and open way, whether or not they aligned with traditional Marxist positions.

I joined the ISO in the mid-1990s, thrilled to find a group that aimed to put into practice Marxist ideas that I had only learned about in graduate school. Over its forty-two years the ISO remained a relatively small group, with less than one thousand dues-paying members spread across forty-odd branches at its height. But we punched well above our weight and, if I may say so, were visible in the US far left for our presence in a variety of movements, our attention to political education, our publications, and our annual Socialism conferences which drew around two thousand people in the last few years of the ISO's existence. The importance we placed on understanding and organizing against white supremacy fueled my twenty-four-year commitment to the group. By engaging with Black liberation and anti-racist struggles, Palestine solidarity work, anti-war and anti-Islamophobia efforts, and the fight for immigrant rights, I learned to connect my homegrown anti-colonial and pro-immigrant politics with the struggles of *other* people of color. The model of solidarity we put forward, one in which all workers had an interest in fighting racism, in all its forms, was refreshing in an activist environment dominated by theories and practices emphasizing insurmountable difference and the impossibility of revolution.

And yet there were signs that all was not well. Over time, several leading comrades of color left the group or became inactive after disagreements about the ISO's policies and practices around race. Others rose to positions of leadership only to find they either suppressed their disagreements for the sake of moving on or were marginalized when they chose to assert themselves. I have first-hand experience of much of this, sometimes making arguments despite opposition and sometimes keeping my mouth shut, not wanting to go against the tide or believing in good faith that things would resolve themselves in the long run. It all came to a head at a session called "Building a Multiracial Organization" at what ended up being the ISO's final national convention in February 2019. Leading members, myself included, described grievances ranging from individual acts of racism and microaggressions; articulated long-standing problems with recruitment, retention, and development of BIPOC members; and identified how the organization regularly suppressed questions and debates by dismissing them as mere "identity politics."

At the session, it felt like a dam had burst as pent-up frustrations and grievances, particularly among Black, Muslim, and Latinx comrades, were articulated openly. It is not an exaggeration to say that a certain euphoria took hold among comrades of color after the convention session, especially among many long-time members, as we formed a national "POC Caucus" for the first time. At the end of the convention, which was contentious for a great many reasons beyond the issues of race, delegates elected a new Steering Committee that consisted of more than 50 percent Black/POC and Indigenous cadre, myself included. We were poised to project a very different face to the left than the white and/or male image usually associated with Marxist leadership in the United States—even as we thought through a number of long-held positions and readied ourselves for a new era defined by mass movements against police brutality and white supremacy, social-democratic upsurge, crises in reproductive rights, deepening economic crisis, and far-right mobilization.

Unfortunately, we didn't get a chance to experiment with new approaches. A few weeks after the convention, reports of the botched handling/active cover-up of a 2013 sexual assault case involving an ISO member were brought to our attention, implicating members of both the old and new leadership. The ISO hemorrhaged members as efforts to create forums for accountability failed. In the following weeks, those of us remaining as members pulled together proposals for potential next steps, including those who had resigned in protest. A few hundred people participated in these least-ditch efforts—but we ultimately voted to dissolve the ISO.[2]

The hushing up of the sexual assault case in the name of "due process" was, in fact, a product of our "nuanced" class reductionism. Despite the group being active in initiatives against rape culture, sexual assault, and gender oppression, comrades' and allies' own physical safety and bodily autonomy was sacrificed for the "greater good" of keeping the ISO together. What good was an organization, comrades rightfully asked, whose members couldn't trust it to be vigilant about their safety? It is only by centering the most vulnerable, being vigilant about their safety and well-being, and most crucially, advancing their leadership, that a radical group can become fit to organize and lead.

Four Questions

The ISO's successes and its struggles with questions around race, as reflected in contemporary debates among socialists about class reductionism and class primacy, are a small instance in a much longer history of Marxist and socialist theory and practice.

Since the mid-nineteenth century, Marxists have linked colonialism and slavery to the rise of industrial capitalism, explored multiracial and international solidarity, and participated in anti-racist, anti-colonial, and anti-imperialist struggles. This has not merely been the work of white socialists and communists but, quite often, of Black and brown comrades. Throughout Latin America, Africa, and Asia, and within radical anti-racist struggles in the United States and other imperialist countries, the deep connections between imperialism, racism, and capitalist exploitation have pulled people of color into engagements with Marxism, socialism, and communism in different forms (see Bartolovich and Lazarus 2002). At the same time, the achievements of Marxism with respect to questions of racism, colonialism, and social oppression in general have often had to battle various strains of racism and Eurocentrism within white-majority socialist and communist organizations in Europe, in the United States, in South Africa, and elsewhere. And in socialist and communist groups of the Global South, rising under the shadow of Stalinism and Maoism, working-class majoritarianism has often meant using anti-racist and anti-imperialist language to cover up caste chauvinism, hetero-patriarchy, Islamophobia and, as Ryan effectively explores with regard to South Africa, offering a straight-up defense of bourgeois nationalism and state-led capitalist development.

Here I outline four major questions and areas where debates *within* Marxism about class, race, and other social oppressions and identities have often come to a head. How Marxists have approached and responded to these, over time, has had real implications in terms of organizing. Please note that my broad sketch here comes from many years of engaging with political writing, academic scholarship, and activist practice, and an effort to link them together in a comprehensive way. But each of these areas is the subject of extensive research and fierce debate, much more than this chapter can take up. While I offer a few reference points, readers interested in these topics should pursue them independently and make up their own minds.

Question 1: Do all workers share a material interest in common?

The exploitation of all workers under capitalism gives the working class, across social and national divisions, a shared potential and a common material interest in acting as a unified, revolutionary force—that's the classic Marxist position. But doesn't the prevalent idea that white workers in the United States benefit from racism contradict the slogan "Workers of the World Unite"? Many Marxists have grappled with this question. W. E. B. Du Bois wrote about the "public and psychological wage" that white workers receive, while asserting a deeper, common working-class unity ([1935] 1999), whereas Claudia Jones—decades before the term "intersectionality" was coined by Black feminist Kimberlé Crenshaw—spoke of the "triple oppression" of Black working-class women (Jones 1949: 4–7; see also Lynn 2016). The ISO "resolved" this conflict by readily acknowledging the "special oppression" of BIPOC workers and others but denied that white workers benefited from or were privileged in a racist society, as if admitting this would be to threaten the idea of workers' solidarity across the board. This fairly idiosyncratic position—one, it is important to emphasize, Ryan does *not* hold—both failed to explain reality and created unnecessary obstacles for comrades of color within and around the group.

How socialists understand the issue of workers' common interests has implications for organizational strategies. Does a multiracial/white-majority group encourage BIPOC caucuses or argue against them as being detrimental to unity—as I did, regrettably, for years? Does the socialist group engage in mutual aid work and support BIPOC communities in general or seek out connections only when there is a crisis—a police shooting, a US military attack, a surge in anti-immigrant activity? Does the group "allow" its BIPOC members to freely engage with the various (non-socialist) formations emerging organically in their communities or effectively pull BIPOC members away from such activity? Simply doing "good" anti-racist activist work will not provide suitable answers to these questions.

Question 2: Was the emergence of industrial capitalism "revolutionary"?

A core pillar of Marxist historiography is that the emergence of industrial capitalism, though violent and brutal, was revolutionary. For the first time in human history, a system of production existed that could harness the collective power of labor and, if fully developed and governed by the producers, could meet the material needs of people everywhere. Despite Marx's own emphasis that capitalism's rise was *contradictory*, and later Marxists' understanding that progress to socialism was not inevitable, many socialists over time have put themselves squarely on the side of modern, national development as essential to socialist liberation.³ This has meant, disturbingly, that some Marxists have often found themselves siding with (settler) colonialism and even imperialism, seeing them as necessary vehicles for the supposedly desirable spread of capital.⁴

In a 2002 article, I investigated the complexities and nuances of this problem in an article on Marx's writings on India, before and during the 1857 Rebellion there (Jani 2002). In an 1853 commentary on colonial India, which Edward Said described as "Orientalist" with good reason, Marx wrote: "Whatever may have been the crimes of England, she was the unconscious tool of history in bringing about [a social] revolution" (Jani 2002: 81). While Marx's attention to popular struggle and his constant critique of the motives and practices of the British moved him away from this position after the 1857 Rebellion in British, as I argue in the piece, the problem of (white) Marxists seeing colonialism as progressive persisted into the early twentieth century. For example, the European socialist parties of the Second International, led by the German SPD, made similar arguments about the progressive nature of imperialism when they backed their own governments in the First World War, betraying the long-held principle of socialist internationalism.⁵

V. I. Lenin and the Third International contested these betrayals, opposing these imperialist-socialists and differentiating between the nationalism of the oppressor and the nationalism of the oppressed. Lenin's characterization of the Great War as a "war between slave-owners for fortifying and strengthening slavery," and his political defense of resistance in colonized lands, underlined the importance of fighting racial and national oppression, not just class exploitation (Lenin 1915). This position went along with Lenin's theorizing of imperialism as "the highest stage of capitalism" and an emphasis on the need to *fight* imperialism in order to struggle for socialism.⁶ However, it remains the case that the emphasis that Marxism places on modern, capitalist development as laying the groundwork for future progress constantly creates questions concerning those hurt most decisively by it. A pro-development emphasis allows governments and parties today to justify atrocities—from the violent suppression of farmer protests in Nandigram by the Communist Party of India (Marxist) in 2007 to the Chinese Communist Party's current pursuit of imperialist aims across Africa.⁷

Marxists' focus on industrial capitalism within Western Europe often means that Asian, African, Latin American and/or Indigenous peoples do not figure prominently in many histories until the point of European contact through slavery and colonialism. Such Eurocentrism has a negative impact on comrades of color. As we know from discussions of diversity and social justice in both K-12 and university education, BIPOC students benefit from seeing themselves in the curriculum, from learning about cultures, histories, and societies that reflect their worlds.⁸ Marxist historiography and socialist educational within organizations ought to include, as a regular feature, opportunities to learn about the non-European world before 1492, integrating that knowledge into how we understand history, including the rise of capitalism and the many diverse struggles for liberation in every place and time.

The problem is not insurmountable. Marxism is not endemically Eurocentric because of its focus on capitalism; rather, the choice to focus primarily on Europe when seeking to understand capitalism and world history more broadly needs to be challenged. One approach might be to pay more attention to pre-capitalist forms of exchange, labor, and profit—as scholars like Jairus Banaji (2010) and Eric Wolf (1983) do—and look at industrial capitalism as not exclusively the product of Europe but as one that was actually constructed through a global process involving many different peoples over centuries. The history of non-European people and who they were before Europe came is not only important for avoiding Eurocentrism but also for telling the history of the world in a more complex and accurate way.

Question 3: Is the proletariat the revolutionary class?

Who makes up the revolutionary subject of Marxism? Classical Marxism is unequivocal: the revolutionary class, which has the potential, the interest, and the placement to overthrow capitalism and create a new world, is the proletariat, or the working class. Capitalist society itself creates "a class of labourers, who live only so long as they find work, and who find work only so long as their labour increases capital," and capitalism creates its own "gravediggers" by concentrating greater and greater numbers of workers within the same conditions as industry expands (Marx and Engels 2000). While workers as a whole form the revolutionary class, the specific role of *industrial* workers is central in Marx and later Marxists. But from early on Marx recognized that it was not enough that the working class was formed by capitalism: workers had to become united through struggle, across many social divisions, and to build growing awareness of their own power, in order to *become* revolutionary subjects (Marx 1999). Only then could they seize the productive forces of capitalism in the interest of human need, not capitalist profit.

How does this model of revolution fit a complex world, in which rebellions and revolutions frequently do *not* follow obvious or predictable paths in which contending classes line up neatly against each other? How does it account for the fact that capitalism spread quite unevenly across the world, as did, consequently, the (industrial) proletariat? Over the course of Marxism's history, debates have emerged around defining the relationship between workers in highly industrialized societies (i.e., the imperialist countries) and (a) other exploited and oppressed groups within these highly industrialized nations, including people of color, (b) agricultural workers and non-industrialized workers in the "Global South," and (c) the marginalized in terms of gender, sexuality, caste, and ability.

Let's take a few examples of these debates and their resolutions. The success of Bolshevik revolutionaries in 1917, for instance, depended on abandoning the idea that only the Western European working class could lead a struggle for socialism. In his famous "April Theses," Lenin stunned his comrades by advocating, amidst the devastations of the First World War, that "the power pass to the proletariat and to the poor section of the peasants aligned to the proletariat" (Lenin 1999). This notion of a workers' seizure of power in Russia was contested by contemporary Marxists, including Russians, as it went against prevailing ideas that made highly industrialized Western Europe the center of world revolution.

Leon Trotsky's innovative concept of "combined and uneven development," formed many years before but refined in the 1920s and 1930s, provided the necessary theoretical and historical support for Lenin's argument. Rather than moving across the world in a linear, uniform way, capitalism had spread unevenly; pre-capitalist and capitalist forms of production sat alongside each other, creating differences not only between nations but also within nations. Heterogeneity, thus, was a *feature* of capitalism. At the same time, capitalism was a "combined" system; all of these complex forms of production existed in the same world, which was increasingly interdependent. In such a view, "stages" of development could not be applied rigidly; even a country with a less industry and a small proletariat could lead a revolution toward socialism (see Trotsky 2008). The (industrial) proletariat was still central, but its relatively small numbers did not mean it could not take power.

Mao Zedong took a different approach to the problem of socialist revolution in a poorly industrialized country. Living through the Chinese Revolution of 1925–7 and the slaughter of Chinese communists after the disastrous advice from Moscow (James 2017), Mao turned to the peasants and advocated a shift from the traditional idea of the proletariat as the revolutionary class (e.g., Mao 1927). Maoism has a strong hold across the Third World precisely for this reason: it gives a clear role to the peasant/farmer majority and its repeated demonstrations of radicalism.

The long debate within Marxism around whether the industrial working class should be viewed as the revolutionary subject is itself a product of capitalism's uneven global spread, as is the problem of how exactly social movements and labor struggles come together. On the one hand, cross-class anti-colonial struggle across the colonized world in the early twentieth century, a world that was underdeveloped by definition, challenged the new Bolshevik state and the Communist International (Comintern) to find ways to link working-class struggle in the imperialist countries to the anti-imperialist movement.[9] On the other hand, evolving struggles against racism, patriarchy, xenophobia, and militarism within the imperialist world demanded the existing labor and socialist formations to think critically and expansively about liberation—though they did not always succeed.[10] All of this, as the twentieth century progressed, occurred as manufacturing and production were transformed by new technologies.

In this regard, it has been important for both theory and ongoing organizing to expand the definition of "working class" to include those employed in the industries of social reproduction (including educators) and in the service sector, as well as those working in informal systems of labor and in agrarian industries. The compatibility of Marxism and intersectionality, as Ashley Bohrer (2020) explains, serves to further break down artificial divisions between workers' movements and wider social movements. But more than attention to relevant theory, it is the actual work of organizing around capitalist exploitation and social oppression simultaneously that will prevent the idea of a revolutionary proletariat from being an exclusive and "color-blind" one, centered around (white) workers in imperialist countries.

Question 4: Should Marxists support nationalism?

Marxism has been associated with internationalism from the very start. The second part of *The Manifesto of the Communist Party* bluntly states: "The workers have no country" (Marx and Engels 2000). However, the sharp rise of anti-colonial struggle and nationalist consciousness in the early twentieth century, directly responding to an era of heightened imperialist war, challenged Marxists to refine their views on nationalism. In the 1920s, Lenin and the Communist International, with the active involvement of Black and brown radicals, turned Marxism toward a defense of national self-determination and away from the positions associated with the Second International's apologists for empire (see Riddell 2011). However, amidst the demise of the Bolshevik project, Joseph Stalin began to put forward the idea in the 1920s of "socialism in one country," linking the project of socialism to that of modern development within a single nation (Stalin 2000).

The combination of these two dynamics—the defense of anti-colonial nationalism and the justification of nation-centered socialist development—meant a sharp turn in how Marxists thought about nationalism (see Mandel 2016). Supporting national liberation movements in colonized countries, often crucial to their victory, also became an extension of Soviet foreign policy as the USSR sought to build alliances with the new postcolonial bourgeoisie of the Global South. As Ryan discusses in his section on South Africa, the South African Communist Party (SACP)'s anti-apartheid work and solidarity with the African National Congress soon turned it into an uncritical supporter for bourgeois nationalism. The factors outlined here meant that the defense of national self-determination, previously viewed as central to a deeper internationalism, was turned on its head.

The problem the SACP faced was not, however, that of competing primacies—"race primacy" over "class primacy," or vice versa. The "two-stage theory" of revolution followed by the SACP and many Communist Parties in the colonized world amounted to a rigid economic determinism—a return to the old, mechanical idea of historical progress in which "advanced" countries would have socialist revolutions before "backward" ones, who had to have bourgeois revolutions first.[11] While this position may appear to value anti-colonial and anti-racist politics and avoid class determinism, historically it ended up orienting communists around what amounted to the aims and objectives of the elites among the colonized *at the expense of* workers and the poor. In the case of South Africa, a combined attention to race and class would have meant challenging *both* the apartheid state and the capitalist economy that kept the Black working class down.

In my final article for the ISO's *Socialist Worker* newspaper, "Towards a Critical Defense of 'Identity Politics'" (2019), I suggested, as others have previously, that the Leninist defense of national self-determination in the 1920s represented a contemporary path forward for Marxism with respect to discussions concerning race and identity. This model, as a critical defense of left-wing nationalism, provides a framework for understanding the indivisibility of anti-capitalist and anti-racist/anti-imperialist struggle, the importance of political independence even within a capitalist world, and, correspondingly, the importance of *self-determination*. Consider the epigraphs that open this chapter, pairing the Combahee River Collective's 1977 call for centering Black women in the general fight for liberation in the United States with Karl Marx's growing understanding, in the 1860s, of the importance of the Irish colonial question for the English working-class movement. Without equating Black women in the United States with the colonized Irish, we can see a common structure of thought in the two quotations that allow us to consider genealogies of race/class that can bridge the divides between classical Marxism, Black feminism, and other traditions of anti-racism and anti-colonialism.

Conclusions

Marxists, and socialists more broadly, engage most successfully with questions of social oppression when we center the struggles of the oppressed within struggles of the working class. But we fall short when we become so focused on championing "the working class" as an abstract whole that we minimize racial and other social oppressions—when we ignore or dismiss the real benefits and advantages that accrue to working-class groups who are part of the racial, gender, and social majority in a given national space.

It is both a curse and a blessing to read that C. L. R. James, at the 1939 convention of the Socialist Workers Party (SWP-US), had to convince his comrades to understand the limits of a white-majority socialist organization in relation to the Black liberation struggle and to support independent Black organizing:

> The awakening political consciousness of the Negro not unnaturally takes the form of independent action uncontrolled by whites. The Negroes have long felt, and more than ever feel today, the urge to create their own organizations under their own leaders and thus assert . . . their claim to complete equality with other American citizens. Such a desire is legitimate and must be vigorously supported. . . . Under any circumstances, it would have been a task of profound difficulty, perhaps impossible, for a revolutionary party composed mainly of whites to win the confidence of the American Negro masses, except in the actual crises of revolutionary struggles. (James 1939)

Well into the twenty-first century, it can feel disempowering to recognize that we are rehashing debates from generations ago, going in circles while trying to accommodate white-majority groups that do not and cannot center BIPOC cadres. Despite a century of proclamations that Marxists support the independent struggle of the oppressed, we continue to be unable to account for the deep rifts that racial capitalism causes within the working class.[12] And yet, reading this quotation from James is also a blessing. It illustrates to those of us raising such questions within Marxist circles that our concerns are legitimate, and that we are following a path forged by giants.

Ten years after James's address to the SWP, Claudia Jones found herself engaged in a very similar struggle against chauvinism and arrogance in the Communist Party USA (CPUSA). As she said to her comrades in 1949: "We must end this practice in which Negro women who join our party, and who in their churches, communities, and fraternal groups are leaders of masses, with an invaluable mass experience to give our Party, suddenly find themselves viewed in our clubs, not as leaders, but as people who need 'to get their feet wet' organizationally" (Jones 1949: 18). While understanding the need for political education, Jones argued that the party's approach reflected "chauvinist disdain for the organizational talents of new Negro members, or for the necessity to promote them into leadership" (Jones 1949: 18).

As James and Jones both suggest, it is not enough to foreground the importance of fighting racism. Rather, it is necessary, they contend, that Black people in socialist groups have the freedom to follow their own political insights and direction. The leadership talent that Black women exhibit in their own spaces, Jones argues, ought to be recognized—rather than being suppressed within white-majority organizations. Centering the oppressed, as the Combahee River Collective propose with respect to Black women, allows the entire edifice of power in society to be illuminated. Our liberation and our struggles are intertwined, but without paying special attention to social oppression, Marxist appeals to the power of the working class will fail, at best, and mimic majoritarian biases, at worst.

Can multiracial socialist groups be built that respect Black/Indigenous/POC knowledge and experience—and truly practice self-determination? While I remain active in anti-racist, anti-imperialist, and labor organizing, I am less confident today about the socialist movement than when I began my journey into those circles in 1995. Yet, the Black-led and multiracial uprisings of the summer of 2020 were inspiring and pointed to what solidarity and joint, radical organizing could look like. Indeed, as I argued in my piece on fighting anti-Asian racism after the Atlanta spa killings of March 2021, the Summer 2020 actions created the context in which violence against Asian Americans became visible (Jani 2021). Socialist groups today ought to reject all models of organizing and struggle that are based upon "class primacy," as these easily turn into "color blindness" and center, implicitly, the experience of white workers as normative. Centering the oppressed—through an intersectional approach to race and social oppression—is the only approach by which one can begin to combine anti-racist politics with BIPOC leadership in the US socialist left.

Acknowledgments

Many thanks to Akunna Eneh, Khury Petersen-Smith, and Joe Ponce for thoughtful comments on the draft. And to the many comrades and colleagues who have directly or indirectly shaped these views.

Notes

1 I'm alternating between the newer acronym BIPOC (Black, Indigenous, People of Color) and the older POC (People of Color) for reasons of style.

2   To see the ISO Steering Committee's account of these developments, see the collection of articles "Reflections on the ISO Crisis" (ISO Steering Committee 2019).
3   See *The Communist Manifesto* (Marx and Engels 2000), among other texts, for Marx's understanding of capitalism as both violent and progressive. Rosa Luxemburg's famous phrase "socialism or barbarism" is an important example of socialists definitively challenging the notion that there is anything inevitable about the end of the capitalist society (Luxemburg 2010). Nevertheless, the linear model of change persists, with modern (capitalist) development seen as crucial for socialism. Debates about socialism and development are extensive; see Wen (2007) for an articulation of pro-development socialism in twenty-first-century China.
4   The extreme example is Warren (1980), arguing in a deliberately polemical tract that imperialism has been beneficial to development and social change. But the question applies to any Marxist history that, despite being troubled by colonial conquest, sees the process as inevitable for the establishment of capitalism and, eventually, socialism. My discussion of Marx and India (Jani 2002) below addresses this. See Churchill (1999) and Dunbar-Ortiz (2016) for discussions on Marxism, settler colonialism, and Native liberation.
5   Day and Gaido (2012) trace debates about socialists about colonialism, including some SPD leaders' open advocacy of (and others' debates against) a "socialist colonial policy."
6   Warren (1980) explicitly challenges Lenin's perspective, arguing, from a supposedly Marxist position, that imperialism has been progressive.
7   See Bidwai (2007) for an Indian leftist critique of the Nandigram massacre and the CPIM Central Committee's statement (Communist Party of India (Marxist) 2007). China's role in Africa is hotly debated on the left and puts on display core theoretical debates, including the very definitions of socialism, imperialism, and self-determination. Umi (2019) is an example of a critical, pan-Africanist perspective.
8   Any perusal of books on diversity in education reveals the need for diversity in the curriculum, not just the student body. See, for instance, NYC Coalition for Educational Justice (2018) and Keengwe (2020).
9   For a study of Asian revolutions with attention to the Comintern, see Harper (2021).
10 For one example, see Rhoads (2002) for a study of white/Chinese labor conflict in the late nineteenth century.
11 See Desai (2008) for an Indian communist's position on the problems of the "two-stages" theory, written in the 1970s and reflecting on the Global South as a whole.
12 The work of Cedric Robinson in "Black Marxism" and the concept of "racial capitalism" is crucial to this discussion, but is beyond the scope of this paper.

4

"Race," Class, and Education in South Africa

Salim Vally

Howard Ryan's substantial and significant essay resonates, despite some contextual differences, with the issues and concerns of many scholar-activists in South Africa. His hope that the essay might facilitate a productive interaction "with others who are interested in integrating class, race, and anti-capitalism—in theory and practice" is appealing and welcomed.

Neglecting social class has contributed to failures with respect to addressing and overcoming the deep and seemingly intractable inequalities that characterize South Africa's society and its education system. This omission of considerations of social class, we have previously suggested (Motala and Vally 2010)—in the wake of the euphoria about the "miracle" of the "new" South Africa—was and is related to the ruling African National Congress's refusal to acknowledge the class nature of the post-apartheid state. To locate and understand the present reality, including inequalities in schooling, means locating and understanding the straitjacket of dominant class relations and the political economy that shaped the transition from apartheid to democracy. The African National Congress (ANC) government came to office in 1994 on the back of promises to prioritize the redistribution of wealth and resources as the means of achieving equality. The years since have witnessed the state's clear, even if at times contested, political, and ideological acceptance of the broad framework of a globally dominant, neoliberal political and economic orthodoxy (Bond 2000; Marais 2001; Alexander 2003).

Apartheid-era racial legislation has been removed from the statute book, access to schooling has increased and there is gender parity in schooling, but quality education for the vast majority of the Black population remains elusive. While a mélange of new official policies covering every conceivable aspect of education exists, the education system as a whole reflects and reproduces the wider inequalities in society. Although a minority of schools in South Africa can favorably compare with the best in the world, quality public education remains unequally distributed along social class, racial, and geographic lines.

My response to Ryan's essay is influenced by the late revolutionary scholar, former political prisoner and educationist Neville Alexander's designation of South Africa's social formation as *racial capitalism* (Alexander 1985: 23). Alexander's use of this term and his analysis of educational and other social issues acknowledges the weaving of structural racism into the warp and woof of South African capitalism without eliding the primacy of class.[1]

The lens of racial capitalism will inform my chapter's analysis of the nexus between "race" and class and the unfulfilled promise of a quality public education in South Africa. Although implicated by it, Ryan's essay does not seek to address whether or not constructions of "race" are at the same time a validation of the classifications of "race" sought by old and new eugenicists and racist pseudo-science. Explanations of racism based solely on itself—that is, the existence of racist stereotypical ideas among racists—can only be sustained to a logical end if the idea of "race" is itself validated. Explanations of racist ideology and practice based on racism alone are therefore hoisted on a tautology. The scare quotes signal my rejection of "race" as a biological concept but not as a social construct. While racism is all too real, "race" as a biological concept is not (Montagu 1952; Fields and Fields 2012; Vally and Motala 2017).

Just over twenty-five years since the first democratic elections, the combined weight of apartheid's legacy, exacerbated by neoliberal policies in the post-apartheid period, has meant that the hopes invested by many who supported the liberation movements' pledge to create "a better life for all" remains a chimera. The "new" South Africa has largely benefited traditional white South African capitalists, global capital, and a thin layer of a new Black elite. South Africa is consistently ranked as one of the most unequal countries in the world and inequality remains the most salient feature of South African society. Although an elaborate system of social grants has mitigated protracted poverty levels under ANC rule, incomes, wealth, and unemployment remain racialized, gendered, and spatialized, as they were in the apartheid era.

As consequences of the 1996 adoption of Growth, Employment, and Redistribution (GEAR) strategy—a neoliberal macroeconomic strategy—South Africa experienced the acceleration of the marketization of public services, stringent budgetary constraints and fiscal "austerity," "public-private partnerships," cost recovery, and cuts to education and other social services. Human capital theory[2] conceptions of development were embraced (Vally and Motala 2014). These strategies were pursued simultaneously with rhetorical support for redistribution and redress (Spreen and Vally 2006) and expressed the contradictory impact of the "negotiated settlement" reached by the ANC and its allies with the apartheid regime and importantly, national and multinational corporate interests.

The political outcome of the settlement ensured that the interests of old and new elites were not only protected but also extended, albeit through new configurations of power sharing with new Black elites. Alexander (2003: 59) argued that despite changes in the racial composition as to who is in power (and not just in government but in the economic spheres as well), the South African government and the new Black elites represent "the very same capitalist class that profited from the system of overt and systematic racism which the world called apartheid and which is now allegedly a thing of the past." Alexander described how South Africa is a rather "ordinary" nation insofar as the imperatives of globalization and neoliberalism drive it "towards becoming a deeply divided society in which, as in all countries today, the divisions are determined by class." Furthermore, because social relations were mystified as "race relations," there was a need to "illuminate the character of the *real* (socio-economic) basis of inequality and the *real* (ideological) forms in which it is expressed" in pursuing liberation, even after the demise of apartheid (2003: 96). Later, Alexander (2012: 34) wrote:

> Ardent as well as "reluctant" racists of yesteryear have all become convinced "non-racialists" bound to all South Africans under the "united colours of capitalism" in an egregious atmosphere of Rainbow nationalism. The same class of people, often the very same individuals, who funded [apartheid government leaders] Verwoerd, Vorster and Botha are funding the present regime. The latter has facilitated the expansion of South African capital into the African hinterland in ways the likes of Cecil John Rhodes or Ernest Oppenheimer could only dream. . . . In this connection, it is pertinent to point out that the strategy of Black Economic Empowerment—broad-based or narrow is immaterial—is no more than smoke and mirrors, political theatre on the stage of the national economy. The only way that erstwhile Marxist revolutionaries in the liberation movement can justify their support and even enthusiastic promotion of these developments is by chanting the no longer convincing mantra: *There is no alternative!* (emphasis in original)

Minister of Mineral Resources and Energy, Gwede Mantashe—the chairperson of the ruling party, the African National Congress (ANC), and a current South African Communist Party (SACP) Politburo member—unwittingly confirmed Alexander's prescience in a recent revealing interview:

> One of the mistakes we make in talking about broad based black economic empowerment is making as if it is a social programme that will benefit everyone. Until we are categorical that [the] programme is about creating black capitalists, once we understand that, then we'll assess its success and failure on the correct basis. (Seccombe 2019: 2)

South Africa is a classic example of the failure of a "race-reductive" theory and confirms Ryan's essential thesis. In the South African instance, Alexander illustrates how pre-existing social relations were transformed by the development of mining capitalism at the end of the nineteenth century, drawing a necessary connection between the development of capitalism and racism. The conclusion, for him, was that it is not possible to eliminate racism without dealing with its capitalist underpinnings in South Africa. For Alexander:

> At certain times racial ideology was and is functional for the accumulation of capital, whereas at other times it could be dysfunctional. So there is no necessary connection, it is a contingent one. . . . This is of course a different thesis from the liberal thesis, which is that racism is allegedly dysfunctional in regard to capital accumulation. (Alexander interviewed by Callinicos 1992: 115–16)

I will discuss this contingent relation later, in the context of the race/class "fusion" referred to by Ryan. First, I provide some historical background and outline a few contemporaneous developments pertinent to how class, "race," and capitalism play out in South Africa's education policy and practice.

Predating apartheid, from the first school for slaves in the Western Cape province opened in 1658 through the colonial period, education was designed to fit Black people into subordinate positions in the racially structured division of labor and through doing so aimed to reproduce this structure. The roots of segregated schooling were tied to a particular form of extractive mining capitalism and the nature of the state and its social policy in the late nineteenth and early twentieth centuries (Cross and Chisholm 1990). Education and schooling were predicated on maintaining a Black migrant workforce and a stabilized white working class. Schooling was to ensure the reproduction of this labor structure along racially defined lines. The gold mining industry in the late nineteenth century, in particular, relied on a rigid and pervasive racial division of labor into "occupations with different functions, income and status" (Cross and Chisholm 1990: 45). Colonial practices suffused with racial prejudices were systematized and formalized to regulate migrant labor in the mining industry and extended into political and social life, including education. Referring to later education developments, Christie and Collins (1990: 182) asserted that "the central continuing feature remains, namely that schooling for the indigenous people of South Africa is in the main for the purpose of reproducing a certain kind of labour, as required by the particular form taken by the accumulation process at a particular time." These policies in education and beyond were not ends in themselves but effectively served the purpose of the super-exploitation and control of Black labor and the rapid accumulation of capital in the hands of a few white mining and agricultural capitalists.

The overt white supremacy social policies of the National Party, which came into power in 1948, extended previous colonial segregationist policies through its program of "separate development" or apartheid. Several laws were passed which enacted segregation in the education system under the apartheid state's ideology of "Christian National Education," which implemented separate education systems for each "population registration group" (in the nomenclature of apartheid officialdom—Africans, whites, coloreds, and Indians).

The expansion of poor-quality education in the context of political and economic oppression resulted in the growth of massive resistance among youth, of which the watershed mark was the 1976 Youth Uprising spearheaded by the Black Consciousness Movement (BCM). Resistance within education to the goals, control, and quality of education was a feature throughout the 1970s and 1980s. In Black schools, apartheid education meant minimal levels of resources, inadequately trained and few staff, poor-quality learning materials, shortages of classrooms, and the absence of laboratories and libraries. Besides these tangible deprivations, schools also inculcated unquestioning conformity, rote learning, autocratic teaching, and authoritarian management styles; syllabi replete with racism and sexism; and antiquated forms of assessment and evaluation (Vally 1998).

In their eagerness to participate in the international political and economic arena, the new post-apartheid policy planners adopted educational reforms that emulated those in industrialized countries and also spoke to vested class interests. The influence of World Bank consultants and other private international consultants was key (Spreen and Vally 2006).

Besides Alexander, a number of other educationists have written about the problems besetting the post-apartheid education system in South Africa. While many analyses of South African education have great merit, they have largely ignored any direct reference to, or analysis of, the social pathologies and structures created by racial capitalism in South Africa. Consequently, they have not provided a theoretical or practical basis for understanding the pervasive phenomenon of class and its relevance to an analysis of school reform in South Africa. These social pathologies are an expression of society's more fundamental cleavages; and unless these are understood and analyzed more fully, interventions in the schooling system alone will have only a limited effect.

Neglecting social class has contributed to the failure by the post-apartheid government to address and overcome the deep inequalities that continue to characterize the South African education system. The absence of class analysis prevents policy actors from seeking more penetrative social interventions in education and social policy in general.

Elsewhere, in an article on class, "race," and state in post-apartheid education, we lamented the fact that social class as an analytical and conceptual category "has been a casualty of the post-apartheid period" (Motala and Vally 2010: 93):

> Post-modern theory, in vogue during this period, was used as a justification for the retreat from class, made even more seductive by its coincidence with the negotiated settlement.... It could be argued that intellectuals in South Africa have themselves been complicit in the elision of class as an analytical category, quite often consciously and disparagingly. There is also the possibility of timidity in the face of the avalanche of academic and public voices representing capital, which have made any reference to class seem both archaic and "ideological," as though these voices are themselves not ideological.

The "free from class" analytical paradigms, based on consensual notions that dismiss the salience of class, fail to understand why class analysis would enhance knowledge of specific local school communities both individually and in relation to society, including with respect to issues of "race" and gender. Class analysis also implies a critical ability to interact with the experiential knowledge of marginalized communities and the ability to embrace the praxis of the initiatives in the educational field that engage democratically with working-class communities. These class struggles in the educational field encompass a focus on concrete issues such as user fees, the cost and commodification of education, the governance of education institutions, and epistemological concerns.

The patent failure of the public education system to provide quality education for the majority of learners has spawned a number of suggestions that their proponents claim will rectify this situation, including the crude resort to an apartheid-like disciplinary regime and the privatization of education.

Although their number is small in relation to their presence in other countries, South Africa has, in recent times, witnessed a mushrooming of private schools. My recent article on both the size and shape of privatization of education in South Africa and the Global Education Reform Movement (GERM) provides relevant details (Vally 2018). The article also provides an analysis of how the state has encouraged the growth of private education by using government employees' pension funds, as well as funding from South African financial companies. Further, the article considers the roles that are played by multinational corporations, such as Pearson, and multilateral organizations, such as the World Bank. Importantly, I also show how the new private schools, supported by the various actors mentioned above, are aimed at finding a market among the growing Black middle class.

Against Both "Race" and Class Reductionism

Although there exists in the South African education literature a wide range of references to "race" and gender, and a great deal of statistical information of value relating to these social characterizations, they remain de-linked from any conscious appreciation of the impact of social class and its deeper structural implications on the very communities of the poor and disadvantaged which are the subject of educational theory, policy, and practice. "Race," in particular, is examined primarily in relation to the achievement of greater "race" equity and the quantification of educational improvements in relation to it.

Analyses of social issues, including education in the post-apartheid period, are dominated by an uncritical focus on racial factors while often ignoring underlying class issues. This is not meant to imply that racial and gender issues are mere distractions from basic issues of inequality. The view of the Trinidadian Marxist C. L. R. James, quoted in Walter Rodney's (Rodney 1983: 100) seminal work, *How Europe Underdeveloped Africa*, is apposite here:

> The race question is subsidiary to the class question in politics, and to think of imperialism in terms of race is disastrous. But to neglect the racial factor as merely incidental is an error only less grave than to make it fundamental.

While "race" on its own is not an adequate explanation for exploitative processes or for the structural components of capitalist political and economic systems, this does not automatically imply that it has no explanatory value in relation to "class" and to processes of exploitation. Indeed, it is precisely because racist policies and strategies have come to be utilized in societies, both for capitalist accumulation engendering social conflict and by the ruling class of global hegemonic states like the United States to advance their global exploitative interests, that ideas about "race" have such powerful meanings in the public consciousness, in global politics, and ultimately in struggles for control over resources. Saul in his essay, "Identifying Class, Classifying Difference" (2006: 64–5), grapples with the relationship between social categories:

> Bannerji has underscored the "absurdity" of attempting to see "identity and difference as historical forms of consciousness unconnected to class formation,

development of capital and class politics." But in doing so she also emphasizes the impossibility of considering class itself outside the gendering (and "race-ing") that so often significantly characterizes it in the concrete.

Ryan usefully describes how:

> The "new social movements"—addressing race, gender, sexuality, ecology, peace, democracy in the university—stretched left and Marxist theory in new ways and beyond an historic tendency to focus narrowly on workplace organizing. Yet, when mass action receded and corporate power reasserted itself, the new bodies of thought generated by the social movements lost their radical edge and, in particular, their connection to Marxism and class politics.

A brief autobiographical note might be pertinent here. I came of age politically as a member of the South African Students Movement (SASM). SASM represented Black school pupils, and the South African Students Organization (SASO) founded by the likes of Steve Biko—who was later murdered in prison—represented Black tertiary students. Both student organizations embraced the philosophy of Black Consciousness. At the age of sixteen, after the watershed moment of the 1976 high school student uprising which started in Soweto, I was imprisoned along with many of my contemporaries. Despite extreme state repression, including the massacre of hundreds of children and youth, torture, and the banning of our organizations, it was also a period of intense education and ideological debate. The BCM was not ideologically homogeneous. We sought answers, enthusiastically debated and read widely and eclectically, influenced by anti-colonial struggles in Africa, Asia, and South America as well as anti-racist struggles in the United States and Europe. Some of us were attracted to Marxism—not through the writings of those situated in Western academies but by the praxis of those involved in national liberation and anti-racist struggles: Amilcar Cabral, Samora Machel, Paulo Freire, Che Guevara, Ho Chi Minh, Walter Rodney, C. L. R. James, George Jackson, Angela Davis, and others. It is much too simplistic to characterize the BCM as narrow "Black nationalism" solely occupied with "Pan-African" issues and an expression of a "race-based" theory. Although there were, indeed, elements of such tendencies, they were not dominant at all times.

Ideological, cultural, and political issues all play a role in shaping historical conjunctures and these must be understood as in complex interplay with issues of class, "race," and gender. I do not accept class-reductionist approaches as adequate explanations for all issues and conflicts, although there is no doubt that many "race," gender, caste, and even religious and regional conflicts are likely to be exacerbated by the underlying contradictions of capitalism, as they may well be an expression of conflicts over social resources and wealth, and as such, conflicts germane to class analysis. Other research is necessary to understand the nature of "outside of class" conflicts, which often express themselves in factionalist, sectarian, religious, territorial, ethnic, and other forms of division—no doubt receiving added ballast in the age of Trump, Johnson, Modi, and other ascendant regressive and racist right-wing leaders and regimes. What is certain is that many of the answers cannot be found at the point of production alone. Tithi Bhattacharya (2017) posed the question: "When we write the memory of class struggle of our era shall we abandon the struggle for Palestine, antiracism and feminism to the margins of our chronicle and await the purely magical workplace struggle to emerge out of a vacuum? Or shall we try again to reread Marx and think about the relationality of struggle?"

Regrettably, even many left-leaning scholars and activists, especially those who are schooled in Marxism in the West, continue to be dismissive of racism as intrinsic to global capital's agenda. As a consequence, they do not understand the specificities of capitalist accumulation in so-called developing societies or the majority world as these are affected by globally organized structures in which forms of difference—"cultural," "racial," "religious," and so on—are fundamental to such accumulation.

While "race" is not adequate to explain relations of production and the processes of exploitation, it has explanatory value in the analysis of particular forms of power—which class analysis *alone* cannot sufficiently explain. Marxist approaches to theorization are considerably more enriching and explanatory of the complex relationship of the forms of capital accumulation and power in developing societies. To wit, the experiences of racialized and gendered workers are important as a source of knowledge of the processes of exploitation, the state and cultural practices that reproduce an inequitable hierarchy of racialized and gendered workers, and these experiences need to be understood within the framework of the social relations of production—that is, in Marxist terms. These racialized and gendered experiences also have a crucial role to play for praxis and solidarity.

The veteran Tanzanian educationist Karim Hirji (2019: 248–9) insists that supporting historically constituted and discriminated against "identity groups"—given this reflects real problems on the ground and thus should not be abandoned—"has to be conducted within a universal framework that will unite hitherto conflicting identities." Hirji discusses how in many African countries, "ethnic," "tribal," xenophobic, and religious differences, as well as justified grievances, are manipulated by governing elites. He provides a left critique of identity politics:

> As people at the bottom bicker about their grievances in restricted ways, the local and global economic, political and military overlords continue to rule over humanity. Perpetually peddling exclusive identity politics will convert our struggles into a grand illusion. Like the frog that burnt to death as the water in which it floated was heated gradually, humanity will remain unperturbed as the planet burns up politically, socially, economically, militarily and physically. Our narrow-mindedness will render us clueless and powerless to confront the mighty corporations and governments that control the world for the benefit of a few billionaires. This is as true in Africa as it is in Asia, Latin America and the Western nations. (2019: 249)

While it is true that contemporaneous sectional identity politics "marks a retreat from the crucial passage of identity to solidarity, and from individual recognition to the collective struggle against an oppressive social structure" (Haider 2018), both Haider today and Kelley previously, like Hirji, are clear about concrete practice, struggle, and principled solidarity. Kelley (1997:11) emphasizes that

We simply can't afford to abandon the subway, with all of its multicultural messiness to jump on board the Enlightenment train of pure, simple, color- and gender-blind class struggle. . . . Attempts to "transcend" (read: outgrow) our race and sex does not make for a unified working class. What does is recognition of the multiplicity of experiences and perspectives and a willingness to struggle on all fronts. . . . Recognizing the importance of environmental justice for the inner city; the critical role of antiracism for white workers' own survival; the necessity for men to fight for women's rights and heterosexuals to raise their voices against homophobia. It's in struggle that one learns about power and how it operates, and that one can imagine a different world.

Notes

1. This is different from Cedric Robinson's understanding of racial capitalism, as referenced in Ryan's paper. While the analyses of both Alexander and Robinson examined the racialized process of accumulation by dispossession and coercive labor regimes, Alexander's vision of an alternative society to that of racial capitalism was unambiguously based on class struggle. Kelley (2017) writes that Robinson developed the concept during a sabbatical year in England, where "Robinson encountered intellectuals who used the phrase 'racial capitalism' to refer to South Africa's economy under apartheid. He developed it from a description of a *specific* system to a way of understanding the *general* history of modern capitalism." Alexander established a lively correspondence with members of the "Race and Class" collective in London in the late 1970s at the same time Robinson was both working on his book *Black Marxism* and also in contact with members of the collective. This was shortly after Alexander's six-year period of forced confinement to his house subsequent to his release from Robben Island, having served a ten-year sentence. In a recent discussion, Kelley and I speculated that it was likely that Robinson was familiar with Alexander's use of the term developed in the mid-1970s to late 1970s.
2. Human capital theory, tied to neoclassical economics and neoliberal discourse, reduces the value of education to the labor market requirements of business. In this conception, education is blamed for not supplying the skills business needs—that is, education is blamed for the mismatch between what education produces and what business wants. Within this framework, unemployment is blamed on an individual's skill deficit and not understood as a structural problem of capitalism.

5

A Marxist Challenge to the Concept of "Race"

Antonia Darder and Rodolfo D. Torres

> *In short, we need to study each domain in which corrective action is to be undertaken in detail, so that we can identify the real sources of disadvantage suffered by the relevant individuals and groups. By using the shorthand of "race" . . . we also entrench—avoidably—the very racial categories that undermine the possibility of attaining a truly non-racial democratic [society].*
>
> —Neville Alexander (2006: 11)

Howard Ryan's essay featured in this volume represents an excellent contribution to the kind of comprehensive analyses still required within the field, in order to more deeply engage the relationships, contradictions, and questions that exist between the categories of class, "race," and school reform. And, as such, it provides a compelling beginning from which to launch a variety of responses speaking to the purpose and aims of this book. However, despite sharing a Marxist lens of analysis, there are a few significant points of departure in our work, which we began almost twenty years ago with our book, *After Race: Racism after Multiculturalism* (2004). For example, although Ryan speaks definitively about the retreat from class in many perspectives related to "race," we argue that it is not solely a retreat from class but also the insidious racializing logic of capital or capitalism as an ideology that makes it difficult and at times even impossible for scholars and activists to speak across our differing perspectives. In fact, our longstanding efforts to enter constructive exchanges across differing perspectives of class and "race"/racism in education and society have nearly always proven futile, given the highly contentious nature of the debate.

Nevertheless, we believe it important to point to the myriad ways in which capitalism occupies a very distinct analytical space, in that all structures and social phenomena are directly shaped by the totalizing logic of capital and capitalism as a system of economic, political, and social life. From this vantage point, it is difficult to imagine that we can reach an understanding of globalized conditions of inequality created by capital without the existence of a grand theory to bring together our engagements with what remains an internationalized system of capitalist oppression. Most recently, we've witnessed the destructive impact of globalized conditions as put into motion by the political economy of the pandemic and the disparate responses of governments around the world. Consequently, already existing conditions of extreme inequality have been severely exacerbated by the pandemic. For example, Oxfam (2021, 2017) reports that eight men now own more wealth than 3.6 billion people. The richest 1 percent have more than twice as much wealth as 6.9 billion people, while almost half of humanity survives on $5.50 a day.

As would be expected, poor and racialized populations globally have faced overwhelming negative consequences associated with Covid-19 and its variants, with statistics showing staggering disparities in infection rates and death rates (Booth and Barr 2020). However, despite arguments that suggest "race" is the primary cause of widespread poverty and health disparities among oppressed populations, it has been people with disabilities who have had the highest rates of Covid-19 deaths (Clegg 2020). In an effort to address harmful racializing notions, Chowkwanyun and Reed (2020) argue that disparity figures without explanatory context can erroneously suggest that certain problems are "primarily racial" and, thus, undermine efforts to eliminate inequities. So, whether we are focusing on health or educational disparities, their analysis points to an urgent need for a social critique that is explicitly grounded in unpacking the unrelenting impact of the structural dynamics and material consequences of capitalism in the world today.

At the core of our response is the belief that a Marxist class-conflict analysis is indispensable to understanding not only racism but all forms of human oppression in society. Due to the nature of the task at hand, we are unable to respond to Ryan's essay in a complete and comprehensive manner. So, in an effort to be concise, we focus on several salient points that we believe are significant to scholarly or community efforts to engage in comradely dialogue across differing viewpoints. These include the retreat from class, concerns tied to perpetuating the concept of "race," the importance of understanding racism (not "race") and racialization, some underlying concerns with race-based theories, and a note regarding the need for a socialist perspective in progressive discussions of educational reform.

Retreat from Class

In his excellent and well-researched discussion, Ryan unapologetically critiques the retreat from class in scholarly discussions of both "race" and educational reform—a phenomenon that has prevailed across the literature during the past three decades. In agreement with his concern, we reassert the importance of class and production relations, particularly with respect to the process of racialization within education, despite tendencies to interpret our position as an attempt to return to an outdated paradigm of economic determinism. Yet, Marxism has been an important site of conflicting and competing readings of Marx, and also of its various interpretations of "race," as Ryan has noted.

Our position here is to draw attention to the importance of class in any educational analysis that positions itself as contributing to a political project of liberation, in that the majority of racialized students continue to be differentially located within the structures of capitalist social relations of production. Hence, their experiences of alienation and repression cannot be definitively characterized as being fundamental or intrinsic across class, skin color, or gender. This is generally overlooked or ignored among race-based theories that tend to discount the ways in which the material conditions of impoverished white populations around the world are more similar to impoverished populations of color than to their more affluent counterparts (Moss 2003). To not acknowledge this shared condition of economic, political, and societal oppression in schools and on the streets is to ignore the organizing potential of bringing together subaltern populations across differences and diverse perspective. In the final analysis, the project of liberation must be inherently anti-capitalist and seek to reimagine the meaning of a democratic socialism is the twenty-first century.

Further, one of our concerns with the way notions of "race" and "race relations" have been deployed over time, by critical race theorists and other race-based scholars, is the manner in which the political and economic spheres are theorized as separate spheres in their treatments of "race." This is to say that notions of "race" or "race relations" in traditional discourses, more often than not, fail to systematically counter the racializing logic of capital, where such ideas are mobilized insidiously and invisibilized within education and other social contexts by way of neutral, common-sense, and meritocratic rationales. In *Democracy against Capitalism*, Wood (1995: 19) argues that this practice serves the deeply anti-democratic aims of capitalism by transfiguring the "economy" into an abstract entity and "emptying capitalism of its social and political content." What Wood seeks to reveal is the manner in which the false separation of the political and the economic obscures and distorts the fragmenting nature of social life within capitalism. Hidden behind this abstraction, as Parenti (1995: 81) asserts, are the class-driven interests of the economy. Yet, frequently, when the "problem of the economy" is mentioned in academic and even activist discourses, it is spoken of in generalized terms that render it a neutral entity, not as "the problems of the capitalist economy with a specific set of social relations and a discernible distribution of class power." Along with this retreat of class politics, there has also been a "licensed disregard and, in some cases, outright contempt for working-class and poor people irrespective of race" (Reed 2020: 162).

These critiques serve to highlight that the act of simply referring to a population's economic status or social class in discussions of "race" and racism does not constitute employing a political-economic lens of analysis in one's interpretation of social phenomenon, nor does it entail challenging the logic of capitalist ideology. It is interesting to note that even Ryan, who carefully moves to challenge race-based theories, does not foreground this issue in his treatment of Cedric Robinson's (2019) implicitly race-based criticism of Marx's anti-Eurocentric argument. Given Ryan's central concern with a return to class, he could have offered a more robust challenge in his analysis of Robinson's work. For example, in "Rethinking Black Marxism: Reflections on Cedric Robinson and Others," Meyerson (2000: 2) critiques theorists like Robinson who enable the relative autonomy of "race" through a reductionist and distorted analysis of class and its primacy. He counters this tendency by noting that an emphasis on the primacy of class and the working class as revolutionary agent does not "render women and people of color 'secondary'" in Marxist analyses. Rather, he argues,

> The primacy of class means that building a multiracial, multi-gendered international working-class organization or organizations should be the goal of any revolutionary movement: the primacy of class puts the fight against racism and sexism at the center. The intelligibility of this position is rooted in the *explanatory* primacy of class analysis for understanding the structural determinants of race, gender and class oppression. Oppression is multiple and intersecting but its causes are not.

The bottom line of this analysis is a focus on the manner in which the logic of capital and the primacy of class fuel racism, in contrast to an analysis that focuses on the socially constructed and fictitious phenotypical category of "race," an idea grounded in an oppressive dualistic epistemology that ultimately bolsters conditions of racialized oppression. This exacerbation occurs through the pernicious process of racialization, an underlying belief system that equates the color of people's skin—including those labeled as white—with essential or intrinsic group characteristics. As Alexander (2006) notes, this system of "race" categorization functions to undermine democratic life. It is, therefore, not surprising to find that within schools and society more broadly there is a deeply imbedded or implicit ideological structure of thought that is enacted materially, attributing to particular groups (depending on who is doing the signification) an inherently evil or dangerous nature, along with judgments made about their innate intellectual inferiority or superiority. For this reason, we insist that unjust capitalist relations are perpetuated not by "race" but by the ideological institutionalization of racism, whose true constitutive foundation is unquestionably tied to material subjugation.

Materiality of Racism

Traditional and popular conceptual formations utilized up to the present day to define "race" within the United States have generally concealed the deeply embedded relationship that exists between racism and class. For this reason, Miles and Brown (2003: 137) assert that one of the major analytical tasks before us is "the historical investigation of the interpolation of racialization and racism in political and economic relations." Regrettably, despite the contemporary glut of literature on critical race theory (CRT), it remains the case that there are few treatments of "race" that offer a systematically grounded and theoretically informed account of the intricate relationship at work between racism, power, and class and its articulation within capitalist social relations. In considerable part, this is because there remains a conventional separation of economic and political spheres in both theory and practice. To Ryan's credit, we believe he attempts, through his discussion, to break with this duality, but because of his sympathy with the category of race, the separation persists.

Historically, the separation of economic and political spheres has been underscored in the United States since the civil rights movements of the mid-twentieth century.

Although these movements sought to address the impoverished material conditions of African Americans and other economically oppressed populations, their persistent emphasis on a liberal, rights-centered political agenda served to undermine the persistent development of a coherent working-class movement in the United States, as it has in other parts of the world. Unfortunately, opposition to a class-based politics, resulting from an ideological separation of the economic and political spheres, reinforces a division between economic and political action—a division inherent in capitalist appropriation and exploitation. In fact, as Wood (1995: 20) argues, "This 'structural' separation may, indeed, be the most effective defense mechanism available to capital," in its perpetuation of economic inequalities and its longstanding assault on working people.

Our rejection of the separation of political and economic spheres echoes Marx's notion that the ultimate aim of capitalist production, with its incessant focus on capital accumulation, is political control. A central claim of this argument is that the well-camouflaged overlap that exists between what we term economic and political spheres must be exposed with specificity and commitment. In Marxist analysis, the economy is viewed as a set of social relations. This view is in sharp contrast with classical views of the economy that "fail to treat the productive sphere itself as defined by social determinations and in effect deal with society 'in the abstract'" (Wood 1995: 22). Consequently, when theories of "race," racism, and other forms of inequality and oppression (no matter how progressive or radical such theories claim to be) fail to counter the oppressive structures of capitalism, their critical edge is assimilated by mainstream ideologies that categorically obscure class struggle.

In contrast, we argue for a materialist understanding of the world in which we grapple forthrightly with the impact of racism upon our material lives. This entails two significant principles of analysis. The first requires us to engage the social relations and practices by which human beings interact with the world and which are thereby implicated in producing the life conditions we are seeking to remedy. And second, we argue for a historical understanding of human life that recognizes that all products of social activity and all social interactions between human beings are manifested as material forces of production. By all social forms, that is, all products of social activity and all social interactions between human beings, we mean to encompass all ideologies and practices that sustain and perpetuate racism and other forms of human inequalities as direct products of a particular social system of production.

Wood (1995: 27) sheds light on this relationship by directly linking the mode of production to questions of power relations and exploitation.

> A mode of production is not simply a technology but a social organization of productive activity, and a mode of exploitation is a relationship of power. Furthermore, the power relationship that conditions the nature and extent of exploitation is a matter of political organization within and between contending classes. In the final analysis the relation between appropriators and producers rests on the relative strength of classes, and this is largely determined by the internal organization and the political forces with which each enters into the class struggle.

As such, we argue that all forms of social inequality are defined by class relations and, in other respects, motivated by the persistent drive to perpetuate class inequality within the context of the capitalist state, a phenomenon of social class warfare that is perpetuated by the ongoing construction and reconstruction of capitalist class relations. Thus, racism, in the form of social policies and practices, is operationalized through racialized class relations. Sexism is operationalized through gendered class relations. Heterosexism is operationalized through homophobic or transphobic class relations. Islamophobia is operationalized through Judeo-Christian class relations. In turn, all of these inequalities function to sustain cultural, political, and economic stratification within societies at large.

To reiterate, everything functions within the context of material conditions—whether one is talking about corporeal, psychological, or spiritual dimensions of culture. We understand culture as a social phenomenon produced at the point of production through the particular configuration of social-material relations, which include the particularities of the region's historical and social-material arrangements and organization. Hence, we argue that class is implicated across all social arrangements of oppression, including racism. Nothing occurs without implicating the material conditions that shape the way individuals and groups locate themselves (and are located) in the context of the body politic of the nation state. What, then, is the motivating force for the construction of particular social arrangements, whether these are marked nationally or internationally by physical, social, or ideological signifiers? Simply put, it is the exploitation and domination of the majority of the population in the interest of sustaining unequal capitalist accumulation—an accumulation that sustains extreme disparities of wealth and power between the haves and have-nots. This is inextricably tied to elite dominion over the majority of the world's populations and natural resources. The global pandemic fiasco of inequality tied to (in)adequate access to vaccination, for example, well illustrates the manner in which this phenomenon is systematically enacted and extended, even during moments of world crisis.

The origin of nation states must be understood within the wider history of capitalism and colonialism (Berger 2001), in that racialized class relations, anchored within and camouflaged by historical and contemporaneous events, were constructed within the social-material milieu of nation states, at the moment of colonization (Blaut 1989). Further, Virdee (2019: 3) reminds us that within the processes of colonialism an "intimate relationship between capitalism, class struggles and racism" was forged—a relationship solidified through the forceful introduction of capitalist modes of production into each region. Moreover, we cannot overlook the interdependency of nation state formation and capitalist formation in our conceptualization of inequalities—along with the manner in which liberalism "served as capitalisms humane face, made to conceal capitalism's inhumane aspects" (Hadžidedić 2022: 3) including genocide, colonization, and slavery. Hence, to speak of the political sphere as being separate from the economic sphere is to create an illusion that fundamentally serves the interests of capitalist exploitation and the accumulative drive for capital and power by the few. This abstract separation conceals unjust processes of capitalist accumulation, of both material and political power—an accumulation sustained by asymmetrical class relations firmly anchored to social practices of racism, sexism, homophobia, ethnocentrism, and other forms of social inequality and exclusion.

A central tenet of contemporary capitalism as a global system, now vastly intensified under the neoliberal offensive and underpinning reform efforts, is the aggressive dismantling of the welfare state, with major cuts made to all public services. During the Covid-19 pandemic we have witnessed this phenomenon just about everywhere, to varying degrees. Responses to the pandemic must be understood as based on particular histories, including constructed social, cultural, and political traditions, and nation state locations, within global production chains embedded in the capitalist world economy. In broad terms, this has resulted in the failure of state revenues to keep up with the costs of publicly funded health services due to reduced tax revenues from capital, and in many cases also political pressures to lower income tax rates under the neoliberal logic of individuals choosing and purchasing services, rather than relying on public provisions (Wallerstein 2013).

However, it must also be clearly noted that poorly resourced nation states often cannot afford to adequately fund health and other public services; while wealthier nations—the United States and the United Kingdom as two prominent examples—clearly *choose* not to—yet, also disingenuously citing lack of state revenues for public services. One clear example is the increasing amount of taxpayers' money funneled into the military, while support for public services dwindles. Furthermore, over the last three decades, the pressure on public expenditure has been exacerbated by capital's demands for increased public spending on private ventures that subsidized corporate activities, including for-profits education, health and prison initiatives. Wallerstein (2013) elaborates this tension as one of several "secular tendencies" of the capitalist world economy approaching absolute limits and contributing to systemic pressures on capitalism's intrinsic requirement of endless accumulation of capital. During the pandemic, the global production and distribution of ventilators, personal protection equipment, and vaccines to the majority of the world's most impoverished populations were negatively affected as a result.

Under conditions of seemingly permanent budget crises of national governments, impelled and reinforced by market-inspired "solutions" to problems that the neoliberal offensive to restore profits has created, the provision of public education was also flung into permanent crisis. Neoliberal educational "solutions," as is well explicated by Ryan in his chapter, leaned heavily on the application of market principles for the provision of education, which in policy terms favored ostensibly diverse and competing, public and private, and increasingly specialized, educational providers. This firmly established market premise was tied to the notion that diversity and competition would lead to more efficient and higher-quality education. This market-driven approach has been consistently employed in response to education's move to virtual education in Covid-19 pandemic contexts, which was responsible for creating a learning crisis for almost half of all students globally (World Economic Forum 2022), particularly where students not only had limited access to computer technology but were unprepared to contend with the isolation and demands of online instruction (International Teacher Task Force 2022). This has often been spoken of as technological inequities based on students' race (Rafalow 2020). Again, we strongly disagree, arguing that to understand the gross inequalities visible in health care and education during the pandemic, for example, requires a serious engagement with the materiality of racism within capitalist rule, which simultaneously produces conditions that perpetuate sexism, disablism, and other forms of social inequalities as well.

Racisms NOT "Race"

Another epistemological duality in Ryan's work that needs to be challenged, also present across much other work whose intent is to address the phenomenon of racism, is the unproblematized acceptance of "race" as a legitimate category to frame social relations. Its expression is prevalent in schools, as much as it is prevalent in discourses related to educational reform. Since education mirrors the ideological and material structures of the larger society, schools and other institutions powerfully socialize and condition students' perceptions of themselves by way of the hidden racialized perspectives that inform the curriculum, textbooks, and classroom life. These racialized perceptions are projected and internalized by both students of subordinate and dominant populations and, in turn, are used to reach conclusions about social relationships, including how students define racism and how they perceive and respond to racialized discourses and events that involve racialized populations.

In the early 1980s, Robert Miles (Miles 1993) blew open the debate concerning the analytical utility of "race" as a suitable construct for the sociological analysis of human populations. He also called into question the "race-relations" paradigm that dominated the field at that time. His efforts aided Marxist scholars in recovering class analysis as a significant analytical tool in the examination of racism, at a time when postmodern theories had begun to severely curtail and erode the analytical power of class in scholarly examinations of culture (Wood 1998). Miles also pointed to the need for scholars to engage historical specificity, rather than adhere to a view of singularity, in theorizing racism. He argued that historically specific racisms possess their own "effectivity" and, as such, could operate as a constitutive (determinant) force in shaping the ideologies of the time. Four decades later this critique remains compelling and instructive but is still conspicuously missing as we navigate through contemporary debates.

Today, as then, traditional arguments about "race" dominate the educational literature and debates tied to educational reform, wherein primary analytical status is attributed to the idea of "race." The use of "race" as an analytical category, here, refers to the practice of positioning "race" as the central organizing principle in explanatory deconstructions of social relations in the world. For several decades our work has challenged schools of thought that employ this idea of "race" within the social sciences. Similarly, we disagree with the traditional use of "race relations"—the social relations between people of different "races"—as the object of study (for many of the reasons noted earlier), in that we consider the use of these terms as the primary locus for the analysis of racism ineffective in moving toward a more materially and politically just world. Instead, we employ the concept of racism and recognize a plurality of historically specific racisms, unhinged from the idea of the existence of such a thing as "race."

Unfortunately, the persistent use of the notion of "race" in educational practice and educational reform discussions serves in consequence, if not necessarily intent, to uphold a definition of "race" as a causal factor. In other words, meaning and significance is attributed to phenotypical features, rather than the relationship of difference with respect to the historically reproduced complex processes of racialization, predicated on its materiality. For generations, disturbing "scientific" assertions, based on biological claims found on notions of genetic superiority or inferiority, well illustrate the theoretical minefield of perpetuating "race" as an analytical category in the social sciences, and the attendant negative consequences this has had on students from racialized groups. The use of "race," in fact, serves to hide the truth; that it is not a person's skin color that determines academic performance but rather the interplay of complex social processes, one of which is premised on the articulation of racism in order to perpetuate the exclusion of populations deemed as deficit and inferior.

This habitual practice of framing social relations as "race relations" in educational discussions of racialized groups both compounds and obscures the complexity of the problem. Here, educational theorists assign significance to "racial" characteristics or behaviors rather than connecting student responses to the economic and political limitations that determine the unequal material realities in which students strive to achieve educational success. The unfortunate persistence of "race" interpretations inadvertently veils the real reasons why racialized students in the United States, for example, underachieve, perform poorly on standardized tests, are overrepresented in remedial programs, underrepresented in AP courses, and continue to drop out of high school at alarming rates (Darder 2012).

Accordingly, educational reform solutions are often derived from distorted perceptions of the problem. The politics of busing in the early 1970s and the multicultural debates of the 1980s, spearheaded by social scientists and educators utilizing a "race-relations" paradigm, provide excellent examples of race-centered reform efforts that have failed to effectively ameliorate racism within schools or society. Yet, despite the distortions that arise from the use of "race" as a central analytical category in educational reform efforts, scholars, reformers, and policymakers have been unable to break with the hegemonic tradition of its use. Moreover, efforts to problematize the reified nature of the term "race" and consider its elimination as metaphor in our work have been quickly greeted with major resistance, even among progressive educators across all communities—a resistance expressed through responses of anxiety, trepidation, fear, and even outrage. So much so that critical conversations related to differences that exist in framing racism are seldom possible. Instead, responses to such efforts frequently evidence a fear of delegitimating historical movements that have principally been defined in terms of "race" struggles. Undoubtedly, there is a tenacious and adhesive quality at work in socially constructed or fabricated ideas, which through their historical usage become so fixated and commonsensical that they not only resist deconstruction but even serious dialogical efforts.

What cannot be missed here is that to combat racism we must contend with both the ways in which it is informed and through which it manifests as both ideology and institutional practices. About this, Graves Jr. and Goodman (2022: 242) argue, in their book *Racism not Race*:

> Racism has its origins in the worldview that races are biologically real and differ in abilities. The view of humankind provided false justification for enslavement and colonization. It still functions in providing cover for police violence and countless everyday acts that promote that status quo. The most important step to combat racism, therefore, is to expose racial ideology to the light of facts and science.

To do this requires a willingness to shift our thinking from talking about "race" to talking about racism (and, we would insist, racisms in the plural), and to employ the concept of racialization as a historically specific ideological process. In other words, we maintain that what is needed is not a critical theory of "race," for this can only leave us stuck in an intellectual quagmire, and further disillusioned by our failure to effectively organize a political offensive against conditions of racism in this country and abroad. Instead, efforts with an anti-racism intent should embrace a global perspective of historically defined racialized relations and acknowledge the conceptual and material plurality of racisms at work across societies. This is anything but a matter of mere semantics; rather it is a call for a new analytic framework from which to identify those structures and representations that preserve racialization—the latter being a process that infuses an essentialized racial character to particular group phenomenon, by categorizing, marginalizing, or regarding certain outcomes as "race" determined.

To construct a new language for examining the nature of racisms requires an understanding of how complex relationships of exploitation and resistance, grounded in differences of class, gender, and ethnicity, give rise to a multiplicity of ideological constructions meant precisely to racialize the other. This knowledge challenges traditional notions of racism as solely a Black/white dichotomous phenomenon and directs us toward a more accurately constructed, and hence more politically useful, idea of racism as a plural construct. In this way, we can contemplate more earnestly radical calls for educational reform, where the relations of power that shape the institutional relations that racialized students must face in schools and society are engaged straightforwardly through the materiality that gives rise to their everyday experience of racism in schools and in the world.

Toward a Democratic Vision of Educational Reform

In the sphere of US education today, we believe there is a dire need to provide an ideological critique of educational reform and the role of the state in systematically perpetuating inequality. That said, Ryan's chapter is an excellent treatise that correctly touches on this need, through his comprehensive discussion of class, race, and education reform. More critiques, similar to his contribution, are required, critiques that can assist us to recast, in more inclusive and contextual ways, educational debates related to public schooling and the academic achievement of students from subaltern communities. By so doing, educational reform discussions about the curriculum, textbooks, teacher education, and classroom initiatives can be directly linked to political power and its material consequence to students and their communities. Hence, as Ryan argues, debates related to educational reform cannot be single-issue oriented, in that, when we treat questions of educational reform in isolation, we are unable to effectively mobilize a political project that supports educational justice and democratic schooling, precisely because the question of economic democracy is left off the table.

Instead, the relationship between a variety of educational reforms must be addressed contextually with respect to the oppressive structural conditions that impact all working people within the US political economy. What underpins the necessity for such an approach is the recognition that similar hegemonic forces of social control move across all public reform arenas. This reinforces the need for coalition and social movement building across cultural, ethnic, and national ties, in efforts to address the social inequities inherent in the educational experience of students from racialized populations. This, of course, requires that questions of racism and other forms of social inequalities be integrated, explicitly as constitutive of all platforms associated with educational reform.

Central to this vision of educational reform is a reconceptualization of the role of the state, in ways that expand the boundaries of participatory democracy, cultivate a genuine sense of the commons across our differences, and initiate organization structures that promote a genuine spirit of collective ownership of schools within communities. This is truer today than ever before, as we contend with the troublesome impact of almost two years of virtual education during the pandemic and the serious consequences resulting for working-class students and, in particular, racialized students. This articulation calls for infusing educational reform debates with a new set of frameworks from which to embark on a genuinely radical democratic educational project. More specifically, this points to a political process that incorporates a radical understanding of social change, political practices of teacher unions, community movements for social justice, structural educational reform efforts, and an overall commitment to genuine equality across American society. Further, education reform debates must be formulated in conjunction with a clearly focused social change strategy, given that ongoing contemporary reform programs are devoid of a politics of social change and a theory of social movements and thus constitute a limited approach toward democratizing education.

Unfortunately, most educational reform efforts today are predominantly grounded in a neoliberal reform paradigm. This inevitably leads to limited reform outcomes, due to the failure to challenge fundamentally the long-standing and persistent economic and political practices of the ruling class. Further, despite the contribution of identity politics to rethinking "race" and schooling, educational reform efforts informed by decontextualized, homogeneous and homogenizing, static, and monolithic views of racialized subjects inadvertently function as analytical and political traps that can lead to a dead-end system of reform. That being the case, despite decades of educational campaigns for reform, an educational system of inequalities persists, excluding genuinely diverse perspectives (despite more than fifty years of institutional rhetoric supporting multiculturalism, diversity, social justice, and more recently decolonization), and reproducing a discriminating structure of rewards and punishment, all of which serve to perpetuate repressive and dehumanizing conditions for all students and teachers, but in particular working-class students from economically impoverished, racialized communities.

Unfortunately, as Ryan implies in his work, the majority of current reform efforts in the United States are not linked to social justice practice or community movements for educational equity, let alone concerted efforts to end racism. Instead, most are overwhelmingly driven by the political and economic interests of the existing social order, which most often places them in direct opposition to radical social movements striving to democratize public institutions, including public education. Although it can be said that in recent years the work of social movements, most recently that of Black Lives Matter, has indeed generated increasing numbers of conversations concerning "race" and some changes in institutional practices, these reforms have been limited and have failed to transform the fundamental nature of structural inequalities in the United States—attributable to deeply rooted structures that are overwhelmingly steeped in the logic of capital. There is no question that educational policy reform efforts need to be radically democratized. However, to accomplish this, educational reformers must acknowledge and incorporate, in concrete ways, the political concerns and economic realities of communities and social movements in their articulation and redesign of the policies and practices advocated. Along the same lines, community and social movements must acknowledge the political centrality of their role in shifting educational reform debates away from the hands of elite policymakers and toward radical political processes and practices of democratic participation.

The absence of a systematic analysis of class and its antagonisms, along with its inequalities of material and political power, represents a serious shortcoming of contemporary educational reform efforts. Given the absence of more substantive analysis, it is imperative that educational movements for social justice be uncompromisingly committed to the goals of structural economic reform. An understanding of the political economy of schooling and the history of current educational practices can better enable educators to reconceptualize the roles of public policy reform, the systematic rethinking of education, and the reconstruction of an educational political project anchored to principles of social justice and economic democracy. This implies conceptualizing the classroom as a powerful political arena of production, along with the integration of cooperative structures of communal school ownership, leadership, teaching, and learning. This rethinking of schools is essential to any critically economic and democratic political vision of education.

Furthermore, to fully understand embedded inequalities, particularly racialized inequalities in education today, requires that we comprehend educational institutions as the direct result of inherent structural features, themselves shaped by macroeconomic forces and trends. Tackling the problems of educational reform, understood as rooted in profound structural inequalities of class and power, also requires the marshalling of new social formations and movements across society with a consciously articulated democratic agenda to end not only racism but every other form of human oppression perpetuated within schools and society.

We believe it is time to seriously consider socialist alternatives that ask tough questions concerning: What works and what doesn't? Who benefits and who does not? How can we create a just system of education within inherently unjust economic conditions of the state? How do we contend with the debilitating antagonisms fueled by identity politics? How do we confront openly recalcitrant practices and policies of meritocracy that perpetuate racism? How can we build a common vision across our differences, despite differing discourses and interpretation of racism? And, in so doing, how do we build the kind of critical solidarity that can contend with the intellectual tensions of differing interpretations of "race," while keeping focused on our shared political vision?

The urgency we are facing today—given the certainty of Covid-19 becoming endemic with more pandemics expected in the future and the consequences of ineffective educational policies over the last two years (Asher 2022)—requires that such questions be widely discussed and linked to political struggles focused on the radical democratization of education. Ryan's work highlights key concerns, particularly with respect to contestations at work across class and racialized debates. About this, Reed (2020: 14) rightly argues that "a policy agenda that seeks only to redress disparities will be incapable of ending precarity for the masses of Black and brown workers." The bottom line concerns the urgency of a return to a public-good model of governance, which requires going beyond solely anti-discrimination policies, toward "a robust public sector and direct state intervention" to support a just educational system. This is fully in line with a Marxist call for educational reforms founded on principles of class struggle—where racism and other forms of human oppression are engaged consistently. This would entail the status quo conceding reforms, obviously to its hegemonic disadvantage, by way of pressures from educational and wider societal struggles focused on establishing conditions for economic democracy and educational justice in this country and abroad, as a vital aspect of realizing the potential for wider transformative economic and democratic possibilities.

6

Race, Class, and Accumulation in Education

A Decolonial Marxist Perspective

Noah De Lissovoy and Adam Martinez

Education is a crucial site for critical, including Marxist, analysis, not only because teaching represents a unique nexus of spheres of social action, including ideological, cultural, and epistemological ones, but also because education's controlling metaphors and dominant policy frameworks have been very durable, resting on a remarkable consensus across elite sectors and parties in the United States. In this context, Ryan offers a useful analysis and argument for centering class in critical analyses of schooling. His arguments imply that we need to attend to the organization of capitalism as a whole and to recognize that analyses focused primarily on race may not necessarily be incompatible with the impulses of neoliberalism. However, Ryan's caution regarding the current tendency to resist "grand narratives" (in particular, Marxism) does not quite go far enough. We argue that the grand narrative of critical theory needs to become even "grander"; that is, it needs to *reach further back*—to capitalism's origins in the colonial encounter—and to *reach deeper*—toward the ground of familiar social categories, especially race and class. These categories form part of what is a complex capital system rather than a simple contest between fractional interests.

If the logic of expanded reproduction is already presupposed in capitalism's accomplished categories and processes, as Marx showed ([1885] 1978), then we have to consider closely the complex interplay between the capital system's different moments and mediations. From this perspective, we can see that race, in addition to class, is central to the determination of schooling, and that it crucially articulates the system's intelligibility. This is so at both the broad structural level and at the level of the phenomenology of schooling, which is saturated by racial meanings and purposes. Considering these effects in connection with the role of schooling as a moment of reproduction of labor power points to a logic of injury—within which race and class are ultimately inextricable—that aims both to prepare and to demoralize, to produce and to decompose.

Finally, we argue, a full reckoning with the particular depth and organization of violence in capitalism means recognizing that this system has been, from its origins, in fact a system of *capitalism-coloniality*. This reckoning argues for an epistemological shift that opens Marxism to a decolonial and pluriversal standpoint—one that builds always from hemispheric and global experiences, and which is shaped by perspectives located in the so-called global "periphery," a space which capitalism has, from its beginning, absolutely depended on for its becoming and expansion. As we note in our conclusion, our reframing of the problem of capitalist schooling has important implications for practice in addition to theory.

Race and Class in the Capital System

It is important, in analyzing education from a Marxist perspective, not to reduce the complex field of schooling to the conflicts between narrow, even if class-based, *interest groups*. The logic of accumulation is embedded in and constructive of every moment and social register in capitalism, and this is true for education as well—perhaps even more so, considering the way that education is involved in the reproduction of the system at the ideological and epistemological levels, in addition to the material one. In this regard, we need to speak in terms of a total "capital system" (Mészáros 1995) which includes numerous mediations in the social and cultural spheres. No special theoretical innovations are necessary in this regard. Marx is clear throughout his work that the familiar categories through which society is organized, and by means of which we understand it, already *presuppose* accumulation—which is to say they presuppose the development of the accomplished system of capitalism, the system of expanded reproduction.

For instance, in volume II of *Capital* ([1885] 1978), in analyzing the circuit of capital, particularly in its paradigmatic form of commodity capital, Marx shows that the very stock of commodities through which an individual capitalist realizes the surplus value created in production presupposes the existence of other (prior) industrial capitals that have supplied the means of production for these commodities. Furthermore, even as the starting point for the circulation process, this commodity stock always already represents an *expanded* capital value, inasmuch as it includes surplus value in addition to a simple capital value. In short, the commodity in capitalism is never simply equal to itself, as it were, but rather testifies to the prior fact and logic of accumulation. Similarly, classes (including the working class) are never simply equal in a transparent sense to a set of interests or intentions but rather bear the traces in their very constitution of the extended capital system of which they are the effect.

In the same way, the elements, rituals, and personae of schooling are not just an occasion or scene for political struggle but also already encode in their very intelligibility the deep logic of capital, which is why it is so difficult in practice to interrupt the process of social reproduction. For instance, the problem with curriculum is not just that it is ideologically oriented in favor of powerful groups but rather that we confront knowledge in the first place *as curriculum*—that is, as a determined content and program separate from the rest of experience. Even teachers and students themselves, who suffer the impositions of capitalist schooling, also embody and refer to—in their status *as teachers and students*—the circuit of capital on the terrain of knowledge. More than simply people in schools, teachers and students are determined as beings in relation to the knowledge-commodity—that is, they are the agents who process and circulate this commodity. In this context, the class determination of education has to be complexly unpacked, since it is present for instance in schooling as warehousing—as well as in attacks on critical teaching. This determination is likewise expressed in vibrant progressivisms that revivify the apparatus of the institution—as well as in authoritarian pedagogies. Furthermore, the class determination of education is an ontological question relating to the kinds of identities and objects that are possible on this terrain (Brown 2018); in this regard, we can recognize the politics of race and racialized identities in schooling as central to class struggle itself, and as a crucial starting point for revolutionary theory and practice.

There are two ways to understand the centrality of race and racism within capitalism—and thus the necessary centrality of an analysis of race within Marxist theory. First, in a "structural" sense, race is a key ontological, symbolic, and ideological building block of the capital system. Race is much more than an instrument to divide the working class; it is rather a fundamental aspect of the content and meaning of this class. In other words, the working class, as such, in addition to functioning economically (in a narrow sense), also functions *racially*—that is, it expresses in its constitution and action a logic of race. Exploitation is from the start a project of racial domination, and the class antagonists on this terrain are always already involved in struggles within and about race (Robinson 2000). Second, in a historical sense, capitalism is from its beginnings in fact a system of capitalism-coloniality. Its original metabolism and ongoing reproduction depend on an internal differentiation that is racially articulated. Thus, Quijano (2000a) shows that from its inauguration in the colonial encounter, capitalism was a system of accumulation that complexly coordinated diverse systems of production, including wage labor, serfdom, and slavery, each of which functioned as an integral component of the total structure. Importantly, the coordination of these different forms of production was racially organized, with wage labor being generally reserved for whites. In this way, coloniality was expressed already in capitalism's fundamental architecture and organization.

Likewise, education in the modern period has been built on and through race and racism. As a privilege originally of the white elite, education was in a sense *for* racism; even now, as a carefully calibrated system of resource and knowledge distribution, education is centrally a system for articulating and enforcing racial differences and racial power. How else can we explain the virulence of the resistance to desegregation and racial justice in schooling? The problem for whites has not only been to preserve their monopoly of access to education against movements for equity; in addition, racial justice struggles, for them, threaten the very epistemological integrity of education insofar as it is determined as a colonial enterprise at the levels of policy and curriculum. Further, if we want to claim that, however powerful racism has been as a factor in schooling and society, it is a separate dynamic from that of class struggle and capitalist reproduction proper, then we still must confront the way that a narrow sense of reproduction is always haunted by and dependent on its (colonial) outside, from the moment of "primitive accumulation" up to the present.

Even beyond his discussion of that initial historical stage, Marx's analyses of accumulation necessarily refer to the colonial world, which already enables, in supplementing the "home" market with raw materials and special commodities, the paradigmatic processes of expanded reproduction within metropolitan capitalism that he uncovers. For others, like Luxemburg (2004), European capitalism depends on an even more intimate integration with its outside, as non-European economies quickly become indispensable markets for commodities from the metropole, as well as key sources of labor power. Likewise, in education, a critical analysis of educational institutions and experiences, even as class projects, has to immediately confront and consider race, insofar as race makes these projects possible, and insofar as race constructs, in a phenomenological sense, the world of education for all who are involved in it. Separating class from race in this context is analytically dubious to the extent that these categories are mutually determining, codependent, and deeply collaborative in constructing the meanings of school.

Neoliberalism and the Logic of Violation

In thinking about the relationships between race, class, and capital in education, it is important to consider the terrain of teaching, as an enacted set of dispositions and relationships, in addition to the broad field of institutional structure and policy. In the teaching context, the historical and geographic organization of capitalism as a colonial project is expressed in the immediate processes of domination that simultaneously reproduce "human capital" (i.e., trained labor power) in a positive moment, while also, in a negative moment, working to demoralize and decompose subjectivity. In other words, in a process that is deeply racially inflected, contemporary schooling works both to prepare students for a future as workers in the capitalist economy (through familiar processes of socialization into work-related skills and dispositions) and also to isolate and exclude them (through processes of hyper-punishment, labeling, and stigmatization)—in the context of a neoliberalized economy marked by deindustrialization, flexibilization, and precaritization.

On the one hand, we can understand this as a historically specific reorganization of the reservoir of workers that Marx ([1867] 1976) called the industrial reserve army—which is now progressively deskilled and made more desperate, in preparation for the vicissitudes of the low-wage and insecure service economy. On the other hand, we can understand the systematic demoralization of students as producing its own specific and immaterial "surplus". In this connection, the fusion of the constructive and deconstructive moments of capitalist production (which is also the production of selves and identities) can usefully be conceptualized in terms of a process of *violation* (De Lissovoy 2012, 2018). Drawing on anti-colonial theories of violence as essential to the rule of capital in the colonial context (see Fanon 1963) as well as Marxist accounts of the centrality of annexation and appropriation in neoliberalism (see Harvey 2005), the theoretical framework of violation argues that capitalism pursues a project of plunder that works across material, psychic, and symbolic registers, and which, through processes of imposition just as much as incorporation, realizes a diverse range of accumulations that support the dominative logic of whiteness at the same time as they reproduce and expand capital values in a narrowly economic sense.

From this perspective, at the level of the basic organization of the capital system, it becomes again difficult to separate race and class. On the one hand, from the starting point of this framework, we can see that proletarianization is as much a process of exclusion from the social metabolism (for instance, through school push outs, permanent unemployment, and incarceration) as it is a process of inclusion or incorporation into regimes of work. On the other hand, racism becomes a central axis and strategy of accumulation, inasmuch as it provides a rationale for shifts to industries like the prison industrial complex and serves as an ideological pillar of neoliberal projects of gentrification and privatization, while also directly reproducing the value system of white supremacy, a system which in the United States has from the beginning always been a system of production as well as a system of violence (Davis 2005).

At the classroom level, it is clear that the key initiatives of neoliberal education—in particular, accountability and discipline—are from the outset racial projects (Lipman 2011; Stovall 2015). This does not mean that white people are not hurt by them (as Ryan points out, white students also face, to a lesser degree, negative consequences from the testing regime, for instance) but rather that these regimes are *organized around* the punishment and stigmatization of communities of color. This is different than arguing that domination in capitalist society and schooling is only or essentially a question of race; rather, we mean to point to the way that capitalism as a whole *depends on and works through* the logic of racism as a condition of its overall reproduction and intelligibility.

Considering capitalist education and society from the starting point of the framework of violation also allows us to make sense of the depth of irrationality that characterizes these systems, especially in the context of neoliberalism. If capitalists were solely interested in preserving and expanding profit (understood narrowly), their collective obliviousness to the systemic risks of extreme inequality, ecological collapse, and hyper-financialization would be inexplicable, since these conditions pose existential threats to society and thus to continued accumulation in the long term (and even medium term). But if elites realize a kind of spiritual or ontological surplus through the distance they attain from working people (see Piketty 2014, for a dramatic account of this distance in material terms), as well as through the injuries that these elites visit upon communities, then we can see that these very crises offer their own particular rewards and opportunities.

Capitalism in this way feeds on its own decay. For instance, the prison system, which is a warehouse for the increasing number of people cast out of production proper, becomes at the same time an essential *industry* (Gilmore 2007). Racism is a central and animating rationale for this complex process of production/decomposition. Likewise, schools, under the official rubric of preparation and qualification, work at the same time to *undo* and disorganize the working class—both at the level of the class itself and at the level of the person. In this way, if violation or injury, as a material and symbolic process, is a central purpose of capitalism, then this means that the value system of capitalism is immediately an ethical problem as much as a narrowly economic one (De Angelis 2007). Furthermore, this means that we have to investigate, as a central aspect of our commitment as Marxists, the dominative ethics that have organized the categories of human being and society that are constitutive of capitalism and colonialism across societies—from their origins in the moment of so-called "primitive accumulation" and colonial encounter.

Exteriority and the Project of Liberation

At issue in the investigation of domination in contemporary education is not just the sociological register of injustice but the cultural and spiritual life of a people as well. We live in a world in monologue with itself, obsessed with maneuvers that will ensure its hegemony and perpetuate its solipsism, unable to see beyond itself or hear the clamor for justice of its victims, in schooling and beyond. The pathology of this world is that it has fetishized itself since its conception, believed in itself as *uni-versal*, according to the megalomaniacal order of modernity in which the sacrifice of the Other is not only the source of capital but also constitutes this world ontologically (Dussel 1994, 2007). Efforts to address issues of race and class in the United States are shaped by these limitations.

Marx's critical-ethical phenomenology challenges us to see past reified notions of these categories and to consider the creative source of capitalism—*living labor*—that is outside, prior to, and after capital. Living labor is excluded life, within and outside the *fronteras* (borders) of the Global North, life that is materially exploited as well as culturally and spiritually sacrificed. Instead of asking how capitalism can be modified so that there is space for the Other to be recognized and made intelligible to the system, we should ask how the Other might rupture *my* world, making *my* humanity possible. This position—one of emancipation—has emerged from the Global South, with the growing awareness of its own sacred distinctions and infinite dignity, as well as the ontological ugliness of *this* world.

In attending to *exteriority*, to what is excluded and un-subsumable by the Totality, it is important to keep track of the conditions through which capitalism has arisen. In this regard, understanding coloniality and its interpretation of the Other is crucial. In the justification for the plunder that inaugurates modernity, race emerges as an answer to the question of who is killable and violable, who can be sold and dispossessed—and on the other hand, who should be brimming with confidence, who should command and be respected—in short, whose life will be affirmed and whose will be denied. As Quijano (2000c) describes, invasion generates a world in which European Being is centered and the Other is relegated to poverty and nothingness. Otherness, as interpreted by the invader, becomes written on bodies, ascribed to the phenotypes that distinguish the colonized from Europeans. Inferiority and Otherness, superiority and whiteness become matching pairs.

Intimately entangled with the issue of Eurocentrism is the question of religion and culture. From the perspective of the Catholics and Protestants who arrived from Europe, worshippers of the "one and only" God, the Others they encountered—in their languages, traditions, writings, songs, and *cosmovisiones*—were demonic. The demonic status of the non-Christian then justifies the burning of the great and ancient libraries of the *Nahuatl*-speaking peoples of Mexico, the prohibition on Indigenous cultures, forced conversions, *encomiendas* and *mitas*—in short, a second inquisition across Abya Yala/Cemanahuac/Turtle Island (Galeano 2010; Quijano 2000b, 2007). This history is rendered obscure within the circuits of capital, and the contemporary moment subsumes it in easy accounts of race and class in particular. However, our analysis aims to expose the more basic condition in which the Other is circumscribed by a Totality for which a beyond is impossible or, at best, irrational.

We live, breathe, drink, and speak the invasions of our worlds—that is, coloniality. It is the movies, news, and TikToks we watch, the sexual icons we admire, the money we wish we had, and the drone strikes that kill innocents. It is crossing *el rio bravo*, bones in the desert, and the University itself. It is diverse youth in US schools promised a future if they study STEM, work hard, and turn their backs on their families and communities—or if they join the military—while other youth lack even these false promises, as they travel thousands of miles to the outposts of the metropole only to be turned away, or arrested and disappeared. Youth, the world over, immersed in this necrophilic condition, suffer the curtailing of their imaginations and curiosities (Freire 1998). They are conscripted into the belief that the world they have inherited is natural and/or divine, and suffer indignity and contempt even as they are assimilated into the cult of whiteness.

Educational critiques and programs based on isolated notions of class and race, while potentially extending some of the benefits of the globally privileged, perhaps toward a minimum of equality in the center, fail to understand the Totality. More importantly, these analyses fail to see an outside beyond the given system, an *exteriority* from which the *new* might emerge, and from which any authentic project of emancipation must depart. In this way, in their provinciality, reform efforts narrowly focused on race and class disparities generally end up aligning with capitalism and whiteness to secure global relations of domination and exploitation (see Dussel 1998; Levinas 1969).

In sum, the *pro-ject* of liberation, as the great Latin American philosopher Enrique Dussel reminds us, is not a prolongation of this unjust system (as the reformist imagination proposes) but rather a new order born from the rupture of *this* world and its ontological *fronteras*. The essential category here is *exteriority*. A new world only emerges from an outside/beyond—not purely geographical—that is incommensurate with the Whole, and from those who suffer the system in their *nothingness* and *poverty*. In this context, while race and class are important to investigate, including in education, we must do so without reaffirming the categories and closed world of capitalism as Totality, as Marx himself showed clearly. Without affirming Otherness-for-itself, which ruptures the given and which requires the denial and destruction of coloniality, we can only reproduce what Dussel calls "the Same."

Conclusion

Capitalism systematically obscures the conditions of its own becoming and reproduction. In education, this can be seen in the way that unceasing efforts at ameliorative reform crash against the rocks of the system's underlying organization.

In this context, Ryan helpfully interrogates the often unreflective impulses of progressivism and returns our attention to the elite interests and class antagonisms that structure the terrain of schooling and contests over it. However, if we aim at a truly critical understanding of this terrain, we must inquire into the fundamental determination of its familiar categories. Hence, radical efforts in theory and practice must avoid reaffirming the order and elements of the capital system, even as we try to interrupt the injustices it produces. In the process, our critical inquiry has to *go back* to the inauguration of capitalism in order to uncover its colonial roots and has to *go deep* in order to expose the complex order of social "reality" itself as an effect of the logic of expanded reproduction.

Race, class, school, teaching, and learning are in this context at once the stakes of the battles we engage and also artifacts in themselves of exploitation and accumulation. While this inquiry may seem theoretical or abstract, we argue that it is in fact eminently practical, since without an understanding of the depth of the challenge we confront, our efforts at transformation will fail, as shown by the dismal record of educational reform (including most radical efforts) in the contemporary era. In contrast to initiatives captured within the limits of the system's vocabulary, we believe that revolutionary projects need to be conceived that look beyond the Totality and envision a form of education that forms part of a broad "third nomos" (Mignolo 2020) outside of capitalism-coloniality. These projects would include coalitions that challenge the arbitrary divisions of race- and class-based strategies (as Ryan suggests), but they would also involve linking struggles in the United States to hemispheric and global ones, in a process that would not just enlarge our sense of the social field on which we operate but also expand the epistemological frame which organizes our efforts.

Revolutionary educational struggles need to expose both the material exploitation and immiseration that capitalist schooling takes for granted, and also the spiritual and ontological poverty that it produces. We can see glimmers of this project in recent struggles by teacher unions that center the communities their students come from (even if these unions also generally accept the underlying parameters of the meaning of teaching) and in new ethnic studies curricula that connect struggles for justice with global and Indigenous vocabularies of survivance (even if these movements also sometimes fall back on a reductionist vocabulary of race). These efforts and others need to be continued, expanded, and more ambitiously imagined. It is not enough to challenge the inequalities that capitalism produces, even at the "systemic" level. Instead, we need a socialist education that refuses the basic rules of the game, but it must be a creative and pluriversal socialism that thinks and fights from a standpoint rooted in geopolitical and epistemological exteriority. From this perspective only can capitalism's "hidden aims" become visible, and from this perspective only can an emancipatory alternative be envisioned and enacted.

7

A Marxist Critical Realist Perspective on Social Class and "Race"

Alpesh Maisuria

The feature chapter by Howard Ryan engages five dynamics in the context of "Race, Class, and the Hidden Aims of School Reform": social class, neoliberal capitalism, Marxism, "race"[1] and racism. There are many topics that Ryan assiduously tackles, and many more that he provokes, with the stated objective of promoting a "progressive dialogue" that includes discussion of his proposal concerning the *primacy* of social class and the understanding of racism as rooted in the neoliberal capitalist mode of production. For those familiar with my work on Marxism (e.g., Maisuria 2022a), it will come as no surprise that my margin annotations of Ryan's chapter are enthusiastic affirmations. Ryan's is one of the most plausible and compelling treatments of the "race"/class bun fight that I have read in some time—and for being such, it will probably receive much pushback. The research that informs his argument is extensive (covering the United States, England, and South Africa), and also intensive—the subsection entitled "Neoliberal School Reform as a Global Movement" is demonstrative of the forensic examination contained in Ryan's chapter. In my response, I further extend and intensify Ryan's critique by offering succinct commentary and contribution with respect to the first two areas that he places under the microscope: "race" and then social class. I do this through a Critical Realism framework, which distinguishes between the "real" (or unobservable) world and the "observable" world.

Ryan rightfully points out that "Race-based theory is reflected in several frameworks." I will now add some remarks with respect to the all-important question: *What is "race"?* The contribution that follows is a cursory but important historicizing of the question, and it introduces some new points to the ongoing dialogue on the Left, in order to distill the problems of biological categorization, and the social construction, of "race." I begin by noting that in many "race" frameworks, "race" has been taken as a natural and biological category of differentiation. A decade ago, I wrote that "race" is

> used to identify genetically given phenotypes that can be used to distinguish people from one another to establish taxonomies of "race." "Race" in this conceptualisation is a scientific category that is determined by DNA and genetic makeup. Following this conceptualisation of "race" explorer Francis Galton (1882–

1911) established the eugenics movement (Chitty, 2001). The proposition was that some "races" were genetically dispositioned to inferiority in every aspect of being a human being. Humans, in this way, were born with a given quota of superior or inferior traits, and categories of "race" were used to differentiate between these . . . Adherents to this scientific conceptualisation of "race" claimed that some people were *naturally* predetermined to be culturally, socially, educationally and physically in deficit compared to others. Eugenics, it seemed, had a revolutionary mission, which was not only to preserve racial purity through selective breeding (Chitty 2001: 115) but also "to improve the innate quality of the human race" (Chitty 2009: 51). The eugenics movement became the mainstream of the academy and politics and it influenced many governments' decisions about issues such as sterilisation, even in traditionally progressive countries in Scandinavia. This was even after the National Socialists in Germany in the 1930s and 40s used it to justify a hierarchy of Aryan supremacy based on somatic features, such as skin colour, shape of nose, size of skull, which culminated in six million Jewish people perishing. In sum, the basic idea of eugenics was that the human gene pool had to be protected from bastardisation by allowing breeding between the weak and fit. The profound effects of this human interference with nature begged for appraisal, and eugenics, as a form of social Darwinism, became the subject of critique itself. (Maisuria 2012: 80)

Historicizing the Social Construction of "Race"

Prior to the Second World War, critiques of "race" were not widespread. But in the wake of Nazism, scholars and international institutions were alert to the need for analyzing the biological basis of "race," an analysis which would render eugenics, as the reason for genocide, to be falsified. This rethinking of eugenics included a comprehensive and conclusive determination by UNESCO, in 1952, that "race" is unlikely to be biological, and drawing on this work, I've noted, in a previous publication (Maisuria 2012: 81):

Carl Linnaeus's valuable [eighteenth-century] research on plant categorisations was being misused, which was significant because it had the unfortunate effect of creating four taxonomies of the human "race": White Europeans, Red Americans, Yellow Asians, Black Africans, . . . [and later] being divided into four categories: American Indian, Caucasian, Mongol and Negro. However, the scientific credibility of these broad categorisations was being questioned universally by the 1950s, and eventually these taxonomies had become obsolete by the 1970s. The prevailing accepted position after the 1970s was that DNA makeup did not suggest biological predestination and ultimately the science behind hundreds of years of research into "race" was rejected. The conceptualisation of "race" as a social construction, rather than a biology, became officially doctrinal when the United Nations declared that "the biological fact of race and the myth of 'race' should be distinguished" and that "it would be better when speaking of human races [*sic*] to drop the term 'race' altogether . . . According to present knowledge there is no proof that the groups of mankind [sic] differ in their innate mental characteristics". (Banton 2010: 137)

I went on to say that this rendered "race" as only skin deep—a construction only, but one with political and ideological value for justifying domination and oppressive power dynamics. It must be stressed that this perspective does not purport that racism is not lived; indeed, many of us have suffered because of it. Rather, the point is that the biological modeling of "race" needs to be invalidated despite its appearance as being real—in which case, the foundations of "race" frameworks are problematized (see Darder and Torres 2004). Ryan's opening chapter specifies critical race theory (CRT) as the "race" framework for particular critical examination, and it is CRT that I now turn to.

Underlaboring CRT

To Ryan's exposition and critique, I elaborate by adding the necessity of philosophical *underlaboring*. The architect of Critical Realism[2] was Roy Bhaskar, who, following the eighteenth-century philosopher John Locke, argued that to know reality, one must clear the ground of "rubbish ideas" that get in the way of knowing reality—this is called *underlaboring* (Bhaskar 2017: 7). A second feature of Critical Realism is *seriousness*. This is a concern with the unity of theories of what the world is like, and the reality of the world[3]; if there is a disunity, then *un*seriousness occurs. In sum, *un*seriousness means there is a problem with the efficacy of arguments about reality. When both of these features of Critical Realism (underlaboring and seriousness) are applied to CRT, then one must ask: If CRT is based on defunct ideas about "race" (as argued above), then can it grasp *reality*? Similarly, do the CRT tenets of whiteness and white supremacy adequately explain reality? When these questions are used to immanently critique CRT, then it seems to be fundamentally flawed.

In the Western intellectual social science traditions, the rejection of positivism[4] has led to a situation where ontology (i.e., reality) has either been conflated with or replaced by epistemology (i.e., knowledge claims); this is termed the epistemic fallacy in Critical Realism (see Bhaskar 2008). Knowledge and reality are not the same and should not be conflated and treated as homologous. Employing white supremacy/whiteness claims is an example of this conflation, because it does not adequately grasp or explain reality and its complexity, and therefore seems to fall afoul of the *epistemic fallacy* (see Bhaskar 2008: 37). As Ryan elegantly explains (as do others in this volume) this is not to say that racism does not matter, but rather that CRT's propagating of the epistemology of white supremacy and whiteness is a philosophical *idealism*. This idealism that is clearer in some versions of CRT (e.g., with respect to Bell's rules of racial standing (1992a); for more on this see Maisuria 2022b) tries to impose a static white supremacy/whiteness idea to a reality that is highly complex, open, and perpetually changing/changeable—it is maladroit. This is made evident by Ryan, when he refers to CRT advocates' claim that school test scores in California provide evidence of whiteness and illustrates that there is an alternative to CRT's "white winners and Black/brown losers" analysis. He posits the possibility of "An alternative class-based narrative [that] points to capitalist winners and working-class losers, with racial and other differentiations (e.g., by language, immigration status, national origin) among the losers."

CRT would benefit from inserting a dialecticism to accounts for and subsequently explain the complexity of reality. CRT does not do this because there seems to be no fallibility principle built-in to the advocacy of white supremacy/whiteness. In other words, for CRT, white supremacy/whiteness is universally true without exception. This insistence is problematic *when* white supremacy/whiteness is *not* empirical reality in specific conditions of time and space. In these instances, for CRT there appears to be an ontological shyness where reality either does not exist or cannot be known, particularly if it challenges the reality of white supremacy/whiteness. Therefore, there are only knowledge claims—the central one of which is that white supremacy/whiteness is ubiquitous rather than context specific. There is an absence of epistemological relativity, meaning that knowledge claims (i.e., white supremacy/whiteness) supersede reality. This aspect of CRT is presupposing instead of emergentist. What is missing from CRT is an *ontology* (or, *reality of being*), one in which it is acknowledged that reality is an open system[5] and mind-independent (see Bhaskar 2017).[6]

One of the important contributions of Critical Realism is the instance that *seriousness* comes from having rigor, achieved through a deep excavation of reality in order to expose the causal mechanisms of events and experiences, such as racism. This is a quest for seeking the dominant causal mechanisms and structures by asking the fundamental question about generative powers: *What must reality be like for x to be possible?* There are many *explanations* for racism that are possible, and in order to establish epistemological relativism and ontological realism[7] for making a rational judgment about causal explanations, a retrodictive reasoning approach must be adopted (see Bhaskar 2017: 28). This is achieved by employing a schema that includes a process of: Description (D), Retroduction (R), Elimination (E), Identification (I), and Correction (C)—known by the acronym *DREIC*. Isaksen (2016: 249) summarizes the implementation of this process:

> First we start with a previously accepted *Description* of some empirical regularity or pattern, then we imaginatively conceive of mechanisms which, if they were real, would cause the events as described to occur (this mode of inference is *Retroduction*). The next step is to *Eliminate* the imagined mechanisms through further empirical analyses until we are left with one mechanism or a combination of mechanisms which is then *Identified* as real. This new knowledge will normally necessitate the *Correction* of previous theories. (My emphases)

Of course, in CRT, the *description* of experiences and events of racism are important, but there is a lack of rigor and seriousness because there is a lack of depth—there is no focus on explanation of generative mechanisms. Put simply, CRT never goes beyond the *D* in retrodiction and therefore cannot provide explanations and relies on descriptions/appearance of white supremacy/whiteness.

CRT, even in its racial realism form (see Delgado and Bell 2021), operates with a flat ontology rather than a stratified and differentiated one (see Maisuria 2018: 183–92 for a modeling of this). This is a kind of naïve realism,[8] which is supported in empirical work by a hard interpretivism/constructivism methodology and the use of methods such as observations and interviews. In Critical Realist language this is called ontological monovalence, meaning there is one version of reality, and for CRT this is always stridently framed by white supremacy/whiteness.[9] CRT lacks *explanatory critique* (Maisuria 2018), which is an attempt to *explain* the conditions that enable accounts of experiences (e.g., of racism) and what the alternatives to these mechanisms and causal powers are. The necessity that I am drawing attention to is for a shift from unserious epistemological knowledge claims to one that focuses on *explanations* of reality. It is only when these explanations are unveiled that progress can be made toward challenging the mechanisms that create the conditions of reality for racism rather than for human well-being.[10]

The strength of Ryan's critique lies with its objective of trying to obtain ontological polyvalence, which is about recognizing that there are *many* deep and transient mechanisms that create the conditions of existence at play at any one moment in history. These mechanisms cannot be eyeballed because they are not discoverable through direct observation, nor are they available directly through interviews/storytelling, because these methods can only gather data for the *D* in DREIC. But crucially, it is the dominant mechanisms from among these which create the conditions for racism to emerge, and as Ryan argues, these have and do include, at specific times and in specific spaces, the primacy of class and capitalism—and it is exactly this kind of uncovering of proximate and root structural causes that the retrodictive approach can unveil to lay a strong claim on grasping reality. A vital aspect of engaging in such work concerns strategically locating the most promising opportunities for struggle. So, Critical Realism is not merely a philosophical exercise; it is one for activating the pulse of freedom (see Bhaskar 1993).

Underlaboring Social Class

Ryan rightfully points out that it is not only "race"-based frameworks that provide a challenge to Marxism. I agree with him that between Marxist and non-Marxists, there are "competing definitions of class, which can interfere with productive conversations." Moreover, Webber (2015), drawing on the work of Ellen Meiksins Wood, writes: "There are really only two ways of thinking theoretically about class: either as a structural location or as a social relation." The point being made is that gradational schemes that try to measure social class actually measure *status* and sociocultural *markers*, which may be interesting and useful points of departure, but, Webber goes on:

there is a very long way to travel in order to identify how a class "in itself" becomes a class "for itself," to use Marx's terminology for the movement between an objective class situation and class consciousness, or from social being to social consciousness. In order to get there, we need to think of class as a social-historical process and relationship.

Webber (2015) then cites E. P. Thompson, who foregrounds the importance of social class being understood historically, dialectically, and as materially emergent in/through human relationships. Echoing Marx, social class is entangled in a web of relations that are always conditioned by the history of capitalism. The masses have been purposefully encouraged by the global ruling class to have a self-perception of freedom and agency to be individuals acting voluntarily as consumers and rational beings—*homo economicus*, rather than being socio-economically related *for* capitalism.

It may be true that British people are infatuated with social class, but like most others, they do *not* have a fulsome understanding of it. The vast majority of people in Britain point to *income* as the most significant *marker* of social class, and this is discussed as part of expressions of wealth indicated through private possessions. Income and wealth are perceived to denote social class; but very few people explicitly discuss social class as a *relational* social structure essential *for* capitalism and social relationships beyond superficial sociocultural markers (e.g., house size/type/location, brand/cost/model of car, etc.). These markers are also used to argue that social class is either important, or unimportant (for instance, as compared with ethno-racial identity), or that we live in a post-class society (including those who unconvincingly promote Posthumanism/New Materialism). In general, workers are far from being a class for itself—they do not have consciousness of the connection with each other and their own labor power *for* neoliberal capitalism.

The promotion of post-class was pursued by former Conservative prime minister John Major in 1990 through claiming he would propel us into a "classless society." And in 1999, giving ballast to this post-class zeitgeist, subsequent Tony Blair claimed, "I want to make you all middle class," in an effort to flatten any sense of social class stratification and differentiation. By so doing, both Major and Blair were seemingly promising the expansion of the middle segment of the social structure. After almost two decades of the aggressive pursuit of neoliberalism with its concomitant market policies, promotion of self-interest and individualization, accompanied by a heavy dose of laissez-faire governance (Maisuria 2022c), their promises were framed in terms of remedying social inequality. Yet in practice, Major and Blair expressed fundamental political antipathy toward working-class issues, solidarity, empathy, and comradeship. This antipathy had been stridently promulged by Thatcher in her now infamous 1987 statement that clearly placed collectivization—such as Trade Unionism, rather than the government's pursuit of neoliberalism—at the center of social ills. On society, Thatcher (1987) stated:

> There is no such thing! There are individual men and women and there are families and no government can do anything except through people and people look to themselves first. It is our duty to look after ourselves and then also to help look after our neighbour and life is a reciprocal business.

For Thatcher, the "pursuit of equality itself is a mirage" (Thatcher 1975), which she considered as the cause of "damage to the economy." As such, the notion of a "caring and sharing society" was propagandized as an anathema in the 1980s.

Social class as something that is individualistic/subjective and gradational is now the most common way that it is understood by those within and beyond academia. For instance, in comparison to previous years, the titles of the presentations at the 2021 Working Class Studies Conference reflect a negation of the relational/Marxist approach to social class. None of the papers had Marx in their title, only five included the word "neoliberalism" (four were on the same panel), and only one had the word "capitalism." A similar shift can also be witnessed more widely, including in the design of official/popular class schemas, such as the Registrar General, Goldthorpe, and the Great British Class Survey, each of which places people in a grade of class (with such grades/"classes" ranging in number from five to seven)—a gradational approach.

Popular class schemas (like the ones mentioned above) and mainstream responses to the question *"What social class are you?"* tend to very sporadically engage with social class—in that they are actually attempting to ascertain social status by means of a *gradational* way of thinking, with no qualitative depth or historical contextualization. In this way, the popular class schemas here suffer the same epistemological limitations related to CRT as discussed above. Thus, we make the point in Hill and Maisuria (2022: 627) about grades of social status:

> They are actually not classes, but rather they are gradational categorisations based on the sociologist Max Weber's theory of status. Importantly they are not articulated as part of a relationship of social groups, so it is unclear how one "class" relates to another—these gradational schemas hide the essential connective economic relationships between groups. . . . In these [neo-Weberian] schemas, people are graded in a hierarchy but they are missing the essential relation, the Capital-Labour Relation.

"Neoliberalism" is a term that is more likely used by those considered progressives who are interested in education reform. For example, Stephen Ball's (e.g., 2012, 2017) work on the marketization of education over many years has been rightfully celebrated, but his work does not adequately make the articulation that neoliberalism concerns the social relations of production. Ball's work is maladroit in showing that the relationship between the workers and the capitalists is exploitative and based on value creation through the production of commodities (Maisuria 2022a). What needs to be made clear is that neoliberalism is all-encompassing; and importantly, within neoliberal contexts, racism is understood not an end in itself for the perpetuation of hierarchy but a way to service economic production very effectively through the process of racialization and xeno-racialization[11] (Cole and Maisuria 2010; Darder and Torres 2004; Ogunrotifa 2022). Moreover, as Ryan points out, an absence of substantive engagement with neoliberalism and its social relations of production in discussions of racism renders the analysis far less useful to organizational and movement efforts.

Final Comments on School Reform

In such a brief response, I have been unable to offer thoughts on the "Hidden Aims of School Reform" aspect of Ryan's chapter. But I will close by offering a few points here to temper Ryan's important claim that school "privatization is far more advanced" in England than in the United States. Presupposing that private means the capacity to be for-profit, independent from central government control and oversight, there is a legal aspect, with respect to the schooling in England, that has considerable bearing on Ryan's claim. Schools in England are registered charities, which means that they are legally prohibited from reaping a financial profit. I must stress, all revenue has to be reinvested back into the school, and there are not and cannot be shareholders to pay dividends because the schools are not private for-profit entities. This is rendered by the fact that they are regulated, and importantly funded through the taxpayer's money, by the central government. In saying this, Academy schools, considerably more so than State comprehensive schools, have significant, though not unlimited, freedom and autonomy to act *like* (though legally they are not) a private business. As such, Academy schools can govern themselves in terms of admission, discipline, budgeting, and curriculum; and they are mostly run by the for-profit private sector (individuals and companies) rather than the state (though the state funds them) non-profit third sector organizations. In the United States, charter schools, irrespective of proprietorship, *can, if they so wish*, be profit-making. For example, those in Arizona, where there is no national or state legal embargo on this. Importantly they can also be as guarded as they like with respect to how they are run and are thus able to avoid government and public accountability and scrutiny. Even those that are designated as not-for-profit charters can be profit-making, through establishing their own education management organizations (EMOs), which can also be secretive about their own and the schools' operation.

Academies are not fully privatized, not within the British definition, as offered above.[12] As such, in England, the shift to Academies represents a right-wing shift that moves schooling away from the duopoly that the state/central government and private fee-paying schools previously had on education provision to a *Third Way* approach—an approach that relies on the claim that it effectively combines state/central government (money) with private sector (business acumen) to deliver public services. This was a hallmark of Tony's Blair's ideology, which he implemented across the entire public sector, during his ten years in office (1997–2007) as prime minister of the UK. There is also a clarification that needs to be made here concerning nomenclature. In Britain, precisely because funding comes from the national government, it would not be accurate to characterize Academies as privatized. As noted above they cannot be financially profit-making and they are regulated by the national government, for instance, through government school inspection, in exactly the same way as comprehensive state schools that are fully under government control. If an international ideological comparison is sought, Academies are more like the Swedish social-democratic model of Free Schools (though these can be legally profit-making) than the US charter school model (within which schools are also legally entitled to be profit-making). Of course, these three types of schools tend to coexist on the same conservative ideological and political plane and so, we may be splitting hairs in attempting to disaggregate them on the grounds of which is more or less privatized—we can agree that they are all bad.

In terms of politics, Academies are experiments concerning decentralization and a pulling back of the frontiers of the state, more than they are examples of profit-making, because they promote a laissez-faire approach to governance, marketization, and individualism (see Maisuria 2014). The enrichment of a limited few that own and control the relevant businesses/corporations is the traditional function of privatization; that cannot happen with the establishment and running of Academies, at least not on paper (though there are underhanded ways of doing this[13]). Though that is not to say that they will not become profit-making in the future through changes to the law—especially given that the likely public reception for just such an idea has already been tested through the media. So, for now at least, it is more accurate to describe Academies as quasi or pre-privatized, as schools that have been placed in the hands of neoliberal capitalists via the right-wing political ruling class, over the past twenty-five years. This kind of analysis is difficult to make without an understanding of the primacy of social class and capitalism, and precisely because of this, Ryan's objective of a "progressive dialogue" with "race" frameworks in order to constructively and collectively navigate through the impasse, that has been posed as class v "race," is not going to be easy.

Notes

1 I have used "race" with quotation marks to recognize the sociopolitical and ideological nature of this particular term. The challenge to the biological modeling of "race" is discussed below, and also see Maisuria (2012: 80–1) for an extended discussion.
2 I now draw here on the philosophy of science called Critical Realism to provide a critique of CRT. While there are many texts that outline the basic architecture of Critical Realism (see Bhaskar 2017), it needs to be highlighted that Critical Realism shows that rigorous scholarship is about *explaining* the nature of things, their generative foundations, and their constitutive causal powers that are rooted in reality, things such as "race." The aim of Critical Realism is to provide a philosophical and scientific framework to grasp reality, and to do this Critical Realists distinguish *essence* from *appearance* and prioritize the former over the latter. The aim of rigorous research must be to unearth the deep mechanisms that generate the conditions for reality to be experienced in the way that it is. There are very few scholars who have examined CRT's philosophical and scientific foundations and even fewer who have applied a Critical Realist-inspired critique to CRT, especially from a Marxist perspective.
3 To make judgments about un/seriousness, Critical Realism has a schema—DRIEC, which I outline below.
4 Positivism's main characteristics include experimentation as its central instrument, a reliance on laboratory-like conditions, the search for laws/patterns/regularity, and a quest for generalizability. The strength of positivism is the identification of causes, but it tends to do this only within closed condition, for example, controlled experiments and labs that do not reflect the complexity of reality. This complexity is captured in the concept of reality being an *open system*, which is discussed in this chapter.

5   This is to denote that the reality is complex, changeable/changing, and stratified. On the latter, stratification is by classified by domains of reality: real (deep generative mechanisms), actual (events and experiences), empirical (experiences). The level of the actual and empirical emerge from the level of the real, but this causation cannot be said to be a *law* because the world is complex and history can unfold in mostly unpredictable ways (see table 0.1, Bhaskar 2008).
6   These fundamental features of Critical Realism are not in any way to be confused with an endorsement of postmodernism and/or its twin post-structuralism; both reject the existence of an objective reality. Critical Realism makes the case for the existence of a differentiated experience of reality and the critical realist call is for explaining causal mechanisms, as argued below.
7   Epistemological relativism is about the acknowledgment of many knowledge claims about reality; ontological realism is about the acceptance of an objective reality that exists beyond experience and/or knowledge of that reality. The challenge for a social scientist aiming for rigor is to establish the efficacy of knowledge claims about reality, and DREIC is a method to facilitate this.
8   An example of naïve realism is Bell's Racial Realism (Bell 1992b), which, while it is based on "empiricism," doesn't attempt to go deeper and identify the causal mechanisms of injustices. See the discussion above, relating to DREIC.
9   More generally, the rejection of positivism, on the basis that it is appropriate only for the study of the natural world, has led to social researchers applying a hard version of hermeneutics. This is commonly operationalized in the guise of strong versions of interpretivism, which lead researchers to make dubious philosophy of science statements, such as: "I believe all knowledge is socially constructed, and therefore ungeneralizable." These are dubious because the claim is that reality does not exist beyond people, their relationships, and their consciousness. It has meant a rejection of structuralism, for example. Marxism *in toto*. This is termed ontological shyness, and it has led to an uncritical rejection of the existence of objective reality and an embrace of postmodernism and its twin, post-structuralism. CRT suffers from some of these philosophical problems.
10 See Maisuria and Beach (2017) for a discussion on method and critical realist ethnography.
11 Preston (2010) provides a unique Marxian take on this issue, one that incorporates the idea of *abstract* racial domination in the form of whiteness, which is disentangled from its *concrete* forms of racial domination.
12 Howard Ryan has usefully brought my attention to an important distinction between England and the United States: "One important way that we [in the United States] distinguish public from private schools is the labor law that applies. So, if the teachers want to unionize in a charter school, including non-profit ones, the private-sector labor law applies, that being the National Labor Relations Act. On the other hand, when teachers in the public schools unionize, then the state public-sector labor law applies" (private correspondence). In England, all schools, including Academies, have to recognize the national *Trade Unions and the Labour Relations (Consolidation) Act 1992*. There is no private-sector industrial relations legislation that demarks public (State) and private (Independent) schools. Furthermore, teachers in Independent schools (the private sector) can join State school teachers in the national trade union body (the "National Education Union"). These wider points seem to add ballast to my counter to the statement that "privatization is far more advanced" in England than the United States. More widely, I agree that there are definitional differences between

the use of the terms: "public," "private," "State"/"federal" that could have a significant bearing on substantive understanding and subsequent analysis.

13 For example, Academies have the autonomy and freedom to award contracts for essential services (such as catering, cleaning, estate maintenance and uniform provision) to whom they desire. Unlike State comprehensive schools, they do not engage in a competitive tending process designed to get value-for(taxpayers)-money. Thus, what Academy leaders can do is award their *own* companies these contracts. This process in the United States is called "Sweeps contracts," because they sweep up the contracts and the public money that comes with them. The report "Chartered for Profit" (Burris and Cimarusti 2021) powerfully documents this. This can be financially lucrative, especially in the case when the school leader has jurisdiction over a Multi-Academies Trust that includes many schools. In summary, financial profit is available via nefarious means, and such has been the problem with these so-called "related-party transactions" that the government has very recently been forced to introduce legislation to curb their freedoms and autonomy (see Academy Trust Handbook, section 5.35).

8

The Exigency of Radical Class Politics

A Personal Journey

Kevin D. Lam

I believe a personal framing is essential for understanding why we do the work we do and why we think about the world as we do. In this response, I trace a personal genealogy (both familial and intellectual) of my formation as a critical scholar and educator and how and why I came to a Marxist understanding of racism. In doing so, I attempt to think through Ryan's articulation on race/class tensions and their relationship to school reform in ways that are theoretically grounded and deeply personal. I hope to evoke a sense of praxis—the dialectical relationship between theory and practice. I frame school reform as vis-à-vis a racializing mechanism, and I view this phenomenon not as an "act of white supremacy" or a "white" racial project but, in fact, a capitalist one. Hence, there is a need to center capitalism (or rather, a critique of capitalism) as "the most totalizing system the world has ever known"—that seeps into every aspect of our lives, as both a local and global phenomenon (Wood 1994: 28).

There are two parts to this chapter. I begin with a focus on my initial thinking on race and class, when I first started doctoral work in 2003. I have spent the last fifteen years trying to make sense of the tensions between the two seemingly competing theoretical analyses and approaches, that are Marxism and critical race theory (CRT), while thinking about "race" and racism in the United States. These theoretical and philosophical traditions attempt to capture the "hearts and minds" of those invested in the work, on both an academic and personal level. While such conversations on race and class stems from academic and legal circles (Cole 2009), yet they extend beyond the academy. Here, I offer a window into my own engagement with questions concerning racism and class relations. I theorize my own family history and its relation to class struggle at a particular time and place. I hope to connect this conversation to working people outside of the university, in ways that help us to think about "history from below."

To this end, the second part of the chapter traces my intellectual and political genealogy, as grounded in a specific understanding of a Marxist analysis of racism within a political economy of migration framework. I engage Ryan's lead chapter on school reform, relative to racialization, political economy, and social movements, and hope to add to the conversation on racialized identities in the midst of major demographic changes and shifting class relations in the United States over the last four decades (Darder and Torres 2003, 2004; Lam 2015, 2019). Intellectual and political work evolves over time, given the nature of our own always evolving histories and *unfinishedness* (Freire 2018; Darder 2018). However, what has remained constant for me is the necessity of striving for economic democracy. It is from such a positionality that I call for a renewal of historical materialism and for a return to the radical class politics of the 1960s and 1970s, as a means for critical scholars and educators (especially of color) to analyze material and human conditions—and more.

Personal Narrative

I share two moments that have informed my initial thinking on academic discourses concerning racism and class relations. The first moment was the start of doctoral work and my desire to understand the politics of graduate funding: Why did certain students receive funding, while others did not? The department I was in was unique at the time, in the sense that we had a large number of faculty and students of color. In particular, there was a large contingent of Black and Latino faculty and students. As an "Asian American" subject, I occupied a very peculiar space as a "person of color" within an oftentimes Black/white context, or at moments, within a Black-brown/white binary narrative (Chang 2020). As someone from the West Coast, where Asian Americans are highly visible and prominent, this was unfamiliar terrain for me. More importantly, what is being stressed here is that these issues and concerns speak to larger questions concerning identity politics.

As I was trying to make sense of my place as a graduate student (and who I was/am) during the first couple of years of graduate work, I was keenly aware that a number of my Black and brown colleagues in the department were receiving full funding in order to pursue their studies (in addition to being provided with graduate and teaching assistantship opportunities). To be sure, this had a lot to do with who was in charge of those funding opportunities. I was aware that some of my colleagues of color were middle class and came from very different material conditions than my own. This included, but was not limited to, having parents who attended college (often with advanced degrees) and/or had middle-class jobs, having lived in relatively affluent neighborhoods, knowing how to ask for things or frame certain questions, and being considerably better prepared to navigate the landscape of higher education.

I am a political refugee from Vietnam and first-generation college student, the first in my family to receive a university degree and the only one with a PhD. My frustration with (and perhaps even envy of) others receiving funding when I did not (I eventually did get partial funding and took out loans) as a working-class Asian American student became motivation for me to understand, or at the very least grapple with, racialized difference within academia and beyond. This experience is one example of how the process of racialization within the context of capitalism informs and impacts notions of "race" and racialized populations in the United States. As such, identity politics in higher education gets played out in very real and material ways.

The second moment (certainly tied to the first) carries a much longer and substantive history for me. It is informed by parents who labored in menial work, were on welfare, and trying to scrape together a livable income to support and provide for their five children. In addition, they were also sending remittances back to their siblings in Vietnam and China. Ten people living together in roach-infested two-bedroom apartments was all I knew during much of my formative years. Growing up in an immigrant/refugee context and working-class Los Angeles in the 1980s served as the basis for understanding and engaging in class struggle. My mother worked as a garment worker in downtown Los Angeles during the day and would continue this work at night. She had a sewing machine hidden in her bedroom closet behind a sliding door, as she was concerned that benefits would be reduced or altogether cut if Aid to Families with Dependent Children (AFDC) discovered that she was working. She would do piecemeal work—getting paid for individual pieces that would later be sewn together as dresses to be sold in department stores. She worked where she slept, and her bedroom was covered with dust particles from her sewing machine.

My father worked for years as a butcher in Asian supermarkets, in LA's San Gabriel and San Fernando valleys. I remember the stench of raw meat from the carpet of his car when getting dropped off at school in the morning before he would go to work. He was able, at times, to bring home steak (filet mignon or another prime cut) purchased at a reduced price. These were special occasions. As kids, we never went out to eat. Now, as a certified academic and middle-class intellectual, I go out to eat/take out frequently with my wife and our two children. I, however, am sure to take home a lot of napkins, so we can use them at a later time.

This personal narrative evokes much pain, shame, and trauma. It speaks to how understanding material conditions in the context of inequality has been, for me, lived and embodied. It is also a source of great pride and serves as the basis for struggle. Indeed, the personal is political (and pedagogical). These experiences of racialized identities, spatial relations, and class formation are mapped on my body and face and in how I talk and move. This narrative informs my history—how I have come to be in the world—and how I think about "race" and class in the context of capitalism and economic restructuring in the metropole. I have worked as a youth worker and, for a couple of years, a middle school social studies and math teacher in my communities. In making the decision to pursue doctoral work, I wanted to teach, write, and research about things that matter to me. Perhaps this is my way of honoring my parents' labor and our history.

Intellectual and Political Genealogy

I began graduate work with the intent of studying critical pedagogy, and along the way, I discovered a critical theory of racism. As I wrestled with questions related to race and class, I came across a body of literature that helped inform and shape my thinking. Given my own history, I was struggling to think about questions of identity and difference beyond the US nation state, as theorizing political economy, colonialism, and imperialism is always relational and comparative. Ngin and Torres's (2001) work on racialized Asian American and Latino identities in Southern California, and on labor/immigrant rights and class formation was one of the first pieces that began the process of critical inquiry for me.

After Race by Darder and Torres (2004), along with the work of British sociologist Robert Miles from the 1980s and early 1990s (Miles 1982, 1989, 1993, 2003), changed everything for me. It provided me with a language for a Marxist understanding of racism and racialization, as the critical pedagogy literature had previously provided me with a language of hope and possibility. Working within a political economy of racism and migration framework, I find this body of scholarship to be theoretically nuanced and historically grounded. It speaks to me at both a theoretical and visceral level. It gives me a way to understand my own contexts and history, as I engage in a Marxist articulation of racialization.

My initial engagement with this area of study left me unsettled, and at moments disturbed, because it went against what I believed firmly to be true. To be sure, I was learning to be a student and how to read theory. Nonetheless, it shook every fiber of my body (and it still does) as I engaged in an ongoing process of attempting to understand this critical theory of racism—with a genealogy originating with the Frankfurt School and a British and French Marxist sociology of the 1960s and 1970s. I decided to stick with it because of my faith in the political project of Darder and Torres (Darder was also my doctoral advisor), which sought to challenge notions of "race" that retreated from class analysis. This particular Marxist/critical orientation, as articulated by Miles (1982, 1989, 1993, 2003), Guillaumin (1995), Darder and Torres (2004), Cole (2009), Wood (1994, 1998), Gilroy (2002), Fields (1990, 2012), Reed, Jr. (2012, 2020) and others, helped to frame my philosophy of praxis. There is something in the literature that moved me, that spoke to the essence of who I am as a working-class and colonized subject of the United States.

Toward a Marxist Understanding of Racialization

Ryan engages race and class with respect to school reform by challenging the "retreat from class" (Wood 1998) which, according to him, has shaped the global left since the rise to prominence of neoliberalism. He wants to better understand the social, economic, and political factors behind the corporate assaults on schools (Ryan 2016). Ryan's research illustrates how many progressive approaches to school reform view "race" as the central unit of analysis. He has encountered progressive race-based analyses that view corporate-influenced contemporary school reform, with its high-stakes testing and focus on privatization, as essentially a "white phenomenon" and an "act of white supremacy." To be sure, the multiple contexts that he engages with are highly racialized. However, Ryan challenges such race-based theorization and argues for the significance of class analysis in his study of education and politics. As a labor organizer, Ryan is interested in finding ways to make sense of these matters theoretically, while also focusing on practical issues concerning education practices for working people in the United States and around the world.

Ryan's central thesis is that the organized business sector "seeks reform primarily for curricular purposes: it wants curriculum that fosters a subordinate working class and that, in other ways, advances capitalist hegemony." Ryan draws on US, British, and South African contexts to substantiate his argument concerning the need for class analysis. He proceeds by acknowledging the three different theoretical approaches, traditions, and bodies of work that have helped inform and shape the spectrum of progressive discourses on educational reform: (1) Marxism, which centers class and a critique of capitalism (Miles 1993; Darder and Torres 2004; Scatamburlo-D'Annibale and McLaren 2005); (2) race-based theory, with CRT as the predominant explanatory tool and mode of analysis for scholars and educators (with its genesis in the progressive spectrum of US legal studies from the late 1980s) (Matsuda, et al. 1993; Delgado and Stefancic 2000; Picower and Mayorga 2015a); and (3) intersectionality approaches (with its trinity of "race, class, gender" argument), having roots in US Black feminist thought (Crenshaw 1989; Carbado, et al. 2013; Collins and Bilge 2016).

Each of these traditions, frameworks, and paradigms are rooted in particular struggles. Ryan is interested in linking both race and class, in a fashion similar to that of Virdee (2014), Marable (2015), Roediger (2006, 2007, 2017), the London-based Institute of Race Relations (home of the journal *Race and Class*), the Centre for Contemporary Studies (the Birmingham School), and others working within and around the Marxist/critical traditions. "Race relations" refers to a sociological paradigm that utilizes race as a central tool of analysis to explain how racialized groups relate to one another and how race impacts social behavior (Darder and Torres 2004; Miles 1993). "Race relations" sociology has dominated much of social sciences, humanities, and educational research, on both sides of the Atlantic (Miles 1993).

In contrast, I offer a different articulation by engaging with a specific understanding of Marxist analyses, grounded in the racism paradigm developed in the UK in the late 1970s and early 1980s (Miles 1993, 1982). I draw from the work of Miles, Darder and Torres, Fields, and others who assert problems with and limitations of "race relations" sociology. Miles places political economy at the center of his study of racism (Ashe and McGeever 2011). Miles (1993: 1) notes that while some social scientists have sought to construct a theory of "race relations," other thinkers have forcefully moved to a more appropriate object of analysis. He argues that beyond the paradigm of "race relations" there is another, more critical, way of understanding social relations, one that does not employ the deeply problematic idea of "race" as an analytical concept.

In an interview with Ashe and McGeever (2011: 2018–19) on his use of the concept of "racialization," Miles distinguishes between the *idea* of "race" and the *concept* of "race":

> I resist talking about the concept of "race." I will talk about the idea of "race." And I try consistently to talk about the idea of "race" and never talk about the concept of "race" because here I like to think that I am rigorous in believing that there is

a very clear distinction between an idea and a concept. What I was trying to do was to create a conceptual language that made it much easier to understand that the idea of "race" is a historical reality; that what is meant by it changes over time; that the contexts in which it is used and therefore applied to create typologies of human beings is always a process; that as a historical process it has a particular determinants at particular moments in time ... that opens the door to history, that opens the door to understanding the complexities of who get racialized when and for what purpose, and how that changes through time.

Miles attempts to understand the complexity of identity by problematizing and disrupting the Black/white binary, which serves to open up the discourse on the complexity of identity. Here, I think about the ways in which Asians and Asian Americans have been racialized historically in the United States—and to some extent globally. The process of racialization across history (e.g., immigration, labor, geopolitics, education, etc.) is informed and shaped by how we think about a particular group of people. As I have noted elsewhere, "Asia," "Asians," and "Asian Americans" have always been on contested and tenuous terrain in their relationship with the US nation state (Lam 2015: 47). The development of capitalism and its relationship to labor (intellectual, manual, and otherwise) has always been at the forefront of that conversation. Immigration exclusion, naturalization laws, and education policies and practices continue to police Asian bodies, though how they have been racialized has varied historically and contextually.

The process of signification for Asian and Asian Americans is tied to a political economy of racism and labor migration. For example, the Naturalization and Immigration Act of 1965 profoundly impacted "Asian America," and more specifically Asian American students and how they are viewed and represented. This 1965 law marked a turn to "new" Asian migration in the US diaspora, which is signified as encompassing both "good" and "bad" subjects. Some Asians are "good" because they hail from a highly educated professional class (hence they are viewed as desirable and "model" workers and citizens). The recruitment of doctors, engineers, nurses, computer scientists, graduate students, and others was deemed necessary to compete internationally with the Soviet Union, the decade or so after the Cold War ended. At the same time, Asians were also "gooks" for US soldiers in the jungles of Vietnam and Americans here at home. In the aftermath of US involvement, more than 3 million political refugees from Vietnam, Cambodia, and Laos resettled in the "belly of the beast" after 1975 (Lam 2015).

As a way to further substantiate the racialization of Asian and Asian American students, I draw from Ryan's analysis of test scores (high school standardized exams) in California and how the concept of "race" is reproduced in mainstream thinking about "student success," and, diametrically, "student failure." Ryan notes, for example, that California's "white" students produced a composite pass rate of 59.5 percent, roughly double that of "Blacks" (26 percent) and "Latinos" (33 percent). Ryan also notes the higher Asian pass rate of 75 percent, partly attributable to the immigration of highly educated, higher-wealth families from China, Taiwan, and South Korea. Indeed, there are many complexities and layers to these racialized categories, including major class difference and experiences within each umbrella term. It is not about "race"; it is about political economy. For instance, immigrants accounted for 81 percent of the growth in the US adult population from 1970 to 2016, and the foreign-born proportion of Asians increased from 45 percent to 78 percent in this same period (Kochhar and Cilluffo 2018). Not surprisingly, Asians are the most economically divided group in the United States and, according to the Pew Research Center, have displaced Blacks with respect to this distinction in the process (Kochhar 2018; Lam 2019).

Further, through analyzing educational and structural inequalities in the United States, it is clear that Asian Americans are racialized as the "good race" and African Americans as the "bad race" (Lam 2015: 13). Asian Americans, racialized as the "model minority," have historically been used as a political wedge—to create division against African Americans (and to some extent Latinos), as a way to control the masses and social relations of power (Chang and Au 2009). It is the oldest trick in the book, and this "divide-and-conquer" colonial logic continues to have a deeply harmful impact on how we think about solidarity and struggle among "people of color" in the United States. Moreover, when discussing difference, Ellen Meiksins Wood's (1994:1) work speaks to both the impossibility and undesirability of such "totalizing knowledges." Wood (1994: 1) affirms the reality of many "particular identities and forms of domination" and succinctly points to an overarching system of identity that "imposes" itself on us all.

The myth of meritocracy, which presupposes a level playing field for all, suggests that if you work hard, you can and will succeed in capitalist America, even in the midst of massive economic inequality and racism (Guinier 2016). Conversely, if you do not succeed, your failure is blamed on your individual deficit. This distortion has left a mark on how racialized populations are signified (as a historical process) relative to "white" people and to other people of color. Given widespread skepticism with respect to class politics and Marxist analyses in the United States (Au 2018), people of color are discouraged from uniting along class lines. Consequently, there is also mistrust among people of color, partly because we do not readily see our commonalities or find opportunities to learn about each other's histories and struggles. Oftentimes, popular discourses include both a depiction of racialized populations as acting only to serve "their own agenda" (often "to the detriment" of other groups) and a "flattening" of diversity within each group in order to homogenize them (Chang 2020). There is a need to challenge and shift the paradigm and to ask different questions—because the world requires us to do so. While the "race relations" paradigm has been dominant in how we make sense of and engage in multiracial and multi-ethnic coalitional work, Gilroy (2000) challenges this with a call for a "planetary humanism"—for us to move beyond a certain parochialism and regionalism that has created stagnation in our political work (Fanon 1963).

The Exigency of Radical Class Politics

Ryan notes that some scholars, within what he describes as the "race-based" theory camp, move back and forth between "a position of race primacy and that of race/class or race/class/gender equivalence." In the process of attempting to combine race and class analysis, he argues, race-based theorists have "short-changed" or retreated from class as a central unit of analysis. Ryan is also concerned that race-based theorists are at times vague about the *who* behind educational school reform and *who* benefits. Undoubtedly, some white people have benefited greatly from such reform. However, in agreement with Maisuria (2010) as cited by Ryan, school reform is less a "white phenomenon" than a capitalist one—and racism is best understood as a "mechanism of ruling-class social control."

To be clear, I am working from a Marxist articulation of racialization that foregrounds political economy and a sustained critique of capitalism. Hence, this is not about "race" and class as categories but about the *process* of racialization and the attendant gesture toward a political economy-inspired class analysis. Ryan argues that the neglect of class analysis is often related to an effort to sustain a political base that was first developed through the civil rights movements of the 1960s in the United States and reaffirmed during the 1980s, when neoconservatism and electoral politics reigned supreme, including for people of color (Taylor 2016). When class *is* mentioned by race-based scholars, it is generally through "race, class, and gender" intersectionality, which combines different systems of oppression (Carbado et al. 2013). Such an approach reinforces the idea that class should be treated as one of many equally valued components of analysis when, as myself, Ryan and others have argued, it is not an equally valuable category of analysis, when rather, as Darder and Torres (2004: 128) contend, "class and 'race' are concepts of different sociological order . . . and do not occupy the same analytical space."

Despite the fact that "race" and gender invariably intersect with class, they are not co-primary. These antagonisms are indeed dialectical in nature. However, what cannot be ignored is the manner in which class struggle as the primary antagonism, gives shape and form to the specificities of antagonisms such as racism, ethnocentrism, and sexism (McLaren and Jaramillo 2003; Lam 2015: 146). Darder and Torres (2004: 127) speak about class "not as an identity or a phenomenon equal to other forms of oppression, but rather as relations of power that encompass social processes that reproduce structural inequality. . . . Class is tied intrinsically to material conditions and asymmetrical structures of power that shape daily life in very concrete ways."

This chapter, as does Ryan's work, situates class struggle/conflict as the starting point of analysis. As such, it calls for a renewal of approaches grounded in historical materialism and insists on the exigency of radical class politics for analyzing contemporary and historically marginalized and dispossessed communities across time. In agreement with Ryan, it may be a worthwhile project for minoritized groups to return to the radical class politics of the late 1960s and 1970s, when issues of class were central to analyses of inequality. Ryan rightfully notes that race-based scholars typically, when they engage issues of class, use the stratification model of class that is predominant across society rather than a Marxian class-conflict model. Darder and Torres (2004: 128) distinguish mainstream definitions of class from one that recognizes the "social relations of production":

> Class is a material space, even within the mainstream definition that links the concept to occupation, income status, and educational attainment—all of which

reflect the materiality of class, though without analytical specificity. Hence, class can only be rigorously analyzed by recognizing that the social relations of production are germane to a social justice or emancipatory political project.

Mainstream understandings of class include factors such as occupation, markers of income, and categories of classes (upper, middle, working). In doing so, these ways of defining class obscure economic interests and capitalist relations. Part of the problem, Barbara Fields explains, has to do with liberal anti-racists "evacuating" the class content of American society, and in the process, talking about race and racism in a vacuum (Fields and Fields 2018).

Ryan goes to great lengths, in his argument, to engage the simultaneous significance of race and class. In contrast, the argument I have provided here does not signal a similar corresponding relationship between race and class in analyzing school reform and "student achievement." Much of the school reform conversation is framed through a "race relations" paradigm. This framework implies that the "problems of race in America are based on some unfortunate interpersonal lack of understanding, rather than in racism and the capitalist order that racism helps maintain" (Fields and Fields 2018: 2). The (over)development of "white supremacy" and "whiteness" as catch-all terms is disconcerting. It connotes the existence of an ideology that has "Black" people as the primary object of racism and "white" people as perpetrators of racism. The reification of skin color as the most active determinant of social relations between Black and white populations ignores the historical and contemporary oppression of those who have been treated as "inferior" or "distinct" without such a reference to skin color (Miles 1993; Darder and Torres 2004; Lam 2015).

This dichotomy, which presupposes Blacks as victims and whites as perpetrators, tends to homogenize the objects of racism: "As soon as you do it that way you are in a self-defeating cycle because then you have people you've identified as a race who are permanent targets and victims. . . . You have no access to politics—you don't even conceive it as a political situation" (Fields and Fields 2018). Hence, the removal of politics and history is troublesome, and perhaps just as problematic is the separation of politics from economics. While acknowledging that "post-all" frameworks (e.g., post-structuralism, postmodernism, etc.) and culture-based analyses have done much to advance our understanding of difference and representational politics, we have been "woefully remiss in addressing the constitution of class formations and the machinations of capitalist social organizations" (Scatamburlo-D'Annibale and McLaren 2005: 42).

The unrelenting power of "race" as common sense and the consequent "race relations" paradigm have pervaded all levels of the academy, as well as mass and popular media. "Race" as an object of analysis is a source of theoretical disagreement. In addressing that disagreement, I have argued here that an anti-racism, firmly grounded in anti-capitalist and anti-imperialist (and always internationalist) struggle, is more urgent and necessary than ever before. Miles was aware of "ploughing a more lonely furrow or ploughing a furrow in which there were fewer people around" (Ashe and McGeever 2011: 2024), to which I can also attest. Nevertheless, this work must be done. It is not a matter of choice, if we desire a truly democratic and economically just world for all.

Part III

Responses from Critical Race Theory and Allied Perspectives

9

Significance of a Race-Based Approach to Teacher Mobilization

Margarita Berta-Ávila

Dominant racial frames, therefore, provide the intellectual roadmap used by rulers to navigate the always rocky road of domination.
—Bonilla-Silva (2006: 26)

In response to Howard Ryan's premise that the dialogue around school reform and the progressive movement in education should center on a class-based analysis with an acknowledgment of a race-based framework, the focus of this chapter aims to address the troublesome impact of his position when preparing preservice students/students of color and providing in-service to teachers/teachers of color. Moreover, in response to the seemingly purposeful invisibility of race often at work in approaches to educational movement work, this response describes the intentional actions of teacher/faculty unions to employ a social justice unionism framework that makes race central in mobilizing within communities of color. Teacher/faculty unions are centering race in organizing members around working conditions and their link to student learning conditions, bread and butter concerns, including equity pay, addressing inversion/compression, and issue-based initiatives such as rent stabilization and the disinvestment of pension funds from the financing of detention centers holding migrant communities.

As a teacher educator, I have always held the belief that in-service/preservice teachers (and educators more broadly) should develop a critical discourse related to schooling and inequity, one which is specifically grounded in a critique of hegemonic social relations coupled with an analysis of power relations both within education and across society. Such an analysis is necessary to counter processes of social reproduction that use schools to preserve the status quo and a system of social and economic control. The historical infrastructures of schools do so by serving as a key institutional vehicle for perpetuating the stratification of political, social, and economic structures. As such, administrators and teachers are often implicated in a structure of oppression that perpetuates institutional racism through valorizing hegemonic culture (i.e., white privilege), marginalizing students of color (i.e., as viewed through a deficit lens), and reinforcing false myths of meritocracy (i.e., neoliberal multiculturalism).

Although I have held steadfast to a critical framing of inequalities, as a Xicana/person of color I have come to realize that, for doing so, a critical economic analysis alone is insufficient. For example, Ryan fails to consider what is systemically perpetuated when race is not centered and attendant issues of ethnicity, culture, language, immigration are not central to our analysis of educational reform. Moreover, in Ryan's analysis, race is situated as being incidental to or a derivative of class, which intentionally or not leads to a racialized form of anti-racist theorizing. Kohli, Pizarro, and Nevárez (2017) argue that such perspectives amplify how schools, as institutions, are race neutral or race evasive. As a result, institutional practices that are in fact racializing are not addressed systematically because they are strategically framed as individual problems and thus individualizes responsibility for addressing them, the pervasive neoliberal bootstrap rationale and solution.

Simultaneously, it is critical that we reframe the narrative that there is not active resistance in and across our communities. Day in and day out, schools and teachers are enacting forms of resistance. More specifically, teachers, including teachers of color, are doing so through teacher unions, as arguably the strongest political avenue available to them. As such, union members (first nation/people of color/and whites) are mobilizing together, through consciously centering race and providing an analysis of labor anchored to a race-based lens.

Significance of a Race-Based Approach to Teacher Mobilization

Breona Taylor--George Floyd--Trayvon Martin--Sandra Bland--Tamir Rice--Rekia Boyd--Sean Monterrosa--Shantel Davis--Michael Brown--Shelly Frey--Eric Garner--Kayla Moore--Philando Castile--Alverta Spruill--Seven Generations Past . . . We Remember!!

At the forefront of my work is the belief that the political is personal and the personal political. That could not be truer today, in that I write this reflection in the midst of the rise of a movement in which collectives in the United States and around the world are demanding and fighting for Black lives. Communities are hitting the streets, shouting out with every being of who they are—of who *we* are—BASTA!!! No more talk, no more finding a middle ground, transformation is needed now!!! Concomitant with this powerful movement's rise we are enduring a pandemic that is taking the lives of Black and Brown bodies at an exasperating rate due to racial economic inequities already in existence pre-Covid-19. So, as I sit with all this, it has not been an easy endeavor to write this response. I am not sure if I would have felt otherwise in a time and space that is not the present—but it feels as if it is likely that this is true, that this is different. As such, there is no way I can ignore the current national politics of hate, or detach myself from this work, as if I was not living in the conditions of which I am writing. As I write, my response here coexists simultaneously with the pain and trauma of contending daily with the hatred and inhumanity associated with white supremacy, racism, and race-based disparities. I am cognizant that these contexts and issues are not new, but they never fail to enrage me; it is as if the air I breathe is being sucked out of me.

These racializing and inhumane acts, as we know, are not always exaggeratedly overt; often they impact subtlety and can be portrayed as non-existent or imaginary, with such rationales for language and behavior serving to deny that systemic racism is at work. When I reflect on "to deny systemic racism is at work" there are countless experiences that come to mind, in which I was meant to feel illogical and irrational. During my second year of teaching, I had already made it clear that I viewed my teaching role as a political act. As such, providing an equitable education to my students, addressing systemic racism, and the intersectionality of other unjust practices went hand in hand. Though I was scared to speak up, I did so anyway, even when doing so isolated and marginalized me. One day, the principal called me into his office. He had me sit across from him and asked me to take the dictionary that was on top of the desk. When I had the dictionary in hand, I was instructed to open it, look up the word "aggressive," and to read aloud the definition. At that point, the principal looked at me and stated that several of my colleagues had gone out of their way to speak to him about their serious concerns about me. At the center of their concern was my "aggressive" behavior toward them. Aggressive apparently, as they had explained, because I would challenge statements they made about students and attribute them to racism, when they were not racists. Moreover, he explained, he was now having to speak on their behalf because I had scared them.

With these sentences, the principal had succeeded in humiliating me; he had made me out to be the aggressor, the bully of the piece, and catered to the discomfort of his white teachers. This necessitated that he put me in my place and be the savior for the teachers who did not want to be confronted with their own acts of racism—not only toward their students but toward me as well. I offer this brief narrative as a starting point because, throughout this experience, that which failed to be centered in these conversations was race/racism, and ultimately white supremacy. The principal rationalized the racism that was being played out by evading that as being the central issue, silencing the analysis of the racism that was taking place, and making the issue out to be one of a problematic personal character trait or individualized personality flaw on my part. By reducing the issue to my supposed "aggressiveness," there was no attempt to hold accountable the systemic structures that are responsible for much of the racialized inequities Black/Indigenous/students of color and teachers of color experience, particularly in K-12 schools.

Politics of Evasion

To that end, Howard Ryan's premise that the dialogue around school reform and progressive movements in education should center a class-based analysis with an acknowledgment to a race-based framework has to be challenged. There is no question that an analysis of political-economic conditions contributes to understanding the lives of marginalized communities; indeed, Zavala (2018) would argue that one cannot partake in a critical analysis of power without situating capitalism. Moreover, he and Lipman (2020) would add that these dialogues concerning power cannot ignore the use of capitalism to other, justify violence, oppress, and dehumanize via racial superiority, given that capitalism is "tied to historically formed racist discourse, which in turn is bound to the political and economic histories of how 'minority' groups are incorporated into a racialized society" (Zavala 2018: 24). Similarly, Mayorga, Aggarwal, and Picower (2020) adhere to an interlocking connection between racism and capitalism but are clear to note that they are not offshoots of one another. As Zavala (2018: 42) explains, "Understand that race is not epiphenomenal or an extension of capitalism or class struggle . . . It is key in seeing these as distinct forms of oppression." Or as Lipman (2020: 133) eloquently states, "Capitalism and White supremacy are co-constituted." Thus, the white supremacist framing at the core of Racial Capitalism in which "the winners and losers are racially and economically categorized and sorted with relentless efficiency; [utilizes] all of the traditional markers of inequality—starting with race and class" (Ayers and Ayers 2020: 195).

As such, myths (particularly racial narratives) have been normalized to justify the ongoing processes of the racialization of communities. In the last three decades, these myths have deeply influenced neoliberal laws and policies related to schooling. These myths are perpetuated through a white imaginative that "seeks to normalize a world where people of color have been racialized and minoritized as inferior to people racialized as whites" (Wright et al. 2018: 9). Moreover, this serves to perpetuate a "colonial, white supremist relations of oppression and marginalization" (Ayer and Ayer 2020: 195). Such colonized relations have become systemic, integral to the fabric of the US societal imagination. Ultimately, these myths justify the framing of an ideal humanity based on white standards, which in turn works to fortify the invisibility of racism: "Normalizing social spaces in a way that perpetuate white power and privilege while making it look that that's not what is happening" (Allen 2004; as cited in Wright et al. 2018: 9).

Ultimately, what becomes most dangerous, here, is that, in a classroom setting, this normalization of racialized myths (e.g., meritocracy, deficit intelligence, etc.) concerning students of color becomes translated into everyday classroom acts (e.g., high-stakes testing, restrictive language practices, the hidden curriculum, etc.) by teachers and then rationalized by the hegemonic discourse of schooling, while most teachers remain oblivious to their participation in this disabling system of education (Sleeter and Owuor 2011). Through such processes it becomes the demand of students to assimilate and embody white colonial norms (Dominguez 2017). Bettina Love (2019a) refers to these acts of racism in the classroom and across wider school structures as "spirit murdering," particularly with respect to the lives of students and teachers of color. Moreover, they function to hide "the punitive disparities of neoliberal ideologies" (Wright et al. 2018: 10) by shaping not only educational policies but also the preparation of teachers and practices within classrooms. For example, sustaining neoliberal policies of accountability and standardization, often justified via "educational reform" processes (Wright et al. 2018), function to erode democratic values by stifling voice and participation.

Accordingly, educational practices are set in place that disrupt, penalize, and criminalize by way of schools rules that disproportionality lead to the suspension of Black/Brown students; expect teachers/schools to "do more with less"; and inequitably punish school districts with a majority of students of color by instituting policies, like those in Detroit, where legislation enforced takeovers of schools in poor communities of color, while other districts with similar economic shortfalls were not subject to such enforced measures(Wright et al. 2018). This iniquitous situation becomes even more complex when a politics of evasion is in play.

A politics of evasion is, more often than not, predicated on attempts to erase racism and white supremacy from the conversation, in order to legitimize actions and invisibilize injustices. A society or community becomes socialized to believe that systemic racism does not exist or that race (and whiteness) is being addressed, while systemic racism is actually being reinforced and perpetuated all along (Patel and Keval 2018). This "illusion" is maintained by either ignoring claims of racism or deeming these delusional, thus ignoring the disabling impact of whiteness and power associated with it. If acts of racism and white supremacy are uncovered and challenged, the psychological practice deployed is to make individuals believe that their complaints are irrational. This racializing practice must be challenged and ended in schools, given that it is detrimental not only to communities of color but also to the framework of our wider society. For too long, the latter has maintained and justified a "White imperial project" that demands of students, their families, and communities that they lose or deny their sense of self, language, culture, history, and so much more (Alim and Paris 2017: 1). As such, it is critical to examine operations of power within institutional policies and practices, by acknowledging the impact of institutional racism, which seeks (consciously or not) to deepen the marginalization of students of color, while proclaiming "all are welcome" (Patel and Keval 2018: 71).

Hence, when examining educational structures (both within and outside of schools), covert or hidden forms of racism (Kohli, Pizzaro and Nevárez 2017) must be uncovered and challenged. Kohli, Pizzaro, and Nevárez (2017) assert that institutionalized racism within K-12 schools exerts its power most effectively when it exists as an "invisible" or denied phenomenon. This is most disconcerting, in that it allows administrators and teachers to wash their hands and abdicate responsibility for injustices by perpetuating deceptive forms of neoliberal anti-racism racism and color-blind practices (Kohli, Pizzaro, and Nevárez 2017)—practices such as high-stakes testing or English-only instruction that on the outside seem harmless but are actually quite disabling to the academic achievement, empowerment, and spiritual well-being of students of color unprepared to contend with the undue stress or linguistic restrictions these can pose upon their learning.

Impact of Teacher Preparation on Future Teachers

Dunn, Sondel, and Baggett (2019) assert that the decisions teachers make are political. All teacher decisions are shaped by the values that inform their sociopolitical understanding of the world. Neutrality with respect to education and to educators, therefore, does not, indeed cannot, exist. As such, if the goal is that of a racially just system of education, the system in question cannot continue to reproduce constructs and practices that perpetuate racism but instead must be focused on the development of a transformative environment in which the social agency of all students and teachers is not just welcomed but also nurtured. However, such transformative education practices are impossible to enact if teachers continue to be socialized into perceiving their role as neutral or non-political, the dominant commonsensical ideological lens of a majority of teachers in public schools today—and a belief and positionality which serves to perpetuate the status quo of a white supremist framework (Kumashiro 2015).

Given these factors, it is essential for teacher educator activists to confront how contemporary student teachers are prepared, a process which generally evades in-depth analysis and dialogues focused on race and racism, while enacting practices of color blindness (Kohli, Nevárez, and Arteaga 2018: 18). More often than not, as Kohli, Nevárez, and Arteaga (2018) and Matias (2015) posit, teacher preparation programs (both at a micro level and at their core) cater to the worldview of white student teachers. Simultaneously, student teachers of color are racialized through the subtle or not so subtle bigotry of low expectations. This is conveyed through a "whitestream framework" (Burciaga and Kohli 2018: 6) that individualizes success and devalues their existing Community Cultural Wealth (CCW) (Yosso 2005). In the process, hegemonic knowledge is valued and the cultural knowledge of student teachers and students of color is invisibilized, marginalized, or denied. A common outcome of such education processes is that future teachers are socialized to not become advocates for their students but rather to embody an assimilationist notion of teacher agency (Hynds et al. 2016), one which, in its turn, ends up openly promoting white nationalist policies and conservative agendas (Ayers and Ayers 2020).

The majority of teacher education programs are grounded in a hegemonic white paradigm. This is made evident by who writes the curriculum, program frameworks, assessments, and standards, as well as the reconstruction of theory and practice, including efforts to transcend or bypass culturally sustaining pedagogy in order to not address the ideology of whiteness (Matias 2015). Moreover, May and Sleeter (2010) argue that the latter is undertaken under the guise of a multicultural education context that has retreated from its core principles tied to transforming schooling and making critical change in educational practices and relations. Though Ryan, in his chapter, accepts that teachers need multicultural education, this is not conducive to supporting the kinds of transformational changes that are necessary, when what is perpetuated under the banner of "multicultural education" is liberal multiculturalism—a multiculturalism based on the notions we are all the same (or a sameness palatable to whiteness) and that racial inequality is simply a matter of insufficient opportunities for minoritized groups (Kincheloe and Steinberg 1997). As such, this approach makes intentional shifts to decenter race and a critical pedagogy while centering white hegemonic practices (May and Sleeter 2010).

More specifically, liberal multiculturalism fails to uncover and address the power relations embedded in institutionalized and systemic structures of racism and how these play out in terms of inequities, including access to education. It does so in such a way that white teachers and administrators do not have to feel or engage with "discomfort"

(May and Sleeter 2010). As a response, needed is an overt anti-racist activist practice focused on challenging student teachers to analyze the macrostructural values at play and how these manifest within the cultures of schools, classrooms, and communities. This is absolutely key to countering systemic oppression (via pedagogy, curriculum, educational resources, policies, organizing, etc.). Moreover, if the white hegemonic paradigm is not addressed, it leaves no room for the healing process necessary (especially for students of color) to effectively address the disabling impact of racism and racialization nor does it ensure that the essential transformative shift in the future preparation of white teachers takes place (Matias 2015).

The preparation of future teachers must then be grounded and intentional. Teacher education programs must work to counter a "technocratic orientation to teaching" (Dunn, Sondel and Baggett 2019: 468). If programs only focus on teaching strategies, lesson planning, and classroom management, and dismiss the need for teacher preparation courses that engage with social justice, the foundations of racism, and with educational history, this will only serve to perpetuate the apolitical paradigm discussed earlier that serves in practice to reinforce a white supremist agenda. As Love (2019a: 75) explains:

> Teachers need to be taught how to question Whiteness and White supremacy, how to check and deal with their White emotions of guilt and anger, and how all these impact their classroom.... White teachers—and, really, all teachers—must unpack how Whiteness functions in their lives, then they can stand in solidarity with their students' communities for social change.

As Sleeter (2012) contends, what is needed are teachers who have a political clarity about who their students are and who affirm that what students bring to their classes is an asset. Alfaro and Bartolomé (2017) build on the latter point by emphasizing the importance of ideological clarity for directly challenging deficit views of students (and teachers) brought about via the ingrained socialization of society's dominant neoliberal paradigm. Toward that end, the preparation of future teachers of color must be concerned with preparing "racially justice-oriented teachers of color" (Burciaga and Kohli 2018: 6). This entails the development of teachers of color who recognize structural racial inequities and strive to strategically counter these through the curriculum and pedagogy they develop, the community relationships they foster inside and outside of the classroom, the relationships they build with families, and the activism/advocacy they enact on behalf of students to counter racist practices.

This points to the importance of teachers of color, in particular, having a command of "racial literacy" (Kohli, Nevárez and Arteaga 2018: 21), which includes "the skill and practice of being able to understand the institutional embeddedness of racism and then process and respond to these experiences." Having the skills to name racism is essential to its eradication. However, it is not enough to be an ally of those suffering from racism (Blaisdell 2018). Blaisdell (2018) builds on this claim, by explaining that white teachers cannot be left out of the mix or released from their responsibility to be accountable for working toward the changes that are required in schools and wider society. White student teachers, as noted earlier, must engage in an analysis of the institutionalized structure at a macro level. Part of this engagement requires learning about and adopting practices that (1) challenge a single story narrative, which in turn requires listening to people of color who have been historically silenced through the marginalizing of their counter stories; (2) incorporate an acceptance, indeed a nurturing, not just mere recognition, of the epistemological differences that people of color bring to the work; and (3) facilitate participation in the acts of insurgency that are necessary in demanding transformation of the hegemonic culture of schooling. To enter into this process, teachers must confront their fears and biases, coupling this with a "vision of hope" (Ayers, Michie, and Rome 2004). This is a call for a critical hope (Duncan-Andrade 2009), one that interrogates our world: What are we teaching against? What are we teaching for? What actions will we take? What steps need to be taken to achieve a more just world?

Unionism, Anti-Racism, and Social Justice Transformation

The movement to transform education must reframe the ill-founded narrative that resistance to anti-racist and social justice efforts is not in play. Schools are sites of resistance, and teachers are enacting resistance daily. More specifically, both teachers of color and white teachers, as well as university faculty, are doing so through one of the strongest avenues that exists for them, through education unions. The neoliberal fallacy "that unions are corrupt" has served to push the agenda of privatization in schools and universities under the guise of education reform (CReATE 2019), and this is being challenged. Moreover, union members are mobilizing through consciously centering race and providing an analysis of their labor (as part of the wider working class) via that lens. This means that union work can no longer just encapsulate bread and butter concerns, without making direct correlation to racial/social justice issues. Nor can unions position themselves as if societal political movements do not coexist with those of labor. As Ayer and Ayer (2020: 197) state: "Unions now are challenging the traditional forms of business in unions." This necessitates a cultural shift in labor unions in order to become not only a service-oriented entity but also a site for mass organizing, for massive mobilizations of workers and the wider public. The call here is for social justice unionism grounded in a paradigm of anti-racism social justice transformation.

Across the nation, this critical shift is evident among teacher and faculty unions. All one needs to do is take note of the school strikes that have taken place across the nation. Whether it be in Los Angeles, Oakland, Sacramento, or Chicago, teachers are joining the picket line to foreground the need to address the inequities found in schools, and specifically those experienced most directly by Black and brown students. By centering institutionalized racism, such actions call not only for improved working conditions for teachers and paraprofessionals but also for more librarians, nurses, and counselors to meet the needs of their students (CReATE 2019). As such, allowing anti-racial social justice unions to forge alliances between teachers, students, parents, and communities (Ayers and Ayers 2020).

As members of the California Faculty Association (CFA), representing over twenty-nine thousand faculty members in the California State University system, we demanded similar changes at a university level (California Faculty Association 2018a). As a member-run union we called on each other to challenge and transform, rather than perpetuate, white dominant spaces, in which people of color are marginalized. In 2015 we passed a resolution by delegates to the 83rd CFA Assembly, announcing our commitment to Anti-Racism and Social Justice Transformation, as guided by ten core principles (California Faculty Association 2016). These guiding principles are:

1. We are a strong social justice organization, but we can be even stronger.
2. We intentionally center Anti-Racism as part of our mission.
3. We acknowledge that even WE in CFA are part of the problem of racism.
4. We acknowledge that WE can be part of the solution by being intentionally committed to addressing it.
5. We engage in courageous conversations about racism and discrimination, in order to transform our union.
6. We adopt changes in organizational values, policies, and practices consistent with principles of anti-racism and social justice.
7. We become a more inclusive Union by focusing on, adopting, and adapting the principles of anti-racism, social justice, and equity to our union and employment work.
8. We practice anti-racism and non-discrimination behavior with one another and others, including our students and colleagues, in order to become more socially just beings and to ensure a stronger and more inclusive union.
9. We ensure that this transformation is sustainable and the philosophy upon which it is based is continually offered to new and emerging leaders in our union and on our campuses.
10. Fairness and Justice should be faculty working conditions!

With racial justice at the center, our social justice unionism is about transforming the academy to justly represent people of color, women, and other oppressed groups. It intersects with what faculty care about (e.g., cultural taxation, exploitation of workload, institutionalized racism, existence of bias in student evaluations, alternatives to campus policing, parental/caregiving support, hostile work environments for faculty/women of color, counselor faculty to student ratio, pathways to tenure line for lecturer faculty), as well as providing an analysis of history, power, and systems that impact our working conditions and thus the learning conditions of students (California Faculty Association 2018a). Most importantly, it is coupled with confronting how white supremacy and racism is implicated in our daily practices, working conditions, and interactions with community, inside and outside of the institution (California Faculty Association 2018b). Such an analysis is weakened if we are not situating an anti-racist paradigm at the very core of what we do as a union. As Sharon Elise (2018: 1) argues, centering race is not about organizing for diversity because that "does not address structural problems that permeate how our educational systems operate, leading up to and through higher education," but rather, it predicates a deeper level of organizing for solidarity and the intentional interruption of racial inequities.

As such, our union has begun to strategically address what it means to center anti-racism in social justice practice. I would like to emphasize that this is work in which we are still actively engaged. One aspect started with our Collective Bargaining Agreement (CBA) and revisiting the composition of the bargaining team—transforming it from being predominantly a white space to a faculty team that reflects the student body, which is now 70 percent students of color. Another component of this work involved addressing how the CBA could be changed and built upon to integrate anti-racism principles, reduce bias, and address inequitable workload conditions (California Faculty Association 2018c). This includes improving on articles in the agreement dealing with non-discrimination, one important aspect of which has then, as Kevin Wehr explains, involved having "parts of the contract referenced back and forth to the article so that the appointment article that talks about how people come in, how they're hired how their contracts are written are linked back to non-discrimination" (California Faculty Association 2018c: 2). This, in its turn, broadens and deepens the categories of protection for workers, especially when working collectively to counter microaggressions against targeted communities. Another focus is on expanding upon the workload article in the agreement, with reassigned time, to address the cultural taxation that many faculty of color, female faculty, and LGBTQIA faculty experience in their efforts to meet the needs of our marginalized students, including being representatives on university/department/college committees (California Faculty Association 2018c: 3).

Part of this effort has also included revisiting the structures of our organization through processes of in-depth dialogue with union leadership and member activists concerning the impacts of institutionalized racism. As Charles Toombs explains (California Faculty Association 2018d: 2), CFA leaders across the state engaged in several rounds of three-day/eight-hour anti-racism training. This training facilitated the creation of an avenue for leaders and activist members to begin the process of actually looking at the issues of race in the United States and how they directly impacted our own organization. As a direct result, our mission statement and bylaws have been revised to make them inclusive. Doing so has functioned to embed greater opportunities for the more underrepresented members to take on leadership roles. In addition, we have developed training workshops aimed at addressing unconscious bias and interrupting racism, which members across our twenty-three campuses have attended. Moreover, because of these changes, we have been forthright in contextualizing our work within larger political concerns, such as the investment of our pensions in CoreCivic and GEO Group, two of the largest corporations in the private prison industry, as well as the operators of the largest migrant detention centers in the country; co-sponsoring bills, such as AB 21, to protect our undocumented faculty, staff, and students on our campus; helping write bills, such as AB 1460, requiring all CSU students to take Ethnic Studies as a required subject in order to graduate; addressing the cost and accessibility issues for students to enter the CSU, especially with respect to food and home insecurities; working with local sibling unions on rent stabilization to address affordability of living conditions for faculty, staff, and students; addressing safety issues for faculty of color, students of color, and targeted marginalized communities on campus—issues which are not new but heighted due to the national political climate.

Has there been pushback and resistance to this transformation, of course. The majority of such stems from white colleagues who have not made the connection between what has been traditionally considered "union work" (California Faculty Association 2018d) and anti-racism/social justice issues, both on campus and off. Our response to such resistance, as Charles Toombs explains (California Faculty Association 2018d: 2), has been to engage in dialogue and to educate members regarding the full scope of labor issues, which, while they have always been about equity and access, have not previously so fully addressed institutionalized racism and done so from within an explicitly anti-racism frame. Therefore, we are asking our members, in particular our white colleagues, to not remain complicit through support for a liberal, multicultural perspective but, instead, be willing to engage in these complex, difficult, but necessary, conversations—and to be willing to share power so that transformative action can be taken to uncover and address the power relations embedded in institutionalized and systemic structures of racism (California Faculty Association 2018d).

Last but not least, at the core of this work has to be relationship building. This cannot take place in isolation, away from other work and engagements, and requires an appropriate level of ongoing analysis and support such that faculty and teachers are retained as educators and as union activists and are sustained and nurtured at a political, personal, and spiritual level. Here, the relationships between the political, spiritual, and personal are overlapping and reinforcing—especially when centering a race analysis. Pour-Khorshid (2018: 319) foregrounds the need to retain teachers of color and the vital role of sustainable working conditions for doing so. She posits that institutionalizing support structures, at a micro level, assists in providing the necessary analysis and developing an intentional strategy in order to organize and build relationships for achieving transformational systemic change in a sustainable manner. She further explains how the use of "Testimonios" (322–6), a form of critical narratives, allows and encourages teachers to name, reflect on, and theorize about their own lived experiences while navigating through schooling's institutional structures. Consistently providing such opportunities fosters environments in which teachers of color can reclaim visibility after their lifelong struggle with invisibilizing oppressions. To successfully do so, teachers of color must not only build community but also be "critical comrades" for each other, affirming that this work cannot be done alone, for it embodies the whole person and its significance within a collective.

Final Thoughts

The movement of anti-racism social justice transformation is about active resistance, a protection of our spirit, and the ascension at an affective level of our political, personal, and spiritual being. To that end, our conversations cannot be about "reform," because ultimately that merely provides a band aid, with serious negative repercussions (Love 2019b). In the contexts in which we examine our realities, as Rios-Reyes (2020: 162) proposes, we have to challenge ourselves to "break out of and break up with power, and enter a third consciousness that's moves us differently within the world we are in." As such, our work has to transcend the conception of education as a human right and lay the foundations for transformational movement building both across education and beyond. I would argue that this has always been a crucial role that educators have played—to provide both the base and the leaders for mass change and revolution. In the context of the United States, until race and racism are centered in such struggles, the outcomes we want to obtain, around broader intersectionality issues of equity, will not reach fruition.

10

Empire, Class, and the Struggle for Value in English Educational Reform

Christy Kulz

Educational reforms have been promoted through policy and political discourse as a progressive development. Former minister of state for education Lord Adonis promised new academies in England would act as "engines of social mobility and social justice," while former British education secretary Michael Gove cast opponents of academization as "ideologues who are happy with failure," particularly the failure of poor and ethnic minority children (Adonis 2008; Harrison 2012). Yet, as neoliberal educational reforms unfold across countries, from North America to Africa to Europe, Howard Ryan highlights how the promises made seldom match the outcomes. We see a narrowing of knowledge and limits placed on critical thinking, as the focus rests on standardized learning and quantifiable outcomes. As Ryan points out, rather than these reforms being necessary to create highly skilled workers for a new economy, they serve to create docile workers willing to accept the precarities of a threadbare welfare state and unstable, exploitative employment conditions. One of the functions of standardized models is that they can be grafted onto any context, as Ryan's example of the Bridge Schools in Uganda highlights.

While there is, given such contexts, an urgent need for political action, progress will not, however, result from assigning either race or class primary causality or by way of developing a grand theory, which appear to be two of Ryan's aims. While I sympathize with his desire to arrive at a theory that would offer a clear route for action, universal certainty over causality is neither possible nor desirable. Standardized educational reforms hegemonically ignore the social and historical contexts to which they are applied. In a rebuttal of this homogenization, it is the role of the sociologist to highlight the importance of the particular through careful reflection on the empirical world, rather than recommending a grand theory with all its attendant universalizing effects (Mills 2000). Any grand theory regarding the hidden aims of school reform must also reflect on the role that raced and classed visions play across different situated localities. As Stuart Hall (qtd. in Virdee 2014: 4) pointed out, "There can be no general theory of racism, only historically specific racisms." This connects to the problem of attempting to understand how educational reforms relate to race and class through the utilization of one theory. A grand theory that tries to establish fundamental historical determinants is unable to respond to historical and contemporary complexities of difference and power (Aziz 1997).

Ryan seems determined to designate class, rather than race, as the primary driver of the hidden aims of educational reforms. I will question the usefulness of undertaking this task by using this chapter to trace the mutual formation of race and class through empire and capitalism, linking this to the historical specificities of the English educational landscape. By taking history, context, and the empirical into account, the sources of causality can be seen to meander across and through categorizations. This highlights how we need to develop a more nuanced way of understanding constantly shifting raced and classed formations, one that also unifies variegated struggles. Sivanandan (1985: 11–12) describes how the theoretical and political severing of race and class becomes a constrictive rupture that dismisses the relationship between racism and imperialism. This chapter will map how this long-term relationship filters into present-day narratives surrounding race and class, in order to show how the designation of primacy that Ryan seeks promotes an ahistorical understanding of these terms.

Recently, Rollock (2014: 449) has pointed out the impossibility of tidily separating race and class as Savage et al.'s (2013) British class survey attempted to do, with its accounts of the Black middle classes acting as "a stark and necessary reflection of the ways in which whiteness continues to be insidiously and silently enacted." The dissociation of racism from other forms of inequality and its portioning into individualized forms becomes "the coat of paint theory of racism" (Gilroy 1992: 52). The historical production of raced, classed, and gendered selves in relation to imperialist conquests and the development of capitalism makes the tidy separation of these categories not just a difficult, but also a detrimental present-day problem.

Finally, we cannot look solely to economics to understand how race and class are currently mobilized to promote neoliberal educational reforms; we must also examine the social and cultural politics of neoliberalism, as promoted since the 1980s. This chapter highlights the need to account for the social and cultural dimensions of class, beyond the economic, in order to understand the significance of these reforms in the English context. Race's deployment through Thatcherism and its neoliberal successors—often via class, or in the guise of culture—is not accorded sufficient attention by Ryan. Race and class have been reunited through the promotion of academies as an antidote to cultures of deprivation in England. From my own research, the prevalent use of the term "urban children" highlights this fusion and how it is negotiated. However, this reunion lacks a progressive or radical critique, instead installing a renewed pathologization that pits inequalities against one another. As Roediger (2017: 44) asserts, we do not need to decide "to organize or to analyze around either racism or class oppression, one to the exclusion of other." Through a situated engagement with English educational reform, I would like to show how we cannot afford to obliterate complexity from our thinking, even when trying to do the vital work of building coalitions across interests.

Historic Formation of Race and Class in the British Context

Understanding the *mutual* formation of race and class is key to present-day projects focused on the building of solidarity. Raced and classed struggles have become disarticulated from one another for a myriad of reasons during the post-war era in England, a division arguably aided by much of anti-racism's central concern being the removal of barriers to individual minority achievement and social mobility. Bonnett (1990) has argued that such anti-racism fits within the context of English liberal educationalism's unresolved ideological conflict between egalitarian impulses and capitalist orientations. We need to understand the conjunction, not delineation, of these interrelated classifications, while not losing sight of their differential effects in the present. Bonnett (1998: 317) describes how the British working class became white and cautions us against using the racial history of the settler colonialist United States as a template for other societies. American workers were "assertively white" generations before their British counterparts, while American white identity was rarely overtly class exclusive as was the case with white identity in Victorian Britain.

These particularities remain important today, and Ryan should be careful not to jump across contexts without acknowledging the specificity of these histories. Bonnett (1998: 318) shows how both metaphorical and literal depictions of racial whiteness, imported from British colonial and settler societies, were employed within Britain as a new paradigm of class hierarchy. Stoler (1995: 87) asserts that discourses of race preceded nineteenth-century social classifications, making race not a resultant function of bourgeois hierarchies but constitutive of those hierarchies. These processes were blurry, as categories were fashioned through the flow between Europe and the colonies, the city and the countryside, as a two-way traffic of materials, persons, and ideas fed one another in creating representations marked by power. From the vantage point of the colonies, all Britons were white, but within Britain whiteness was a contested notion, given that the British working class was frequently excluded from claiming it (Bonnett 1998). We can see this exclusion through a variety of texts written by the Victorian bourgeois regarding their working-class others.

Britain's colonies and urban slums were continually linked through works like social reformer William Booth's *In Darkest England and the Way Out*, whose title is derived from Henry Morton Stanley's *In Darkest Africa* (McClintock 1997: 121). In such texts, the working classes in Britain were frequently likened to natives in the colonies. Henry Mayhew, a middle-class bohemian, used ethnographic sensibilities to create rich narrative portraits of London costermongers, scavengers, and vagrants. In his 1861 preface to *London Labour and the London Poor*, Mayhew (1864) describes himself as a "traveller in the undiscovered country of the poor." The explorer's discovery of their other—both at home and abroad—became critical to the formation of bourgeois individuality. While Mayhew (1864: 118) hoped his text would raise awareness of the poor's plight, these concerns did not disturb his sense of middle-class belonging which he only "wandered out of . . . to regard the other forms of life with the same eyes as a comparative anatomist loves to lay bare the organism and vital machinery of a zoophyte, or an ape in the hope of linking together the lower and higher forms of animal existence." The working classes are simian forms, readily objectified, as race is mobilized to describe the apartness of the working classes.

From a more sympathetic angle, Engels (1892/2000: 99) described the working class as "a race wholly apart from the English bourgeoisie" due to poverty; however, poverty was frequently attributed to poor character rather than structural conditions. Dark spaces of poverty generated substantial middle-class anxiety; there was fear of uprisings both at home and abroad. The Victorian middle classes were fearful of entrenched poverty's effects on the laboring working class, and more specifically, the "residuum" of casual laborers who were deemed lazy and irredeemable (Stedman-Jones 1971). The social question of urban poverty and what to do about this "residuum" permeated political and social thought. The poor were a race apart, yet also dwelling within the modern metropolis and, like their colonial counterparts, might be civilized through corrective training administered by the bourgeoise.

Unstable Categories and Cultural Contamination

This confluence of race and class shows how fluidly these concepts moved across the seventeenth, eighteenth and nineteenth centuries. Stoler (1995) seeks to highlight the fragility, anxiety, and flux through which categories that can now seem self-evident were forged. She contests the positioning of race by many scholars as a "rhetorical political strategy" used to emphasize the enormous gap between bourgeois and working-class cultures; instead, asserting that race being interpreted simply as a metaphor, as in the work of such scholars, assumes that race and class occupied stable, discrete meanings and categories. This ignores how the meanings of these terms and concepts changed over the centuries (p. 109). Bonnett (1998: 318) highlights this categorical instability by charting how the British working class become white. Changes to capitalist socioeconomic organization prompted a shift in focus, "from whiteness as a bourgeois identity, connoting extraordinary qualities, to whiteness as a popularist identity connoting superiority but also ordinariness, nation and community." Virdee (2014: 5) highlights how this process ties to racialization and nationhood, as political reforms improving the economic security of the working classes, in the period spanning the 1850s to the 1940s, allowed the British elite to ideologically incorporate swathes of the working class as citizens into a nation imagined as racially and religiously homogeneous. Through the gains of the welfare state, British national identity is formed in opposition to a racialized other and "in that process, class as representational form and as a material relation was indelibly nationalized and racialized."

Anxieties over the instability of boundaries is brought into focus by the framing of the working-class woman as a conduit for racial pollution. English working-class women were depicted as promiscuous and fecund in comparison to their middle-class counterparts. In 1772, the planter and colonial administer Edward Long commented that such women were "remarkably fond of the blacks . . . By these ladies they generally have a numerous brood" (qtd. in Hall 2020). He worries that over time this blood "contamination" could reach the highest echelons of English society until not only their skin color but also their mental faculties were degraded. Such concerns with blood and nation are foregrounded in MP Enoch Powell's now infamous "rivers of blood" speech, nearly two hundred years later, in 1968. Powell related how watching immigration to England was "like watching a nation busily engaged in heaping up its own funeral pyre," relating how one of his constituents, a "decent, ordinary fellow Englishman," feared the Black man would "have the whip hand over the white man" in fifteen or twenty years. Here the "ordinary" Englishman is naturalized as white.

While Ryan describes Thatcherism as a ruling-class initiative, it was also a regime promoting a particular racialized version of Englishness. Thatcherite politics skillfully mobilized this "ordinary" white Englishman in opposition to a racialized other. Stuart Hall describes how Thatcherism's popularity was tied to its "defense of 'Englishness'" or "of the British feeling 'Great Again'" where cultural racism acted as "one of its most powerful, enduring, effective—and least remarked—sources of strength" (2005: 235). Thatcher's reforms, and the many emanating from both Conservative and Labour parties in the years that followed, were not simply economic but accompanied by a nationalist cultural constellation that celebrated the white Englishman's stoic, robust and respectable qualities in opposition to derided "folk devils" like the Black "mugger," culturally antagonistic migrants and militant trade unionists who threatened the fabric of English propriety (Hall et al. 1978). As Valluvan and Kalra (2019: 2403) remind us, this cultural discourse highlights that Thatcherism should not be "misunderstood as an abstracted exultation of 'homo economicus', lacking in any broader cultural figuration." Thatcherism promoted a form of British nationalism firmly tied to race; Powell's "ordinary decent Englishman" was its hero. We can see the endurance of this feeling "great again" sentiment through the rhetoric of contemporary Brexiteers.

It is also important to mention the Muslim "folk devils" more recently generated through Britain's "war on terror," as older tropes are combined with current anxieties regarding radical Islam (Meer 2014). We can see the intertwined, mutable deployment of race and culture through the heightened surveillance of Muslim students through the implementation of the controversial Prevent program in schools—intended to stop violent extremism but virulently critiqued for its focus on and criminalization of Muslim populations (Kundnani 2009). Since 2015, schools became legally required to curtail extremism through monitoring students for signs of radicalization while promoting the dissemination of "British values"; this policy has resulted in critiques regarding how Prevent can be practically implemented in schools, who it is aimed at protecting and how (see Busher, Choudhury, and Thomas 2019; Davies 2016; Durodie 2016; Winter et al. 2021). Yet this form of racism is often siphoned off into the non-racialized label of Islamophobia, although, as Meer (2013) asserts, it is not separate from racism in its reliance on a dangerous, sexualized masculinity, much like that of the criminal Black folk devil. Race and culture are invoked in order to influence perceptions as to who and who is not a "potential terrorist," as new folk devils come to overlay and augment older versions (Kulz 2018).

Anxiety over racial denigration through class also came to the fore in the wake of widespread civil unrest across British cities in 2011. Tyler (2008: 18) describes how the "dirty white" working classes are held up as central to this denigration, whereby "chav" is a recently developed and derogatory term displaying disgust for white working-class subjects. However, "chav" can also expand to include non-white working-class bodies.

Historian David Starkey described, on BBC Newsnight in 2011, how he believed this poisonous raced and classed mixture was a cause of the rioting:

> A substantial section of the chavs have become black. The whites have become black. A particular sort of violent, destructive, nihilistic gangster culture has become the fashion. Black and white, boy and girl operate in this language together. This language which is wholly false, which is a Jamaican Patois, that's been intruded in England. (qtd. in Quinn 2011)

Starkey posits that through contamination with a racialized other, white working-class people have taken up a pathological Blackness (Quinn 2011). These sentiments recall Long's fears of biological pollution, yet Starkey's contamination fears are also cultural. The nineteenth-century "urban residuum" becomes fused with citizen-migrants from former colonies and is then branded a toxic invasion. Starkey's accusation reflects twentieth-century movements in terminology which have replaced race with culture; Kahn questions the progress it is claimed is signified by these changes by pointing out the continual slippage between race-culture distinctions and the biologizing of cultural differences evident in commentaries such as Starkey's (Kahn 2001: 53). Here, white people can be blackened and devalued through cultural and social proximity; the working classes' security as respectably white is thrown into question as the welfare state is downsized. Haylett (2001: 364) describes the question mark that is established over the quality of the white poor's whiteness, adding that in this "modern multicultural [conditionally 'inclusive society'] there is no legitimate space for class-based discourses; its impulse is for class to be remade as an ethno-difference." Here, we can see the relationship between race and class continuing to shift in the wake of the English welfare state's degradation. The individualization of poverty and cultural racism, as promoted by Thatcher, has continued in a different register through New Labour and subsequent governments, providing an ongoing key rationale for the advent of neoliberal educational structures.

Neoliberalism and Edu-profit as Natural Allies

The fusing of belief, desire, and imagination to market values through neoliberal ideology makes these reforms persuasive, as they work directly on human subjectivity. Ryan differentiates "edu-profit" from "neoliberal ideology" as motivators behind educational reforms, yet separating such theses overlooks the deep interrelation of neoliberalism and profit. Through neoliberalism, the marketplace becomes a way of organizing all social relations, as we are transformed from Kantian individuals into individual units of competing human capitals (Brown 2015). Dean (2009: 49) describes how the presentation of neoliberalism's project as inevitable, as per Thatcher's infamous dictum "there is no alternative," becomes a means of ideologically creating a belief in the necessity and desirability of markets. Market logic becomes penetrative as a value system, which relates to how it can be and is mobilized in support of and through educational reforms. Thatcher's own biographic folk tale was crucial in "legitimating" her political aims as beneficial for ordinary Britons: a petit bourgeois shopkeeper daughter's triumph through hard graft and determination. Neoliberalism's notion of a natural, external economy has financialized "the very scaffolding of our political imaginations," restructuring our very imaginings of how we can live or what we can politically aspire to (Massey 2011: 31).

Rather than the majority of Britons regarding themselves as victims of a politics benefiting the powerful, many were convinced that these educational reforms were necessary or even positive. An emphasis on pride through self-reliance broke down class allegiances while also promoting racial superiority and nationalism. We can see this in the defense of the tripartite system of schooling in England, whereby grammar schools that selected students by exam at the age of eleven were promoted as a ladder to success for clever working-class students, while ignoring the wider damage these processes of selection inflicted, primarily on working class and ethnic minority children. The right's success can be gauged by the extent to which neoliberalism continued under New Labour. Labor came to adopt, augment, and further promote many Conservative initiatives—in particular academies, which were modeled on Thatcher's City Technology Colleges.

It is important to interrogate the "corporate assault on schools" not as something working entirely through a top-down imposition that is passively accepted but something managed by relevant social actors. Audit practices and performativity regimes are embraced, resisted, and negotiated through daily practice; Ball (2002: 217) documents how British teacher subjectivities are shaped as they struggle against these regimes where values are reduced to value. Practices of the everyday have a lot to add to this discussion, as they can illustrate how school reforms are lived in and through social relations and pre-existing historical hierarchies.

Educational Panacea for the Problems of Culture

This section emphasizes the importance of attending to specific contexts when writing about race, class, and education, through a brief exploration of English education's particularities. State-organized education in Britain has frequently monitored populations while also cementing social and racial hierarchies. Nineteenth-century panics regarding working-class degeneration shaped the formation of compulsory schooling. Rather than a straightforward Enlightenment innovation, schooling provided an opportunity to shape and monitor children, with schools functioning as "centres of observation disseminated throughout society" where parenting practices could be supervised (Foucault 1977: 212). Education was viewed as a key means of forming good character in workers, as well as providing a stabilizing force to counteract morally deficient families (Carey 1992). The teaching of morals was included in the syllabus for mass elementary education and "there were similar intentions behind sending missionaries out to moralize to the colonized and teaching the working class to be well behaved and moral" (Tomlinson 2019: 28). This continued moral proselytizing is evident in today's character education initiatives, instructing poor students to resiliently "bounce back" from failure; it is character flaws, not inequality and oppression, holding them back (Bull and Allen 2018; Morrin 2018).

Tomlinson highlights how, meanwhile, in public schools (private, fee-paying schools in US terminology), upper-class boys were groomed to run the British empire. Public schools exhibited and (re)produced the social and political values of the English upper classes (and continue to do so), and these values shaped mass education (and continue to do so). English elites in the nineteenth and twentieth centuries "treated the overseas and internally colonized, and the English working classes, with the same arrogance and contempt" (2019: 58). The public school builds and reinforces students' belief in their own superiority through their privileged white culture, which justifies their reigning above white British subjects at home and racialized natives abroad. While there was pressure prior to the 1944 Education Act to abolish public (i.e., private) schooling, a compromise was reached by offering scholarships to such schools, for some of those whose families could not afford the fees. Rab Butler, Conservative politician and architect of the legislation, expressed his happiness about the fact that the issue could be managed with the "first class carriage" removed from public view (CCC 1981: 59).

In 2020, the "first class carriage" continues to convey elite students to spaces of power, with public schools remaining a preserve of the predominantly white and wealthy. Sixty-five percent of Prime Minister Boris Johnson's cabinet in 2020 attended fee-paying schools, compared with 7 percent of the general population. The UK continues to be governed in large part by an elite who have been trained in spaces of whiteness, as public schools remain often inhospitable spaces for the small minority of students of color who can access them. A recent letter to the Independent Schools Council, which oversees public schools in the UK, signed by 180 former ethnic minority students at elite public schools, documented endemic racist bullying and abuse (Lough 2020). Some have compared the supposed character building that takes place at elite boarding schools to the tough love approach of academies, but this is to grossly ignore the power differentials of the pupils in these respective schools, what they are being trained for and how they are being taught to understand themselves, others, and the world around them.

While the move toward a non-selective comprehensive school system by the Labour Party in 1965 was a step toward a more egalitarian structure, Thatcherite reforms in the 1980s undermined this and altered direction. The Education Reform Act of 1988 signaled the enthusiastic embrace of a quasi-market and introduced City Technology Colleges, the aforementioned template for academies, and themselves inspired by Reagan's charter schools. Ryan describes how notions of educational mediocrity and falling standards tied to the needs of the national economy have been mobilized as a reason for reform in the United States. This rationale requires expansion in the case of England, where mediocrity was also tied to alleged falling standards, supposedly fostered by alternative pedagogies or anti-racist education. In the late 1960s and 1970s, the New Right generated moral panics by framing comprehensive schooling as harmful to intelligent working-class children (Cox and Dyson 1969: 20). Progressive forms of teaching, pedagogy and curriculum were branded as "loony left" by the right-wing press in the 1980s. Left-wing councils were publicly ridiculed as bastions of extremist policies by Conservative politicians and the popular press. Numerous fictitious tales targeted white anxiety, for the purpose of deriding anti-racist education, positioning such education as a key cause of British cultural decline (Gordon 1990). In a similar vein, Ryan shows us how a London local authority's tentative steps to address racial inequality were dismantled as consequences of the actions of a right-wing tabloid press that aligned these moves with left-wing socialist indoctrination. This example also shows how left-wing politics and anti-racism were cohered by the English right and portrayed by them as damaging to white working-class interests.

Ball and Solomos (1990: 12) posit that the political climate of this period tended to frame anti-racists, rather than racist attitudes, as the core problem. The Black papers,[1] an influential series of polemic pamphlets critiquing the comprehensive system through "common-sense" home truths, claimed to speak the fears of a "silent majority" of "ordinary" parents. Here, we have another appeal to the "ordinary" English citizen, understood as white and working class, in opposition to the racialized outsider and unrespectable working classes (Skeggs 1997). The rationale for closer control and centralization with respect to the school sector comes not only from the idea of mediocrity but also from a mediocrity tied to addressing issues like racism or gender equality. The turn to academization offered a technocratic solution to difficult struggles in urban areas, whereby concerns around race and social inequality could be subsumed beneath the rhetoric of social mobility and individual aspiration.

The advent of academies under Prime Minister Tony Blair's New Labour government in 2004 and the rapid extension and revamping of this policy by the Conservatives placed school education further outside of democratic structures and fostered a franchise model, where education chains or Multi-Academy Trusts work as small businesses. Underpinning this model was the idea that academies would "break the cycle of underachievement in areas of social and economic deprivation" by "establishing a culture of ambition to replace the poverty of aspiration" (DCFS 2009; Adonis 2008). Once again, context is important, as a key area where comparisons between England and the United States fall short concerns the capacity to separate actors into neat categories of drivers and implementers of legislative and policy reform as Ryan desires. While this might work in the US context, it cannot so clearly be delineated in England. Ryan seems moderately dismissive of Ball's writing about fragmented networks in England, yet his text is incredibly useful in mapping fragmented, complex, and often oblique relationships between government, academies and the private sector (see Ball 2007; Ball and Junemann 2012). Ryan's attempt to create order in this context is too simplistic, as there is collaboration in England between the drivers and implementers, as well as significant traffic between the public and private sectors. Venture capitalist Lord Nash worked as Parliamentary Under-Secretary of State for the School System, while also founding Future Academy chain and serving as their chair of the board; such conflicts of interest are rife, and similar entanglements many.

Being a Subject of Value: Class, Race, and Culture in Twenty-First-Century Britain

I will now offer a couple of empirical examples from my study of Dreamfields Academy, a celebrated flagship secondary school in an urban area of England, to illustrate the continuing mutual formation of categorizations. These complexities highlight the futility of attempting to find a singular line of causality motivating educational reforms. My study took place between 2009 and 2011 and involved ethnographic research and interviews with over sixty-five parents, students and teachers (Kulz 2017). Rather than referencing occupational stratification models of class, I position class as a site of conflict and struggle—retaining Marxism's concern with capitalism, history, and exploitation. Yet culture and value are also paramount to how classifications are made and how subjectivities are formed, making a Bourdieusian approach helpful, as it broadens the concept of class beyond the relations of production.

Feminist researchers have used Bourdieu to interrogate how value is attributed and to map the affective dimensions of class struggle. Cultural and symbolic mechanisms make social class "real"; class is not marked or achieved through economics alone but through diverse cultural practices marking the subject (Lawler 1999). To be a subject of value is to possess the capacity to act as the arbiter of judgment; it centrally concerns who can claim respectability (Skeggs 1997). Reay and her colleagues (2007: 1042) bring this capacity to value into conversation with race:

> to embody both whiteness and middle classness is to be a person of value. It is also to be a person who makes value judgments that carry symbolic power; a value of others. And despite the rhetorical flourishes around difference and diversity, it is sameness that routinely gets valued.

This mode of conceptualizing class addresses Ryan's frustration that the economic division of society into the 99 percent of workers and 1 percent of owners does not generate working-class awareness among and by groups like teachers. While factually correct in economic terms, this viewpoint misses the more affective and cultural dimensions of class. Focusing on the economic alone does not give a sufficiently nuanced understanding of how class hierarchies are formed in the UK.

Culture is mobilized by Dreamfields' principal Mr. Culford to justify the school's authoritarian discipline; the "structure liberates" ethos claims to free working-class students from unstructured and unhappy backgrounds to lead happier, more productive lives. We can see the cultural significance of class in the term "urban children," used at Dreamfields to describe a predominantly working-class and ethnic minority cohort. This problematic urban child is tied to a city space regarded as regressive; they are today's "urban residuum" who lack value and require modernization through education. Culford describes these children as coming from unstructured, unhappy backgrounds, in contrast to middle-class children from "leafy suburbs" who are assumed to come from more structured and thus happier homes with books. Culford's academy purports to step in as a "surrogate parent" in order to overcome detrimental parenting practices, with Dreamfields providing rigid structure, rituals, and routines that are described as absent from the working-class home. Culford states that class is the issue because: "A child going home to a home which doesn't value education, doesn't support their child, where there are no books, where there is no experience of higher education ... that's the bigger problem."

Culford uses the language of class to justify his disciplinarian approach, yet behind this language lies an implicit reference to race through the use of "urban" and by way of referencing Dreamfields' majority ethnic minority student body. The racialized urban is often conceptualized and spoken through the register of class. Middle-class labeling generally infers whiteness, while speaking race through class appears to be more acceptable in the wake of the resurgence of language like "chavs." Blaming the pathological home for poverty's effects is not confined to being an accusation leveled at the white working class, as a long legacy of the stigmatized Black family is folded into this discourse and can be observed through the practices of Dreamfields (see Gilroy 2002; Lawrence 1982; Phoenix 1991; Reynolds 2005). Aspirational individualism is meant to overcome this cultural deficit; possessive selfhood presents the individual as able to stand outside of themselves, legitimating their interests and establishing their authority by defining themselves against the "mass" (Skeggs 2004: 7). Only certain forms of culture that bear the hallmarks of whiteness and middle classness carry the right sort of capitals and will be recognized as legitimate by educational institutions (Yosso 2005).

The adoption of modes of comportment regarded as white and middle-class also possessed the power to whiten students at Dreamfields. Mixed-race, high-achieving student Olivia described how she had "ended up becoming more white" through her time at Dreamfields; to be an "ideal student" required her to orientate herself away from Black and working-class pupils and culture and orientate herself toward more white and middle-class modes of being. The racialized urban becomes whitened through the application of middle classness (see Reay et al. 2007). Black British Nigerian and high-achieving student Joshua describes how he has actively adopted controlled, compact, concise modes of behavior, or what he calls "the three C's" displayed by a white middle-class student group. This mode of comportment attracts less attention and monitoring, allowing Joshua to escape some of the discipline most frequently directed at students of color. Through becoming exemplary multicultural subjects within Dreamfields, whiteness can be detached from the white body and worn by Black students like Joshua (Nayak 2006). The threat of Black criminality is temporarily undone by the application of middle-class whiteness, and this needs to be middle-class whiteness, as working-class whiteness has negligible value as a racialized form of whiteness (Tyler 2008). Working-class whiteness is frequently regarded as a block to modernity's progress in contrast to the ethnic minority student who can at least proffer valuable culture (Haylett 2001). Yet, this culture must not be too divergent but neutered by middle-class respectability. We can see the complex ways that value is being marked out through complex deployments of race and class that makes their separation difficult.

Conclusion: Routes through Race and Class

This chapter has emphasized the importance of history, context, and the empirical when exploring the aims of neoliberal educational reforms. I approached this analysis through an exploration of the ways in which fragile raced and classed categorizations were initially formed through empire and continue to shift today. Through historian David Starkey's diatribe about chavs turning Black and principal Culford's "urban children" in need of transformation, we can see powerful actors fashioning labels and causalities that go in, around, and through both race and class. Yet these are not liberatory constructions that interrogate the long-term relationship of capitalism with empire, and (neo)colonialism, but obfuscatory and damaging confections that pit people against one another in a bid to retain or gain value and respectability. Virdee (2017a: 11) comments, "I want to suggest that we have to go through race, not around it, if we are to forge a sustainable solidarity between the ethnically diverse proletariat in the imperialist core, as well as with those beyond." This is a recommendation we as researchers, and/or educationalists, and/or activists must take seriously in order to counteract the opportunistic, divisive, and ahistorical ways that race and class are deployed by those in power and mobilized in relation to academization in the UK and beyond.

While Ryan's desire to come to a grand theory regarding education reform that would give us a clear cue for future action is understandable, universal certainty over causality is neither possible nor desirable. A singular theory is incapable of explaining everyday practices across a variety of contexts; some theories have a lot of explanatory power at one juncture but little purchase at another. Gane (2011) explores the importance of both the historical and contemporary contexts of knowledge production through the work of C. Wright Mills (2000) and his seminal text *The Sociological Imagination*. Gane (2011: 161) summates Mills's rejection of universalizing grand theory:

> [T]he key to the development of an imaginative yet systematic and effective sociology lies in our ability to control the level of abstraction at which we work. This means that there can be no universal scheme or system through which problems arising in the empirical world can be understood, for what is needed instead is a "variety of . . . working models" . . . as well as a detailed understanding of the historical contexts and complexities of the phenomena under study.

This assertion takes us back to the importance of complexity when approaching the social world. Like Mills, we should place the empirical problems of these educational reforms before our choices as to methods and theories. We need to understand everyday practices and gauge how such understandings connect with or reshape our theory, rather than cramming the empirical into a preordained schema. We do not need to believe in grand theory to embrace systemic change or have a vision of a just world; transformational systemic change will look different in different places. The task is to hold onto complicated histories, while discerning how diverse alliances can be built in the present. This task is not easy, but we can catch historical glimpses of such radically oriented engagements in the socialist internationalism of the nineteenth century, whereby the struggle of the colonized in Africa was recognized as part of the struggle of working classes in Britain (see Virdee 2017a). Such histories could serve to suggest fruitful future routes of travel while also providing a source of hope.

Note

1 See Cox and Dyson (1969) for a good example of these pamphlets and their contents.

11

The Wall of Whiteness and White Supremacy Persists

A Critical Race Response

Cleveland Hayes II

In this chapter, I turn to important tenets of critical race theory (CRT) to respond to Howard Ryan's feature chapter, as well as contribute to the continued conversation about race in the United States. Love (2004: 228) argues, "CRT is a race-based form of oppositional scholarship developed in the late 1980s because of the perceived failure of traditional civil rights litigation to produce racial reform that could change the subordinated status of people of color in U.S. society." Solórzano and Yosso (2001: 471–2) define CRT as "an attempt to understand the oppressive aspects of society in order to generate societal and individual transformation are [*it is*] important for educators to understand that CRT is different from any other theoretical framework because it centers race." Solórzano and Yosso (2001: 471–2; citing Tierney 1993: 4) define CRT as "an attempt to understand the oppressive aspects of society in order to generate societal and individual transformation." As the timeline in my contextualized discussion below shows, while race may not be the only factor, it is never not a factor. I also hope readers will read this chapter in twenty years and recall that in 2020 and in the middle of a global pandemic in the United States, whiteness and white supremacy received 72 million votes, in the guise of support for Donald Trump's unsuccessful re-election to the presidency.

The Context

In 2008, the United States did something that many did not believe was possible, by electing a Black man as president. As a result of that historic election, there was the release of white rage in various forms (Metzl 2020)—from an increase in the number and size of white supremacist groups to the Senate majority leader and other Republicans meeting the night of the inauguration with the intent of making Barack Obama a one-term president. These actions have nothing to do with class. Or, to the extent that they might do so, perhaps only in the sense that the rich white men involved wanted to remain powerful. Then in 2012, the United States did it again: a Black man was sent back to the White House for a second term. The result of this election, as with the previous one, was the release of white rage. In its wake, the birther movement emerged, with many people in the United States claiming that President Obama was not in office legitimately—claiming, falsely, that he was not a natural-born citizen of the United States and thus had not been eligible to stand as a presidential candidate (Serwer 2020). Many of the people making this claim, along with many others who claimed that their disagreement was with Obama's economic policies (an issue I will return to later in this chapter), would never consider themselves racist.

In 2016, the United States elected Trump, a reality television star, to the presidency, which I argue was a consequence of the white rage following the 2008 and 2012 elections. More disturbing still, the election of Trump seemed to prove that a record of perpetual failure can lead to winning elections. The man bankrupted six companies (Murse 2020), yet succeeded on the biggest of electoral stages. He is indeed the champion of failures. The rise of fascism, illustrated by the Trump presidential win (Giroux 2018), seemed to signal both that white masculinity was in crisis and that there existed a range of economic problems that only powerful Trumpian emotional appeals, which played to and exacerbated feelings of aggrieved white entitlement, could resolve. It is not so much that ultra-conservative whites believed that one economic system has failed them and that they needed to vote for another. Rather, it seemed from their response that sustained unemployment or underemployment, endemic in precisely the parts of the country that won Trump the election, was perceived as humiliating and emasculating to many of his constituency—many who are poor conservative whites who feel they "don't have any say about what the government does" (Thompson 2016).

The considerable national disconnection from party politics must also be highlighted here. Less than one quarter of the US population actually voted for Trump. Moreover, as the historical economic injustices of US society were seemingly obscured by Trump's tweets —designed to create impulsive and emotional, rather than considered and rational, reactions among his voter base—low voter turnout created conditions whereby disillusioned white men and women could decide the result of a presidential election campaign (Anderson 2016; Blaisdell 2020; DiAngelo 2018; Graff 2018). Also of concern here is that many poor white people in this country chose white over their own and their families' well-being, by continuing to support a president who was clearly more concerned with his stock portfolio than the number of poor white people suffering, standing in food lines for hours, in places like Texas (Blaisdell 2020; Metzl 2020). Despite their dire economic circumstances, which were only exacerbated by Trump's actual policies, they supported his racist tirades. When many poor white folks had the choice to do what was right, they chose white. Given this, the rich white elite in this country knows that playing white supremacy cards is a winning hand, regardless of the economic status of the poor whites they seek the vote from—in that, for whatever reason, poor white people seem to believe they will be rewarded by the wealthy elite for upholding white supremacy.

In March 2020, the United States was crippled by a global pandemic. The president was incapable of leading the country in ways that could have potentially mitigated the near eight hundred thousand Covid-19 deaths over the following two years (Centers for Disease Control and Prevention n.d.). Then, in May 2020, the United States witnessed the killing of George Floyd, when a white police officer knelt on his neck for nine minutes as Floyd pleaded for his life. As I sat watching Floyd's life slip away on the television screen I broke down, knowing that could have easily been me. I still worry about my safety, even when I am at home, because we are aware of countless instances of Black men and women killed at the hands of police regardless as to whether they were on the street or in their homes. Breonna Taylor comes to mind—and please let us remember to say her name. Following her death, instead of issuing a message of compassion and unity, President Trump went on television and pandered to white supremacist groups in this country. In response to the news that no police officer would be indicted for Breonna Taylor's death, Trump said he was praying for the two police officers shot in Louisville (Jarvis 2020). In a similar fashion, when it was revealed that a group of white supremacists intended to kidnap—and, it is suspected, murder—Michigan governor Gretchen Whitmer, Trump refused to condemn their kidnapping plot (Wise 2020). We have witnessed powerful "conservative" white men, including Ron DeSantis, the governor of Florida; Tucker Carlson, a commentator on Fox News; and Jim Jordan, a member of the House from Ohio, publicly rallying around white supremacist groups, without offering any critique of them or their actions (Holt 2021). And, even more disconcerting, it is very likely that if President Trump had not so woefully mishandled the pandemic, he would have won re-election for a second term (Parker et al. 2020).

We also cannot ignore that most of the violence during protests that erupted across the United States, in the wake of Floyd's death in 2020, was carried out by white nationalist groups. There is clear evidence that shows that white supremacist groups burned down the police station in Minneapolis, in order to make it appear that the Black Lives Matter movement was responsible for the violence and destruction (Helsel 2021). Once this kind of distorted and fallacious narrative about the Black Lives Movement went mainstream, such accusations stuck. In fact, during the presidential debates, Trump actually told the Proud Boys, a far-right group that endorses violence, to "stand by" (Frenkel and Karni 2020), priming such groups to be ready to commit further violent atrocities. The point here is that many of these groups on the far right are predominantly poor and white. This country has a long history of the white, wealthy elite using poor white people to do their "dirty" work. This is well illustrated by the 1920s massacres of Black people in Tulsa, Oklahoma (Tulsa Historical Society and Museum 2021), and Rosewood, Florida (Glenza 2016)—two vibrant Black communities that were seen as a threat to the dominant order of whiteness and white supremacy in those regions.

The Grip of Whiteness

Through centering the experiential knowledge of subordinated people of color (Delgado 1995), CRT explores the question of white racial domination and domestic terrorism in a forthright manner. Based on commitments to societal transformation,

CRT attempts to foster circumstances within education that eliminate the likelihood that students' race will predict either positive or negative schooling and life outcomes. For CRT scholars such as Cheryl Harris (1993), this begins by acknowledging that no matter where on the traditional political spectrum of left to right people fall, whiteness has a grip on white people that is hard to break. In her seminal article, "Whiteness as Property," Harris (1993: 1713) argues:

> In ways so embedded that it is rarely apparent, the set of assumptions, privileges, and benefits that accompany the status of being white have become a valuable asset that whites sought to protect and that those who passed sought to attain—by fraud if necessary. Whites have come to expect and rely on these benefits, and over time these expectations have been affirmed, legitimated, and protected by law.

The White Racial Frame

The concept of the *white racial frame* (Feagin 2010; Picca and Feagin 2007) explains how individuals of goodwill may often support and affirm racist oppression, despite their anti-racist intentions. Specifically, the white racial frame enables us to highlight and examine the race-based assumptions individuals use to interpret matters concerning racial equality in the world around them. Transmitted from generation to generation, over what is now four centuries, the white racial frame refers to "an organized set of racialized ideas, stereotypes, emotions, and inclinations to discriminate" (Feagin 2006: 25). Five racializing dimensions constitute the white racial frame: (1) assumptions about the overall superiority of whites with respect to culture, achievements, and morality in general, as justifications for white control and dominance of institutions; (2) negative stereotypes related to people of color; (3) emotions that are racialized through their association with racial assumptions or supposed knowledge about people of color, in the form of negative stereotypes; (4) recurring individual, and group enactments and performances of racialized knowledge; and (5) the larger institutional structures in which racialized performances are enacted (Feagin 2006; Picca and Feagin 2007).

Pointedly, the white racial frame is more than a deeply embedded cognitive tool historically used by whites and still in operation today (Picca and Feagin 2007; Feagin 2010); rather, it is a collectively shared perspective that influences how whites, both as individuals and groups, think about and interact with people of color (Feagin 2010; Gillborn 2005; Leonardo 2009). Very importantly, the white racial frame serves as a guide and, therefore, does not determine how whites (or anyone else using the assumptions of whiteness), either individually or collectively, will act and interact with people of color. Accordingly, white people can, and sometimes if not often do, choose to draw on and apply racial knowledge that does not privilege whiteness (Aptheker 1993; Ignatiev and Garvey 1996).

Moreover, not all five dimensions of the white racial frame are evident or implicated in every interaction or speech act that involves whiteness. Here, the focus is on why we can't get to a conversation concerning class until we deal with the social construction of race and the assumptions of white superiority and Black inferiority, given the normalizing function of such race-based knowledge and its ties to individuals' and groups' actions and decision-making processes—for example, poor white people voting against universal health care because they are convinced that it is going to help undocumented Latinos and penalize hard-working white folk—that can be interpreted as a "dying of whiteness" (Metzl 2020). As we learn more about the functions and consequences of white racial knowledge in structuring the distribution of resources and social safety nets, specifically as including education, we may become better equipped to interrupt the processes of race-based dominance which continue to produce inequalities in our society (Dixon and Rousseau 2006; Ladson-Billings and Tate 1995).

The White Problem

Historically, this country has relied on violence to maintain white supremacy. The violence has come in many forms, including the genocide and removal of Indigenous populations, the enslavement and chattel slavery of Africans and African Americans, the conquest of Mexican lands in what is now the Southwest of the United States, Chinese exclusion acts, and Japanese internment camps (Gaskin 2006). Not to be forgotten among this gruesome list is the lynching of Blacks that was carried out as a terrorist form of social control, for one hundred years, during the Jim Crow era of racial apartheid in the United States.

What is white racial knowledge, then, and how does it connect teachers' (and others') racial understandings with the disjuncture between ideals of equality and the patterned realities of racialized inequalities within schooling and across wider society? The answer is best illustrated by the example of *the white problem* (Bennett 1972; Du Bois [1940] 1968; Wright 1957), a concept derived from the Black radical tradition (Dawson 1994; Olson 2004). In response to a reporter's question about race relations in the United States, Richard Wright in 1946 explained: "There isn't any Negro problem; there is only a white problem" (cited in Kinnamon and Fabre 1993: 99). By redefining US society's race *problem* as white instead of Black, "Wright called attention to its hidden assumptions—that racial polarization comes from the existence of blacks rather than the behavior of whites, that black people are a 'problem' for whites rather than fellow citizens entitled to justice, and that, unless otherwise specified, 'American' means 'white'" (Lipsitz 2006: 1).

The racial assumptions identified by Wright are significant because they represent what, at the time of his writings in the 1940s and 1950s, were conventional ideas, beliefs, and understandings or knowledge about race and equality, collectively shared by and drawn on by whites as a group (Feagin 2010; Foner 1988; Frederickson 1997). Both individually and collectively, whites used their racial knowledge—that is to say, their underlying ideas, beliefs, and assumptions about Black people—to interpret, make sense of and justify everyday matters regarding race and (in)equality. Thus, we have white privilege in the form of social, economic, and political opportunities and Black disempowerment in the form of social, economic, and political disadvantages, within a nation supposedly founded on principles of equality (Jacobson 1998; Juarez,

Hayes, and Smith 2016; Roediger 2007). In fact, as Bennett (1972: 1) notes: "It was a stroke of genius really for white Americans to give Negro Americans the name of their problem, thereby focusing attention on symptoms (the Negro and the Negro community) instead of causes (the white man and the white community)."

White racial knowledge, therefore, refers to a concrete set of race-based understandings of ideas, beliefs, and assumptions as noted above, which whites historically created, reinforced, and continue to draw on today to sustain and perpetuate white supremacy—"a racialized social system that upholds, reifies, and reinforces the superiority of Whites" (Leonardo 2009: 127). Adapting itself to shifting historical conditions, white racial knowledge functions as a hidden referent that privileges the interests, values, experiences, and beliefs of whites and the presumed superiority of whiteness (Coates 2008; Yancy 2004). By privileging characteristics associated with understanding whites as normal, and thus conceiving of being white as the state of being human, white racial knowledge is a way of knowing and being in the world that provides whites with an identity and a corresponding sense of earned privilege and therefore rightful belonging, entitlement, and superiority (Bhaba 1989; Omi and Winant 1994; Yancy 2004).

Evaluated against the criteria of such white racial knowledge, centered on understandings of being white as being normal and authentically human, people of color are then racially perceived as interlopers and the denigrated others who do not belong (Bhaba 1989; Lipsitz 2006). Whites, by contrast, are positioned by white racial knowledge as naturally in control of society's institutions and resources (Feagin 2010; Headley 2004). "To be an 'All-American' means, by definition, *not* to be an Asian American, Pacific-American, American Indian, Latino, Arab-American or African-American" (Marable 1993: 113, emphasis in original). As the dominant group in control of societal institutions that generate and police cultural meanings, whites have historically used this position of dominance and the knowledge it generates to justify their dominance and to impose their perspectives on society as being *the* legitimate viewpoint, *the* right way to understand what is truth or knowledge and what defines being human (Darder 1991; Feagin 2006; Morgan 1975; Wise 2005).

Accordingly, white racial knowledge is at the center of processes of race-based domination. According to Leonardo (2009: 75), processes of white racial domination are defined as "those acts, decisions, and policies that white subjects perpetrate on people of color." Thus, white racial domination does not happen behind the backs of white people or through arbitrary acts of race hate committed by individuals (Coates 2008; hooks 1989; Leonardo 2009). As a group and individually, whites make decisions daily about and take "resources from people of color all over the world, appropriate their labor, and construct policies that deny minorities' full participation in society" (Leonardo 2009: 76). Drawing on white racial knowledge, regardless of intent, whites actively recreate and secure supremacy in almost all facets of social life through processes of racial domination (Bonilla-Silva et al. 2003; Gillborn 2005; Leonardo 2009; Mills 1997).

Racial domination is consequently achieved as individuals and groups draw and act on white racial knowledge to maintain, justify, and perpetuate the supremacy of whiteness (Feagin 2010; Jacobson 1998; Lopez 2006; Yancy 2004). Being white, however, doesn't automatically signify the use of white racial knowledge "although there certainly is a preponderance of white people who interpret social life through white racial knowledge" (Leonardo 2009: 109). Here, Leonardo (2009: 109) notes, "white people's racial knowledge is not synonymous with white racial knowledge" or with white people themselves. In other words, as sociologist and educator W. E. B. Du Bois (1924) well knew, status and position in society (i.e., vis-à-vis other groups) determines race; race does not determine status and position in society: "you are not Jim Crowed because you are Black; you are Black because you are Jim Crowed" (cited in Olson 2004: 22). Whites, like all people from whatever background, are concrete, acting, thinking subjects of and within history who make choices according to how they approach and interact with others in the world around them (Coates 2008; Harris, Hayes, and Smith 2020; Lopez 2003; Leonardo and Porter 2010).

Indeed, whiteness as racial knowledge is less about the happenstance of skin color and more about what racial knowledge individuals and groups use and how they use it, in order to interpret and make decisions about the world around them (Hall 1991; Omi and Winant 1994; Yancy 2004). Perhaps Malcolm X (cited in Hare 2002: 9) said it best: "White-ness is a state of mind, not a complexion." People of color may and sometimes do espouse or embody white racial knowledge (Leonardo 2002, 2009). As oftentimes happens with individuals learning to do anti-racist work and working to acknowledge their white privilege and denounce white racism, people who are identified as white may acquire the skills and knowledge required to recognize and apply in their own lives the collective racial knowledge generated from the historical experiences of people of color (Aptheker 1993; Juarez, Hayes, and Smith 2016).

Why Race Still Matters?

A foundational tenet of CRT is the belief that race still matters. With this in mind, Charles Mills's (2015) notion of *global white ignorance* and Charles Metzl's (2020) *Dying of Whiteness* serve as grounding frameworks for why race still matters. While Howard Ryan's introductory chapter provides a valid racial and class analysis of educational reform, race cannot be one silo and class another silo—for they intersect. As noted earlier, for critical race scholars, race may not be the only factor, but it is never not a factor. In this final section of the chapter, I employ key tenets of CRT to respond to Ryan's chapter, in order to argue that race still matters and must remain at the center of any analysis of educational reform.

Racism is endemic: First, racism is at the center of my argument because it remains important to recognize that racism is endemic across American society. However, the problem with whiteness is the continued refusal to consider these everyday realities of race and racism. Racism's pervasiveness, therefore, requires whites to face their own racist behavior and to name the contours of racism, along with the ways that people of color may or may not play into supporting white racial domination and the supremacy of whites (Bergerson 2003; Dei, Karumanchery and Karumanchery-Luik 2007; Gillborn 2005).

Countering Color Blindness: Second, race and racism remain at the center of my argument that, at least in the US context, race still matters and must remain at the center of any analysis of educational reform—for we do not and cannot practice true color blindness. In fact, color blindness is not an appropriate ideal for social justice. According to Bergerson (2003), whites attribute negative stereotypes to people of color, while at the same time espousing their opposition to racism, only associating such with blatant acts of racism. When white liberals fail to understand how they can and/or do embody white supremacist values through this lack of awareness (even though they themselves may not embrace racism), they inadvertently support the racist domination they supposedly want to eradicate (Gillborn 2005; hooks 1989).

Injustice of Meritocracy: Third, racism remains at the center of my argument because the notion of meritocracy is problematic in the United States. It is not enough to merely say that anyone who works hard can achieve success, when students of color are systematically excluded from education and educational opportunities despite their hard work. Our supposed meritocracy operates under the burden of racism; racism thus limits the applicability of merit to people of color (Bergerson 2003). The hard work of some pays off much more than the hard work of Racial Others. Racialized workers remained invisible within their work contexts until they began disrupting whiteness, when they became targets of that very whiteness. Their hard work was not valued by the official discourses of the institutions in which they were employed.

Value of Experiential Knowledge: Fourth, race stays at the center of my arguments because CRT values the role experiential knowledge plays in the discourses and experiences of people of color. As an example, from my own experience, I was having a conversation with a white colleague who was trying to make a class argument in a way that diminished the significance of race. My response to this colleague was, "I have done everything that has been asked. I own my own home, I have a terminal degree, I am a lieutenant colonel in the U.S. Air Force, I have never been arrested, and I pay my taxes." My question remains: Why do I still experience racism?

Limits of Class Arguments: Lastly, keeping race at the center counters the limits of class arguments that can obscure key racial issues and, thus, silence the voices and participation of racialized populations. Ignoring personal lived experience of racism, through focusing on arguments purely concerning class, fails to recognize the knowledge of those who are victims of the brutality of whiteness as legitimate, appropriate, and critical for those who must navigate a society grounded in racial subordination. Whiteness usually postures toward people of color who refuse to remain silent and refuse to serve as the token, well-scrubbed, articulate, racially minoritized person, who is just like us (white folks) apart from skin color (hooks 1989). This is what Hytten and Warren (2003) call an *appeal to authenticity*. In their view, when whiteness is cited to counter or contradict non-white voices, the experiences cited are usually employed to undermine the realities of the others' lived experiences.

Still in a Race State of Mind

Yes! Class is an important construct, as Ryan argues in his work. However, as a CRT scholar, I argue that there is no way to get to an in-depth class analysis until there is a racial reckoning in the United States. A race analysis begins with an understanding of why poor white people in this country continue to maintain and uphold white supremacy, even though it is literally killing them or keeping them materially oppressed. In his work, Metzl (2020: 20) notes "the lengths to which white working-class voters could either have underlying racism or be manipulated to vote in support of wealthy donors and corporations, but against their own lifespans."

As we proceed with caution toward a more nuanced race and class analysis, we must be certain that we don't succumb to racial liberalism. Racial liberalism places emphasis on the individual, thus redefining racism from a matter of institutional structures to a matter of personal biases and prejudice (Goldberg 1993; Guinier 2004; Mill 1997). Race itself, within racial liberalism, is reduced to solely a matter of skin color and therefore anti-racism concerns making skin color irrelevant. Furthermore, claiming that race is irrelevant or a meaningless concept with respect to the statistical measurement of a society's distribution of rewards promotes a color-blind tolerance of inclusivity, one based on race-neutral and universal ideals of equality. As such, equality speaks no race and thus, equality is rendered color blind.

A major impact of assumptions that promote white superiority on one hand, and the inferiority of people of color on the other, is to create a *racialized* or *herrenvolk ethics* (Mills 1997)—a racial division authorizing one set of social rules for whites and another set of rules for racial minorities. The good productive citizen is then a white citizen, because the normative standard by which people of color are judged is the benchmark of whiteness. In this way, equality remains the jurisdiction of whites, who use social rules grounded in the privileging of whiteness in order to racially mark and perpetuate the racialized exclusion of peoples not defined as white. Given these factors, the apparent contradictions between many whites' tolerance of racially inclusive egalitarian ideals and their historical and contemporary intolerance toward race-based policies focused on addressing discrimination and oppression become an understandable, reasonable, and logical outcome of whites' faulty perceptions of race.

It is precisely these faulty perceptions that foster a silent covenant among whites to collectively detach and disassociate themselves from any identification with, or feelings of empathy for, the race-based suffering and inequalities faced by people of color (Bell 2004; King 1991). This silent covenant authorizes whites, individually and collectively, to continue benefiting from an unjust system, which denies the advantages of whiteness to people of color. As long as whites remain the gatekeepers of society's valued resources (Kivel 2004; Shapiro 2004), the negative impact of whiteness will remain far-reaching and profound.

What Is Needed?

Du Bois (1940) argues that, when the American Civil War ended, white landowners created a social order that prevented poor whites from joining political forces with the freed enslaved Africans. Racism is thus a correlate of US constructions, notions, and conceptions of constitutional, liberal democracy that reflects the social order created by white landowners (Cone 2004; Delgado 1989, 1995). When the immensity and depth of the physical and psychological violence continually committed against minoritized peoples is considered, the majority of it perpetrated by *nice* people, we realize that the costs in suffering and lost lives are too high to keep tiptoeing around whiteness and trying to appease and placate (otherwise decent) white people. What is needed is a fundamental dismantling of whiteness and white supremacy.

As James Baldwin (1963; cited in Wise 2005: 61) noted:

> What societies really, ideally, want is a citizenry which will simply obey the rules of society. If a society succeeds in this, that society is about to perish. The obligation of anyone who thinks of [herself or] himself as responsible is to examine society and try to change it and to fight it—at no matter the risk. This is the only hope society has. This is the only way societies change.

For a more authentic conversation about both educational and wider societal reform to include a deeper engagement with class, we must work together to abolish whiteness and white supremacy, rather than replace them with a class argument (Hayes et al. 2013). In order to end white supremacy, there have to be effective, and thus necessarily collective, efforts to transform those structures that reinforce and perpetuate white supremacy in the first place (hooks 1994).

12

Academic Laboring with Critical Social Theories in a Torus of Education Reform

Vonzell Agosto and Ericka Roland

We support Howard Ryan's aim of fostering a discussion on the construction and use of theories to understand education reform, one that considers various ways of knowing and being in the world. Ryan's opening chapter is grounded in philosophical principles linked to a Marxist perspective of the social and material world. While we embrace a view honoring the socio-materiality of oppressions and accept the invitation to participate in the discussion concerning race and class as related to education reform, we reject the terms of engagement: the centering of *Marxism* and *capitalism* as the theoretical core supporting the analysis of both race and class in education reform. Instead, to enter the proposed discussion on education reform, we situate critical social theories as sources for multiple analyses of racism with classism and suggest that these theories provide examples of academic labor mediated within the Global Education Reform Movement (GERM).

Theories are meant to support sense-making about social phenomena and help to explain social life. They can also help deconstruct the premises of common sense that are contradictory and build hegemony (Torres 2012). They filter out other means of understanding, especially those that narrowly focus on one category of social experience while ignoring others. Critical social theories are particularly suited for exploring complex phenomena variously, including how class(ism) and race(ism) operate in service to and in response to educational reform. Critical social theories consider ontology (i.e., histories, humans, spirits, consciousness), epistemology (i.e., faith, reason, doubt, intuition), and axiology (i.e., morals, ethics, kinesthetics, aesthetics). They provide an expansive umbrella of theories, including variations of Marxism, serving as a pluralistic framework with manifold possibilities for comprehending, explaining, and critiquing how existing interwoven social inequities and inequitable systems are implicated in and affected by some aspects of education reform. As such, movement through theories in combination is not only an intellectual engagement but also an outcome and progenitor or historical, political, and transformational engagement.

In our view, critical social theories can be engaged through lines of inquiry that consider how sectors of society, academic disciplines, and sociological scales interpenetrate to use and perpetuate racism and classism as a unified oppressive force. Critical social theories, oppression, and education reform are not static. We advance the *torus* as a metaphor depicting movement, namely heuristic engagement that recycles combinations of critical social theory to address this unified oppressive force associated with the causes of, correlations with, and reactions to education reform. To discuss the relational possibilities of cycling through or struggling with critical social theories heuristically-analytically to examine and ameliorate social oppression (Evans 2006), we turn to metaphor. Metaphors have been used to illustrate the interconnections of multiple oppressions (e.g., racism and classism) and theories (e.g., racist classism, classist racism). Patricia Hill Collins (2019) explains this use of metaphors as the provision of tools that allow us to become familiar with concepts and imagine the relationship among the various theories.

Our metaphor of choice is a torus (see Figure 12.1), a surface of revolution generated by revolving a circle in three-dimensional space. The revolving axis does not touch the circle, thus creating a ring shape of many rings that expand vertically and horizontally. Although the torus shape has boundaries, it is never static like theories. It is a form of continuous multidirectional movement that undermines any attempt to position a single center. Similarly, as a multidisciplinary framework, critical social theory pushes beyond the exclusionary binary logic of either/or (i.e., class or race). It allows inquirers to take theory or theories to their limits by working or struggling with them (Hall 1997), which can serve to expose both their strengths and weaknesses.

Fay (1987: 31) argued that necessary to critical social science is a *complex of theories* that are "systematically related to one another." In other words, movement through theories can be dynamic, as depicted by the shifting shape of the torus, as can the interactions of power from multiple levels and knowledge traditions. The movement comes through moving or laboring variously.

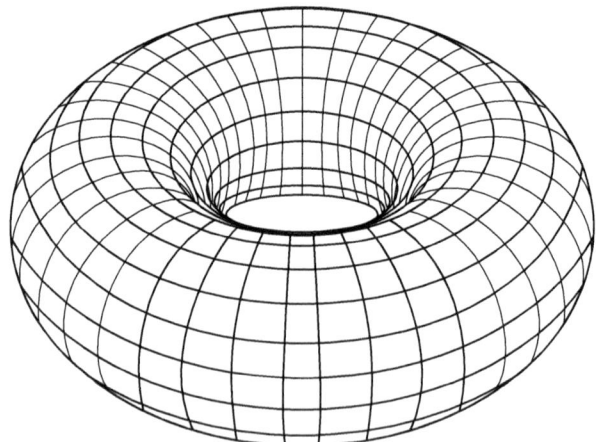

Figure 12.1 A Static Image of a Torus. Source: Public domain via Wikipedia Commons. https://commons.wikimedia.org/wiki/File:Simple_Torus.svg.

Critiquing the Terms of Engagement

There are several terms of engagement provided by Howard Ryan in the grounding essay for these discussions that we address: questioning the primacy of racism or classism, the centrality of capitalism in studying classism, the use of Marxism, and grand theory in general. Rather than center on debates about the primacy of race or class, we accept that both should be continued as raceclass analysis (Leonardo 2012b; Norval 1994) to explore racist classism (Pére 2010) and explore classist racism (Roman 2015).

As Ryan argues, although classism is often included among the oppressions studied (or drawn on) by critical theorists in education, it has not been given equivalent standing or integrated into the problematization of education reform where racism(s) is/are implicated. This, as he describes, is often the case among those who associate themselves with critical race studies, critical ethnic studies, cultural studies (of racism), and critical race theories (i.e., LatCrit, AsianCrit, BlackCrit). Some of the critiques that inform the rejection, avoidance, and adoption of (forms of) Marxism and capitalism and classism, as theoretical guides used to examine K-20 education, help explain why such a position has been and continues to be the case. We engage such critiques along with examples of education reform that rely on theories (some of which are/were *marxish*, if not Marxist) offering powerful explanatory and transformational analyses of racism and classism in education reform (i.e., critiquing domination) not limited to Marxism, singular or grand theories, or a specific set of social relations such as *capitalism*.

Marxism, which focuses on capitalism, has not been the sole bridge used to connect race and class in analyses of education reform. As others have described, in terms of eras, the educational system of the United States is not simply situated in the *capitalocene* but also in the *anthropocene, chthulucene, and plantationocene* (Haraway 2015), the last of which concerns the devastation and transformation of farms and fields into plantations that depended on slave labor and other settler-colonial mechanisms (Taylor, Pacini-Ketchabaw, de Finney, and Blaise 2016). Decolonial critiques of Marxism recognize the limitations of studying capitalism as if it is not also a cultural system. British (Black) cultural studies scholar Stuart Hall (1996: 264) claimed that Marxism's treatment of capitalism was rooted in Eurocentrism, given Marx's suggestion that "capitalism evolved organically from within its own transformation" rather than through conquest and colonization. Hall's decolonial theoretical stance challenged the very basis upon which Marxist theory was built—a Eurocentric understanding of capitalism rather than a dispersion of power unevenly exchanged across cultures and a globalized political economy.

Others have theorized capitalism within racism rather than something apart from it, arguing that racism *is* racial capitalism (Robinson 2000: 77). Therefore, the construction of racial ideology that positioned Indigenous people in Africa, Asia, and the Americas as less than fully human was necessary for colonization (Pulido 2017). According to Pulido (2017: 527), "racial ideology (along with guns) enabled colonization." Echoing Hall's critique of Marxism, Lindner (2010) posed a postcolonial critique of Marx, namely that when referring to Africa and Asia, he treated (1) Europe as a society with superior technology, infrastructure, a legal system, and so on; and (2) its form of property relations (private land ownership) as the basis for social progress.

A significant risk of applying (a single) theory (as a grand theory) is reductionism. By this, we mean (1) reducing the complexity of education systems and how they affect lives and livelihoods and (2) reducing one's ability to be flexible in how they study, communicate, or coalition around education problems. Marxism also suffers from downward reductionism, resulting in caricatures of Marxism as mechanistic materialism (Wrigley 2019), as well as upward reductionism, whereby Marxism is used to explain all educational phenomena (Sayer 2010). For instance, the claim that a grand theory like Marxism can support efforts to understand, analyze/critique, and transform that which promotes inequities that are social, economic, and educational (Hill 2004) is a claim that would apply to various theories. Such avoidance of reductionism further sets the terms of agreement away from single theories to multiple theories, multiple expressions of theories, and theoretical shifts or leanings. Before turning to education reform and the role of critical social theories in examining racism and classism, we discuss theoretical shifts from Marxism to neo-Marxism, and critical social theories not as predetermined but as dialectically determined through the push and pull of their limitations and possibilities.

Neo-Marxism is often used to describe the reinvigoration of Marxism through its extension to mass culture via cultural critique and the adoption of its revolutionary spirit and some of its orienting concepts (e.g., alienation, ideology). Neilson (2017) argues there are two generations of neo-Marxism thus far. First-generation neo-Marxism is typically associated with critical theory, notably the Frankfurt School and its contributors, including Horkheimer, Adorno, Marcuse, Benjamin, Lowenthal, and Fromm. Second-generation neo-Marxism is associated with scholars such as Joan Robinson, Paul A. Baran, and Paul M. Sweezy, whose critiques of the political economy attend to the rise of global corporations, anti-colonial struggles for liberation, and American imperialism (Toscano 2007). In other words, neo-Marxism has been taken up in the social sciences as the application of *herrschaftskritisch* (the critique of rule or critique of domination) to examine problems as social, political, economic, and cultural phenomena.

In education, during the 1980s, Marxist analysis often focused on political economy and social class in schools (e.g., Anyon 1980; Apple 1979; Giroux 1981). Whereas the culture of schools was studied, the cultural heritage and identities of students that were the focus of intercultural education, multicultural education, ethnic studies, and other strands of critical social theory were often ignored. Over time, educational scholars began referring to the political and historical study of power and injustices within formal and informal education from various knowledge traditions as *critical turns* (Apple 1978; Gottesman 2016). Similar to how the Combahee River Collective's liberation praxis extended from and merged Black feminist and Marxist analysis to address issues about race, class, gender, and sexual orientation simultaneously, we consider addressing the compoundness of race and class by way of multiple integrated theories. Instead of solely relying on a grand theory to understand race and class, we suggest educators, researchers, and activists collaborate and cycle through multiple theories across various traditions as a means of challenging the reductionism, individualism, and profit when guided by liberal ideologies that characterize the current GERM.

Cycling through and Combining Critical Social Theories

Critical social theory is associated with the Frankfurt School, a multidisciplinary group of scholars who reconsidered and reformed Marxist social criticism (Agger 2006; Levinson et al. 2015). Neo-Marxism, by way of the Frankfurt School, is the basis of critical social theory/theories (Jay 1973), including cultural studies. Critical social theories invite inquiring into, theorizing about, and problematizing how race/ism and class/ism converge or how scholarship is extended to explore relationships between multiple oppressions (i.e., racism, classism, race-based classism, class-based racism) and theorizing traditions. Social, economic, and cultural analyses underpin critical social theory as a means of critique directed at blights that impinge upon peoples' freedom from domination. The following are heuristic concepts often associated with various critical social theories.

Power

Critical social theories allow for the recombination of ideas supporting efforts to offer a sustained and nuanced critique of power dynamics related to racism, classism, and other social oppressions. In critical social theory, power is frequently referred to as a critique of sociopolitical and material manifestations of structural oppressions (Collins 2019; Foster 2017; Honneth 1991). Education and educational research are social practices, and critical social theories support inquiry into education about power and uneven power dynamics across levels of sociological analysis: micro levels (classrooms), meso levels (school districts, societies), and macro levels (state or national education policies, nation state educational systems). We argue that movement through recombinations of theories and lines of inquiry that scan sectors of society, disciplines, and sociological scales that sustain racism and classism must be guided by power analysis. Power analyses allow a critique of social interactions and manifestations of privilege and oppression. For instance, through a power analysis of class modality connected to college graduates, one is to understand how middle-class white students and women of color are affected by oppressive systems within their various social positions and contexts. As a result, scholars can then study how each group is rendered invisible in the conversation concerning oppression. A consideration of identity politics, for example, would start from power analyses of individual and group experiences of social injustices to redescribe and transform structural oppression.

Identity Politics

The work of the Combahee River Collective and other social critical theorists signals the relationship between identity politics and theorizing (Combahee 2017). Identity politics refers to the shared experiences of oppression by subjugated groups, defined by race, class, gender, and other identities that mark interlocking structures of domination (Young 1990). Identity politics can also be based on multiple identity markers. For example, the Black Lives Matter movement engages identity politics to challenge racial, gender, class, and heterosexual oppressions, politically and socially. Inquiries into education reform often center on understanding the lived experiences of those impacted by oppression(s) in the educational system (e.g., Black students, white poor rural students). Paradoxically, identity politics can be both a safeguard against oppression and a tool of divisiveness—for instance, when researchers or theorists engage in "oppression Olympics" (Yuval-Davis 2012), a term that speaks to the hierarchical treatment of oppressions (i.e., claiming one form of oppression is worse than another).

Higher education reform has focused on reintegrating marginalized people into the education system via admission processes, institutional funding, and student success policies (Brunila and Rossi 2018). Hence, there is a need for structural analyses, as focused on identities or identity politics, to inform challenges to racism, classism, and other interlocking oppressions on structural, political, and representational levels (Collins and Bilge 2016; Crenshaw 1991). With this in mind, identity politics can assist in analyses aimed at recentering political expressions of experiences of oppression in order to theorize structures of domination. Through doing so, an understanding of identity politics and structural oppression can be used to help expose hidden injustices. The same can be said of a range of relevant critical theories.

A recent study illustrates the role of identity (regarding collaborative researchers' positionalities) in research on colonial (linguistic) oppression in education. In this study, three co-researchers (a woman from a Quechua community, a woman from Central Europe, and a man from the United States) cycled through different interpretive frameworks to interpret students' experiences (Levitan 2018). The author, Levitan (2018), illustrated how divergent interpretations, based on different interpretive frameworks, led to the recommendation of divergent policy options. Overall, the study serves as a warning to readers that using a single theory, or even multiple theories in isolation from each other, to interpret students' voices/experiences is dangerous. The same warning extends to the interpretation of education reform more broadly. Cycling through multiple analytic engagements and mergers to explore racism and classism means considering the push and pull of theoretical movements within the current GERM.

Analyzing the Torus of Global Education Reformulations

Our consideration of education reform derives from Pasi Sahlberg's (2016) view that a GERM, which has produced a culture of high accountability focused on assessment (i.e., standardized or high-stakes testing), is well established and increasingly active. The GERM has ensured that its choices, as to current indicators of success and rising importance placed on education standards, were firmly established in the 1990s across continents. These indicators have led to uniformity across educational systems and an attendant worldview that functions to increasingly narrow education discourse (Ydesen and Andreasen 2020). While the market exacerbates inequalities of various types (Hill 2004), an economic interpretation and analysis, such as the one Ryan offers, does not provide a sufficiently comprehensive engagement with such reform and related outcomes. A sociocultural and socioeconomic view, in contrast, attends to the phenomenon at different times, places, and scales. Critical social theory of various strands offers various interpretive or heuristic angles to analyze, critique, and counter complex movements. In other words, the blanket of reform is not a uniformly blanket experience, nor does it result in blanketed outcomes that can be explained all at once or with one theory or set of theories, including critical social theories.

Understanding the influence of the *GERM* and its neoliberal impetus, as primarily concerned with marketplace competition and profit (Hill 2004), begs for both cultural and economic understandings of how mandated testing and standardization of curriculum, pedagogy, and assessment have developed and inspired further reform. Cardoso and Steiner-Khamsi (2017) draw on historiography across various periods, engaging in micro-, meso-, and macro-level analyses to identify the discursive shifts in policy and how educational statistics are situated within the current *GERM*. They engage with historical processes of modernization/nation-building, colonization/development, and standardization/globalization to discuss the role of comparative education. In doing so, they are attentive to cultural-historical networks of power and theory.

Isaac L. Kandel is often noted as one of the founders of comparative education in the United States. His writings express a Eurocentric view in which (modern) countries were more civilized than others (traditional ones), creating *a civilization gap* (Kandel 1932). As such, education reform in colonized countries needed reform but could not be reformed with extraordinary intervention. Cardoso and Steiner-Khamsi (2017: 369) argued that those embracing this theory of civilization maintained it was possible to identify "individuals, groups, or nations" within stages of civilization development. Furthermore, they noted that races (e.g., African Americans, Native Americans, Africans) that "were regarded as being at the same underdeveloped stage of civilisation" could be compared and that such comparison was considered to be a "morally acceptable methodology" (2017:369). Understanding how civilization was imagined within a racialized colonial lens prepares one to critique how development projects used race, class, and religion in their approach to education reform theory and methodology.

Cardoso and Steiner-Khamsi (2017) describe the *Adapted Education* reform movement. *Adapted Education* has its origins within education reform in the United States and provides basic levels of functional education in rural Black communities and Historically Black Colleges (Bude 1983). According to Bude (1983: 396), the transportation of the American Hampton-Tuskegee model (with its focus on a vocational course of study) to the African continent was justified on the basis that the rural context for Black people in the United States was sufficiently comparable, such that the Hampton-Tuskegee model could "be adapted to colonial conditions in Africa (Jones 1923: 141)." As such, the inception of Historically Black Colleges and Universities (HBCUs) can be understood as an education reform that intervened in racialized/classed educational inequities *and* extended racialized/classed education in the colonization of Africa. The *Adapted Education* reform movement stemmed from the British empire's colonizing project and its embrace of positive science alongside the US embrace of the scientific method (Cardoso and Steiner-Khamsi 2017).

Concluding Remarks

A broad and deep understanding of global education reform can be arrived at by studying education from different theoretical and disciplinary vantage points. Critical accounts of education reform include the following intellectual threads: the consideration of history, geographic diversity at the macro level, analysis of power, and attention to socially constructed categories of people (i.e., social groups). In other words, critical social theories offer various ontological angles from which to understand education reform over time and in connection to intellectual movements, including historical and dialectical materialism (associated with Marxism), critical realism (Bhaskar 2016) *and* discursive positions (see Hall 1997). The principles related to critical race theory, for example, guide its users to avoid ahistorical interpretations and embrace the ontological position that racism has some purchase on reality in material ways (Bonilla-Silva 2015). Racism and classism, as systems of oppression resulting from forces ranging across scales (individual, societal, global), concern power, which can be conceived of variously depending on the philosophical (i.e., ontological) and theoretical vantage points one employs.

How inquirers select and represent problems and derive inferences or judgments are neither logically consistent nor devoid of bias. Theorizing, understood as academic laboring, within the politics of conducting inquiry can assist educational researchers in mediating their individual biases, whether planning to investigate alone or with others. The following questions are raised as choices about which theoretical perspectives will be engaged: Which problems and explanations are inquirers willing and able to address and bring comprehension to others? Which problems and explanations are inquirers willing and able to leave aside? These questions involve theory, ability, and will.

Multiple theories can support analyses of education reform and contribute to proposing and making improvements in the conditions of schooling by considering various ways in which people's experiences are constrained by structures, cultures, and actions that operate simultaneously and in reaction to their multiple ways of being, sense-making, relating, and valuing. Both/and inclusive, heuristic-analytic process among educational researchers can help to account for how raceclass (Norval 1994), racist classism (Pére 2010), or classist racism (Roman 2015) are situated and treated within systems, organizations, or other socially reproduced arrangements. This demands that individuals and teams of inquirers draw on multiple resources—theories, histories, forms of discrimination, and processes that foment social inequities and (in)justices and different disciplinary understandings and approaches. Furthermore, because we are alert to the politics of analysis leading to the privileging and hierarchical ranking of theories—while accepting that some use of grand theory contributes to education and educational reform—we are calling for heuristic-analytic processes and politics. These ways of laboring involve processes of engagement and movement, such as navigating meandering intellectual streams to reorient critical social theories despite the pull of (global) education reform. "Such is the nature of the movement of history and intellectual fashion," according to Hall (1996: 266), who was commenting on the emergence of a post-Marxist era.

13

Capitalism and Caste

Christine Sleeter

Howard Ryan rightly argues for a theory that identifies the main drivers of the school reform movement and the forms of power that undergird those drivers, in order to understand how to address them at their root. The problem he sees with posing race as the primary driver is that class then recedes into the background. While he acknowledges that race must be taken seriously, he argues that a class analysis most directly identifies the drivers of the school reform movement of the past three decades. Through utilizing such a class analysis, Ryan identifies the business sector as the main driver and their central motive as being control over the curriculum in order to produce workers for the capitalist economy.

In this chapter, I will argue that a class analysis is hindered by blinders that serve to obscure the important roles played by racism, inevitably so, given that racism and capitalism have been inextricably intertwined from the beginning; hence, they cannot be separated. Drawing on Latin American decolonial work (Mignolo 2018; Quijano 2007), Wilkerson's (2020) analysis of racism and caste and Black Marxists' work that connects race and class (Marable 2015; Robinson 2000), I argue that both racism (understood as caste) and capitalism are ultimately derived from European ontology and that such ontological premises provide the foundations for social structures. While I agree with Ryan that curriculum is a key site of contestation, I argue that its power lies not just in its production of workers but more fundamentally with its role in shaping public consciousness.

Roots of Caste and Capitalism

Foundationally, I view US racism as a caste system, and I will be using it in that sense. Wilkerson (2020: 17) explains: "A caste system is an artificial construction, a fixed and embedded ranking of human value that sets the presumed supremacy of one group against the presumed inferiority of other groups on the basis of ancestry and often immutable traits." She goes on to explain: "In the American caste system, the signal of rank is what we call race, the division of humans on the basis of their appearance. In America, race is the primary tool and the visible decoy, the front man, for caste" (2020: 18). Thus, when we speak of racism, we are speaking not only of discriminatory actions and beliefs but also of an entire system that fixes humans into ranked categories, a system that is so immutable that, from the perspective of the dominant ideology, it is "natural."

Racial caste and capitalism emerged as an interlocking system from roots in European ontology and epistemology. Latin American decolonial theorist Mignolo (2018: 137) explains that European conquest of the world grew out of how Europeans viewed and defined reality. "Western expansion was not only economic and political but fundamentally epistemic," as rooted in Western knowledge as a totalizing enterprise. Christianity defines its epistemic totality as *the* only one, all others being false. Theology "was the overarching cosmological frame for Western Christendom" (2018: 201).

Central to Western Christian ontology is the assumption that everything sits within a hierarchy in which inert matter is at the bottom; God and the angels are at the apex, and everything else is rank-ordered in between. Humans, who rank above and have dominion over other animals, can similarly be further subdivided into rank-ordered races. Within this way of understanding, it is natural to exert dominion over any and all who are below oneself in nature's hierarchy. Europeans viewed themselves as belonging to the most highly developed civilization, thereby holding a right to colonize the rest of the world. They viewed modernity as "the acceptance of Western knowledge as a totalizing enterprise" (Mignolo 2018: 127). Wilkerson (2020: 104) explains: "These tenets, as interpreted by those who put themselves on high, would become the divine and spiritual foundation for the belief in a human pyramid willed by God, a Great Chain of Being." This ontology became the basis through which Europeans, during the Renaissance, viewed their epistemic totality as the only truth, at the same time as Europe was busy colonizing much of the world. Europeans simply dismissed what they regarded as lesser knowledges and knowledge systems that arose outside of Europe.

European colonization and the rise of capitalism, then, were products of a particular, hierarchical view of the world. Western Christian Europeans assumed that how they interpreted others—peoples of the Americas, Asia, and Africa—was in fact how they were. This creation and imposition of a reality is what Mignolo (2018: 196) refers to as the colonial matrix of power (CMP), which selects from all matter what we should see, from all possible ways of thinking what we should believe, and from all human creation (including the creation of economic and political systems) what we should accept. "The CMP created a powerful fiction, marked by a single totality." Quijano (2007: 169) emphasizes how the European colonizers systematically repressed local knowledges, gradually replacing them with their own.

> At first, they placed these patterns far out of reach of the dominated. Later, they taught them in a partial and selective way, in order to co-opt some of the dominated into their own power institutions. Then European culture was made seductive: it gave access to power. . . . Cultural Europeanisation was transformed into an aspiration. It was a way of participating and later to reach the same material benefits and the same power as the Europeans: viz, to conquer nature in short for "development". European culture became a universal cultural model.

Let me be clear about the main point being argued here. How people think is often taken to be a product of the social structure within which they live. From the Marxian perspective of historical determinism, ideology emerges out of location within the economic mode of production. Conversely, decolonialists, such as those from Latin America, argue that social structures emerge from not only ideology but the entire ontology of a civilization, or from the CMP, as Mignolo describes it. We will return to this idea in the last section of this chapter.

Racial Capitalism

If caste and capitalism emerged in conjunction with each other from the same ontology, how did that happen? Terming these interlocking systems "racial capitalism," Robinson (2000) explains that it initially emerged out of feudalism in the context of colonization; both capitalism and racism grew together from the same soil that produced a system dependent on slavery, imperialism, violence, and genocide. While exactly who is racialized has shifted somewhat over time, the process of racialization, the impetus for it, and its interconnection with the economic structure have not changed. Racial capitalism, thus, is a structural product of the Western Christian European imaginary.

Robinson argues that while capitalism displaced feudalism, it did so by extending and repurposing feudalism's basic social relations and logic. Slave labor was a social relation that had existed since the Western Roman Empire; throughout the history of Europe, there was also extensive use of migrant labor from other places, whether as mercenaries, domestic labor, industrial labor, or agrarian labor. Further, in Europe, different ethnic groups tended to specialize—for example, the mercenaries came from one ethnic stock, the merchants from another, the slaves from another. Race was invented to rationalize domination and was, thus, built into the core of European civilization (Quijano 2000; Robinson 2000).

Viewing themselves and their religion as superior, as Europeans came into greater contact with the rest of the world, they regarded it as natural, even God's will, for them to extend control over (or save) "pagans" both within and outside of Europe, and to appropriate their labor and natural resources. For example, Galeano (1973: 24), writing about the European conquest of the Americas, stated: "The epic of the Spaniards and the Portuguese in America combined propagation of the Christian faith with usurpation and plunder of native wealth." Especially in the form of gold and silver, Europe transferred enormous wealth from the Americas. According to Weatherford (1988: 14): "At the time of the discovery of America, Europe had only about $200 million worth of gold and silver, approximately $2 per person. By 1600 the supply of precious metals had increased approximately eightfold." This wealth, which derived from Europeans' assumption that it was theirs for the taking, fueled the development of the capitalist economy.

Within a relatively short period of time, a good deal of money was circulating in Europe, while thousands of native Americans had died mining the silver used to create it. Different colonizing nations used that wealth differently. Spain bankrupted itself. The Dutch, British, and French built large armies and navies for the purpose of expanding their colonial ventures, as well as buying luxury consumption items, such as spices, silk, and porcelain in Asia. The British also directed much of their new wealth into large profit-making companies. While small businesses had been common across England and other European countries for a long time, these nations had not possessed the capital to establish much larger companies. According to Galeano (1973: 40),

> The money in circulation kept multiplying and it was necessary to stimulate the movement of capitalism in the hour of birth: the bourgeoisie took control of the cities and founded banks, produced and exchanged merchandise, conquered new markets. Gold, silver, sugar: the colonial economy supplying rather than consuming, was built in terms of—and in the service of—the European market.

Thus, capitalism was born out of colonization, which itself was the product of a view of reality that placed Europeans (particularly European men) just under God, and as such, destined to control the people and the natural resources of the entire world. As long as Europeans believed in the totality of their own knowledge, they saw no need to pay attention to the knowledges of those they saw as beneath or outside that totality (with the exception of those local knowledge they viewed as useful and subsequently appropriated). This is a legacy we have inherited that continues to buttress both racial capitalism and patriarchy.

Marxism as a Western European Totalizing Theory

Ryan posits Marxism as a useful tool in its offering of a systemic analysis of power relations rooted in the means of economic production, an analysis that helps to identify today's centers of power. I agree that Marxism offers a highly useful analysis and critique of capitalism and its structural consequences. But Marxism is also predominantly a product of Western European ontology and thus possesses blind spots it does not recognize and consequently does not grapple well with the range of issues that concern difference. Robinson (2000) noted that while Engels was aware of a lack of solidarity within the proletariat, he and Marx still believed the economy to be the determining condition of society, and that political issues and cultural traditions, while important, were secondary. However, as Robinson (2000: 2) also notes, what cannot be denied is that

> At base, that is at its epistemological substratum, Marxism is a Western construction—a conceptualization of human affairs and historical development that is emergent from the historical experiences of European peoples mediated, in turn, through their civilization, their social orders, and their cultures.... European Marxists have presumed more frequently than not that their project is identical with world-historical development.

In other words, classical Marxists (who in my experience are overwhelmingly white) tend to position their analysis as a totalizing framework, even while traditional

Marxism does not speak to racism, caste, patriarchy, or colonialism (Robinson 2000). It is important to recognize that Marxism arose from a specific set of contexts, as to time and location, including that of an ethnically homogenous population, and although it provides tools that are useful beyond its origins, it can take the form of an imperial project from the left, rather than a decolonial project that de-links "from the colonial matrix of power" (Mignolo 2007: 455).

While Wilkerson's (2020) discussion of caste does not address capitalism and class relations, Wilkerson pushes us to view racism as the deeply structured product of a Western European ontology that views the world in terms of hierarchy—the same ontology that produced capitalism. Further, the shape capitalism has taken depends on whether and where it has access to a large reservoir of exploitable labor and resources. Such labor pools and the people who occupy land rich with natural resources are generally not white.

Marable (1983) and Robinson (2000) have, perhaps, done the most to advance a way of understanding capitalism as being connected with racial exploitation and racism as interconnected with class. Like Ryan, Marable argues that it is necessary to figure out primacy in order to design an action strategy that aims toward the actual roots of oppression. Marable (1983: 2) further argues that a Marxist analysis does so by locating people (and thus their oppression) within the economy, in relationship to the means of production and the capitalist class. However, "Capitalist development has occurred not in spite of the exclusion of Blacks, but because of the brutal exploitation of Blacks as workers and consumers" (1983: 2). As Wilkerson (2020: 135) notes: "The historic association between menial labor and blackness served to further entrap black people in a circle of subservience in the American mind."

In other words, without the concept of race, and without a racialized class performing menial labor alongside an ideology supporting that racialization, capitalism would not have expanded and ingrained itself anywhere close to the extent that it has done. One can make much the same argument about capitalist exploitation of lands and resources within the "darker nations" (Prashad 2007) and the production of and control over the Third World (Galeano 1973). Capitalism may well have never left the British Isles, were it not anchored in a way of seeing the world that propelled invasion, conquest, and enslavement, all justified as consistent with nature's (and God's) hierarchical creation, known as the Great Chain of Being (Gilbert 2021).

School Reform, Curriculum, and Public Consciousness

Where, then, does this leave us in identifying the main drivers of the school reform movement of the past three decades? Ryan argues that we need to identify a "who" and a "why" in order to know who to counter and on what grounds. He points out, correctly, that with few exceptions, most theorists ignore class/capitalism altogether or dilute class to a form of social stratification, rather than understanding it as a core structure of the social order. Ryan also argues that race-based theorists do not clearly explicate a grand theory of race primacy, and that those who advocate a race/class perspective draw mainly on race when analyzing education policy. So, using a class analysis, he identifies organized business, concerned about attacks on the free enterprise system, as the main driver of education reform. Beginning in the 1970s, business put things into place (establishing think tanks, media outlets, the American Legislative Exchange Council (ALEC), etc.) that eventually enabled them to exert considerable control over school processes, and over curriculum in particular. While I agree that the business community has been a central driver and that curriculum has been a major concern of school reform (privatization of education has been another), I believe Marxism falls short of explaining why this is so.

Bernstein and Solomon (1999: 268) argue that in all societies, groups struggle for the means to control the collective consciousness of people and that education plays a prominent role: "The pedagogic device, the condition for the materializing of symbolic control, is the object of a struggle for domination, for the group who appropriates the device has access to a ruler and distributor of consciousness, identity, and desire." In the United States, there has long been struggle for control over curriculum. Kliebard (1982: 23) identified four main curriculum orientations that drove twentieth-century debates: the *humanists*, "guardians of an ancient tradition tied to the power of reason and what they regarded as the finest in the Western cultural heritage"; the *developmentalists*, who believed curriculum should derive from the interests and growth of the child; the *social meliorists*, who saw the curriculum as a way of preparing citizens to address social issues; and the *social efficiency educators*, who believed the curriculum should be standardized around the needs of an industrial society. By the mid-twentieth century, while all four orientations had influence, social efficiency had become curriculum's "most potent ingredient" (Kliebard 1995: 206).

What Kliebard did not problematize was that *all* of these curriculum orientations are rooted in Western Euro-American thought and share its characteristics: such as, viewing knowledge not as holistic but as divisible into disciplines, each having their own internal structure; viewing humans as above the natural world and the natural world as an object of study and control; viewing time as linear; and viewing knowledge as an objective representation of reality that, as it becomes known and verified, is universalized. The social efficiency orientation packages the dominant group's knowledge, conceived of in this way, into standards that drive curriculum, the teaching of which is reinforced and enforced by mandating high-stakes testing.

While this basic orientation to curriculum has been challenged from time to time, it has become well-embedded in how schooling is constructed in Western nations. For example, following Russia's launch of Sputnik in 1957, the social efficiency orientation drove a wave of school reform in the United States. As Kliebard (1995: 226) explained, "While American schoolchildren were learning how to get along with their peers or how to bake a cherry pie, so the explanation went, Soviet children were being steeped in the hard sciences and mathematics needed to win the technological race that had become the centerpiece of the Cold War." To keep up with the Soviets, standards for learning in American schools were raised, more testing of students was put into place, students were grouped and tracked hierarchically based on their achievement levels, and science was infused more strongly into the curriculum.

Then the Civil Rights movement erupted. The Civil Rights movement was anchored in forms of racial and ethnic consciousness that rejected white American ideology concerning the opportunity structure, the roots of the oppression of peoples of color, personal and collective identity, and visions of a better world. While not all projects of the Civil Rights movement could be described as transformative, much activism was directed toward what Mignolo (2007: 459) terms "de-linking from the colonial matrix of power": "De-coloniality, then, means working toward a vision of human life that is not dependent upon or structured by the forced imposition of one ideal of society over those that differ, which is what modernity/coloniality does and, hence, where decolonization of the mind should begin."

Examples of decolonial work from the late 1960s and early 1970s include the Ethnic Studies movement launched by the Third World Liberation Front in San Francisco which Marable (1983: 196) saw as "a call toward the systematic reconstruction of American learning," Black liberation schools such as the Black Panthers' Oakland Community School, and community-controlled schools such as Ocean Hill-Brownsville. Even the segregated Black education system, including HBCUs, which existed under crushing race/class oppression, provided intellectual space for "the development of militant political reformers, dedicated public school teachers, physicians, and other skilled professionals within the Black community" (Marable 1983: 195). As E. San Juan, Jr. (1992: 77) explains: "Popular memory, a sense of history inscribed in the collective resistance against, racist, patriarchal, and exploitative forces, is one of the necessary means for oppressed peoples to acquire a knowledge of the larger context of their collective struggles, equipping them to assume transformative roles in shaping history."

In spaces such as these, knowledge was drawn not from white disciplinary experts but from lived experience and ancestral knowledge of minoritized communities. While not all curriculum that arose from such spaces was built from knowledge systems outside of the West, strong efforts have been made to achieve this. Speaking of ethnic studies, for example, Abdullah (2016: 7) argues, it "was never meant to be a part of the ivory tower, but to disrupt it. Ethnic Studies scholars who are true to our field are not academics, but intellectuals whose work must challenge the order of things and should contribute to freedom and justice struggles." While most of this work took place in localized spaces, it spilled over into mainstream schools, in forms such as multicultural education, constructivist teaching, and bilingual education. For the overwhelmingly white business sector that depended on the acquiescence of a subordinate working class *and* general public, the power of organized communities of color (as well as labor unions and women) to transform the consciousness of significant segments of the public was downright threatening.

While pushing for the school reforms that Ryan details, the business sector also allied itself with several white academics and journalists to engage in a public campaign to discredit the ideologies of activist educators who were attempting to reshape public consciousness. During the early 1990s, a barrage of critiques appeared in the form of books (e.g., Bloom 1989; D'Souza 1991; Schlesinger 1992), op-eds, and magazine articles (e.g., Ravitch 1990) that were funded by conservative think tanks. The books were reviewed in such highly visible publications as the *New York Times Book Review* and the *New Yorker*. The main targets were curricular changes and policies being instituted in schools and universities on a wide scale, particularly New York state's *A Curriculum of Inclusion* (a framework to guide the development of new

K-12 multicultural curricula), Portland, Oregon's *African American Baseline Essays* (a series of essays that explicate six disciplines from an Afrocentric perspective, designed to help K-12 teachers reconceptualize their own curriculum), Afrocentrism in general, and revisions of core curricula on several university campuses. Essentially, this war on multiculturalism can be seen as a powerful attempt to discredit any work that might de-link curriculum from the CMP.

For about three decades, the business community got what it wanted: a standardized curriculum based largely on Euro-American knowledge and anchored in a Western ontology, enforced through testing regimes that rank ordered schools. Not only are the narratives shaped by those who dominate, but knowledge remains carved into distinct disciplines, the natural world is framed as an object of study and control, and skills such as mathematics and reading are disconnected from meaningful use. Further, racism is rarely examined, class is mentioned even less, and capitalism is so deeply equated with what it means to be American that questioning it invites charges that the questioner hates America.

Conclusion

What we have, then, is a set of reforms that derive from both the business sector's need for a controllable labor force and also the white public's growing fear of losing dominance due to both shifting demographics and the political power of "woke" communities of color. I argue that the most effective pushback necessitates marrying a Marxist analysis with a race/caste analysis of both the structures of power and the public consciousness on which those structures rest.

14

Critical Race Theory, Materialism, and Class

Ali Meghji and Tiger Chan

I believed and still believe that Karl Marx was one of the greatest men of modern times and that he put his finger squarely upon our difficulties when he said that economic foundations, the way in which men earn their living, are the determining factors in the development of civilization, in literature, religion, and the basic pattern of culture. And this conviction I had to express or spiritually die.
—W. E. B. Du Bois ([1940] 2007: 151)

We read Howard Ryan's chapter with great enthusiasm but also with a sense of déjà vu. As Ryan himself notes, the debate in the social sciences and education studies—more specifically, over critical race theory's (CRT's) "race centrism"—has a long intellectual lineage. What troubles us, however, is that many people writing on this supposed tension between the sociology of class and CRT—including Ryan but also Mike Cole (2017), Dave Hill (2009), Carl Parsons (2016), and Trevor Thompson (Parsons and Thompson 2017)—fail to give proper treatment to the critical race canon. This creates grossly exaggerated differences between intellectual traditions such as Marxism and CRT. In this chapter, our aims are to try and clear some of this conceptual mess, in the hope of both contributing to and, through doing so, opening up further possibilities for a more generative study of class and race as it is articulated in CRT. Our intention is not to dismiss the scholarship and intellectual labor of Ryan, something we hope comes through in this piece. Rather, our intention concerns illustrating how some of Ryan's central claims, while often repeated in academic circles, are not necessarily as accurate as many assume. Through destabilizing the idea that CRT is "race centric" and ignores questions of class, we hope to open up a much more generative conversation with scholars whose positionalities are akin to Ryan's school of thought.

Class and "Race-Based Theory": Whatever Happened to Anti-Colonial Scholarship?

Before proceeding to a focused discussion on the materialist approach of CRT, it is worth reflecting on what Ryan refers to in his work as "race-based theory." Ryan offers a working definition of race-based theory as one "which sees race, or white supremacy, as the driving structure," and gives us examples of it: CRT, systemic racism theory, racial formation theory, Pan-Africanism, and Black nationalism. Further, Ryan argues against theory/positions that view race as *the* central, primary, or *only* important lens, with respect to "social thought." Nevertheless, given the manner in which Ryan sets up his argument, there seems to be an underlying tendency to perceive race-based theory as simply any social thought seeking to reflect upon racialization, racism, and race more broadly. The problem with this tendency is that putative race-based theory also, in reality, fundamentally encompasses considerations of class. The reason why Ryan and others overlook questions of class within race-based theory is largely because they pick and choose intellectuals whom they think fit the profile of the argument they are trying to make, and use these thinkers to corroborate their argument.

For instance, Ryan claims that "Black nationalism and Pan-Africanism tend to be vigorous both with grand theory and assertions of race primacy," using the example of Haki Madhubuti, to argue that both traditions can be viewed as predominantly ignoring central questions of class. We could, though, respond to Ryan on this point by suggesting: if you want to talk about class and Pan-Africanism, why not consider the stream of intellectuals, working within that tradition, who put class and a critique of capitalism at the core of their position, those such as Kwame Nkrumah (1971), Eric Williams (1944), Amilcar Cabral (1966), Thomas Sankara (1985), or Julius Nyerere (1963)? Indeed, Ryan labels W. E. B. Du Bois as a classic example of Black nationalism/Pan-Africanism, without mentioning that Du Bois himself was stripped of US citizenship due to his relations with the Communist Party! As highlighted by the opening quote, scholars like Du Bois placed their intellectual faith in Marxist social critique. To dismiss these thinkers as race-centric, simply because they critique the relation between racialization and capitalism, would be fairly crude.

This points to a fundamental flaw in the class-based arguments such as that endorsed by Ryan—a flaw we are arguing is largely one of historical inaccuracy. Arguments like Ryan's rely on a mistakenly perceived historiography, whereby certain intellectuals began to think about "race and class" through Marxist approaches, primarily in the 1960s and 1970s, before retreating back into a race-centrism. As Ryan himself argues:

> The 1960s and 70s were a time of progressive advance, not only in terms of mass action but also for political thought. The "new social movements"—addressing race, gender, sexuality, ecology, peace, democracy in the university—stretched left and Marxist theory in new ways and beyond an historic tendency to focus narrowly on workplace organizing. Yet, when mass action receded and corporate power reasserted itself, the new bodies of thought generated by the social movements lost their radical edge and, in particular, their connection to Marxism and class politics.

Historical accounts like the above engage in *both* a grossly oversimplified bifurcation which ignores copious amounts of intellectual labor from the Global South and obfuscating critical work developed within the Global North/West. We don't have the time or space to excavate all of these traditions, but it seems quite obvious that the historical account above neglects significant anti-colonial struggles since the time of Marx himself, up to the 1960s and 1970s. The Pan-African congresses of 1900, 1919, 1921, 1923, 1927, and 1945, for instance, are just a handful of events which gathered Marxist-inspired anti-colonial intellectuals from across the world to bring together analyses of colonialism and capitalism. Indeed, many of the intellectuals engaging in such work at Pan-African congresses were themselves working within the metropoles and thus influencing nationally specific communist or socialist agendas. These include the aforementioned Du Bois, alongside such thinkers as George Padmore, Ida Gibbs Hunt, Shapurji Saklatvala, and John McNair (Gopal 2019).

For many reasons, it is peculiar that Ryan sees the 1960s and 1970s as a unique point in history where intellectuals thought about race and capitalism in tandem with one another. Ryan is right to shed light upon the anti-capitalist, anti-racist intellectual labor of the 1960s and 1970s, in which he includes "the last years of Malcolm X and Martin Luther King Jr.," "the Black Panthers' joining of black power with a Maoist-influenced Marxism," "the League of Revolutionary Black Workers based in the Detroit auto industry," and Cedric Robinson's influential *Black Marxism: The Making of the Black Radical Tradition*. It is not clear to us, though, why Ryan limits himself to discussions concerning intellectuals working in the United States (even if some of these groups/intellectuals endorsed internationalism). Where, for instance, is mention of the Tricontinental Conference, a 1966 international gathering of anti-colonial activists in Havana, Cuba? There Amilcar Cabral (1966) famously reiterated the Leninist notion of "imperialism [as] the highest stage of capitalism,"[1] in that "imperialism can be defined as a worldwide expression of the search for profits and the ever-increasing accumulation of surplus value by monopoly financial capital, centered in two parts of the world; first in Europe, and then in North America" (qtd. in Gasper 2008).

As one of the largest and most radical gatherings of anti-imperialists in the world, a central aim of the Tricontinental Conference was to work to merge Afro-Asian solidarity with Latin American solidarity and to develop an international communist organization, with an explicit revolutionary condemnation of imperialism, colonialism, and neocolonialism (Mahler 2018). Consideration of these legacies of the Tricontinental Conference leads to an evident conclusion: Ryan is wrong to assume that the 1960s and 1970s were unique in their intellectual trajectory, in that many of those who participated in the conference had been working on the issues decades before the 1960s. Critiques as to the inherent link between imperialism and capitalism have continued to be made, up to and including in the present day, as, for instance, realized in political projects across Bolivia and Chile, to name but two from many available examples. Relevant UK scholars who are worth highlighting include such canonical figures as Stuart Hall (2021) and Ambalavaner Sivanandan (1982), both of whom brought together critiques of race, class, and capitalism well into the twenty-first century (see Virdee 2014). Post/decolonial scholars would rightfully highlight intellectuals such as Utsa Patnaik (see Patnaik and Patnaik 2021) or the wider decolonial school (e.g., Mignolo and Walsh 2018), which continue to conduct research on a variety of issues, including the relationship between imperialism and the drain of resources in the Global South as a direct consequence of the globalized capitalist system.

Even within the geopolitical location of the United States, as Ryan himself consistently notes, historical and contemporary anti-racist movements in the United States have worked with an understanding that capitalism is the root cause of inequality. This is clearly evident with respect to struggles for abolition. As explained by scholars such as Ruth Wilson Gilmore (2007) and Angela Davis (2005), the campaign for abolition of the prison industrial complex is based on a critique of capitalism, whereby the US carceral system—especially with respect to the role of private prison companies—is understood to be a central facet in multinational corporations' exploitation of labor. Hence, it is not fair or accurate to argue (as Ryan does in his critique of Cedric Robinson) that the critique of anti-racist intellectuals is "anti-capitalist, but with a race-based Pan-African vision rather than a class-based vision." As Gilmore (2007) summarizes, incarceration *is* class warfare, and just because it is Black people who are disproportionately incarcerated in this class war does not mean that it is not still a class war.

Intersectionality, Labor, and Capitalist Exploitation

Raising the work of Angela Davis and Ruth Wilson Gilmore is particularly apt, given that Ryan seems to endorse the view that the "rise of intersectionality" gave way to a form of identity politics which prevents class analysis from gaining traction in contemporary social movements. Ryan argues that, from the 1970s:

> When mass action receded and corporate power reasserted itself, the new bodies of thought generated by the social movements lost their radical edge and, in particular, their connection to Marxism and class politics. Delia Aguilar (2012) traces these changes through the evolution of feminist theory and the rise of intersectionality. . . . By the 1990 . . . intersectionality theorists regarded the "trinity" of race, class, and gender apart from any grounding in capitalism. . . . The term *class* was itself stripped of its Marxian class-conflict meaning, replaced by the mainstream sociology definition based on a person's occupation, income, and lifestyle, without addressing systemic power relations.

Again, we take issue with respect to the historical and contemporary accuracy of such a generalized and overly simplified reading of intersectionality. When considering the work of scholars like Davis and Gilmore, two of the leading advocates of intersectional scholarship, it is impossible to separate their analysis of race, gender, and class from their overall critique of capitalist social relations, within which they view these as interlinked, always connected, and evolving aspects of capitalist oppression. We have already mentioned that both Davis and Gilmore developed such critique by focusing on carcerality, but this critique is a constant intellectual current across and throughout their oeuvres. In *Women, Culture, & Politics*, for instance, Davis (1984) shows how the stigmatization of Black women in the United States was being used to justify capitalist expansion of "the right hand of the state"—that aspect of government, according to Bourdieu (Bourdieu, Droit, and Ferenczi 2008), that serves the expansion of corporations and financial institutions, as well as punitive functions and regulatory operations linked to social control.

Davis (1984) notes here that the US government produced a stereotype of the Black welfare queen—work-shy and happy to live on state handouts—in order to justify cuts to social services. These cuts were extended to cover social welfare, subsidized housing, food stamp rolls, and Aid to Families with Dependent Children (AFDC) programs. None of these aspects of the welfare state were relied on exclusively by Black people—as such, we argue, these policies of state retrenchment with respect to social welfare and public services were an act of class warfare. However, in this class warfare, Black people disproportionately suffered (e.g., 50 percent of welfare recipients were Black at this time in the mid-1980s).[2] Furthermore, as Davis argues, at exactly the same time that the United States was cutting its welfare spending, it was also rapidly accelerating spending with respect to one of its most profitable industries, the military. Davis (1984: 136) explains:

> Between 1981 and 1985, military budgets have totalled $1.2 trillion, and the Pentagon has proposed $2 trillion more for the next five year ... $3 million spent every day for the past two thousand years would equal $2 trillion—the amount the Pentagon proposes to spend in the next five years. In 1986, the Pentagon spent nearly $1 billion a day, which amounts to $41 million an hour, or $700,000 a minute.

We have quoted Davis at length concerning the nature and consequences of cuts to social services, viewed alongside concurrent raised spending on the military, because it illustrates something that is extremely pertinent to our reply to Ryan regarding both the saliency of race-based approaches and the inseparability of race, gender, and class in their overall critique. Davis's example shows that an analysis can begin from a centering of the experiences of Black women, as racial subjects. The analysis can then move seamlessly to a critique of state practices—because, of course, they are inherently linked. From this analysis of state practice, it is easy to then move to a critique of militarization and the various global social relations engendered by this. In other words, centering the experiences of a particular social group does not necessarily mean that your research process and conclusions have to be limited to a narrow analysis of identity; rather, as Davis shows, it can become a productive way for reflecting upon key national and transnational phenomena in the capitalist world system.

On to Critical Race Theory

This brings us to the final and most substantive of our responses to Ryan: while CRT is about racism, it understands this critique of racism as is inherently connected to a critique of both class and other systems of inequality and exploitation, such as those built on gender. When Ryan discusses CRT, he largely limits himself to a discussion of the CRT canon as it emerged in critical legal studies in the United States. However, even with respect to such limiting considerations, Ryan does not fully engage with the realities of such studies, in that it was primarily concerned with material forms of inequality which—while focusing on race—were clearly critiques of the capitalist social order. In Crenshaw's (1988: 1333) canonical "Race, Reform, and Retrenchment:

Transformation and Legitimation in Antidiscrimination Law," she points out that twenty years after the introduction of civil rights legislation:

> The African-American socioeconomic position in American society has actually declined.... Average annual family income for African-Americans dropped 9% from the 1970's to the 1980's.... Since 1969, the proportion of Black men between 25 and 55 earning less than $5000 a year rose from 8% to 20.... African-American enrollment in universities and colleges is also on the decline.

In other words, the entire CRT project, as it emerged out of legal studies in the United States, was a critique of how the legal system served to reproduce, evolve, and exacerbate the inequities of the status quo. This is by no means identical to a Marxist theory of law (Hunt 1999), but it is partially so. Indeed, if we examine more closely the original legal studies iteration of CRT, we can see even more similarities with a Marxist position, in a way that makes them epistemic allies. When scholars like Crenshaw (1988) and Derrick Bell (1992) were questioning *why* Black Americans were worse off *after* the introduction of civil rights legislation, part of their critique was aimed at the economic policies and accompanying ideology of neoliberalism. In particular, Crenshaw (1988) argued that the 1970s and 1980s witnessed not only neoliberal policies of state retrenchment (equating to significant cutbacks to welfare and public services, including educational support) but also the diffusion of neoliberal ideology that claimed that inequalities were the result of individual and group traits rather than structural processes. This meant that Black Americans were left in a contradictory position, one in which they were told that as they had been given civil rights in the 1960s, any inequality they faced was no longer the result of structural racism but rather was now the result of their own individual and group traits or cultural failings (Crenshaw 1988).

Further, this ideological side of neoliberalism was by no means limited to the promulgation of stereotypes around race. As authors, such as Wacquant (2008) and Tyler (2013) have highlighted, the neoliberal turn to individualism and groupism *also* facilitated the invention of the "undeserving poor" more broadly—a whole sector of a supposedly work-shy sub-proletariat who were draining state resources, the existence of which was consequently used to justify cuts to social welfare. Thus, while critiques from CRT, as arising in US critical legal studies and as exemplified by Crenshaw et al. (1995), centered on racism, as we have argued here with respect to the case of neoliberalism, their analyses are able to be scaled (locating the individual with the societal) alongside other epistemic traditions, including Marxism.

This leads us to the final point of our argument: that CRT sits very neatly alongside Marxist critiques of contemporary capitalist social relations. In order to fully grasp this argument, it is necessary to appreciate that the CRT approach encompasses far more than the US literature on law and education that Ryan relies on for his analysis. A centrally important approach within CRT scholarship is the racialized social system approach of Bonilla-Silva (2015).[3] We want to highlight the following key premises of CRT as they are articulated in this theoretical approach, for the purposes of explaining why we believe that CRT is complementary with respect to Marxist critiques of contemporary capitalist social relations.

Bonilla-Silva's development of the racialized social systems approach has, as one of the foundational influences for his theory, Karl Marx! Central to Bonilla-Silva's (2017) work is a conceptualization of racism as much more than individual bigotry. Instead, he considers racism a material structure, in which agents have active interests in the reproduction of the social order, with ideologies being disseminated across social space that serve to naturalize this social order. In other words, key to Bonilla-Silva's approach was a shift as to the understanding of racism, away from the interpersonal to one which conceives of it as a *materialist* theory that considers conflict, ideology, and structure as the essential mediums through which racialization and racism take place.

As Bonilla-Silva iterates, once we commit to the idea of racism as being structural, we can begin to see how it works like any other structure of inequality (as Marx describes in his analysis of social class (Milios 2000), for instance). As Bonilla-Silva (2017: 15) poses:

> Why are racial structures reproduced in the first place? Would not humans, after discovering the folly of racial thinking, work to abolish race as a category as well as a practice? Racial structures remain in place for the same reasons that other structures do. Since actors racialized as "white"—or as members of the dominant race—receive material benefits from the racial order, they struggle (or passively receive the manifold wages of whiteness) to maintain their privileges. In contrast, those defined as belonging to the subordinate race or races struggle to change the status quo (or become resigned to their position). Therein lies the secret of racial structures and racial inequality the world over. They exist because they benefit members of the dominant race.

Bonilla-Silva (2017: 15) then goes on to directly evoke Marx when discussing the role of racial ideology in naturalizing the racial order:

> The frameworks of the dominant race tend to become the master frameworks upon which all racial actors ground (for or against) their ideological positions. Why? Because, as Marx pointed out in *The German Ideology*, "the ruling material force of society, is at the same time its ruling intellectual force."

Conceptually, therefore, they share considerably more in common than Ryan supposes when he bifurcates class analysis from CRT. CRT may be, as Ryan claims, "about race," but to accuse it of being a race-centric theory would be myopic. To put it another way, CRT assumes the omnirelevance of race but does not claim that race/ism is the only form of structural inequality in the world system. This is precisely the reason why CRT theories, as provided by scholars from Crenshaw to Bonilla-Silva, are so useful: they stress the specific mechanisms of racial domination, but their methods of analysis make it extremely easy to connect them with other traditions and approaches across the critical social sciences.

Back to the Never-Ending Debate of Race or Class

CRT scholars like Crenshaw and Bonilla-Silva, among others, would likely not waste too much time on debating whether class or race is more "important" with respect to contemporary inequalities. Bhattacharyya challenges "the narrowing of the debate about race and class into a battle between competing affiliations and, sometimes, oppressions." This approach, she writes, "offers almost no insight into what race or class do or how what they do gets done" (2018: 2). In this respect, we find it very interesting that often people engaging in debates concerning the dominance of either "race or class" tend to come from a positionality that is concerned with wanting to "protect" class analysis from approaches like CRT. However, that is perhaps a topic for another paper. What we will briefly conclude this chapter with is a call for a more expanded understanding of "class analysis," which has also been expressed by Ryan.

We want to underscore the works of race scholars—such as Claudia Jones (1949), Stuart Hall (2021), Paul Gilroy (1993), Claire Alexander (1996), and Satnam Virdee (2015)—who provide profound critiques of class and *capitalism through the exploration of racialization and racism*. Indeed, Hall is often quoted with respect to his comment that "race is the modality in which class is lived" (Hall et al. 1978: 394). In this trajectory of scholarship, authors like Virdee (2015: 2262) have stressed the need to "navigate between the Scylla of reducing race to class (as Marxists were and are prone to do) and the Charybdis of studying race in isolation from class (as so many in Sociology continue to do), and instead plough a line of investigation that studied race and class in articulation."

We contend that, despite the critiques leveled by Ryan, CRT and other race-based approaches may actually offer a firm conceptual foundation upon which we can conduct such research on "race and class in articulation." Of course, as with any broad tradition, within CRT there may well be authors who are dismissive of class analysis—in a similar manner as to how some who predominantly focus on a class analysis may neglect the importance of racism. However, especially when you consider the conceptual foundations of CRT and closely related approaches developed firstly by Crenshaw et al. (1995) in critical legal studies, and later by Bonilla-Silva (2015) with respect to an approach that focuses on a racialized social system, it is apparent that there are clear opportunities for working together in ways that utilize such approaches alongside those founded on classical Marxism.

This leads us to conclude and, in doing so, foreground what we see as one of the central takes from our chapter, that social scientists ought to care less about the question, "What is this theory (in the singular) not focusing enough on?," and instead focus on the much more productive questioning that concerns on more productive questions such as, "How can we use multiple theories (in the plural) in tandem with one another for a more complete analysis?"[4] Once we start this more productive line of questioning, we are more likely to expand our epistemic horizons, in the spirit of Du Bois, and to do so in a manner that avoids giving undue prominence to class analysis, as does Ryan—a position which, we have argued, narrows our understanding of the relationship between race, class, and capitalism.

Notes

1 Lenin wrote *Imperialism: The Highest Stage of Capitalism* in 1916. "Lenin's main goal in *Imperialism* was to show how the colonial expansion and imperialist rivalry in the late nineteenth and early twentieth centuries were rooted in profound changes in the nature of capitalism during the same period. That's why he called imperialism at the beginning of the twentieth century a stage of capitalism" (Gasper 2008).
2 For data on "Welfare Receipt by Race, 1970–93," see *Race and the Politics of Welfare Reform* (Schram et al. (2003: 202)).
3 For more detailed discussions of the racialized social systems approach, see Meghji (2021, 2022).
4 For more on this discussion of social theory, see Meghji (2020).

15

Engaging Islamophobic Racism in the Classroom

Shirin Housee

On October 2020, Kemi Badenoch, the Black Minister of State for Equalities for the UK's Conservative Party, denounced Black Lives Matter (BLM) and Critical Race Theory (CRT) in parliament. She stated that BLM is a political movement masquerading as a benign call for equality, describing the movement as a "dangerous trend." This Tory MP punctuated her remarks by saying that any school that teaches "these elements of Critical Race Theory as fact . . . without offering a balanced treatment of opposing views is breaking the law" (Ernst and Morton 2020). The women and equalities minister could not have been clearer: BLM and CRT are political and do not belong in schools.

When I first came across the above parliamentary discussion, I found it both amusing and deeply disturbing. Badenoch's dismissal of BLM actions against the murder of Black folks by the police was accompanied by her saying, "We do not want to see teachers teaching their white pupils about white privilege and inherited racial guilt. And let me be clear: any school which teaches these elements of Critical Race Theory as fact, or which promotes partisan political views such as defunding the police without offering a balanced treatment of opposing views, is breaking the law" (qtd. in Dumas 2020). Given that this was the first time reference to CRT had been made at the level of parliamentary debates, I was pleased the concept was being mentioned, despite it being a negative reference, and it has since led to some debates on what CRT is and "who's afraid of CRT?" (Gillborn 2008).

Contrary to the Badenoch comments, I argue that anti-racism in education needs to be engaged front and center and placed at the core of curriculum and education policy reform. Unfortunately, anti-racist teaching and critical race curricula remain on the margins of most English school and university curricula. Most schools, universities, and colleges will not be offering studies on racism and anti-racism as a central part of their curriculum—if indeed it is there at all. In the light of the disproportional deaths of ethnic minorities, including due to Covid-19, and the 2020 murder of George Floyd, I often comment that our teaching fails to deal with or connect to the realities of our society and world, both historically and currently. Indeed, the mass demonstrations of predominantly young people confirm to me that any teaching exchange on race must engage with the "real" world, with what is actually happening in society, both inside and outside of the classroom. We have to make that connection and argue both for more anti-racist teaching and anti-racist approaches to education policy reform.

As a long-standing academic activist writing on racism in education, I believe it is pertinent to challenge popular "common-sense" racism and offer directions and strategies for anti-racism. Therefore, in my response to Howard Ryan's argument that centers discussions of class rather than race or racism, I explore in this chapter the varied ways that anti-racist classroom teaching tackles racism. I discuss the importance of inclusive anti-racist teaching approaches that involve students' counter-voices and how such student voice can become the instrument for challenging racism from the classroom. Specifically, in this chapter I explore how educators and students can work together to challenge everyday Islamophobic racism that has emerged in UK society. In my job as a teacher, I draw attention to such injustices and through doing so seek to encourage and facilitate anti-racist critical thinking among my students. It is in this context that I discuss the relevance of CRT as a tool for critiquing racism in that, in contrast to Ryan's proposal, it explicitly centers race and racism as central units of analysis in discussions of education.

Critical Race Theory/Feminism

Drawing on the theoretical and methodological tools offered by Black feminism and CRT, and the stories told by my students, I examine experiences of racism and highlight the ways in which critical voices within the academy can open doors to anti-racist work. My anti-racism is built through making student voices and experiences central to my pedagogical engagement. I also make use of Black feminist thought (Davis 1984; hooks 1984, 1994; Collins 1991); critical race feminism (CRF) (Crenshaw 1991; Wing 2003); CRT from the United States (Delgado 1989; Delgado and Stefancic 1999; Dixson and Rousseau 2006); and CRT from the UK (Housee 2012a; Gillborn 2005, 2008; Hylton et al. 2011; and Warmington 2020). The UK work incorporates understandings of new racisms, such as Islamophobia, to provide the lens through which I analyze gender identity with ethnicity.

A central premise of Critical Race Theory and Feminism (CRT/F) perspectives is that racism is endemic in society; it is "normal" and part of everyday life. Bell (1992), Dixson and Rousseau (2006), Delgado (1989), and Delgado and Stefancic (1999) all affirm that, although race is a social and not a biological construct, the experience of race is very real, in that ethnic minorities continue to be discriminated against in the job market, educational institutions, the criminal justice system, and elsewhere across society. A racial hierarchy, they argue, determines who gets tangible benefits, including the best jobs, entrance to the best schools, and so forth (Delgado and Stefancic 1999: 17). CRT is conceived of as reflecting a stance that Bell (1992) describes as "racial realism." An understanding of this "realist" positionality with respect to race ensures that those who struggle against racism—be that in academia, on the streets, or within the legal system—will have no illusions about the persistence of racism and racial inequality. Racial realism's core claim is that, while racial distinctions are socially constructed, they are enduringly important due to contemporary social realities in which dominant social forces continually reinforce them. And, although CRF and CRT reject essentialist racial identity, they assert that people use raced and gendered labels as ways of recognizing common experience as marginalized outsiders (Ladson-Billings 1998; Wing 2003).

With reference to the central question that Ryan poses—as to whether "race" should or should not be granted primacy—in considering different oppressions and specifically with respect to primacy over class in analyses of educational inequality and reform, I argue that race must be considered as one of the intersectional layers of oppression significant to understanding all inequalities. My position is that no one oppression—be it racism, sexism, or the socioeconomic positionality that class inequality throws up—can stand independently of the others. My application of CRT/F, therefore, draws on an understanding of intersectionality that brings together, in an analytical sense, a range of social identities and attendant oppressions, be that class, race, gender, disability, sexuality, or any other form of categorizing identification related to oppression (Gillborn 2016). In this sense, I do not view any of these social identities as representing a category of primacy with respect to oppression.

While Ryan agrees that anti-racist struggles are pivotal, he nevertheless argues for the centrality of class. In contrast, I conceive of race as equal and interlocking. This has proven a particularly useful position for informing my analysis of Islamophobic racism in education, in that this has allowed me to connect it with other forms of inequalities. My research endeavors (Housee 2008, 2010, 2012a, 2018) have been focused on creating the conditions to facilitate voice among my Black and Minority Ethnic (BAME) and specifically Muslim students, so as to hear the stories of their lived experience as layered through with issues concerning class, race, ethnicity/religion, gender, and the positionalities relating to these. I therefore stand in agreement with Collins and Bilge (2016), as referred to by Ryan, who assert that social inequalities are better understood when the layers of oppression—of class, gender, and race—are interrogated together. Using a CRT/F lens, alongside that of Black feminism, has helped me to make sense of class, gendered, racialized and specifically Muslim/Islamic identities, as they are articulated in educational contexts.

I use CRT/F for analyzing racism from the perspective of those that live racism. As these lenses enable me to critically appreciate and understand these lived experiences, I argue that they must be understood as appropriate tools for doing so. And in agreement with Ryan, I too believe that a central importance in writing about racism is to build a movement, through reflecting on our efforts to integrate class, race, and anti-capitalism (and I would also add gender) in the development of our theory and practice. My use of CRT does not privilege race above other identities; rather it focuses "on how racism works with, against, and through additional axes of differentiation, including class, gender, sexuality, and disability" (Gillborn 2008: 36). As Warmington (2020) suggests, a Black radical position on race, gender, and class does not cohere easily with the positions of either a liberal left committed to multiculturalism, or that of Marxists whose primacy of class fails to grapple with pluralities or "to acknowledge the devastating role of racial, gender, and class inequality on the lives of people of color" (Belkhir 1994: 79).

It is worth remembering, with respect to such pluralities, that the racism experienced by Asians, Blacks, and other minorities in the UK context concern race-based identities created by both the racism of the bourgeois state (Hall 1996) and also rejection by predominantly white working-class struggles for equality, from which the BAME working class was largely excluded (Gillborn 2010). This is to say, racism pushed us to organize independently. This need explains my own decision to become a member of the Birmingham Black Sisters, and the decision of others to join the Black Peoples Alliance, Asian youth movements, or the Indian and Pakistani workers' associations. These decisions to struggle separately were partly due to being marginalized within the racism of white spaces and partly due to wider concerns about the need for a space that was more conducive to our voices and our specific struggles. While I uphold the principle of a united coalition movement and seek solidarity with trade union and wider working-class struggles, I am reminded that this has never been an easy path to tread. Racism is deep, lasting, and exclusionary, as evidenced by recent anti-immigration sentiment from the UK's Brexiteers (Creighton and Jamal 2022).

In a British educational context, the marginalization referred to above has also pushed critical academics, particularly BAME academics, to seek theoretical spaces that help to explain nuanced experience of racism that mainstream sociological/educational theories fail to do. Contemporary academia in the UK has also witnessed deepening feelings of racism among students. Given these realities of contemporary UK higher education, it is not surprising that, as Warmington (2020: 15) explains, "CRT has become a rare space for resistance. For race conscious, anti-racist scholars, it has promoted international dialogue and offered conceptual tools with which to bring to the fore issues of race and racism at a time of rising populism and white nationalism." This has never been more important than it is now, in a time when politicians such as Badenoch have decided that CRT, anti-racism efforts, and expressing support for BLM constitute ideological indoctrination. If CRT is being seen as a threat because it is fueling the contemporary movements to dismantle racism in higher education, then I welcome this "threat" with open arms.

My attraction to CRT and CRF for the purposes of research is tied to my central concern with voicelessness. CRT/F promotes the voice of people of color, often referred to as counternarratives. This is an important concept for an understanding of classroom discourse on race issues. Ladson-Billings (1998: 14), one of the first to use CRT to address educational issues, claims that storytelling or naming one's own reality provides for the "psychic preservation of marginalized groups." In the UK, we have begun to see the emergence of CRT scholarship, including that of Gillborn (2005, 2006, 2008), Hylton et al. (2011), Chakrabarty, Roberts, and Preston (2012), Housee (2018), and Warmington 2020), which argues that CRT insights are relevant for analyzing recent education policy trends and the continued existence of inequalities with respect to racialized minorities in the UK. The application of CRT/F, moreover, provides space within the education system and within educational research, where people from racialized minority groups can air their counter stories and have them heard and matter. This is an important endeavor in a world where oppressed minority voices are so often silenced. Educators, however, must be weary of essentializing common-sense experience as knowledge but rather critically interrogate notions with respect to political value and validity. As argued by Darder and Torres (2004), voices from the margins provide clues about the socioeconomic, political, and cultural structures that shape the lives of oppressed minorities. This can enable educators to glean a wider understanding of the actual conditions in which people must survive.

Applying a critical race lens to developing an understanding of the racialized inequalities of education involves making sense of racialized social identities. From a CRT perspective, whiteness is understood as dominant with respect to other racialized identities, such as Blackness and "Muslimness." White supremacy, from a CRT perspective, is not by any means a reference to white people per se, as clearly not all white people from different class backgrounds hold the same economic power or cultural/capital or privilege. Nonetheless, according to CRT, "White Supremacy is systematic and global: a system of power wherein structural racism, white privilege and overt race hate are mutually reinforcing" (Warmington 2020: 6). It is "a political system, a particular power structure of formal and informal rule, privilege, socioeconomic advantages" (Taylor 2009: 4). Hence, white supremacy that encapsulates racism is perceived as normal and persistent, benefiting whites to the detriment of non-whites.

In my view, white supremacy should be seen in the same way as patriarchy: when one critiques patriarchy, one is not necessarily saying that male dominance and privilege resides with all men but in a social system that privileges men. Similarly, when one critiques white supremacy, one is not necessarily saying that white dominance and privilege resides with all who are white but in a social system that privileges whiteness. Whiteness can be understood as a shifting signifier—which echoes Hall's (1997) notion of *race as a floating signifier*—not necessarily equated with skin color but, rather, understood as an ideological representation of a particular set of privileges and power relations.

It is worth noting at this juncture that my intention is not to dismiss the value of Marxist approaches to understanding structures of oppression. Instead, I want to illustrate how an explicit stance against white supremacy/privilege could be adopted by neo-Marxist scholars to enable a more nuanced analysis of racism, one which might appeal more to CRT scholars who are skeptical of Marxism. In agreement with Walton (2020: 13), "White supremacy as a concept should not be dismissed, but incorporated into a neo-Marxist framework for conceptualizing and explaining racism in all its manifestations." This view is in sync with Cabrera (2019), who suggests we should see CRT *not* as a fixed theory but as a "theorizing space," one under continual critical review and development. The assumption here is the need for open dialogue aimed at developing theory that enables us to sharpen our tools of analysis and equip us with the necessary skills to fight racism, be that in the classroom, the streets, or elsewhere across society. With this in mind, what follows is an exploration of the specific racism experienced by my classroom groups, in which my analyses point to how we can turn student exchanges in our teaching into anti-racist moments.

Counternarratives as Classroom Strategy for Challenging Racism in Higher Education

This section provides insights for rethinking pedagogic strategies so that students can more fully participate in teaching and learning moments with respect to issues of race and racism. I discuss the ways in which, based on my experiences, tutors can utilize classroom exchanges/interactions to create and facilitate learning experiences that critically explore racism. The lecturer/teacher has the role of facilitator in the classroom, encouraging students to develop critical ways of learning, as well as the relational skills that are relevant to enabling discussion among a range of students from different backgrounds and contexts. In its search for how anti-racism can be effectively engaged in educational contexts, my work argues that one way of challenging racism is to start where racism(s) lives, in other words, to speak with and to students about their experiences of racism (Housee 2012a). Furthermore, I again contend that the lived experiences of students are essential to anti-racist education policy reform, in that they can provide key sights into their actual educational needs.

This involves those who have lived racism bringing these experiences into the classroom in order to share them with others. This offers a more grounded understanding of students' issues, which can then be engaged critically through dialogue in ways that allow for greater discernment. Viewing BAME experiences as "lived knowledge" provides important epistemological breakthroughs and foregrounds the importance of accessing BAME voices in the making of anti-racist pedagogy. From my experience this process, when BAME students engage their worldviews and question dominant mainstream views, they step into a process of "counter hegemony," which provides them insights more in line with their lives. This is to say, through the work of the educator as critical facilitator, the dialogue with students moves from an initial giving voice to their experiences, to a problem-posing stage in which worldviews are acknowledged, expressed, and challenged, and dominant views uncovered and challenged, in order to create genuine opportunities for counter-hegemonic transformations in the classroom.

While CRT/F places a particular importance on the voices and experiences of oppressed minorities, this is not to say that these experiences are universal (or can be essentialized) but rather that insightful contributions can serve to interrogate racism (Delgado 1989), through critically reflecting on students' specific lived experiences of being marginalized. These accounts are the counternarratives or storytelling that draw on students' autobiographical/daily life experiences. As a tool, storytelling creates a powerful space in which racialized minoritized groups can "speak back" against racism. This is an act that functions as a form of "psychic preservation" (Tate 1997: 220) and a means of psychological empowerment as a response to the impacts of racism. Facilitating the emergence of such counter stories is central to a process which aims to provide opportunities for the lived experiences and realities of the marginalized to be expressed. Hence, storytelling has the potential to act as a persuasive and potentially transformative tool, in struggles that seek to challenge liberal racist ideology (Rollock 2012).

CRT scholars Dixon and Rousseau (2006), as well as Ladson-Billings (1995), have argued for the importance of counternarratives that draw from concrete experiences. As Matsuda also argues, "Those that have experienced discrimination speak with a special voice to which we should listen" (Matsuda 1995; cited in Dixon and Rousseau 2006: 35). I have found this concept of counternarratives helpful, as it legitimizes my students' lived experiences of racism as knowledge to be shared in a classroom setting. In what follows, I outline how I have practiced the above-described processes in my classroom.

Islamophobia and Educational Exchanges

In this section, I discuss a specific form of racism that one could argue adds another layer of identitarian oppression to those based on class, race, and gender: that being Muslim identity. Anti-Muslim racism, often referred to as Islamophobia, has been deeply exacerbated by post-9/11 contexts (Gunter and Kieffer 2021). It is in these contexts that we have witnessed a shift, in which Islam has become the new Black and Islamophobia the new racism, and in which Muslims are claimed to pose a new threat to the stability and security of the state. For centuries, as Said (1978) reminds us, Islam has been represented by the West as evil and threatening, as backward and barbaric with comparison to Western civilization and modernity. This "binary juxtaposition" of the West and the Islamic world provides the dominant background narrative which, alongside the rise of Islamism or Muslim religiosity as an identity for many Muslim students, provides the contexts within which I work, with my students, to make sense of Islamophobia.

The important sociological point that needs to be understood here is that any study of racism in education has to consider differences with respect to social identity(ies), and thus subjectivity(ies), and the relative power positions of diverse groups and communities. To make sense of why students feel marginalized and dismissed, we must be aware of their class positioning *and* their cultural/racialized and gendered differences. This is important in that students' different social, cultural, racial, and gendered identities go beyond merely those associated with students' class positioning. This view also points to the many identities and attendant oppressions that fall within the ambit of intersectionality (e.g., disability, sexuality, age, etc.). Hence, my argument for an anti-racist pedagogy sets out to make sense of student identity and experiences as providing essential educational resources in the micro-context of the classroom. Identities matter when it comes to teaching and learning moments. Identities are salient; they make the classroom a different place for different students—students with different identities within the same classroom will experience and respond differently to potential learning moments.

An appreciation of the nature of different racialized identities and how these are formed and shaped over time and context is important, if we are to understand the experiences students share and how these might relate to the articulation of such identities in the course of pedagogical processes and exchanges in our classroom. This is central for my work on Islamophobia in a higher education context and vitally important for all educators seeking to develop their anti-racist praxis.

Some of our students are very much aware of these issues, as exemplified by this quote from one of my students:[1]

> Knowing about my religion has informed my identity. I now know that being a Muslim adds to the differences articulated by race, nationality, class, and other social differences.

For some of my students, post-9/11 contexts have served to widen and draw attention to cultural differences. Note, in the following extract, how Islamophobic racism makes this student feel like an outsider:

> As a child I thought I was British. Recently, I overheard a conversation about the recent [terrorist] attacks . . . and how the Quran encourages such violence. I was furious and stood up and challenged their ignorance. These incidents made me feel that [because] I am different, I'm not seen as British and [am] a target for racists.

Here, it is beliefs concerning Islam that are central to the experience of being different, with such division leading to feelings of alienation that are compounded by the student becoming a target for racism. It is through such analyses done with students that take account of their positionalities and thus their experiences of different forms of *racisms*, that, within my classroom, understandings have been gained with respect to current societal debates concerning both gender and racialized/ Islamophobic experiences of racism. In order to help students make sense of such experiences and begin to consider ways of addressing their root causes, it is imperative that our teaching seeks to identify and challenge the alienation and othering that occurs within educational institutions, which are always tied to what is happening out in the larger society. In what follows, I propose that an important step in this process is the development of a curriculum that centers critiques of racism.

Teacher-Facilitator: Directing Classroom Dialogue

Here, I reflect on particular teaching moments concerning Islamophobia. I note how student contributions to class discussions raised issues that went beyond the standard seminar curriculum. Some of my Muslim students shared their lived experiences of being at the receiving end of Islamophobia, which were often tense moments. I utilized student exchanges and interactions to help create a learning experience and alternative curriculum that critically explored Islamophobic racism. Through sharing and comparing narratives about their lived experiences of racism, students were able to develop counternarratives that then became a resource for rethinking the relationship between students from different cultural and religious backgrounds.

Several matters are considered next in the development of anti-racist curriculum: the role of the lecturer as facilitator of critical teaching/learning moments; the specific complexities of teaching and learning about racial "difference"; and the classroom as a space for student empowerment. I discuss students' contributions to seminar discussions in terms of these bringing critical understandings voiced concerning Islamophobia. I foreground several aspects of the role of the lecturer in such seminar discussions. I reflect critically on my own positionality as an Asian, Muslim, female lecturer from a working-class background and how that allows my students greater freedom and opportunity to say things (on racialized, gendered, and class issues) in my classroom that they might not voice with other tutors.

My role in facilitating seminar discussions was to help students navigate the various voices, while encouraging students to engage them through critical anti-racist thinking. My teaching role, which sometimes felt like I was the referee in the middle of a playing field of ideas, involved carefully liaising between students by actively listening to each and posing questions or providing clarification where necessary. Forms of critical, engaged dialogue can offer powerful tools for bringing out both the existence of racisms and that of counter anti-racist thinking and struggle in the classroom, dialogues that need to be facilitated in such a way that students' stories are connected to the relevant work and struggles of media commentators, academics, communities, and social movements.

The lived experiences shared by minority students in mixed classrooms are often questioned by other students in the classroom, with regard to both the degree to which these experiences are authentic and as to whether they provide legitimate academic value. I have found that majority (white) students are often ignorant or dismissive of the racialized experiences and views expressed by minoritized students in class. Similarly, many majority (white) students can feel dismissed, misunderstood, defensive, or overwhelmed when students of color share their lived experiences of racism. My experiences of such teaching illustrate that discussions concerning identity can trigger very emotionally driven debates, which have the capacity to lead most students to adopt defensive postures with respect to their own identity, cultures, and religion. For this reason, tutors need to be sensitive to the responses of everyone in the groups they teach, including majority (white) students.

An example of the kind of tension I have just mentioned is provided by an engagement in my class that began when a hijab-wearing female Muslim student argued that racism against Muslims was on the rise and shared an example of her own experience of racism:

> I was on a train on the way to university. There was a little girl who kept smiling at me. I returned the smile; the girl then began to approach me to sit next to me. Her mother [who was white] pulled her away. I then heard her say to her daughter, "You don't sit next to people like that." "People like that" simply meant, for me, Muslim people. I choose to wear a hijab [head scarf]. I did not know what she thought of me: did she think I was carrying a gun or something?

An Asian female student, who agreed that Muslims were being targeted for racist abuse, said:

> But what do you expect, being dressed like that and singling yourself out as being different to other Asians?

She followed this comment by suggesting that such racist abuse could be avoided if Muslim women stopped wearing the hijab. To this Hindu student, assimilation, as opposed to accepting differences, is what makes for peaceful existence. In response, the Muslim student told the class that racism was not her problem and that she should have the right to dress as she pleased, saying: "I am not going to hide my identity now." Another non-Muslim student, of mixed heritage, then made a further and similar controversial comment:

> Yeah, but, why? I'm Catholic and the only time I have worn a scarf is when I visited a Catholic church in Europe out of respect. Anyway, we had to. You're not in a religious place now, so why do you wear one? [sniggering]

This comment was met with a long, drawn-out silence. The majority of the students, who were white, looked uncomfortable, while the minority Muslim students began to appear agitated and looked at each other in disapproval at the comment that had just been made and the reaction to it. This was also an uncomfortable moment for me. I stepped in and made the following comment:

> Surely, this is their freedom of choice; why should it matter to others if they wear the hijab? Freedom of dress, whether of wearing a mini-skirt or a hijab, should be a universal freedom. One should be free to dress as one pleases, so long as we are all free to do so.

This type of educator intervention was clearly needed here to redirect the debate in a constructive direction, through making a political connection to considerations concerning universal freedoms.

The examples provided above suggest that anti-racism reflects a form of political struggle, whether in the classroom or within educational policy arenas—where racializing attitudes and views (such as those expressed above) can arise and influence policies, yet never be discussed or addressed. Moreover, the classroom teaching against racism described here was not solely about sharing a moment but was also about bringing to the fore, acknowledging, and exploring the negative and uncomfortable experiences and emotions that emerged. It is through such exchanges that counternarratives were enabled. My interventions were designed to connect student lived experiences with wider social political issues. Reflecting on these critical moments, the depth and breadth of the sociological analyses developed from the above anti-racist discussions are most transformative when the wider sociopolitical connections are drawn out and linked to students' everyday lives. In contrast, when students' anti-racist experiences are excluded from either the classroom or from debates and decisions related to educational policy reform, as they so often are, processes of racialization are summarily negated, ignored, and go unattended.

Conclusion

The struggle against racism, both within the classroom and society more broadly, can be fraught with contention, as Ryan's work suggests; but if we, as teachers, fail to rise to the challenge of uncovering and undoing racism, we leave such oppressive ideas undisturbed. For carrying out such necessary work within educational settings, the development of counternarratives, as described above, is necessary and not only for providing essential information. More importantly, they serve to provide a challenge to "everyday" "racist" common-sense views, as held by many students. The counternarratives of Muslim students, in this case, served to both inform and challenge the common-sense racism that emerged through others' contributions and interactions. Such sharing of experiences is often considerably more facilitative of rich and deep learning than book learning. My intervention, as the facilitating teacher in the example shared above, was made for the purpose of challenging the bigotry expressed by some students and approved by other students, in an effort to foreground the need to protect democratic freedoms. Further, in my comment to students about "freedom of choice," for example, I also intended my intervention to be a means of assisting students to connect their personal experiences with broader socioeconomic and political issues—in this case, Islamophobia.

Such facilitatory intentions centrally concern a directive form of facilitation that speaks to the development of critical thinking and an encouragement to expand and stretch their views and understanding with respect to culture and religion. In this way, potential exchanges, whether in the classroom or in the education policy arena, can serve to create a pedagogical space for learning about the lives of racialized minorities, which can lead to critical anti-racist learning moments. This concerns a move from what was simply a sharing moment to one that instead becomes a counternarrative and thus anti-racist learning or transformative moment. Such moments speak to critical engagement and the critical evaluation and validation of students' lived experiences of racism.

So, the question here is: What is to be done for this change to take place? I suggest here that universities become serious and insist on teacher training which is more progressive and critical in its strategies. Indeed, as part of such training, the university should also take seriously the process of diversifying and de-colonizing the curriculum, so teachers are more equipped with the learning resources and indeed the mindset that will enable them to undertake a much more critical role in their teaching. Through such processes, we can contribute collectively to move from struggling within schools to wider struggles focused on transforming the societal systems, institutions, and relations that are the root cause of material inequalities and social exclusions.

Note

1   As part of my PhD thesis (Housee 2012b) on anti-racism and critical pedagogy, I observed my classes and received ethical approval from the University of Wolverhampton for this research. Students were fully aware that I was note-taking and recording during seminars. To keep it as "natural" as possible, we would leave the recorder on and continue the class. The students were also aware that the research would be published. I shared the relevant transcripts with the students. A fuller discussion is in the PhD thesis and in other publications which are available. This chapter draws on a few specific moments as examples to show how critical redirection in an anti-racist way can be done in the classroom.

16

An Intersectional Reflection on Race, Class, and Education Reform

Nicholas D. Hartlep and Nicholas C. Ozment

A Black man in a hoodie gets on an elevator already occupied by a white woman. He has a vicious-looking Rottweiler on a leash. She is immediately nervous. As the elevator slowly makes its way up the floors, her blood pressure rises, and her tension builds into full-blown anxiety. Suddenly the man says, "Sit!" Panicked, she obeys the man's command. Imagine her embarrassment when she learns the man is Eddie Murphy, and he was issuing the command to his dog! This urban legend made the rounds back in the 1980s. Sometimes it was another Black person in the story, such as Bill Cosby (although in that case it turned out, in retrospect, the consternation might have been warranted).

The theme of this little bit of urban folklore is clearly race. The woman prejudges a Black man as a threat and is left looking foolish when the Black man turns out to be someone whom popular culture would not perceive as a threat. Yet, upon closer analysis, it is also inextricably tied up with class. When the person is identified as being a professional entertainer or having a solid career, the fear of Blackness is dissipated. It could also be noted that if the person with a scary-looking dog was a young, tattooed white male, the woman alone in this situation might also feel apprehension. Blackness might be the central focus in this story, but there are clearly other markers, those of class, in play as well. This seems to be the crux of Howard Ryan's critique of race-based scholarship that explores education reform—that it myopically focuses on race and misses the ramifications of class. By disregarding class, Ryan further argues, critical race theory has limited its scope of vision when it comes to education reform.

This is the central issue Howard Ryan confronts in his feature chapter. We quote the following passage at length to offer context for our response which, for the most part, aligns with Ryan's critique:

> This chapter challenges what I call *race-based theory* and argues for the validity and importance of class analysis—in the study of education and politics, and in the pursuit of racial and social justice. The chapter does not attempt to provide a comprehensive theory on race and class, or on related topics such as the primacy of one category over the other, or the pursuit of race/class fusion. The aim, rather, is

to foster discussion toward the building of such theory; and it assumes that how we address these theoretical matters, and how we imagine the world is constructed, bears much on how we strategize and organize for social change.

The intent of this chapter is to contribute to the theory-building Ryan proposes. To begin with, we agree with Ryan that class should be centered and is the most critical component of education reform work. Why? Because as we see it, racism in its modern form is a product of capitalism. However, while we center class, we also believe it is important to provide an intersectional understanding of how class converges with other categories such as race, gender, and sexual orientation (Crenshaw 2022). We begin, here, by sharing a schematic (Figure 16.1) that will be used as a frame of reference for our thoughts, in that it illustrates the contexts for our thinking on this issue.

Through the use of this schematic (a representation of a theory in the form of a model), our intent here is to affirm that concerns of race and class, along with gender—rather than being antagonistic—are conceptually compatible in that they are always intersecting. A variety of scholars in education insist on an ironclad division between these two theoretical approaches, but others recognize them as equally relevant tools for understanding inequality and human relations, and the role of power in shaping these (Leonardo 2009: 2012). We understand racism as being inculcated, promulgated, and exploited to divide working-class whites from non-white populations. Consequently, our work denotes capitalism as the environment in which race, class, and gender operate.

Looking back at the elevator anecdote with which we opened the chapter, that story, plucked from modern folklore, might initially seem counterintuitive with respect to Ryan's thesis—given that its fear depends on racial bias—however a more nuanced

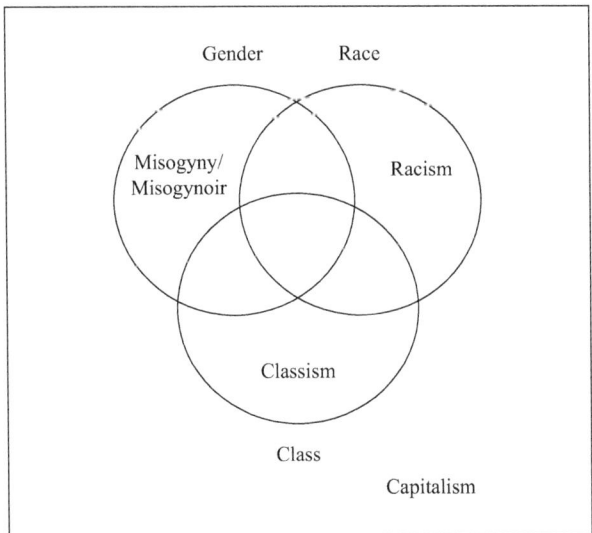

Figure 16.1 Schematic for Understanding Importance of Intersectionality. Authors.

reading reveals that a concurrent factor at play in the story's impact is class. Indeed, class is the bedrock requirement for the "punchline" to work—in that eliminating the aspect of race from the story would shift the story from one concerning the prejudging of a Black person to one concerning the prejudging of a man, though in both cases the "punchline" would concern class.

As suggested by our Figure 16.1, capitalism in the United States is the proverbial water that everyone swims in; American capitalism was built upon a foundation of genocide, that of the Indigenous people who populated the land before colonization (Spring 2016). Capitalism in the United States further expanded when Africans were forcibly transported from their homelands to this colonized territory to serve as chattel slaves (Inikori 2020). It was these enslaved Africans who shouldered much of the burden of building the United States, of physically laying its foundations, without receiving compensation or reward in return for the sweat, blood, and sacrifice of their labor (Banerjee and Johnson 2020). Their free labor was used to enrich the individuals who owned them as property. Slave owners amassed wealth obtained from the crops that were farmed by slaves. Using unpaid slave labor, slave owners also built buildings and established institutions such as colleges and universities, which led to their accruing yet more power and prestige (Smith and Ellis 2017). These are the ugly realities that served as the backdrop to how the enterprise of education was instituted.

With this in mind, we argue here that reforming education policies and practices without taking class into consideration would be a fool's errand. Similarly, when anti-racism scholars or activists accuse poor whites for being part of the problem, this feeds into a divisiveness that only serves to propagate systemic racism. Poor whites arguably have more in common with Black, Indigenous and People of Color (BIPOC) communities than with the elites who possess most of the nation's wealth, in the sense that poor whites have also been used and exploited by those in power—namely, wealthier whites—including in ways that serve to maintain the racist and classist divisions we experience today.

As such, is there a way that education reform can help us to address these divisions? Ryan observes, "reform can have unequal results while still affecting all negatively. An alternative to the race-based formulation—with reform rewarding whites and oppressing non-whites—is that reform oppresses working-class whites, oppresses working-class people of color more so, and with the major rewards accruing to a tiny capitalist class." We agree with Ryan that the current system is detrimental to both people of color and poor whites. Further, we believe it is important to note here, as Noam Chomsky (2015) argues, "America is a plutocracy masquerading as a democracy." As such, those who control the wealth also control the power and this has worked to overshadow the significance of race (Lewis 1996). The artificial divisions that have been created by those in power, between working-class whites and BIPOC communities, continue to be well-entrenched within the educational system, through the policies, actions, and inactions perpetuated by contemporary society's beneficiaries—the economic elites who are considered to have a quite substantial and highly significant impact on policy (Gilens and Page 2014).

Historically an Unequal Opportunity Race

From the beginning of the American system of schooling, there has been unequal access to education. Slaves were forbidden from receiving education because their doing so would be a risk to their owners. Indeed, this was essential to maintaining the myth that Black people were somehow lesser and less capable than whites, through ensuring that there was no, or very limited and controlled, access to what would have been an opportunity for Blacks to prove the myth wrong. When an educated, brilliant thinker and orator like Frederick Douglass came along (escaping from slavery to become a leading voice for abolition), such myths served to facilitate his being viewed as an isolated example of such Black possibilities in the white southern mind, painted as a freak of nature, as an exception that proved the rule. It was believed that, were Black youth to begin receiving equal access to education and demonstrating themselves just as capable as white children, these myths, including the notion that the "negro race" was closer to animals than the "white race" and needed whites to own and govern them, would collapse.

These debilitating myths continued to exist long after struggles over the institution of slavery had been ended—up into and through the twentieth century, as exemplified by Jim Crow laws, and continues to manifest as a range of biased, racist, beliefs, both conscious and subconscious, and their oppressive, violent, consequences, up to the present day. Segregation has always been built on the false narrative that Black people are not as capable as and are more primitive and savage than whites. The central premise of segregation was that Black people and white people should not comingle—this was *not* intended with the benefit of both races in mind but, instead, with a perceived benefit for whites, as this would, purportedly, both help to ensure that their superior bloodlines would not be contaminated and also function to significantly reduce opportunities for being adversely influenced by their inferior Black fellow citizens. When successful Black communities and businesses did manage to establish themselves, they were frequently attacked and burned down. They did not fit with the established white myth of Black inferiority, so had to be eradicated. Black musicians had their music kept separate from mainstream music, Black athletes were prevented from playing in sports' professional leagues, and one consequence of doing so concerned attempting to ensure that Black performers, entertainers, and athletes would not be seen to be as good as or even better than their white counterparts. This bias that has whites as the superior and paternal race still exists today. White couples adopting Black children is a popular trope in television sitcoms and is also common in real life (Willis 2017). But are you aware of similar portrayals or real-life examples of Black couples adopting a white child? Perhaps it has happened; but, like us, you probably cannot think of a single incident either in fact or represented in fiction. You will likely recall more stories of white infants being raised by apes or wolves, than by a Black family.

Key to our discussion is the recognition that Blacks did not go from slavery to a life where they would be able to catch up with whites, who still possessed institutional, including academic, power over them and were able to thus ensure that opportunities were far from equal. One hundred years after the passing of the Thirteenth Amendment, legally abolishing slavery in the United States, in 1965, President Johnson said, in a Howard University commencement address: "You do not take a person who, for years, has been hobbled by chains and liberate him, bring him up to the starting line of a race and then say, 'You are free to compete with all the others,' and still justly believe that you have been completely fair." Yet much social reform has amounted to little. For example, programs that give students laptops are nice, but they won't help students who don't have access to a dependable internet connection. Or educational policies tied to high-stakes testing do little to ensure that students will have adequate opportunities and resources needed to contend with racializing classroom practices that negatively impact their learning.

More disheartening is how inequitable and oppressive conditions of schooling and society persist for Blacks today. Some of the most prestigious colleges/universities, predominantly white institutions (PWIs) like Harvard, have the largest endowments, the most perceived social value, and the most exclusionary admission processes—all founded upon the kind of early exploitation outlined earlier. Harvard, for instance, founded in 1636, has an endowment of $41 billion. With so much money at its disposal, Harvard could serve the interests of many but instead continues to enroll a significant percentage of students from among the affluent class. In essence, this is a continuation of its long tradition: to reproduce the elite class. Writing about Harvard and slavery, Beckert and Stevens (2011) noted that, in fact, "When they graduated, many Harvard students became slave owners themselves" (2011: 8).

In January of 2021, Harvard announced that it would remove standardized testing requirements for class of 2026 (read: students who apply for admission during the 2021-2 year). Will this lead to further reforms at Harvard? Who will likely benefit from reforms? Will reforms lead to more class diversity (read: admitting more low-income students)? Harvard and other "test-optional" universities have an advantage over universities that rely on standardized testing, because they receive many more student applications per available place (Anderson 2021). Aisch et al. (2017) write: "At 38 colleges in America, including five in the Ivy League—Dartmouth, Princeton, Yale, Penn, and Brown—more students came from the top 1 percent of the income scale than from the entire bottom 60 percent." Hence, the role of elite universities such as Harvard is to perpetuate a deeply unequal system, which continues to benefit the interests of the wealthy and powerful.

Education and the Importance of Class Analyses

One doesn't have to look very long to notice how the system of schooling and education more broadly in the United States perpetuates classism, a consequence of such education functioning to support the hegemonic system of capitalism, in its contemporary form, neoliberalism. It is an even worse mutated variant of social Darwinism, wherein an already corrupt system predicated on "survival of the fittest" has been further rigged and exploited by the rich and powerful: America's plutocrats. The ethos of academic competition permeates the education system, with a central role being the continual meritocratic sorting and grouping of students—class ranks, weighted GPAs, SAT, and ACT tests, the list goes on; contestants (read: students) continuously engage in competition with one another, on what is, as described above, anything but a level playing field with respect to their battleground, the contemporary American education system. Contemporary schooling fails to measure what students actually know. Rather, today's educational assessments tools measure if students know what schools decide is legitimate knowledge (Darder 2012). The consequences of doing so are considerable, given that such "measurements" are used to decide which students get tracked into college credit courses and which students do not, thus ensuring that students' circumstances as to upbringing strongly influence decisions that will lead to very disparate life outcomes for different groups of students.

We will share our thinking on why we believe education reform should draw on the intersectionality of class, race, and gender, as it relates to issues of social justice, rather than exclusively situating analyses in either race-centered or class-centered ways. As such, we call for an intersectional approach, given that race and class are so intertwined with each other and with other categories of identity such as gender (as noted above), asking: why cannot we use *both-and*? Within CRT, we contend that intersectionality is a significant principle by which we can consistently consider the ways in which race *and* class *and* gender intersect; and thus, it can help us to both understand and address educational inequality and exclusion within the context of education reform. We wish to further argue that, with an appreciation as to class and race intersectionality, any analysis of race should be understood as a form of class analysis. In other words, we are claiming that race and class are so interwoven that an intersectional analysis is often the most viable way to engage questions of education reform.

University efforts to adhere to test-blindness, a policy of seeking to achieve color blindness in the testing of students, have not shown to foster greater diversity (Plaut et al., 2018). Similarly, holistic admission policies—supposedly meant to get a sense of not only the applicant's academic qualifications but also of what the applicant is like as a person—have not proven to be effective (Bovy 2013). In both examples, these policies do little or nothing to interrupt class privilege from benefiting students from more affluent backgrounds. Research by Bastedo, Howard, and Flaster (2016) has shown that low-income students are less likely to maximize their high school curriculum than affluent students are, while racial minority students are less likely to both maximize their high school curriculum and benefit from doing so when applying to colleges in states that ban affirmative action, than their white affluent counterparts.

Unfortunately, despite well-meaning intentions, contemporary university reforms have failed to ameliorate race or class disparities in higher education. It is for this reason that we stress the importance of the intersectionality of race and class in our efforts to engage with questions of class analysis within the context of education. We draw, in particular, on William Julius Wilson's (2012) seminal book, *The Declining Significance of Race*, originally published in 1980, where he argues that social class had gradually become more important than race in determining the life trajectory of African Americans. At that time, he seemed to be arguing that one's race was less important than one's class. However, in his subsequent article "*The Declining Significance of Race: Revisited & Revised,*" Wilson (2011: 66–7) concluded:

> The point is that a continuous struggle is needed to address the problems of racial inequality—some calling for race-based solutions, like affirmative action, others calling for class-based solutions, such as programs to increase employment in areas with the highest rates of joblessness. Accordingly, if I were writing *The Declining Significance of Race* today, I would provide more balance in my policy recommendations by placing much greater emphasis on the need to *strongly* and *continuously* embrace, as well as advance, both race- and class-based solutions to address life chances for people of color. (italics in original)

With all this in mind, the next section provides an example of how the Covid-19 pandemic has demonstrated the importance of an intersectional understanding of race and class, while highlighting why class analysis remains central to our discussion of education reform.

The Covid-19 Pandemic

The Covid-19 pandemic led to renewed public awareness of the important role that teachers play across globally. When it became the responsibility of parents and guardians to teach their children and explain educational materials at home, many had their eyes opened to the labor teachers engage in every day. Teaching is both difficult and time-consuming—two factors that many already stressed people found difficult to handle in a home situation. Around the world, many people were (and still are) at breaking point (United Nations 2022). Some households do not have internet access, making it impossible to engage properly with the virtual teaching as required. Other homes don't have the necessary computer hardware, be that desktop computers, laptop computers, or smartphones, necessary for students to engage with and complete schoolwork. Consequently, the global education crisis has been worse than anyone ever thought possible (World Economic Forum 2022).

The Covid-19 pandemic, nevertheless, also illustrated the important role that schools play in combating hunger, as the reliance of some on school meals was foregrounded by the additional numbers of pupils going hungry over the period when schools were shut to them. Schools provide breakfast and lunch for many of their students who are living with food insecurity, so considerable numbers of these students were at home during lockdowns, hungry, without any or without appropriated academic support, doing the best they could to learn in difficult and precarious living conditions. The pandemic also served to shed light on how some of the most privileged students benefited from that privilege. If they attended public schools that were closed, they could re-enroll in private, parochial (church affiliated), or independent schools that were open (Sullivan 2020). Other affluent students were homeschooled using curricula that were richer and more robust than those provided for the majority of working-class students attending public schools. Given these factors, many privileged students were able to continue learning uninterrupted, while those lacking in such privilege often fell behind when having to learn at home, due to inadequate support and resources.

The educational consequences of the Covid-19 pandemic serve to reinforce our position: that, educational opportunities are deeply impacted by class in a capitalist society, such as the United States. Families with resources, as per Bourdieu's (1986) various forms of capital, will be able to emerge from this global catastrophe further "ahead" of those less privileged. Given their advantages, wealthier families have been able to appropriately "socially distance" within society, thus keeping their families safe, while also being able to continue to further benefit their children in terms of academic opportunities.

Research by Miller, Wherry, and Mazumder (2021) has documented Covid-19's disproportionate effect on people of color, when compared both to whites in general and particularly with respect to whites from poor working-class communities. Their research finds that you were, for example, less likely to die from Covid-19 as a poor white person than a middle-class Black person. You were also less likely to die from Covid-19 as a white person who had to attend their workplace for work during lockdown than a Black person who was able to work from home. You were less likely to die from Covid-19 as an uninsured white person than a Black person who is insured. These findings suggest that "race" is a more important factor than class when considering those factors most important to predicting death from Covid-19 in the United States. The work of scholars such as Achille Mbembe (2013) has explained that this is one consequence of racism—such that one's "race" can be viewed as an indicator with respect to one's likelihood of premature death. Gilmore (2007) defines racism as "the state-sanctioned and/or extralegal production and exploitation of group-differentiated vulnerability to premature death." Miller et al.'s research, while underscoring the correlation of class and health, also serves to problematize a class-only approach, because race is also clearly a factor with respect to health outcomes across society. With regards to gender, Fisher and Ryan (2021) were able to document glaring gender inequalities that were exacerbated by the pandemic, by considering relevant intersections of identity. Hence, the studies noted here, when engaged together, strongly support an intersectional understanding of race, gender, and class.

Racialized, Gendered, and Classed Outcomes

During the Covid-19 pandemic, US public schools did their best to feed and educate vulnerable students. Buses delivered food to their homes; Electronic Benefit Transfer (EBT) cards were given to needy families; some of the students most in need were picked up and allowed to receive supplemental instruction at school by masked and socially distanced teachers. But this was not enough. What is often missed is that already vast racialized, gendered and classed educational inequities were and continue to be further exacerbated by the pandemic (Perry, Aronson, and Pescosolido 2021).

US schools and universities in the modern capitalist age have been designed to produce workers for the benefit of the American economy. Educational pathways to achieve this begin at preschool and continue through elementary, middle, and high school. After high school, students will either directly enter the workforce or proceed to further study, at a two-year community/technical school or through a four-year degree at a college or university. Following the successful completion of a four-year degree, graduate school becomes an option. These options of degree programs (that include law school, medical school, master's programs, etc.) prepare students for specific careers. The various pathways through and barriers within education just outlined are all shaped by the need for and primarily concerned with narrowly producing what and who is required for the short-term needs of the economy within a US, as well as global, capitalist framework, in which workers' pay is differentiated, often based on their educational credentials.

When looking at the educational pipeline (i.e., movement of students across the P–12 educational process), it becomes apparent that the system has major shortcomings, even when judged by its own claimed standards. Purportedly the system is based on meritocracy, and it is taken on faith by many to be neutral and fair, while its primary purpose is actually linked to providing what and whom US capitalist society needs (Bowles and Gintis 1976). The kind of meritocratic education system that is held out by such rhetoric is color blind and accessible and considered to be available for all who are viewed to be capable of benefiting from it. In such a system the best-performing students are to reap the rewards, and those who do not "win" in this educational competition get what they deserve. It is claimed that everyone has an equal opportunity to succeed, as per the persistent myth of the American dream; however, at the core of meritocracy is the assumption of an equality that does not exist in America (Garber 2017).

The ideology of meritocracy is both color blind and fails to address issues of class. The belief that what one gets is what one deserves is widespread in the United States—and as such, functions to ensure that wealthy, well-resourced, race-privileged individuals do not have to respond to accusations that their position in society is dependent on a system that is rigged in their favor (Sandel 2020). If, in fact, a genuine system of equality existed, there would not be racialized, gendered, and classed outcomes. For instance, with respect to SAT and ACT scores, whites consistently score higher on average than do other racial groups and males tend to score higher than females (Smith and Reeves 2020).

This raises the question: Why are consequential tests racialized, gendered, and classed? While correlation does not prove causation, we can surmise much from the fact that these tests produce predictable outcomes. These include buttressing notions of white superiority, that they are likely racist because white students tend to score higher than students of color. They, similarly, buttress the class system, given that students from wealthier backgrounds score higher than students from poor ones. Coming from a wealthy family would seem to provide a major advantage to students. Carnevale et al., (2019: 1) note: "Among children with similarly high academic potential, the test scores of economically disadvantaged students are most likely to decline and stay low as they move through the K–12 system." The questions in these important exams have been found to be culturally biased (see Santelices and Wilson 2010), in that the knowledge expectations of standardized tests are informed by the dominant cultural and linguistic worldview (Darder 2012). One finding of the research conducted by Santelices and

Wilson (Darder 2012) was that SAT questions in the verbal tests tend to favor white subgroups over African American ones, in that white examinees are used to reference these tests.

However, it is not just testing that ensures racist outcomes in education; another prominent example is provided by the way high schools administer Advanced Placement (AP) courses. Using critical race theory as a framework, Solórzano and Ornelas (2004) examined the availability of and the nature of access to AP courses and how these considerations impact educational outcomes for Latina/o and African American students. They found that Latina/o students and African American students were disproportionately underrepresented in AP enrollment right across the district that was the subject of the research: schools that primarily served urban, low-income Latina/o and African American communities had low student enrollment in AP courses as compared to schools in predominantly white affluent communities; and even when Latina/o and African American students attended high schools with high numbers of students enrolled in AP courses, they were disproportionally underrepresented on such courses. Solórzano and Ornelas termed the result of such processes and structures, "Schools within School," given that blatant disproportionate conditions of students' opportunities within the same school.

Racialized structures and processes such as those that created "Schools within School" are similar to those Jeanie Oakes found over decades of research (see Oakes 1984, 1992; Oakes and Wells 1998). In her book, *Keeping Track: How Schools Structure Inequality* (1984), Oakes identified how schools, through tracking structures that group students based on achievement, widen rather than reduce inequalities. Tracking is so commonplace in K–12 education that it has become normalized as "best practice" (Oakes 1984). This internal tracking within schools may explain why we see males overrepresented in fields such as STEM and why wealthier children are overrepresented in programs designed for those labeled gifted and talented (see Grissom, Redding, and Bleiberg 2019; Hill, Corbett and St. Rose 2010). Gendered and racialized outcomes also persist with respect to college education, with women carrying more student loan debt than men and Black collegians carrying more than white collegians (see AAUW 2017; Murakami 2021). While student loans supposedly exist to help students access higher education, it appears that they help women differently than they do men; women, who earn 84 percent of what men earn (Barroso and Brown 2020), experience, in the long run, greater economic burden.

Conclusion

"Operation Varsity Blues" is the name given to the 2019 college admissions bribery scandal that involved many wealthy and powerful people working with William "Rick" Singer—a college admissions counselor who admitted in court to being behind the scheme, who bribed exam administrators to facilitate cheating on entrance exams for college and university and bribed coaches and administrators to nominate unqualified applicants as elite recruited athletes—so as to facilitate their offspring's smooth entry into the best colleges (Kasakove 2021). The scandal, which led to a documentary film entitled *"Operation Varsity Blues,"* (Smith 2021) illustrates how, like many others throughout the long histories of these institutions, these parents sought to leverage their wealth to unfairly benefit their children when it came time to apply for admission to them. Class—in effect, the financial wealth of the implicated families—was what this admissions scandal boiled down to. Herein lies the issue: It wasn't exclusively wealthy white families, there were also families of color who participated in this illegal behavior, but these were people of color with money.

In Ryan's opinion: "The predominant trends in race-based theory . . . diminish class. Race-based theorists sometimes shortchange class even as they mindfully seek a race-class synthesis." We find Ryan's assessment to be grounded and cogent and agree with his belief in the significance of class in discussions of education reform. Even when one is mindful that class has deep and consequential ramifications, we recognize that it can be easy, particularly given controversy-creating coverage in the media, to pay much more attention to the deeply emotional issues surrounding race in the United States. Given the issues we have raised on our intersectional discussion, this has led us to tentatively conclude that class should be central. However, because other factors, particularly in this instance race and gender, interact with class, intersectionality is a necessary heuristic for engaging, critiquing, and proposing education reform. In a capitalistic system that values profit above all else, (income-based) class becomes the defining hierarchy. However, within and around this class hierarchy are overlapping hierarchies of race and gender, tightly intertwined like choking vines on the social good that go beyond race and gender.

Afterword

Cheryl E. Matias

Academia was initially conceptualized as a space for intellectual symposia wherein ideas were to be freely brought forth to enlighten, provoke, dispute, or contest. Yet, as times have changed and practices evolved, these open intellectual spaces have been reduced to the holding of private discussions among a few. Insofar as these spaces have been reduced, so too has our capacity to disagree. It is almost as if we cannot disagree, provoke, or entertain that which is controversial anymore for fear of being canceled (see Brown 2020). And yet, as academics, scholars, and advocates for educational justice, this is precisely what we must do to achieve a better humanity. Let me be clear. We, as critical scholars, do not put our reputations on the line, our safety at risk,[1] or sacrifice our more than twelve years in higher education to sit in silence, idly watching injustice take place. Alas, we find ourselves in a situation where we must come to reclaim this space, to honor what it was and should be—to say that which must be said, to think that which should be thought, and to write that which needs to be written. Despite the occasional open dissertation defense or public plenary that allows for dissent and critique, the academy is now deeply colonized by neoliberal policies and practices focused on eagerly churning out the next set of passive laborers for the capitalist economy, armed with PhDs, with little concern, support, or regard for the transformative efforts and ideas of professors themselves.

Indeed, many scholars are but public servants, serving the public with hopes of loan forgiveness. However, we are, in truth, so much more. From being the first one to attend college in our families to transforming our past educational traumas to creating new future visions for educational policies so that others will never have to experience those same traumas, many scholars have committed themselves to the struggle for educational justice not simply because it is our job but because it is our life's passion.

Thus, one can understand how refreshing it is to read a book that honors what the academy was initially designed for: to present, contest, and encourage possibilities for thinking anew. Within this complexity, there is never solely one view or perspective that rings true. There is no simple how-to guide for traversing the real tensions and anxieties generated by the experiences of racism and other inequalities we face. Instead, embedded in *On Class, Race, and Educational Reform* is a strategy for how to engage in an intellectual dialogue that respects a range of expertise, theoretical perspectives, and academic journeys, as well as acknowledges the difficulties at work in our lives as educators and activists for social justice.

Unlike a social climate in which cancel culture demands we pick a side, wherein white supremacy reduces us to binaries of white and non-white, and in which capitalism bifurcates us into the haves and have-nots, this text weaves the multiplicity of ideas, the complexity of issues, and the challenge to disagree rightfully and respectfully. Although I have my own thoughts on Ryan's commitment to a grand theory that gives primacy to class analysis (which I will share below), my main desire here is to congratulate the editors, Antonia Darder, Cleveland Hayes, and Howard Ryan. Through convening a variety of scholars across perspectives to contribute to the dialogical purpose and content of this book, they have, in an explicit, conscious, and very deliberate manner provided both academia and the wider society an open approach, by which we can come together to push, challenge, and rethink anew. Isn't that what critical scholarship is supposed to do?

As the editors remind us: "only through dialogue grounded in a deep sense of love for the world (Freire 1971) can we engage the true culprit of the oppressive divisions fabricated in our society." As such, the critical labor of academia requires dialogue, which all scholars should embrace, along with a grounded commitment to just educational reform. And we must approach this labor with profound love for world, despite the controversies, imperfections, contentiousness, and, at times, the plain ugliness that such dialogues may portend. I say this because in critically engaging the age-old quandary over race-versus-class or class-versus-race, the ultimately outcome we seek is justice, whether in schools or the wider society.

From Race-versus-Class/Class-versus-Race to *RaceClass*

Ryan's argument with respect to the primacy of a class analysis in our struggle for educational reform is bold, especially at a time when critical race theory (CRT) is rapidly becoming central to educational debates and, simultaneously, notorious among conservatives. In his critique of Leonardo's (2009) analysis of No Child Left Behind, Ryan claims what is missing is the leading role of business. In fact, he doubles down by stating, "policy is made by people, not by ideology per se." Indeed, big business has always played a role in education. Apple and Christian-Smith (1991), for instance, detail how the production of textbooks is not exempt from the sways of business profiteering. Similarly, Symcox (2002) traces how classroom history standards are also at the whims of party politics, many of which are swayed by donations of big business. Here, the role of business is considered a key component of how educational reform is made, maintained, and operated.

Yet, in this acknowledgment, Ryan misses the mark in presuming that policies—made by people—are without ideological tendencies. In fact, Leonardo (2003) argues that "ideology *is* the relations that subjects live out" (p. 38); stated otherwise, "ideology is anchored in real practices and institutions like schools" (p. 39) or, by extension, like policies themselves. That is to say that people in and of themselves act in ways that adhere to their long-held ideologies. Therefore, it is more apropos to say that people *do* make policy but that which aligns with their ideologies, many of which are in sharp contrast to the ideologies of those such policies are supposed to help.

What is also evident, across the contributions in this volume, is the quandary about whether reform benefits whites and the need to contend with the differences between working-class and middle-class whites. Indeed, class positionality (and difference) is a significant factor in how people experience the world. As an example, Lareau's (2000) study reveals the differences that exist between the ways in which middle-class white parents engage in dialogue with their children, as opposed to how working-class parents do. In doing so, parents provide their children with varied access to the social capital needed for educational success. Therefore, it is not surprising that contributors here consistently note that scholarly engagement with class analysis is of utmost importance and failure to do so, as Darder and Torres argue in this volume, weakens our capacity to "counter the oppressive structures of capitalism . . . that categorically obscure class struggle."

Further, Allen (2009) work, which investigates the dynamics of how poor whites socialize whiteness at the expense of their own economic interest, also comes to mind. Allen concludes that in using the racial presumption that despite being poor they are still *white*, poor whites inadvertently throw their self-interests on the petard of racism, rather than politically aligning themselves with people of color, in order to improve their access to social institutions such as schools and health care. From a CRT perspective, Hayes here reminds us that just as class analysis reveals the economic inequities behind the brutality of free-market capitalism, it can also fail to reveal why "when many poor white folks had the choice to do what was right, they chose white."

Hence, a perspective that intersects the dynamic relationship between class and race is paramount in our struggle for racial justice. So, rather than a grand theory of class primacy reigning supreme, perhaps what is needed is a concept beyond class or race supremacy; this to say, we need a deeper understanding of what class dynamics entails in the face of racism. Sleeter's contribution to this volume, for example, does an excellent job of reminding us that "capitalism was born out of colonization," and that the structure of class dynamics, particularly within the United States, is perpetually bound to white supremacy. In lieu of arguing over the either/or race or class position, various contributors to this book argue that we must accept a both/and perspective. We cannot forget, for example, that chattel slavery was *both* a capitalistic act *and* a racist endeavor; the ideology of Manifest Destiny and the genocide of the American native population were *both* projects grounded in capitalism *and* a racist social policy endeavors; the annexation of the southwest from Mexico, the colonization of the Philippines and Puerto Rico, and the cultural imperialism forced upon students of color via Eurocentric curricula are *both* a capitalistic act *and* a racist endeavor.

In his work, Leonardo (2012a) argues that in any analyses of race, a Marxist and critical social theory of class must be entertained; and in analyses of class, a critical social theory of race must be employed, lest we overlook the impact that each have on the other. In forgoing the idea of solely a race analysis or a class analysis, Leonardo (2012) challenges us with a *raceclass* analysis whereby we acknowledge that both constructs exist as "two intimately related points on one axis" (p. 429). In his critique, he exposes how class is underutilized in CRT and how race is underutilized in Marxism. As such, Leonardo (2012a) argues for a concept that "locate[s] the unity between studies of capitalism, such as the division of labor, and themes of racialization, such as philosophies of personhood," hence, *raceclass* (p. 438). In this endeavor, both race-and-class and class-and-race are acknowledged in equal weights; or, as Leonardo (2010) states, "It is an argument for . . . necessitating attention to both race and class dynamics" (p. 162). Therefore, to remain in the age-old chicken-egg quandary of which came first, class or race, will keep us trapped in a cyclic argument where we remain fixated on the theoretical argument, while educational injustice persists. In fact, it is also the very quandary that Darder, Hayes, and Ryan seek to shatter through creating an arena for greater dialogue across perspectives that seldom engage one another in a serious and sustained manner.

Toward Educational Reform Research as Humanity

Recently, I have noticed a disturbing trend. There are critical scholars who claim to be "the real" social justice warriors, yet engage in the very oppressive mechanisms that they claim to abhor via their articulations of justice. I have witnessed scholars, all doing critical work from different angles, theoretical points, and methodologies, calling each other out in such inhumane ways that it becomes divisive of the very community we so require in order to struggle effectively against the forces of oppression. In the midst of the pandemic, we've been reminded of our mortality. So why is it that we still allow ourselves to get swept away in the fanaticism of cancel culture? As Brown (2020) reminds us, "Cancelling is punishment, and punishment doesn't stop the cycle of harm, not long term" (p. 75). In this punishment, our humanity goes out the window, as if the common courtesies of giving the benefit of doubt, humanizing a situation, and, perhaps, simply picking up the phone to call someone directly are no longer relevant to our larger political struggles. It has made me wonder, at times, if we, as critical scholars, have moved beyond our capacity for solidarity—for engaging in radical ways of educational reform and justice, for thinking beyond impossibilities or being tolerant of that which discomforts us—to a space whereby we reduce each other to nothing more than who's in or who's out?

Through cultivating a space for divergent voices, Darder, Hayes, and Ryan encourage critical scholars to not fixate on defending one absolute position, but rather that our very survival demands that we focus together on thoughtful and respectful engagements across our differences. In his chapter, "Afrolantica," Bell (1992) contends that too often in the work for social justice we become fixated on an intellectual utopia that simply does not exist. By doing so, we overlook where humanity and hope truly lie: within our collective emancipatory struggles. Moreover, we often forget that we come to this struggle because we so love each other and refuse to leave anyone at the "bottom of the well" (Bell 1992). Drawing on Freire, Darder (2017) writes, "A pedagogy of love must encompass a deep unwavering commitment to social inclusion and economic democracy—a revolutionary commitment to release our humanity from the powerful death grip of capitalism and to dismantle the coloniality of power that persists today." What an exciting vision for our future: to be free from the death grips of white supremacy, capitalism, patriarchy, hetero-

aggressive heteronormativity, gender binaries, ableism, linguistic dominance, and citizenship bias.

Yet, such a vision is impossible unless we seek to overcome this hateration across critical scholarly communities that seek liberatory ends. Unfortunately, I know many of us will continue to critique for the sake of furthering our class or race arguments—and, upon receiving critiques, become reactive and resistant to open dialogue. Indeed, conclusions made by others may trigger responses tied to our individual and collective traumas. Nevertheless, we cannot live our lives hiding behind our psychological triggers. With this in mind, *Class, Race, and Educational Reform* invites us, as critical scholars, to embrace one another's work with a *both/and* complexity, instead of dividing ourselves within *either/or* frameworks. To heal, to learn, to fight, we must bring a pedagogy of love to our practice and our scholarship. For, to remain imprisoned in a divide-and-conquer mentality places us in danger of disabling our communities further, which only causes us to lose focus of the reason why we struggle: we *do* love each other and the world. If two years of Covid-19 isolation has taught us anything, it is that we *need* each other. There is no question that this message is implicit to the very ethos of this book—in that critical scholars committed to just educational reform are encouraged to respectfully push, critique, contest, or challenge one another, not to hate on each other, but all in the name of building a more empowered, liberated, and loving humanity *together*.

Special Note

To Marxists and critical race theorists alike, contest and critique to push us closer to a more loving humanity.

Note

1 In times where CRT is under attack by the government, professors are being put on national watchdog lists and scholars are being stalked and bullied for doing their job.

Bibliography

AAUW (2017), "Deeper in Debt: Women and Student Loans." Washington, DC: AAUW. Available online: https://www.aauw.org/app/uploads/2020/03/DeeperinDebt-nsa.pdf (accessed March 30, 2022).

Abdullah, M. (2016), "What the Black Lives Matter Movement Demands of Ethnic Studies Scholars." *Ethnic Studies Review*, 37–38 (5): 5–9.

Abrams, M., J. J. Pedulla, and G. F. Madaus (2003), "Views from the Classroom: Teachers' Opinions of Statewide Testing Programs." *Theory into Practice*, 42 (1): 18–29.

Academy Trust Handbook (2021), "Testimony of Education and Skills Funding Agency." London: UK Parliament. Available online: https://www.gov.uk/guidance/academy-trust-handbook/part-5-delegated-authorities

Adams, M., L. E. Hopkins, and D. Shlasko (2016), "Classism." In M. Adams and L. A. Bell, eds., *Teaching for Diversity and Social Justice*, 3rd ed. New York: Routledge. 255–97.

Adonis, A. (2008), "Academies and Social Mobility." Speech to the National Academies Conference. Available online: www.standards.dfes.gov.uk/.../Andrew_Adonis_Speech_feb08.doc

Agee, J. (2004), "Negotiating a Teaching Identity: An African American Teacher's Struggle to Teach in Test-Driven Contexts." *Teachers College Record*, 106 (4): 747–74.

Agger, B. (2006), *Critical Social Theories*. Virginia: Paradigm Publishers.

Aguilar, D. D. (2012), "From Triple Jeopardy to Intersectionality: The Feminist Perplex." *Comparative Studies of South Asia, Africa and the Middle East*, 32 (2): 415–28.

Aisch, G., I. Buchanan, A. Cox, and K. Quealy (2017), "Some Colleges have More Students from the Top 1 Percent than the Bottom 60." *The New York Times*. January 18.

Alemán, E., Jr., and S. M. Alemán (2010), "Do Latin@ Interests Always Have to 'Converge' with White Interests?: (Re)Claiming Racial Realism and Interest-Convergence in Critical Race Theory Praxis." *Race Ethnicity and Education*, 13 (1): 1–21.

Alexander, C. (1996), *The Art of Being Black: The Creation of Black British Youth Identities*. Oxford: Oxford University Press.

Alexander, M. (2010), *The New Jim Crow: Mass Incarceration in the Age of Colorblindness*. New York: The New Press.

Alexander, N. (1985), *Sow the Wind: Contemporary Speeches*. Braamfontein: Skotaville Publishers.

Alexander, N. (2003), *An Ordinary Country: Issues in the Transition from Apartheid to Democracy in South Africa*. New York: Berghahn.

Alexander, N. (2006), "Racial Identity, Citizenship and Nation Building in Post-Apartheid South Africa." Lecture delivered at East London Campus, University of Fort Hare. March 25. Available online: https://www.marxists.org/archive/alexander/2006-racial-identity-citizenship-and-nation-building.pdf

Alexander, N. (2012), "South Africa Today." In Foundation for Human Rights, *Enough Is a Feast: A Tribute to Neville Alexander*. Braamfontein: Foundation for Human Rights.

Alfaro, C., and L. Bartolomé (2017), "Preparing Ideologically Clear Bilingual Teachers: Honoring Working-Class Non-Standard Language Use in the Bilingual Education Classroom." *Issues in Teacher Education*, 26 (2): 11–31.

Alim, H. S., and D. Paris (2017), "What is Culturally-Sustaining Pedagogy and Why Does it Matter?" In D. Paris and H. S. Alim, eds., *Culturally Sustaining Pedagogies: Teaching and Learning for Justice in a Changing World*. New York: Teachers College Press. 1–25.

Allen, R. L. (2001), "The Globalization of White Supremacy: Toward a Critical Discourse on the Racialization of the World." *Educational Theory*, 51 (4): 467–85.

Allen, R. L. (2009), "What about Poor White people?" In W. Ayers, T. Quinn, and D. Stovall, eds., *Handbook of Social Justice in Education*. New York: Routledge. 209–30.

Allen, T. W. (1998), "Summary of the Argument of *The Invention of the White Race*." Part One. *Cultural Logic 2*. Available online: https://ojs.library.ubc.ca/index.php/clogic/article/view/191851/188820

Allen, T. W. (2012), *The Invention of the White Race*, 2nd ed. New York: Verso.

Altwerger, B., ed. (2005a), *Reading for Profit: How the Bottom Line Leaves Kids Behind*. Portsmouth, NH: Heinemann.

Altwerger, B. (2005b), "The Push of the Pendulum." In L. Poynor and P. M. Wolfe, eds., *Marketing Fear in America's Public Schools: The Real War on Literacy*. Mahwah, NJ: Lawrence Erlbaum. 31–49.

Amalgamated Transit Union (2020), "George Floyd's Words a Reminder of the Racism and Hatred Yet To Be Overcome." *ATU Media Center*. May 28.

American Legislative Exchange Council (2016), *Report Card on American Education: Ranking State K–12 Performance, Progress and Reform*, 21st ed. Washington: ALEC.

Amrein, A. L., and D. C. Berliner (2002), *An Analysis of Some Unintended and Negative Consequences of High-Stakes Testing*. Tempe, AZ: Education Policy Studies Laboratory, Arizona State University.

Anderson, C. (2016), *White Rage: The Unspoken Truth of Our Racial Divide*. New York: Bloomsbury.

Anderson, J. D. (1988), *The Education of Blacks in the South, 1860–1935*. Chapel Hill, NC: University of North Carolina Press.

Anderson, K. B. (2010), *Marx at the Margins: On Nationalism, Ethnicity, and Non-Western Societies*. Chicago: University of Chicago Press.

Anderson, N. (2021), "Applications Surge after Big-name Colleges halt SAT and ACT Testing Rules." *The Washington Post*. January 29.

Anft, M. (2013), "The STEM Crisis: Reality or Myth?" *Chronicle of Higher Education*. November 11.

Ansley, F. L. (1989), "Stirring the Ashes: Race, Class and the Future of Civil Rights Scholarship." *Cornell Law Review*, 74 (6): 993–1077.

Anyon, J. (1980), "Social Class and the Hidden Curriculum of Work." *Journal of Education*, 162 (1): 67–92.

Apple, M. (1979), *Ideology and Curriculum*. Boston, MA: Routledge and Kegan Paul.

Apple, M. (1993), *Official Knowledge*. New York: Routledge.

Apple, M., and L. Christian-Smith, eds. (1991), *The Politics of the Textbook*. New York: Routledge.

Apple, M. W. (1978), "Ideology, Reproduction, and Educational Reform." *Comparative Education Review*, 22 (3): 367–87.

Apple, M. W. (2006), *Educating the "Right" Way: Markets, Standards, God, and Inequality*, 2nd ed. New York: Routledge.

Applebaum, A. (2021), "Democracies Don't Try to Make Everyone Agree." *Atlantic*. June 28. Available online: https://www.theatlantic.com/ideas/archive/2021/06/milley-critical-race-theory-marxism-racism-fox-news/619308/

Aptheker, H. (1993), *Anti-Racism in U.S. History*. Westport, CT: Praeger.

Asante, M. K. (2003), *Afrocentricity: The Theory of Social Change*, rev. ed. Chicago: African American Images.

Ashe, S. D., and B. McGeever (2011), "Marxism, Racism and the Construction of 'Race' as Social and Political Relation: An Interview with Professor Robert Miles." *Ethnic and Racial Studies*, 34 (12): 2009–26.

Asher, G. (2022), "Working, In, Against and Beyond the Neoliberal University: Critical Academic Literacies as a Pedagogical Response to the Crisis of the University." In G. Asher, S. Cowden, A. Maisuria, and S. Housee, eds., *Critical Pedagogy and Emancipation: A Festschrift in Memory of Joyce Canaan*. Oxford: Peter Lang.

Au, W. (2006), "Against Economic Determinism: Revisiting the Roots of Neo-Marxism in Critical Educational Theory." *Journal for Critical Education Policy Studies*, 4 (2): 11–35.

Au, W. (2008), "Between Education and the Economy: High-stakes Testing and the Contradictory Location of the New Middle Class." *Journal of Education Policy*, 23 (5): 501–13.

Au, W. (2009), *Unequal by Design: High-Stakes Testing and the Standardization of Inequality*. New York: Routledge.

Au, W. (2015), "High-Stakes Testing: A Tool for White Supremacy for over 100 Years." In B. Picower and E. Mayorga, eds., *What's Race Got to Do with It? How Current School Reform Policy Maintains Racial and Economic Inequality*. New York: Peter Lang. 21–44.

Au, W. (2018), *A Marxist Education: Learning to Change the World*. Chicago: Haymarket.

Au, W., and J. J. Ferrare, eds. (2015), *Mapping Corporate Education Reform: Power and Policy Networks in the Neoliberal State*. New York: Routledge.

Ayers, R., and W. Ayers (2020), "Afterword: A Letter to the Resistance." In E. Mayorga, U. Aggarwal, and B. Picower, eds., *What's Race Got to Do with It? How Current School Reform Policy Maintains Racial and Economic Inequality*, 2nd ed. New York: Peter Lang. 195–200.

Ayers, R., G. Michie, and A. Rome (2004), "Embers of Hope: In Search of a Meaningful Critical Pedagogy." *Teacher Education Quarterly*, Winter: 123–30.

Aziz, R. (1997), "Feminism and the Challenge of Racism." In H. S. Mirza, ed., *Black British Feminism*. London: Routledge. 70–9.

Bagdikian, B. H. (1983), *The Media Monopoly*. Boston, MA: Beacon Press.

Balingit, M. (2017), "DeVos Rescinds 72 Guidance Documents Outlining Rights for Disabled Students." *Washington Post*. October 21.

Ball, S. (2002), "The Teacher's Soul and the Terrors of Performativity." *Journal of Education Policy*, 18 (2): 215–28.

Ball, S. (2007), *Education Plc: Understanding Private Sector Participation in Public Sector Education*. London: Routledge.

Ball, S., and C. Junemann (2012), *Networks, New Governance and Education*. Bristol: Bristol University Press.

Ball, S. J. (2012), *Global Education Inc.: New Policy Networks and the Neo-Liberal Imaginary*. New York: Routledge.

Ball. S. J. (2017), *The Education Debate*. Bristol: Policy Press.

Ball, W., and J. Solomos, eds. (1990), *Race and Local Politics*. Basingstoke: Macmillan.

Banaji, J. (2010), *Theory as History: Essays on Modes of Production and Exploitation*. Leiden: Brill Publishers.

Banerjee, A., and C. Johnson (2020), "African American Workers Build America." *CLASP: The Center for Law and Social Policy*. February. Available online: https://www.clasp.org/blog/african-american-workers-built-america

Bannerji, H. (2005), "Building from Marx: Reflections on Class and Race." *Social Justice*, 32 (4): 144–60.
Banton, M. (2010), "The Vertical and Horizontal Dimensions of the Word Race." *Ethnicities*, 10: 127–40.
Barroso, A., and A. Brown (2021), "Gender Pay Gap in U.S. Held Steady in 2020." Pew Research Center. Available online: https://www.pewresearch.org/fact-tank/2021/05/25/gender-pay-gap-facts/
Bartolovich, C., and N. Lazarus, eds. (2002), *Marxism, Modernity and Postcolonial Studies*. Cambridge: Cambridge University Press.
Bastedo, M. N., J. E. Howard, and A. Flaster (2016), "Holistic Admissions after Affirmative Action: Does 'Maximizing' the High School Curriculum Matter?" *Educational Evaluation and Policy Analysis*, 38 (2): 389–409.
Baynes, C. (2013), "Headteacher 'Farce' Proves Harris Federation Consultation Is Sham, Claim Angry Roke Primary School Parents." *Croydon Guardian*. April 25.
Beal, J. (1970), "Double Jeopardy: To Be Black and Female." In R. Morgan, ed., *Sisterhood Is Powerful: An Anthology of Writings from the Women's Liberation Movement*. New York: Random House. 340–53.
Beckert, S., and K. Stevens (2011), "Harvard and Slavery: Seeking a Forgotten History." *Harvard and Slavery*. Available online: http://www.harvardandslavery.com/wp-content/uploads/2011/11/Harvard-Slavery-Book-111110.pdf
Belkhir, J. (1994), "The 'Failure' and Revival of Marxism on Race, Gender and Class." *Race, Sex and Class*, 2 (1): 79–107.
Bell, D. (1992a), *Faces at the Bottom of the Well: The Permanence of Racism*. New York: Basic Books.
Bell, D. (1992b), "Racial Realism." *Connecticut Law Review*, 24 (2): 363–79.
Bell, D. (2004), *Silent Covenants*. Oxford: Oxford University Press.
Bell, D. (2009), "Who's Afraid of Critical Race Theory?" In E. Taylor, D. Gillborn, and G. Ladson-Billings, eds., *Foundations of Critical Race Theory in Education*. New York: Routledge. 37–50.
Bell, D. A., Jr. (1980), "Brown v. Board of Education and the Interest-Convergence Dilemma." *Harvard Law Review*, 93 (3): 518–34.
Bell, T. (1988), *The Thirteenth Man: A Reagan Cabinet Memoir*. New York: Free Press.
Bennett, L. A., Jr. (1972), "The White Problem in America." In L. A. Bennett, ed., *The Challenge of Blackness*. Chicago: Johnson Publishing. 117–27.
Benson, R. (2016), "'School-in-a-Box' Tech Is Helping Teaching Children in Asia and Africa." *Wired*. June 3.
Berger, M. T. (2001), "The Nation-State and the Challenge of Global Capitalism." *Third World Quarterly*, 22 (6): 889–907.
Bergerson, A. A. (2003), "Critical Race Theory and White Racism: Is There Room for White Scholars in Fighting Racism in Education?" *Qualitative Studies in Education*, 16 (1): 51–63.
Berliner, D. C., and B. J. Biddle (1995), *The Manufactured Crisis: Myths, Fraud, and the Attack on America's Public Schools*. Reading, MA: Addison-Wesley.
Bernstein, B., and J. Solomon (1999), "Pedagogy, Identity, and the Construction of a Theory of Symbolic Control: Basil Bernstein Questioned by Joseph Solomon." *British Journal of Sociology of Education*, 20 (2): 265–80.
Bhaba, H. (1989), "The Commitment to Theory." In J. Pines and P. Willeman, eds., *Third Cinema Reader*. London: British Film Institute. 111–32.
Bhaskar, R. (1993), *Dialectic: The Pulse of Freedom*. London: Verso.

Bhaskar, R. (2008), *A Realist Theory of Science*. London: Routledge.
Bhaskar, R. (2016), *Enlightened Common Sense: The Philosophy of Critical Realism*. New York: Routledge.
Bhaskar, R. (2017), *The Order of Natural Necessity: A Kind of Introduction to Critical Realism*, G. Hawk, ed. London: CreateSpace Independent Publishing Platform.
Bhattacharya, T. (2017), "Ragpicking through History: Class Memory, Class Struggle and Its Archivists." *Salvage*. May 24.
Bhattacharyya, G. (2018), *Rethinking Racial Capitalism: Questions of Reproduction and Survival*. Lanham, MD: Rowman & Littlefield.
Bhorat, H., C. van der Westhuizen, and T. Jacobs (2009), "Income and Non-Income Inequality in Post-Apartheid South Africa: What Are the Drivers and Possible Policy Interventions?" August 31. Cape Town: Development Policy Research Unit, University of Cape Town, SSRN. Available online: https://papers.ssrn.com/sol3/papers.cfm?abstract_id=1474271
Bidwai, P. (2007), "Learning Nandigram Lessons" The Transnational Institute. March 24, 2007. https://www.tni.org/en/article/learning-nandigram-lessons. Retrieved October 19, 2022.
Black, D. (2016), "Office for Civil Rights Releases Annual Report and Reflections on Past Eight Years, Citing Accomplishments and Lingering Challenges." *Education Law Prof Blog*. December 9.
Blaisdell, B. (2018), "The New One-Drop Rule: Challenging the Persistence of White Supremacy with In-Service Teachers." *Teaching Education*, 29 (4): 330–42.
Blaisdell, B. (2020), "Cupcakes, White Rage, and the Epistemology of Antiblackness." *Taboo*, 19 (1): 70–90.
Blaut, J. M. (1989), "Colonialism and the Rise of Capitalism." *Science and Society*, 53 (3): 260–96.
Bloom, A. (2017), "Ofsted to Use 'Strong Pass' of GCSE Grade 5 to Judge Schools." *Times Educational Supplement*. September 8.
Bloom, A. C. (1989), *The Closing of the American Mind*. New York: Simon & Schuster.
Bloom, E. (2015), "Introduction: Forewarned is Forearmed." In K. VanSlyke-Briggs, E. Bloom, and D. Boudet, eds., *Resisting Reform: Reclaiming Public Education through Grassroots Activism*. Charlotte, NC: Information Age. 1–13.
Blume, H. (2015), "Backers Want Half of LAUSD Students in Charter Schools in Eight Years, Report Says." *Los Angeles Times*. September 21.
Blume, H., and A. M. Phillips (2017), "Charter Backers Win Their First L.A. School Board Majority." *Los Angeles Times*. May 17.
Bohrer, A. (2020), *Marxism and Intersectionality: Race, Gender, Class, and Sexuality under Contemporary Capitalism*. New York: Columbia University Press.
Bond, P. (2000), *Elite Transition: From Apartheid to Neoliberalism in South Africa*. London: Pluto Press.
Bond, P. (2003), *Against Global Apartheid: South Africa Meets the World Bank, IMF and International Finance*, 2nd ed. New York: Zed Books.
Bonnett, A. (1998), "How the British Working Class Became White: The Symbolic (Re)formation of Racialized Capitalism." *Journal of Historical Sociology*, 11 (3): 316–40.
Bonnett, A. (1990), "Anti-Racism as a Radical Educational Ideology in London and Tyneside." *Oxford Review of Education*, 16: 255–67.
Bonilla-Silva, E. (2006), *The Central Frames of Color-Blind Racism*, 2nd ed. New York: Rowman & Littlefield Publishers, Inc.
Bonilla-Silva, E. (2015), "More than Prejudice: Restatement, Reflections, and New Directions in Critical Race Theory." *Sociology of Race and Ethnicity*, 1 (1): 73–87.
Bonilla-Silva, E. (2017), *Racism without Racists: Color-Blind Racism and the Persistence of Racial Inequality in America*, 5th ed. Lanham, MD: Rowman and Littlefield.

Bonilla-Silva, E., T. A. Forman, A. E. Lewis, and D. G. Embrick (2003), "It Wasn't Me! How Will Race and Racism Work in 21st Century America." *Research in Political Sociology*, 12: 111–34.
Booth, R., and C. Barr (2020), "Black People Four Times more likely to Die from Covid-19, ONS Finds." *The Guardian*. May 7.
Bourdieu, P. (1986), "The Forms of Capital." In J. G. Richardson, ed., *Handbook for Theory and Research for the Sociology of Education*, Westport, CT: Greenwood. 241–58.
Bourdieu, P. (1987), "What Makes a Social Class? On the Theoretical and Practical Existence of Groups." *Berkeley Journal of Sociology*, 32: 1–17.
Bourdieu, P. (2000), *Pascalian Meditations*. Cambridge: Polity Press.
Bourdieu, P., R. P. Droit, and T. Ferenczi (2008), "The Left Hand and the Right Hand of the State." *Variant*, 32: 3–4.
Bovy, P. M. (2013), "The False Promise of Holistic College Admissions." *Atlantic*. December 17.
Bowles, S., and H. Gintis (1976), *Schooling in Capitalist America: Educational Reform and the Contradictions of Economic Life*. New York: Basic Books.
Brabazon, T., S. Redhead, and R. Chivaura (2018), "Trump Studies: The Double Refusal and Silent Majorities in Theoretical Times." *Cultural Studies Review*, 24 (2): 3–25.
Bradbury, A., M. Brenner, J. Brown, J. Slaughter, and S. Winslow (2014), *How to Jump-Start Your Union: Lessons from the Chicago Teachers*. Detroit: Labor Notes.
Brantlinger, E. (2004), "An Application of Gramsci's 'Who Benefits?' to High-Stakes Testing." *Workplace*, 11: 78–103.
Breitman, G., ed. (1965), *Malcolm X Speaks: Selected Speeches and Statements*. New York: Merit Publishers.
Breitman, G. (1970), *Last Year of Malcolm X: The Evolution of a Revolutionary*. New York: Pathfinder.
Brenner, R. (2006), *The Economics of Global Turbulence*. New York: Verso.
Bridge International Academies (2016), "Our Philosophy." March 3. Available online: https://web.archive.org/web/20160313222546/http://www.bridgeinternational academies.com/academics/philosophy
Brown, A. (2020), *We Will Not Cancel Us: And Other Dreams of Transformative Justice*. Chico, CA: AK Press.
Brown, A. L. (2018), "From Subhuman to Human Kind: Implicit Bias, Racial Memory, and Black Males in Schools and Society." *Peabody Journal of Education*, 93 (1): 52–65.
Brown, W. (2015), *Undoing the Demos: Neoliberalism's Stealth Revolution*. New York: Zone Books.
Brunila, K., and L. Rossi (2018), "Identity Politics, The Ethos of Vulnerability, and Education." *Educational Philosophy and Theory*, 50 (3): 287–98.
Bruns, B., D. Filmer, and H. A. Patrinos (2011), *Making Schools Work: New Evidence on Accountability Reforms*. Washington: World Bank.
Bude, U. (1983), "The Adaptation Concept in British Colonial Education." *Comparative Education*, 19 (3): 341–55.
Bull, A., and K. Allen (2018), "Introduction: Sociological Interrogations of the Turn to Character." *Sociological Research Online*, 23 (2): 392–8.
Bunting, B. (1975), "Freedom Charter." In *Moses Kotane South African Revolutionary, A Political Biography*. London: Inkululeko Publications. Available online: https://www.marxists.org/subject/africa/bunting-brian/kotane/ch13.htm
Buras, K. L. (2015), *Charter Schools, Race, and Urban Space: Where the Market Meets Grassroots Resistance*. New York: Routledge.

Burciaga, B., and R. Kohli (2018), "Disrupting Whitestream Measures of Quality Teaching: The Community Cultural Wealth of Teachers of Color." *Multicultural Perspectives*, 20 (1): 5–12.

Burke, E. (1976), "Frantz Fanon's 'The Wretched of the Earth.'" *Daedalus*, 105 (2): 127–35.

Burris, C., and D. Cimarusti (2021), *Chartered for Profit: The Hidden World of Charter Schools Operated for Financial Gain*. Network for Public Education. Available from: https://networkforpubliceducation.org/wp-content/uploads/2021/07/Chartered-for-Profit.pdf

Busher, J., T. Choudhury, and P. Thomas (2019), "The Enactment of the Counter-Terrorism 'Prevent Duty' in British Schools and Colleges: Beyond Reluctant Accommodation or Straightforward Policy Acceptance." *Critical Studies on Terrorism*, 12 (3): 440–62.

Business Coalition for Education Reform (1999), "Letter to Representative William Goodling of Pennsylvania." June 28.

Business Roundtable (1996), *Business Leader's Guide to Setting Academic Standards*. Washington: BRT. Available online: http://files.eric.ed.gov/fulltext/ED400588.pdf

Cabral, A. (1966), "The Weapon of Theory." Address to the Tricontinental Conference of the Peoples of Asia, Africa and Latin America. Havana, Cuba. January. *Marxists Internet Archive*. Available online: https://www.marxists.org/subject/africa/cabral/1966/weapon-theory.htm

Cabrera, N. L. (2019), "Critical Race Theory v. Deficit Models." *Equity and Excellence in Education*, 52 (1): 47–54.

California Department of Education (2018), "State Schools Chief Tom Torlakson Announces Results of California Assessment of Student Performance and Progress Online Tests." Press release. October 2. http://cde.ca.gov. The specific page is no longer available; document is in the author's possession (Accessed November 1, 2018).

California Faculty Association (2016), "Anti-Racism Social Justice Transformation Guiding Principles." California Faculty Association. Available online: https://www.calfac.org/pod/guiding-principles

California Faculty Association (2018a), "Stronger Together, Episode 1 Transcript." *Radio Free CSU*. Available online: https://archive.org/details/podcast_radio-free-csu_stronger-together-episode-1_1000394009656

California Faculty Association (2018b), "Stronger Together, Episode 2 Transcript." *Radio Free CSU*. Available online: https://archive.org/details/podcast_radio-free-csu_stronger-together-episode-2_1000397193556

California Faculty Association (2018c), "Stronger Together, Episode 3 Transcript." *Radio Free CSU*. Available online: https://archive.org/details/podcast_radio-free-csu_stronger-together-episode-3_1000405229311

California Faculty Association (2018d), "Stronger Together, Episode 4 Transcript." *Radio Free CSU*. Available online: https://archive.org/details/podcast_radio-free-csu_stronger-together-episode-4_1000408724386

Callinicos, A. (1983), "The 'New Middle Class' and Socialist Politics." *International Socialism*, 2 (20): 82–119.

Callinicos, A., ed. (1992), *Between Apartheid and Capitalism*. London: Bookmarks.

Camfield, D. (2016), "Elements of a Historical-Materialist Theory of Racism." *Historical Materialism*, 24 (1): 31–70.

Cano, R., and J. Hong (2020), "Mind the Achievement Gap: California's Disparities in Education Explained." *Cal Matters*. Available online: https://calmatters.org/explainers/achievement-gap-california-explainer-schools-education-disparities-explained/

Carbado, D., K. W. Crenshaw, V. M. Mays, and B. Tomlinson (2013), "Intersectionality: Mapping the Movements of a Theory." *Du Bois Review*, 10 (2): 3003–312.
Carbado, D. W. (2011), "Critical What What?" *Connecticut Law Review*, 43 (5): 1593–643.
Carbado, D. W., and M. Gulati (2004), "Race to the Top of the Corporate Ladder: What Minorities Do When They Get There." *Washington and Lee Law Review*, 61 (4): 1645–93.
Cardoso, M., and G. Steiner-Khamsi (2017), "The Making of Comparability: Education Indicator Research from Jullien De Paris to the 2030 Sustainable Development Goals." *Compare: A Journal of Comparative and International Education*, 47 (3): 388–405.
Carey, J. (1992), *The Intellectuals and the Masses: Pride and Prejudice among the Literary Intelligentsia, 1880–1939*. London: Faber & Faber.
Carmichael, S., and C. V. Hamilton (1967), *Black Power: The Politics of Liberation in America*. New York: Vintage.
Carnevale, A. P., M. L. Fasules, M. C. Quinn, and K. P. Campbell (2019), "Born to Win, Schooled to Lose: Why Equally Talented Students Don't Get Equal Chances to be All They Can Be." Washington, DC: Georgetown University Center on Education and the Workforce. Available online: https://1gyhoq479ufd3yna29x7ubjn-wpengine.netdna-ssl.com/wp-content/uploads/ES-Born_to_win-schooled_to_lose.pdf
Carson, C. (1992), *In Struggle: SNCC and the Black Awakening of the 1960s*. Cambridge, MA: Harvard University Press.
Carter, B. (2000), *Realism and Racism: Concepts of Race in Sociological Research*. London: Routledge.
CCCS (Centre for Contemporary Cultural Studies), ed. (1981), *Unpopular Education: Schooling and Social Democracy in England since 1944*. London: Hutchinson in association with the Centre for Contemporary Cultural Studies, University of Birmingham.
Centers for Disease Control and Prevention (n.d.), "COVID Data Tracker," Centers for Disease Control and Prevention. https://covid.cdc.gov/covid-data-tracker/#datatracker-home
Center for Education Policy (2006), *From the Capital to the Classroom: Year 4 of the No Child Left Behind Act*. March. Washington: CEP. Available online: http://www.ccp-dc.org/nclb/Year4/Press/
Chakrabarty, N., L. Roberts, and J. Preston (2012), "Critical Race Theory in England." *Race Ethnicity and Education*, 15 (1): 1–3.
Chang, B. (2020), "From 'Illmatic' to 'Kung Flu': Black and Asian Solidarity, Activism, and Pedagogies in the Covid-19 Era." *Postdigital Science and Education*, 3 (3): 741–56.
Chang, B., and W. Au (2009), "You're Asian, How Could You Fail Math?: Unmasking the Myth of the Model Minority." In W. Au, ed., *Rethinking Multicultural Education: Teaching for Racial and Cultural Justice*. Milwaukee, WI: Rethinking Schools. 207–17.
Chang, H.-J., and I. Grabel (2014), *Reclaiming Development: An Alternative Economic Policy Manual*, 2nd ed. London: Zed Books.
Chibber, V. (2020), "Capitalism Is Complex – But Not Difficult to Understand: An Interview with Vivek Chibber." *Verso Books*. May 18.
Chicago Teachers Union Research Department (2014), *Twelve Months Later: The Impact of School Closings in Chicago*. Chicago: CTU. Available online: https://ctulocal1.org/wp-content/uploads/2018/10/TwelveMonthsLaterReport.pdf
Chitty, C. (2001), "IQ, Racism and the Eugenics Movement." *FORUM*, 43 (3): 115–19.
Chitty, C. (2009), *Eugenics, Race and Intelligence in Education*. London: Continuum.

Chomsky, N. (2015), "America is a Plutocracy Masquerading as a Democracy." *Salon*. October 6.

Chowkwanyun, M., and A. Reed (2020), "Racial Health Disparities and Covid-19: Caution and Context." *New England Journal of Medicine*, 383: 201–3.

Christie, P., and C. Collins (1990), "Bantu Education: Apartheid Ideology and Labour Reproduction." In P. Kallaway, ed., *Apartheid and Education: The Education of Black South Africans*. Johannesburg: Raven Press. 160–83.

Churchill, W., ed. (1999), *Marxism and Native Liberation*. Boston, MA: South End Press.

Clawson, D., and A. Neustadtl (1989), "Interlocks, PACs, and Corporate Conservatism." *American Journal of Sociology*, 94 (4): 749–73.

Clegg, R. (2020), "Covid: Learning Disability Deaths Rates 'Six Times Higher.'" *BBC News*. November 13.

Coates, R. (2008), "Covert Racism in the USA and Globally." *Sociology Compass*, 2 (1): 208–31.

Coates, T. (2016a), "Why Precisely Is Bernie Sanders Against Reparations?" *Atlantic*. January 19.

Coates, T. (2016b), "Bernie Sanders and the Liberal Imagination." *Atlantic*. January 24.

Cohen, C. (1999), *The Boundaries of Blackness: AIDS and the Breakdown of Black Politics*. Chicago: University of Chicago Press.

Cole, M. (2009), "'The Color-Line and the Class Struggle: A Marxist Response to Critical Race Theory in Education as It Arrives in the United Kingdom." *Power and Education*, 1 (1): 111–24.

Cole, M. (2011), *Racism and Education in the U.K. and the U.S.: Towards a Socialist Alternative*. New York: Palgrave Macmillan.

Cole, M. (2017), *Critical Race Theory and Education: A Marxist Response*, 2nd ed. New York: Palgrave Macmillan.

Cole, M., and A. Maisuria (2010), "Racism and Islamophobia in Post 7/7 Britain: Critical Race Theory, (Xeno-) Racialization, Empire and Education: A Marxist Analysis." In D. Kelsh, D. Hill, and S. Macrine, eds., *Class in Education: Knowledge, Pedagogy, Subjectivity*. London: Routledge. 108–28.

Collins, P. H. (1991), *Black Feminist Thought: Knowledge, Consciousness, and the Politics of Empowerment*. New York: Routledge.

Collins, P. H. (1993), "Toward a New Vision: Race, Class, and Gender as Categories of Analysis and Connection." *Race, Sex and Class*, 1 (1): 25–45.

Collins, P. H. (1997), "On West and Fenstermaker's 'Doing Difference.'" In M. Roth Walsh, ed., *Women, Men and Gender: Ongoing debates*. New Haven, CT: Yale University Press. 73–5.

Collins, P. H. (2019), *Intersectionality as Critical Social Theory*. Durham, NC: Duke University Press.

Collins, P. H., and S. Bilge (2016), *Intersectionality*. Malden, MA: Polity Press.

Combahee River Collective ([1977] 2017), "The Combahee River Collective Statement." In K.-Y. Taylor, ed., *How We Get Free: Black Feminism and the Combahee River Collective*. Chicago: Haymarket. 15–27.

Communist Party of India (Marxist) (2007), "Central Committee Statement on Nandigram." April 4. Available online: https://www.cpim.org/content/central-committee-statement-nandigram

Cone, J. H. (2004), *Martin and Malcolm and America: A Dream or a Nightmare*. Maryknoll, NY: Orbis Books.

"COSATU Spells Out Its Aims to the ANC" (1985), *Star Weekly* (Johannesburg). December 23.

Cox, C. B., and A. E. Dyson, eds. (1969), *The Crisis in Education*. London: Critical Quarterly Society.

CReATE (2019), "Statement in Support of the Chicago Teachers Union (CTU)." CReATE. Available online: https://docs.google.com/forms/d/e/1FAIpQLSfKZdMBJAVaCf2cYDuv0wd27w2KT8WrzALIXiKqACtyUPfRbg/viewform

Creighton, M. J., and A. A. Jamal (2022), "An Overstated Welcome: Brexit and Intentionally Masked Anti-Immigrant Sentiment." *Journal of Ethnic and Migration Studies*, 48 (5): 1051–71.

Crenshaw, K. (1989), "Demarginalizing the Intersection of Race and Sex: A Black Feminist Critique of Antidiscrimination Doctrine, Feminist Theory and Antiracist Politics." *University of Chicago Legal Forum*, 140: 139–67.

Crenshaw, K. (1991), "Mapping the Margins: Intersectionality, Identity Politics, and Violence against Women of Color." *Stanford Law Review*, 43: 1241–99.

Crenshaw, K. (1995), "Mapping the Margins: Intersectionality, Identity Politics, and Violence against Women of Color." In K. W. Crenshaw, N. Gotanda, G. Peller, and K. Thomas, eds., *Critical Race Theory: The Key Writings that Formed the Movement*. New York: New Press. 357–83.

Crenshaw, K. (2011), "Postscript." In H. Lutz, M. T. H. Vivar, and L. Supik, eds., *Framing Intersectionality: Debates on a Multi-Faceted Concept in Gender Studies*. Burlington, VT: Ashgate Publishing. 221–33.

Crenshaw, K. (2022), *On Intersectionality: Essential Writings*. New York: The New Press.

Crenshaw, K., N. Gotanda, G. Peller, and K. Thomas, eds. (1995), *Critical Race Theory: The Key Writings that Formed the Movement*. New York: New Press.

Crenshaw, K. W. (1988), "Race, Reform, and Retrenchment: Transformation and Legitimation in Antidiscrimination Law." *Harvard Law Review*, 101 (7): 1331–87.

Crenshaw, K. W., L. C. Harris, D. M. HoSang, and G. Lipsitz (2019), "Introduction." In K. W. Crenshaw, L. C. Harris, D. M. HoSang, and G. Lipsitz, eds., *Seeing Race Again: Countering Colorblindness across the Disciplines*. Oakland, CA: University of California Press. 1–22.

Cross, M., and L. Chisholm (1990), "The Roots of Segregated Schooling in Twentieth-Century South Africa." In N. Nkomo, *Pedagogy of Domination: Toward a Democratic Education in South Africa*. Trenton, NJ: Africa World Press. 43–74.

Crowe, J. (2019), "Sanders Backs Committee to Study Slavery Reparations." *National Review*. April 5.

Cruz, N. S. (2010), "Arizona Bill Targeting Ethnic Studies Signed into Law." *Los Angeles Times*. May 12.

Cucchiara, M. B. (2013), *Marketing Schools, Marketing Cities: Who Wins and Who Loses When Schools Become Urban Amenities*. Chicago: University of Chicago Press.

Darder, A. (1991), *Culture and Power in the Classroom: A Critical Foundation for Bicultural Students*. Santa Barbara, CA: Bergin & Garvey.

Darder, A. (2012), *Culture and Power in the Classroom*, 2nd ed. Boulder, CO: Paradigm Press.

Darder, A. (2017), *Reinventing Paulo Freire: A Pedagogy of Love*. New York: Routledge.

Darder, A. (2018), *The Student Guide to Freire's Pedagogy of the Oppressed*. London: Bloomsbury Academic.

Darder, A., and R. D. Torres (2003), "Shattering the 'Race' Lens: Toward a Critical Theory of Racism." In A. Darder, R. D. Torres, and M. Baltodano, eds., *The Critical Pedagogy Reader*. New York: Routledge. 245–61.

Darder, A., and R. D. Torres (2004a), *After Race: Racism after Multiculturalism*. New York: New York University Press.

Darder, A., and R. D. Torres (2004b), "What's So Critical about Critical Race Theory? A Conceptual Interrogation." In A. Darder and R. D. Torres, *After Race: Racism after Multiculturalism*. New York: New York University Press. 97–117.

Darder, A., and R. D. Torres (2008), "After Race: An Introduction." In A. Darder, M. P. Baltodano, and R. D. Torres, eds., *The Critical Pedagogy Reader*, 2nd ed. New York: Routledge. 150–66.

Davidson, M., S. Fielden, and A. Omar (2010), "Black, Asian and Minority Ethnic Female Business Owners." *International Journal of Entrepreneurial Behavior and Research*, 16: 58–80.

Davies, L. (2016), "Security, Extremism and Education: Safeguarding or Surveillance?" *British Journal of Educational Studies*, 64 (1): 1–19.

Davis, A. Y. (1984), *Women, Culture & Politics*. New York: Vintage.

Davis, A. Y. (2005), *Abolition Democracy: Beyond Empire, Prisons, and Torture*. New York: Seven Stories Press.

Dawkins, P. (2007), *Federalist Paper 2: The Future of Schooling in Australia*. Melbourne: Department of Premier and Cabinet. April. Available online: https://apo.org.au/node/3139

Dawson, M. C. (1994a), *Behind the Mule: Race, Class, and African American Politics*. Princeton, NJ: Princeton University Press.

Dawson, M. C. (1994b), "A Black Counterpublic? Economic Earthquakes, Racial Agenda(s), and Black Politics." *Public Culture*, 7: 195–223.

Dawson, M. C. (2001), *Black Visions: The Roots of Contemporary African-American Political Ideologies*. Chicago: University of Chicago Press.

Dawson, M. C. (2011), *Not in Our Lifetimes: The Future of Black Politics*. Chicago: University of Chicago Press.

Dawson, R. (2017), "An Open Letter to Dolores Huerta." *Huffington Post*. Available online: https://www.huffpost.com/entry/an-open-letter-to-dolores-huerta_b_9538994

Day, R. B., and D. Gaido (2012), *Discovering Imperialism: Social Democracy to World War I*. Chicago: Haymarket Books.

DCFS (Department for Children, Schools and Families) (2009), *What Are Academies?* London: DFCS. Available online: www.standards.dfes.gov.uk/academies/what_are_academies/?version

Dean, J. (2009), *Democracy and Other Neoliberal Fantasies: Communicative Capitalism and Left Politics*. Durham, NC: Duke University Press.

De Angelis, M. (2007), *The Beginning of History: Value Struggles and Global Capitalism*. London: Pluto Press.

Dei, G. J. S., L. L. Karumanchery, and N. Karumanchery-Luik (2007), *Playing the Race Card: Exposing White Power and Privilege*. New York: Peter Lang.

Delgado, R. (1989), "Storytelling for Oppositionists and Others: A Plea for Narrative." *Michigan Law Review*, 87 (8), 2411–41.

Delgado, R. (1995), *Critical Race Theory: The Cutting Edge*. Philadelphia, PA: Temple University Press.

Delgado, R. (2003), "Crossroads and Blind Alleys: A Critical Examination of Recent Writings about Race." *Texas Law Review*, 82: 121–52.

Delgado, R. (2011), "Rodrigo's Reconsideration: Intersectionality and the Future of Critical Race Theory." *Iowa Law Review*, 96 (4): 1247–88.

Delgado, R., and D. Bell (2021), "Realism, Idealism, and the Deradicalization of Critical Race Theory—Rethinking the CRT Debate, Part 2." *Monthly Review*. Available online: https://mronline.org/2021/09/11/realism-idealism-and-the-deradicalization-of-critical-race-theory-rethinking-the-crt-debate-part-2

Delgado, R., and J. Stefancic, eds. (1999), *Critical Race Theory: The Cutting Edge*, 2nd ed. Philadelphia, PA: Temple University Press.

Delgado, R., and J. Stefancic, eds. (2000), *Critical Race Theory: The Cutting Edge*, 2nd ed. Philadelphia, PA: Temple University Press.

Delgado, R., and J. Stefancic (2017), *Critical Race Theory: An Introduction*, 3rd ed. New York: New York University Press.

De Lissovoy, N. (2012), "Education and Violence: Conceptualizing Power, Domination, and Agency in the Hidden Curriculum." *Race, Ethnicity and Education*, 15 (4): 463–84.

De Lissovoy, N. (2018), "Value and Violation: Toward a Decolonial Analytic of Capital." *Radical Philosophy Review*, 21 (2): 249–70.

Department for Education (2016a), *Educational Excellence Everywhere*. March. Available online: https://www.gov.uk/government/uploads/system/uploads/attachment_data/file/508550/Educational_excellence_everywhere__print_ready_.pdf

Department for Education (2016b), *Schools, Pupils and Their Characteristics: January 2016*. Available online: https://www.gov.uk/government/statistics/schools-pupils-and-their-characteristics-january-2021

Derman-Sparks, L., and C. B. Phillips (1997), *Teaching/Learning Anti-Racism: A Developmental Approach*. New York: Teachers College Press.

Desai, A. R. ([1974] 2008), "Two Stages Theory of Revolution in the Third World: Need for Evaluation." *Marxists Internet Archive*. Available online: https://www.marxists.org/subject/india/positive-programme/ch03.htm

Devi, M., et al. (2007), "Reading Nandigram Wrongly." *Economic and Political Weekly*, 42 (48). December 1.

DfE (Department for Education) (2014), *Measures to Help Schools Instill Character in Pupils Announced*. Department for Education. December 8. Available online: https://www.gov.uk/government/news/measures-to-help-schools-instil-character-in-pupils-announced

DiAngelo, R. (2018), *White Fragility: Why It's So Hard for White People to Talk about Racism*. Boston, MA: Beacon Press.

Dixson, A. D., and C. K. Rousseau (2006), "And We Are Still Not Saved: Critical Race Theory in Education Ten Years Later." In A. D. Dixson and C. K. Rousseau, eds., *Critical Race Theory in Education*. New York: Routledge. 31–54.

Dixson, A. D., and C. K. Rousseau Anderson (2006), *Critical Race Theory in Education: All God's Children Got a Song*, 1st ed. New York: Routledge.

Dixson, A. D., C. K. Rousseau Anderson, and J. K. Donnor, eds. (2017), *Critical Race Theory in Education: All God's Children Got a Song*, 2nd ed. New York: Routledge.

Dixson, A. D., and C. Rousseau Anderson (2018), "Where Are We? Critical Race Theory in Education 20 Years Later." *Peabody Journal of Education*, 93 (1): 121–31.

Dixson, A. D., D. Gillborn, G. Ladson-Billings, L. Parker, N. Rollock, and P. Warmington, eds. (2018), *Critical Race Theory in Education: Major Themes in Education*, Vols 1–4. New York: Routledge.

Docksai, R. F. (1981), "The Department of Education." In C. L. Heatherly, ed., *Mandate for Leadership: Policy Management in a Conservative Administration*. Washington: Heritage Foundation. 163–211.

Domhoff, G. W. (2005), "Power at the Local Level: Growth Coalition Theory." *Who Rules America?* April. Available online: http://www2.ucsc.edu/whorulesamerica/local/growth_coalition_theory.html

Domhoff, G. W. (2013), *Who Rules America? The Triumph of the Corporate Rich*, 7th ed. New York: McGraw-Hill.

Dominguez, M. (2017), "Se Hace Puentes al Andar: Decolonial Teacher Education as a Needed Bridge to Culturally Sustaining and Revitalizing Pedagogies." In D. Paris and H. S. Alim, eds., *Culturally Sustaining Pedagogies: Teaching and Learning for Justice in a Changing World*. New York: Teachers College Press. 225–46.

"Dorset School Praised by David Cameron 'Isolates' Up to 40 pupils for 'Pencil Case Infringements'" (2015), *Telegraph*. September 8.

DSA AfroSocialist and Socialists of Color Caucus (2020), "In Reed's Opinion, Are We Ever Allowed to Talk about Race?" May 30, Statement linked at Facebook page: https://www.facebook.com/AFROSOCDSA/posts/it-is-tone-deaf-and-unproductive-that-lower-manhattan-dsa-and-philly-dsa-are-hol/609102526363867/

D'Souza, D. (1991), *Illiberal Education: The Politics of Race and Sex on Campus*. New York: The Free Press.

Du Bois, W. E. B. (1924), *The Gift of Black Folk*. Boston, MA: Stratford.

Du Bois, W. E. B. ([1935] 1999), *Black Reconstruction in America*. New York: Simon and Schuster.

Du Bois, W. E. B. ([1940] 2007), *Dusk of Dawn: An Essay toward an Autobiography of a Race Concept*. Oxford: Oxford University Press.

Dumas, D. (2020), "UK Women and Equalities Minister Torches BLM Movement, Critical Race Theory in House of Commons Floor Speech." *Blaze Media*. October 20. Available online: https://www.theblaze.com/news/ready-uk-equalities-minister-torches-blm-movement-critical-race-theory-in-house-of-commons-floor-speech

Dumas, M. J. (2009), "How Do We Get Dictionaries at Cleveland? Theorizing Redistribution and Recognition in Urban Education Research." In J. Anyon, ed., *Theory and Educational Research: Toward Critical Social Explanation*. New York: Routledge. 81–102.

Dumas, M. J. (2010), "What Is This 'Black' in Black Education? Imagining a Cultural Politics without Guarantees." In Z. Leonardo, ed., *Handbook of Cultural Politics and Education*. Boston, MA: Sense Publisher.

Dumas, M. J. (2011), "A Cultural Political Economy of School Desegregation in Seattle." *Teachers College Record*, 113 (4): 703–34.

Dumas, M. J. (2013), "Doing Class in Critical Race Analysis in Education." In M. Lynn and A. D. Dixson, eds., *Handbook of Critical Race Theory in Education*. New York: Routledge. 113–25.

Dunbar-Ortiz, R. (2016), "'A Sense of Hope and the Possibility of Solidarity.'" Interview with R. Johnson and B. Ward. *International Socialist Review* 103. Winter.

Duncan-Andrade, J. M. R. (2009), "Note to Educators: Hope Required When Growing Roses in Concrete." *Harvard Educational Review*, 79 (2): 181–94.

Dunn, A. H., B. Sondel, and H. C. Baggett (2019), "I Don't Want to Come off as Pushing an Agenda: How Contexts Shaped Teachers' Pedagogy in the Days After the 2016 U.S. Presidential Election." *American Educational Research Journal*, 56 (2): 444–76.

Durodie, B. (2016), "Securitising Education to Prevent Terrorism or Losing Direction?" *British Journal of Educational Studies*, 64 (1): 21–35.

Durvasula, R. (2022), "Turn Off the Gaslight." *Aeon*. Available online: https://aeon.co/essays/what-gaslighting-does-in-exploiting-trust-therapy-can-repair

Dussel, E. (1994), *1492: El Encubrimiento del Otro: Hacia el Origen del Mito de la Modernidad*. La Paz, Bolivia: Plural Editores.
Dussel, E. (1998), *Ética de la Liberación en la Edad de la Globalización y la Exclusión*. Madrid, España: Editorial Trotta.
Dussel, E. (2007), *Política de la Liberación: Arquitectónica*. Madrid, España: Editorial Trotta.
Dyson, M. E. (2006), *Is Bill Cosby Right? Or Has the Black Middle Class Lost Its Mind?* New York: Basic Books.
Eagleton, T. (2011), *Why Marx Was Right*. New Haven, CT: Yale University Press.
Education Commission of the States (1984), "Task Force on Education for Economic Growth." *Journal of Children in Contemporary Society*, 16 (3-4): 11-47.
Ehrenreich, B., and J. Ehrenreich (1979), "The Professional-Managerial Class." In P. Walker, ed., *Between Capital and Labor*. Boston, MA: South End Press. 5-45.
Ehrenreich, B., and J. Ehrenreich (2013), *Death of a Yuppie Dream: The Rise and Fall of the Professional-Managerial Class*. February. New York: Rosa Luxemburg Stiftung. Available online: https://www.rosalux.de/fileadmin/rls_uploads/pdfs/sonst_publikationen/ehrenreich_death_of_a_yuppie_dream90.pdf
Elias, S., and J. R. Feagin (2016), *Racial Theories in Social Science: A Systemic Racism Critique*. New York: Routledge.
Elise, S. (2018), "Diversity, Equity and Justice: Framing Our Work for Social Justice." California Faculty Association. Available online: https://www.calfac.org/magazine-article/diversity-equity-and-social-justice
Elkind, P. (2015), "Business Gets Schooled." *Fortune*. December 23.
Ellison, R. (1972), *Invisible Man*. New York: Vintage Books.
Ellner, S. (2004), "Leftist Goals and the Debate over Anti-Neoliberal Strategy in Latin America." *Science and Society*, 68 (1): 10-32.
Emery, K. (2002), "The Business Roundtable and Systemic Reform: How Corporate-Engineered High-Stakes Testing Has Eliminated Community Participation in Developing Educational Goals and Policies." PhD diss., University of California at Davis. Available online: http://educationanddemocracy.org./Emery_dissertation.html
Engels, F. ([1892] 2000), *The Condition of the Working Class in England*. London: Swan Sonnenschein.
Ernst, D., and V. Morton (2020), "Kemi Badenoch, British Equalities Minister, Denounces Black Lives Matter and Critical Race Theory." *Washington Times*. October 20. Available online: https://www.washingtontimes.com/news/2020/oct/20/kemi-badenoch-british-equalities-minister-denounce/
Esch, E. D. (2018), *The Color Line and the Assembly Line: Managing Race in the Ford Empire*. Oakland, CA: University of California Press.
European American Collaborative Challenging Whiteness (2010), "White on White: Developing Capacity to Communicate about Race with Critical Humility." In V. Sheared et al., eds., *The Handbook of Race and Adult Education: A Resource for Dialogue on Racism*. San Francisco, CA: Jossey-Bass. 145-57.
Evans, J. St. B. T. (2006), "The Heuristic-Analytic Theory of Reasoning: Extension and Evaluation." *Psychonomic Bulletin and Review*, 13 (3): 378-95.
Fabricant, M., and M. Fine (2012), *Charter Schools and the Corporate Makeover of Public Education: What's at Stake?* New York: Teachers College.
Faku, D., and Bloomberg (2015), "Ramaphosa Sells Majority Stake in Shanduka." *IOL Business Report*. June 2.
Fanon, F. (1963), *The Wretched of the Earth*. New York: Grove Press.

Fasching-Varner, K. J. (2009), "No! The team Ain't Alright! The Institutional and Individual Problematic of Race." *Social Identities*, 15 (6): 811–29.
Fay, B. (1987), *Critical Social Science: Liberation and Its Limits*. New York: Cornell University Press.
Feagin, J. R. (2006), *Systemic Racism: A Theory of Oppression*. New York: Routledge.
Feagin, J. R. (2010), *The White Racial Frame*. New York: Routledge.
Feagin, J. R. (2014), *Racist America: Roots, Current Realities, and Future Reparations*, 3rd ed. New York: Routledge.
Feagin, J. R., H. Vera, and P. Batur (2001), *White Racism: The Basics*, 2nd ed. New York: Routledge.
Feinberg, L. (1983), "Panel Urges Measures to Halt Decline of Education in America." *Washington Post*. April 27.
Feistritzer, C. E. (2011), *Profile of Teachers in the U.S. 2011*. Washington: National Center for Education Information, The Heartland Institute. Available online: https://www.heartland.org/_template-assets/documents/publications/Profile_Teachers_US_2011.pdf
Ferguson, D. E. (2013–14), "Martin Luther King Jr. and the Common Core: A Critical Reading of 'Close Reading'." *Rethinking Schools*, 28 (2): 18–21.
Fields, B. (1990), "Slavery, Race and Ideology in the United States of America." *New Left Review*, 181: 95–118.
Fields, B., and K. Fields (2018), "Beyond 'Race Relations': An Interview with Barbara J, Fields and Karen E. Fields by Daniel Denvir." *Jacobin*. January 17, 2018. Available online: https://www.jacobinmag.com/2018/01/racecraft-racism-barbara-karen-fields (accessed March 13, 2022).
Fields, E. F., and J. B. Fields (2012), *Racecraft: The Soul of Inequality in American Life*. London: Verso.
Figazzolo, L. (2009), *Impact of PISA 2006 on the Education Policy Debate*. Brussels: Education International.
Fine, M., and M. Fabricant (2013), *The Changing Politics of Education: Privatization and the Dispossessed Lives Left Behind*. Boulder, CO: Paradigm.
Fisher, A. N., and M. K. Ryan (2021), "Gender Inequalities during COVID-19." *Group Process and Intergroup Relations*, 24 (2): 237–45.
Fiske, E. B. (1983a), "Commission on Education Warns 'Tide of Mediocrity' Imperils U.S." *New York Times*. April 26.
Fiske, E. B. (1983b), "Study Says Weaknesses of Schools Pose Economic Threat." *New York Times*. May 4.
Foner, E. (1988), *America's Unfinished Revolution, 1863–1877*. New York: Harper & Row.
Foner, E. (1998), *Reconstruction: America's Unfinished Business 1863–1877*. New York: Perennial Classics.
Foster, R. (2017), "Freedom's Right: Critical Social Theory and the Challenge of Neoliberalism." *Capital & Class*, 41 (3): 455–73.
Foucault, M. ([1977] 1991), *Discipline and Punish: The Birth of the Prison*. Harmondsworth: Penguin.
Frankenberg, R. (1997), *Displacing Whiteness*. Durham, NC: Duke University Press.
Frederickson, G. (1997), "White Images of Black Slaves: Is What We See in Others Sometimes a Reflection of What We Find in Ourselves?" In R. Delgado and J. Stefancic, eds., *Critical White Studies: Looking behind the Mirror*. Philadelphia, PA: Temple University Press. 38–45.
Freeman, R. B. (1976), *The Overeducated American*. New York: Academic Press.

Freire, P. (1971), *Pedagogy of the Oppressed*. New York: Herder and Herder.
Freire, P. (1997), *Pedagogy of the Heart*. New York: Continuum.
Freire, P. (1998), *Pedagogy of Freedom: Ethics, Democracy, and Civic Courage*. Lanham, MD: Rowman & Littlefield.
Freire, P. (2018), *Pedagogy of the Oppressed*. New York: Bloomsbury Academic.
Frenkel, S., and A. Karni (2020), "Proud Boys Celebrate Trump's 'Stand By' Remark about Them at the Debate." *New York Times*. September 29.
Friedman, G. (2013), "Collapsing Investment and the Great Recession." *Dollars and Sense*. July/August.
Gaines, K. K. (1996), *Uplifting the Race: Black Leadership, Politics, and Culture in the Twentieth Century*. Chapel Hill, NC: University of North Carolina Press.
Galeano, E. (1973), *Open Veins of Latin America*. New York: Monthly Review Press.
Galeano, E. (2010), *Las Venas Abiertas de América Latina*. Mexico, DF: Siglo XXI.
Gane, N. (2011), "Measure, Value and the Current Crises of Sociology." *The Sociological Review*, 59 (2): 151–73.
Garber, M. (2017), "The Perils of Meritocracy." *The Atlantic*. June 30. Available online: https://www.theatlantic.com/entertainment/archive/2017/06/the-perils-of-meritocracy/532215/
Gaskins, A. (2006), "Putting the Color in Colorado: On Being Black and Teaching Ethnic Studies at the University of Colorado-Boulder." In C. E. Stanley, ed., *Faculty of Color: Teaching in Predominantly White Colleges and Universities*. Boston, MA: Anker Publishing. 139–52.
Gasper, P. (2008), "Imperialism: The Highest Stage of Capitalism." *Socialist Worker*. December 2. Available online: https://socialistworker.org/2008/12/02/imperialism-the-highest-stage-of-capitalism
Gates, B. (2007), "Remarks of Bill Gates, Harvard Commencement 2007." *Harvard Gazette*. June 7. Available online: https://news.harvard.edu/gazette/story/2007/06/remarks-of-bill-gates-harvard-commencement-2007/
Gates, B. (2009), "Prepared Remarks at the National Conference of State Legislatures." July 21. Seattle: Bill & Melinda Gates Foundation. Available online: https://www.gatesfoundation.org/ideas/speeches/2009/07/bill-gates-national-conference-of-state-legislatures-ncsl
Georgakas, D., and M. Surkin (2012), *Detroit: I Do Mind Dying: A Study in Urban Revolution*, 3rd ed. Chicago: Haymarket.
Geschwender, J. A. (1977), *Class, Race, and Worker Insurgency: The League of Revolutionary Black Workers*. Cambridge: Cambridge University Press.
Gewirtz, S. (2001), "Cloning the Blairs: New Labour's Programme for the Re-socialization of Working-Class Parents." *Journal of Education Policy*, 16 (4): 365–78.
Gilbert, S. F. (2021), "Systemic Racism, Systemic Sexism, and the Embryological Enterprise." *Developmental Biology*, 473: 97–104.
Gilens, M., and B. I. Page (2014), "Testing Theories of American Politics: Elites, Interest Groups, and Average Citizens." *Perspectives on Politics*, 12 (3): 564–81.
Gillborn, D. (2005), "Education Policy as an Act of White Supremacy: Whiteness, Critical Race Theory and Education Reform." *Journal of Education Policy*, 20 (4): 485–505.
Gillborn, D. (2006), "Critical Race Theory and Education: Racism and Anti-Racism in Educational Theory and Praxis." *Discourse: Studies in the Cultural Politics of Education*, 27 (1): 11–32.
Gillborn, D. (2008), *Racism and Education: Coincidence or Conspiracy?* New York: Routledge.

Gillborn, D. (2009), "Who's Afraid of Critical Race Theory in Education? A Reply to Mike Cole's 'The Color-Line and the Class Struggle.'" *Power and Education*, 1 (1): 125–31.

Gillborn, D. (2010), "The White Working Class, Racism and Respectability: Victims, Degenerates and Interest-Convergence." *British Journal of Educational Studies*, 58 (1): 3–25.

Gillborn, D. (2013), "The Policy of Inequity: Using CRT to Unmask White Supremacy in Education Policy." In M. Lynn and A. D. Dixson, eds., *Handbook of Critical Race Theory in Education*. New York: Routledge. 129–39.

Gillborn, D. (2016), "Intersectionality, Critical Race Theory, and the Primacy of Racism: Race, Class, Gender, and Disability in Education." *Qualitative Inquiry*, 2 (3): 277–87.

Gilmore, R. W. (2007), *Golden Gulag: Prisons, Surplus, Crisis, and Opposition in Globalizing California*. Berkeley, CA: University of California Press.

Gilroy, P. ([1987] 2002), *There Ain't No Black in the Union Jack: The Cultural Politics of Race and Nation*. London: Routledge.

Gilroy, P. (1992), "The End of Anti-Racism." In J. Donald and A. Rattansi, eds., *"Race," Culture and Difference*. London: Sage. 46–61.

Gilroy, P. (1993), *Small Acts: Thoughts on the Politics of Black Cultures*. London: Serpent's Tail.

Gilroy, P. (2000), *Against Race: Imagining Political Culture Beyond the Color Line*. Cambridge, MA: Harvard University Press.

Gimenez, M. E. (2007), "Back to Class: Reflections on the Dialectics of Class and Identity." In M. D. Yates, ed., *More Unequal: Aspects of Class in the United States*. New York: Monthly Review Press. 107–17.

Giroux, H. (1981), *Ideology, Culture and the Process of Schooling*. Philadelphia, PA: Temple University Press.

Giroux, H. (2018), "Donald Trump's Fascist Politics and the Language of Disappearance." *Salon*. November 18. https://www.salon.com/2018/11/18/donald-trumps-fascist-politics-and-the-language-of-disappearance/

Givan, R. K., and P. Whitefield (2018), *Women's Work? Voices of Vermont Educators*. Piscataway Township, NJ: Rutgers School of Management and Labor Relations. Available online: https://www.nea.org/sites/default/files/2020-06/RU_SMLR_Womens_Work.pdf

Glenza, J. (2016), "Rosewood Massacre a Harrowing Tale of Racism and the Road toward Reparations." *The Guardian*. January 3. Available online: https://www.theguardian.com/us-news/2016/jan/03/rosewood-florida-massacre-racial-violence-reparations

Goldberg, D. T. (1993), *Racist Culture*. Oxford: Blackwell.

Goldberg, D. T. (2002), *The Racial State*. Malden, MA: Blackwell Publishers.

Gonzalez, J. (2012), "Hedge Fund Executives Give 'Til It Hurts to Politicians, Especially Cuomo, to Get More Charter Schools." *New York Daily News*. March 11.

Goodman, D. (2016), "Critical Literacy, Democratic Schools, and the Whole Language Movement." In H. Ryan, *Educational Justice: Teaching and Organizing against the Corporate Juggernaut*. New York: Monthly Review. 156–85.

Gopal, P. (2019), *Insurgent Empire: Anticolonialism and the Making of British Dissent*. London: Verso Books.

Gordon, L. (2014), "The Women's Liberation Movement." In D. S. Cobble, L. Gordon, and A. Henry, *Feminism Unfinished: A Short, Surprising History of American Women's Movements*. New York: Liveright Publishing. 69–145.

Gordon, L. R. (2000), *Existentia Africana: Understanding Africana Existential Thought*. New York: Routledge.

Gordon, P. (1990), "A Dirty War: The New Right and Local Authority Anti-Racism." In W. Ball and J. Solomos, eds., *Race and Local Politics*. Basingstoke: Macmillan. 175–90.

Gorlewski, J. A. (2011), *Power, Resistance, and Literacy: Writing for Social Justice*. Charlotte, NC: Information Age.

Gorski, P. C., and K. Zenkov, eds. (2014), *The Big Lies of School Reform*. New York: Routledge.

Gottesman, I. (2010), "Sitting in the Waiting Room: Paulo Freire and the Critical Turn in the Field of Education." *Educational Studies*, 46 (4): 376–99.

Gottesman, I. (2016), *The Critical Turn in Education: From Marxist Critique to Poststructuralist Feminism to Critical Theories of Race*. New York: Routledge.

Graff, G. (2018), "The Name of the Game Is Shame, Part II: From Slavery to Obama and Now Trump." *Journal of Psychohistory*, 45 (3): 154–62.

Graves, J. L., Jr., and A. H. Goodman (2022), *Racism not Race*. New York: Columbia University.

Greany, T., and J. Scott (2014), *Conflicts of Interest in Academy Sponsorship Arrangements: A Report for the Education Select Committee*. London: Institute of Education, University of London and London Centre for Leadership in Learning.

Green, A. (1990), *Education and State Formation: The Rise of Education Systems in England, France and the USA*. Basingstoke: Palgrave Macmillan.

Green, E. L. (2017), "Education Department Says It Will Scale Back Civil Rights Investigations." *New York Times*. June 16.

Greenhouse, S. (2009), *The Big Squeeze: Tough Times for the American Worker*. New York: Anchor.

Grissom, J. A., C. Redding, and J. F. Bleiberg (2019), "Money over Merit? Socioeconomic Gaps in Receipt of Gifted Services." *Harvard Educational Review*, 89 (3): 337–69.

Guillaumin, C. (1995), *Racism, Sexism, Power and Ideology*. New York: Routledge.

Guinier, L. (2004), "From Racial Liberalism to Racial Literacy: *Brown v. Board of Education* and the Interest-Divergence Dilemma." *Journal of American History*, 91 (3): 92–118.

Guinier, L. (2016), *The Tyranny of the Meritocracy: Democratizing Higher Education in America*. Boston, MA: Beacon Books.

Gunter, B., and C. Kieffer (2021), "Islamophobia after 9/11: How a Fearmongering Fringe Movement Exploited the Terror Attacks to Gain Political Power." *Southern Poverty Law Center*. September 17.

Guthrie, J. W., and M. G. Springer (2004), "A Nation at Risk Revisited: Did 'Wrong' Reasoning Result in 'Right' Results? At What Cost?" *Peabody Journal of Education*, 79 (1): 7–35.

Hadžidedić, Z. (2022), *Nations and Capital*. London: Routledge.

Haidar, A. (2018), *Mistaken Identity: Race and Class in the Age of Trump*. London: Verso.

Hall, C. (2020), "Mother Country." *London Review of Books*, 42 (2). January 23. Available online: https://www.lrb.co.uk/the-paper/v42/n02/catherine-hall/mother-country

Hall, S. (1978), "Racism and Reaction." In CRE (Commission for Racial Equality), ed., *Five Views of Multi-Racial Britain: Talks on Race Relations Broadcast by BBC TV*. London: CRE. 23–35.

Hall, S. (1991), "Ethnicity: Identity and Difference." *Radical America*, 23 (4): 9–20.

Hall, S. (1993), "The West and the Rest: Discourse and Power." In S. Hall and B. Gieben, eds., *Formations of Modernity*. Cambridge: Polity Press.

Hall, S. (1996a), "Cultural Studies and Its Theoretical Legacies." In K. Chen and D. Morley, eds., *Stuart Hall: Critical Dialogues in Cultural Studies*. London: Routledge. 262–75.

Hall, S. (1996b), "New Ethnicities." In K. Chen and D. Morley, eds., *Stuart Hall: Critical Dialogues in Cultural Studies*. New York: Routledge. 441–9.

Hall, S. (1997), "Race, the Floating Signifier Featuring Stuart Hall [Transcript]." *Media Education Foundation*. Available online: http://www.mediaed.org/assets/products/407/transcript_407.pdf (accessed March 28, 2022).

Hall, S. (2005), "The Meaning of New Times." In D. Morley and K. Chen, eds., *Stuart Hall: Critical Dialogues in Cultural Studies*. London: Routledge. 223–37.

Hall, S. (2021), *Selected Writings on Marxism*. Durham, NC: Duke University Press.

Hall, S., C. Critcher. T. Jefferson, J. Clarke, and B. Roberts (1978), *Policing the Crisis: Mugging, the State, and Law and Order*. London: Palgrave Macmillan.

Hamilton, C. V. (1992), Afterword to K. Ture and C. V. Hamilton, *Black Power: The Politics of Liberation in America*. New York: Vintage. 201–18.

Haraway, D. (2015), "Anthropocene, Capitalocene, Plantationocene, Chthulucene: Making Kin." *Environmental Humanities*, 6 (1): 159–65.

Harc, B. (2002), *2001 Race Odyssey: African Americans and Sociology*. Syracuse, NY: Syracuse University Press.

Harper, T. (2021), *Underground Asia: Global Revolutionaries and the Assault on Empire*. Cambridge, MA: Harvard University Press.

Harris, B. G., C. Hayes, and D. T. Smith (2020), "Not a 'Who Done It' Mystery: On How Whiteness Sabotages Equity Aims in Teacher Preparation Programs." *Urban Review*, 52: 198–213.

Harris, C. I. (1993), "Whiteness as Property." *Harvard Law Review*, 106 (8): 1707–91.

Harrison, A. (2012), "Michael Gove: Academy School Critics 'Happy with Failure.'" *BBC News*. January 4.

Harvey, D. (2005), *A Brief History of Neoliberalism*. Oxford: Oxford University Press.

Harvey, D. (2016), "Neoliberalism Is a Political Project." *Jacobin*. July 23.

Hatcher, R. (1995), "The Limitations of the New Social Democratic Agendas: Class, Equality and agency." In R. Hatcher and K. Jones, eds., *Education after the Conservatives: The Response to the New Agenda for Reform*. Stoke-on-Trent: Trentham Books.

Hayes, C., B. G. Juarez, M. T. Witt, and N. D. Hartlep (2013), "Toward a Lesser Shade of White: 12 Steps Toward More Authentic Race Awareness." In C. Hayes and N. D. Hartlep, eds., *Unhooking from Whiteness: The Key to Dismantling Racism in the United States*. Boston, MA: Sense Publishers. 1–16.

Hayes, C., and N. D. Hartlep (2013), *Unhooking from Whiteness: The Key to Dismantling Racism in the United States*. Rotterdam: Sense Publishers.

Haylett, C. (2001), "Illegitimate Subjects? Abject Whites, Neoliberal Modernisation, and Middle-Class Multiculturalism." *Environment and Planning D: Society and Space*, 19: 351–70.

Headley, C. (2004), "Delegitimizing the Normativity of Whiteness: A Critical Africana Philosophical Study of the Metaphoricity of Whiteness." In G. Yancy, ed., *What Whiteness Looks Like: African-American Philosophers on the Whiteness Question*. New York: Routledge. 87–106.

Helsel, P. (2021), "Man Sentenced to 3 Years in Minneapolis Police Precinct Fire after George Floyd's Death." *NBC News*. May 6.

Herrnstein, R. J., and C. A. Murray (1994), *The Bell Curve: Intelligence and Class Structure in American Life*. New York: Free Press.

Hess, M. E. (2019), "Using Digital Storytelling to Unearth Racism and Galvanize Action." In S. D. Brookfield and Associates, *Teaching Race: Helping Students Unmask and Challenge Racism*. San Francisco, CA: Jossey-Bass. 253–72.

Hill, C., C. Corbett, and A. St. Rose (2010), "Why so Few? Women in Science." In *Technology, Engineering, and Mathematics*. Washington, DC: AAUW.

Hill, D. (2001), "The National Curriculum, the Hidden Curriculum and Equality." In D. Hill and M. Cole, *Schooling and Equality: Fact, Concept and Policy*. London: Kogan Page. 95–116.

Hill, D. (2004), "Educational Perversion and Global Neo-Liberalism." *Cultural Logic: A Journal of Marxist Theory & Practice*, 11: 1–41.

Hill, D. (2009), "Race and Class in Britain: A Critique of the Statistical Basis for Critical Race Theory in Britain." *Journal for Critical Education Policy Studies*, 7 (2): 1–40.

Hill, D., and A. Maisuria (2022), "Education, Social Class and Marxist Theory." In A. Maisuria, ed., *Encyclopaedia of Marxism and Education*. Leiden: Brill. 624–43.

Hirji, F. K. (2019), *Under-Education in Africa: From Colonialism to Neoliberalism*. Montreal: Daraja Press.

Hoff, D. J. (2006), "Big Business Going to Bat for NCLB." *Education Week*. October 18.

Holmstrom, N., ed. (2002), *The Socialist-Feminist Project: A Contemporary Reader in Theory and Politics*. New York: Monthly Review Press.

Holt, J. (2021), *After the Insurrection: How Domestic Extremists Adapted and Evolved after the January 6 US Capitol Attack*. Washington: Atlantic Council. Available online: https://www.atlanticcouncil.org/wp-content/uploads/2022/01/After-the-Insurrection.pdf

Honneth, A. (1991), *The Critique of Power: Reflective Stages in a Critical Social Theory*. London: MIT Press.

hooks, b. (1984), *Feminist Theory: From Margin to Center*. Boston, MA: South End Press.

hooks, b. (1989), *Talking Back: Thinking Feminist, Thinking Black*. Boston, MA: South End Press.

hooks, b. (1994), *Teaching to Transgress*. New York: Routledge.

hooks, b. (1996), *Killing Rage*. New York: Henry Holt.

Horn, J. (2016), *Work Hard, Be Hard: Journeys through "No Excuses" Teaching*. Lanham, MD: Rowman and Littlefield.

Horne, G. (1990), "Re-Educating the U.S. Working Class on Race and Class." In S. H. London, E. R. Tarr, and J. F. Wilson, eds., *The Re-Education of the American Working Class*. New York: Greenwood Press. 171–81.

Horne, G. (1997), *Fire This Time: The Watts Uprising and the 1960s*. New York: Da Capo Press.

Horsford, S. D. (2011), *Learning in a Burning House: Educational Inequality, Ideology, and (Dis)Integration*. New York: Teachers College Press.

Housee, S. (2008), "Should Race Matter When We Teach Race and Racism in the Classroom." *Race Ethnicity and Education*, 11 (4): 415–28.

Housee, S. (2010), "'To Veil or Not to Veil': Students Speak Out against Islam(ophobia) in Class." *ELiSS*, 23. http://www.eliss.org.uk/CurrentIssueVol23/tabid/280/Default.aspx

Housee, S. (2012a), "What's the Point? Anti-Racism and Students' Voices against Islamophobia." *Race, Ethnicity and Education*, 15 (1). Available online: https://www.tandfonline.com/doi/abs/10.1080/13613324.2012.638867

Housee, S. (2012b), "Identity and Pedagogy in a University Context: A Study of Student Experiences and Critique in the Work of Anti-Racism in Education." PhD thesis. University of Wolverhampton. Available online: https://ethos.bl.uk/OrderDetails.do?uin=uk.bl.ethos.576679

Housee, S. (2018), *Speaking Out against Racism in the University Space*. London: Trentham Books.

Howard, G. R. (2016), *We Can't Teach What We Don't Know: White Teachers, Multiracial Schools*, 3rd ed. New York: Teachers College.
Hunt, A. (1999), "Marxist Theory of Law." In D. Peterson, ed., *A Companion to Philosophy of Law and Legal Theory*. Malden, MA: Blackwell Publishing.
Hunt, T. (2014), "Speech to Character Conference." Demos Conference, London. December 8. Available online: www.demos.co.uk/files/TristramHuntspeech.pdf
Hyland, T. (1994), "Teaching, Learning and NVQs: Challenging Behaviourism and Competence in Adult Education Theory and Practice." Paper presented at the 1994 Standing Conference on University Teaching and Research in the Education of Adults, University of Hull, England. Available online: https://citeseerx.ist.psu.edu/viewdoc/download?doi=10.1.1.1001.3691&rep=rep1&type=pdf#page=66
Hylton, K., A. Pilkington, P. Warmington, and S. Housee, eds. (2011), *Atlantic Crossings: International Dialogues on Critical Race Theory*. Birmingham: The Higher Education Academy Network, University of Birmingham.
Hynds, A. S., R. Hindle, C. Savage, L. H. Meyer, W. Penetito, and C. E. Sleeter (2016), "The Impact of Teacher Professional Development to Reposition Pedagogy for Indigenous Students in Mainstream Schools." *The Teacher Educator*, 51 (3): 230–49.
Hytten, K., and J. Warren (2003), "Engaging Whiteness: How Racial Power Gets Reified in Education." *International Journal of Qualitative Studies in Education*, 16 (1): 65–89.
Iglesias, E. M. (2000), "Global Markets, Racial Spaces and the Role of Critical Race Theory in the Struggle for Community Control of Investments: An Institutional Class Analysis." *Villanova Law Review*, 45 (5): 1037–73.
Ignatiev, N., and J. Garvey, eds. (1996), *Race Traitor*. New York: Routledge.
Inikori, J. E. (2020), "Atlantic Slavery and the Rise of the Capitalism Global Economy." *Current Anthropology*, 61 (22): 159–71.
International Finance Corporation (2014), "IFC Supports Expansion of Primary Education with Investment in Bridge International Academies." Press release. January 21. Washington: IFC. Available online: https://www.ifc.org/wps/wcm/connect/news_ext_content/ifc_external_corporate_site/news+and+events/news/bridgeschools_feature
Isaksen, R. (2016), "Reclaiming Rational Theory Choice as Central: A Critique of Methodological Applications of Critical Realism." *Journal of Critical Realism*, 15 (3): 245–62.
ISO Steering Committee (2019), Series: "Reflections on the ISO Crisis." *Socialist Worker*. Available online: https://socialistworker.org/series/reflections-on-the-iso-crisis
Jacobson, M. F. (1998), *Whiteness of a Different Color: European Immigrants and the Alchemy of Race*. Cambridge, MA: Harvard University Press.
James, C. L. R. ([1937] 2017), *World Revolution 1917–1936: The Rise and Fall of the Communist International*. Durham, NC: Duke University Press.
James, C. L. R. (1939), "The SWP and Negro Work." *Marxists Internet Archive*. Available online: https://www.marxists.org/archive/james-clr/works/1939/07/negro-work.htm?fbclid=IwAR2cFFtxzlSdTHX6guMXoQeNe9NHH8zpSzbn28mQdxM14PNlc_YVjaIUzDY
Jani, P. (2019), "Towards a Critical Defense of 'Identity Politics.'" *Socialist Worker*. April 19. Available online: https://socialistworker.org/2019/04/03/towards-a-critical-defense-of-identity-politics
Jani, P. (2002), "Karl Marx, Eurocentrism, and the 1857 Revolt in British India." In C. Bartolovich and N. Lazarus, eds., *Marxism, Modernity, and Postcolonial Studies*. Cambridge: Cambridge University Press. 81–97.

Jani, P. (2021), "Atlanta Was a Watershed: Lessons for Fighting Anti-Asian Racism." *Tempest*. August 30.

Jarvis, J. (2020), "Trump 'Praying for' Louisville Police Shot amid Breonna Taylor Protests, Demands Law and Order." *Newsweek*. September 24.

Jay, M. (1973), *The Dialectical Imagination: The History of the Institute for Social Research and the Frankfurt School, 1923–50*. Berkeley, CA: University of California Press.

Jesse-Jones, T. (1923), "Education in Africa: A Study of West, South and Equatorial Africa by the African Education Commission under the Auspices of the Phelps-Stokes Fund and the Foreign Missions Society of North America and Europe." *African Affairs*, XXIII (LXXXIX). October 1. https://doi.org/10.1093/oxfordjournals.afraf.a099952

Jones, C. (1949), "An End to the Neglect of the Problems of the Negro Woman." In *National Women's Commission*. New York: CPUSA. 1–19.

Jones, K. (2016), *Education in Britain: 1944 to the Present*, 2nd ed. Cambridge: Polity Press.

Jones, O. (2015), *The Establishment: And How They Get Away with It*. London: Penguin.

Juarez, B. G., and C. Hayes (2014), "On Being Named a Black Supremacist and a Racist against Your Own Kind: The Problem of White Racial Domination and the Domestic Terrorism of White Supremacy in U.S. Teacher Education and Colleges of Education." *Urban Review*, 46 (2): 2–20.

Juarez, B. G., C. Hayes, and D. T. Smith (2016), "Just Do What We Tell You: White Rules for Well Behaved Minorities." In N. D. Hartlep and C. Hayes, eds., *Unhooking from Whiteness: Resisting the Esprit de Corps*. Boston, MA: Sense Publishers. 101–16.

June, S. (2017), "Oregon Is Now Currently the Only State to Have Required Ethnic Studies Curriculum for K-12 Students." *Willamette Week*. July 1.

Kahn, J. (2001), *Modernity and Exclusion*. London: Sage.

Kandel, I. L. (1932), "Introduction." In I. L. Kandel, ed., *Educational Yearbook of the International Institute of Teachers College, Columbia University, 1931*. New York: Columbia University.

Karis, T., and G. M. Carter, eds. (1973), *From Protest to Challenge: A Documentary History of African Politics in South Africa 1882–1964*, vol. 2. Stanford, CA: Hoover Institution.

Kasakove, S. (2021), "The College Admissions Scandal: Where Some of the Defendants Are Now." *The New York Times*. October 9.

Kasrils, R. (2013), "How the ANC's Faustian Pact Sold Out South Africa's Poorest." *Guardian*. June 24.

Keengwe, J. (2020), *Handbook of Research on Diversity and Social Justice in Higher Education*. PA: IGI Global.

Kelley, R. D. G. (1997), "Identity and Class Politics." *New Politics*, 6 (2). Winter.

Kelley, R. D. G. (1999), "Building Bridges: The Challenge of Organized Labor in Communities of Color." *New Labor Forum*, 5: 42–58.

Kelley, R. D. G. (2002), *Freedom Dreams: The Black Radical Imagination*. Boston, MA: Beacon Press.

Kelley, R. D. G. (2016), "Cedric J. Robinson: The Making of a Black Radical Intellectual." *Counterpunch*. June 17.

Kelley, R. D. G. (2017), "What Did Cedric Robinson Mean by Racial Capitalism?" *Boston Review*. January 12.

Kelliher, D. (2017), "Solidarity, Class and Labour Agency: Mapping Networks of Support between London and the Coalfields During the 1984–5 Miners' Strike." PhD thesis. University of Glasgow. http://theses.gla.ac.uk/8030

Kendhammer, B. (2007), "DuBois the Pan-Africanist and the Development of African Nationalism." *Ethnic and Racial Studies*, 30 (1): 51–71.

Kendi, I. X. (2019), *How to Be an Anti-Racist*. New York: One World Books.
Kincheloe, J. L., and S. R. Steinberg (1997), *Changing Multiculturalism*. Philadelphia, PA: Open University Press.
King, J. (1991), "Dysconscious Racism: Ideology, Identity, and the Miseducation of Teachers." *Journal of Negro Education*, 60 (2): 133–46.
Kinnamon, K., and M. Fabre, eds. (1993), *Conversations with Richard Wright*. Jackson, MS: University Press of Mississippi.
Kivel, P. (2004), *You Call This a Democracy? Who Benefits, Who Pays, and Who Really Decides*. Lexington, KY: The Apex Press.
Kliebard, H. M. (1982), "Education at the Turn of the Century: A Crucible for Curriculum Change." *Educational Researcher*, 11 (1): 16–24.
Kliebard, H. M. (1995), *The Struggle for the American Curriculum*, 2nd ed. New York: Routledge.
Knapp, M. S., and S. Woolverton (2004), "Social Class and Schooling." In J. A. Banks and C. A. M. Banks, eds., *Handbook of Research on Multicultural Education*, 2nd ed. San Francisco, CA: Jossey-Bass. 656–81.
Kochhar, R., and A. Cilluffo (2018), "Income Inequality in the US is Rising Most Rapidly among Asians." Pew Research Center. July 12. Available online: https://www.pewresearch.org/social-trends/2018/07/12/income-inequality-in-the-u-s-is-rising-most-rapidly-among-asians/
Kohli, R., A. Nevárez, and N. Arteaga (2018), "Public Pedagogy for Racial Justice Teaching; Supporting the Racial Literacy Development of Teachers of Color." *The Assembly: A Journal for Public Scholarship on Education*, 1 (1): 17–27.
Kohli, R., M. Pizarro, and A. Nevárez (2017), "The 'New Racism' of K-12 Schools: Centering Critical Research on Racism." *Review of Research in Education*, 42: 182–202.
Kozol, J. (2012), *Savage Inequalities: Children in America's Schools*, reprint ed. New York: Broadway.
Kristal, G. (2017), "A Working-Class Strategy for Defeating White Supremacy." *Working In These Times*. August 10.
Kulz, C. (2017), *Factories for Learning: Making Race, Class and Inequality in the Neoliberal Academy*. Manchester: Manchester University Press.
Kulz, C. (2018), "Mapping Folk Devils Old and New through Permanent Exclusion from London Schools." *Race Ethnicity and Education*, 22 (1): 93–109.
Kumashiro, K. (2015), *Against Common Sense: Teaching and Learning Toward Social Justice*, 3rd ed. New York: Routledge.
Kundnani, A. (2007), *The End of Tolerance: Racism in 21st Century Britain*. Ann Arbor, MI: Pluto.
Kundnani, A. (2009), *Spooked! How Not To Prevent Violent Extremism*. London: Institute of Race Relations.
Ladson-Billings, G. (1998), "Just What Is Critical Race Theory, and What Is It Doing in a Nice Field like Education?" *International Journal of Qualitative Studies in Education*, 11 (1): 7–24.
Ladson-Billings, G. (2001), "Teaching and Cultural Competence: What Does It Take to Be a Successful Teacher in a Diverse Classroom?" *Rethinking Schools*, 15 (4): 16–17.
Ladson-Billings, G. (2006), "They're Trying to Wash Us Away: The Adolescence of Critical Race Theory in Education." In A. D. Dixson and C. K. Rousseau, eds., *Critical Race Theory in Education: All God's Children Got a Song*. New York: Routledge. v–xiii.
Ladson-Billings, G., and W. F. Tate (1995), "Toward a Critical Race Theory of Education." *Teachers College Record*, 97 (1): 47–68.

Lafer, G. (2017), *The One Percent Solution: How Corporations Are Remaking America One State at a Time*. Ithaca, NY: ILR Press.
Laffer, A. B., S. Moore, and J. Williams (2016), *Rich States, Poor States*, 9th ed. Washington: ALEC. https://www.alec.org/publication/rich-states-poor-states
Lam, K. D. (2015), *Youth Gangs, Racism, and Schooling: Vietnamese American Youth in a Postcolonial Context*. New York: Palgrave Macmillan.
Lam, K. D. (2019), "Asian American Youth Violence as Genocide: A Critical Appraisal and Its Pedagogical Significance." *Equity and Excellence in Education*, 52 (2–3): 255–70.
Lapper, R., and T. Burgis (2008), "South Africa Urged to Beware of Left Turn." *Financial Times*. October 27.
Lareau, A. (2000), *Home Advantage: Social Class and Parental Intervention in Elementary Education*. Lanham, MD: Rowman & Littlefield Publishers.
Lawler, S. (1999), "Getting Out and Getting Away: Women's Narratives of Class Mobility." *Feminist Review*, 63 (1): 3–24.
Lawler, S. (2000), *Mothering the Self: Mothers, Daughters, Subjects*. New York: Routledge.
Lawler, S. (2005), "Disgusted Subjects: The Making of Middle-Class Identities." *Sociological Review*, 53 (3): 429–46.
Lawrence, E. (1982), "In the Abundance of Water, the Fool Is Thirsty: Sociology and Black 'Pathology.'" In CCCS (Centre for Contemporary Cultural Studies), ed., *The Empire Strikes Back: Race and Racism in 70s Britain*. London: Routledge in association with the University of Birmingham. 93–141.
Lawrence, S. M., and B. D. Tatum (1998), "White Racial Identity and Anti-Racist Education: A Catalyst for Change." In E. Lee, D. Menkart, and M. Okazawa-Rey, eds., *Beyond Heroes and Holidays: A Practical Guide to K-12 Anti-Racist, Multicultural Education and Staff Development*. Washington: Network of Educators on the Americas. 45–51.
Layton, L. (2014), "How Bill Gates Pulled Off the Swift Common Core Revolution." *Washington Post*. June 7.
Lee, E., D. Menkart, and M. Okazawa-Rey, eds. (2008), *Beyond Heroes and Holidays: A Practical Guide to K-12 Anti-Racist, Multicultural Education and Staff Development*, 4th ed. Washington: Teaching for Change.
Legassick, M. (2007), *Towards Socialist Democracy*. Scottsville: University of KwaZulu-Natal Press.
Lenin, V. I. ([1916] 2005), "Imperialism: The Highest Stage of Capitalism." Marxists Internet Archive. Available online: https://www.marxists.org/archive/lenin/works/1916/imp-hsc/
Lenin, V. I. ([1915] 2005), "Socialism and War." Marxists Internet Archive. Available online: https://www.marxists.org/archive/lenin/works/1915/s-w/index.htm
Lenin, V. I. ([1917] 1999), "The Tasks of the Proletariat in the Present Revolution." Marxists Internet Archive. Available online: https://www.marxists.org/archive/lenin/works/1917/apr/04.htm
Leonardo, Z. (2002), "The Souls of White Folk: Critical Pedagogy, Whiteness Studies, and Globalization Discourse." *Race, Ethnicity, and Education*, 5 (1): 29–50.
Leonardo, Z. (2003), *Ideology, Discourse, and School Reform*. Westport, CT: Praeger.
Leonardo, Z. (2009), *Race, Whiteness, and Education*. New York: Routledge.
Leonardo, Z. (2010), "Afterword." In K. L. Buras, J. Randels, and K. ya Salaam, eds., *Pedagogy, Policy, and the Privatized City: Stories of Dispossession and Defiance from New Orleans*. New York: Teachers College Press.

Leonardo, Z. (2012a), "Black Education in the Interest of Black Folks." In E. Thomas and S. Brooks-Tatum, eds., *Reading African American Experiences in the Obama Era: Theory, Advocacy, Activism*. New York: Peter Lang. 261–6.

Leonardo, Z. (2012b), "The Race for Class: Reflections on a Critical Raceclass Theory of Education." *Education Studies*, 48 (5): 427–49.

Leonardo, Z. (2013), *Race Frameworks: A Multidimensional Theory of Racism and Education*. New York: Teachers College.

Leonardo, Z., and R. K. Porter (2010), "Pedagogy of Fear: Toward a Fanonian Theory of 'Safety' in Race Dialogue." *Race, Ethnicity and Education*, 13 (2): 139–57.

Lévinas, E. (1969), *Totality and Infinity: An Essay on Exteriority*. Pittsburgh, PA: Duquesne University Press.

Levine, M. V. (2013), "The Skills Gap and Unemployment in Wisconsin: Separating Fact from Fiction." February. Milwaukee, WI: Center Economic Development, University of Wisconsin-Milwaukee. Available online: https://dc.uwm.edu/cgi/viewcontent.cgi?article=1017&context=ced_pubs

Levinson, B. A., J. P. K. Gross, C. Hanks, J. H. Dadds, K. Kumasi, and J. Link (2015), *Beyond Critique: Exploring Critical Social Theories and Education*. New York: Routledge.

Levitan, J. (2018), "The Danger of a Single Theory: Understanding Students' Voices and Social Justice in the Peruvian Andes." *Teachers College Record*, 120 (2): 1–36.

Levy, J. (2014), "The Politics of Honduran Schoolteachers: State Agents Challenge the State." PhD thesis. University of Western Ontario. Available online: http://ir.lib.uwo.ca/etd/2142

Lewis, D. L. (1996), "The Promise and Peril of Class in the Problem of the 20th Century." *The Journal of Negro Education*, 65, no. 2 (Spring): 111–21.

Lindner, K. (2010), "Marx's Eurocentrism, Postcolonial Studies and Marx Scholarship." *Radical Philosophy*, 161: 27–41.

Lipman, P. (2009), *Making Sense of Renaissance 2010 School Policy in Chicago: Race, Class, and the Cultural Politics of Neoliberal Urban Restructuring*. January. Chicago: Great Cities Institute.

Lipman, P. (2011), *The New Political Economy of Urban Education: Neoliberalism, Race, and the Right to the City*. New York: Routledge.

Lipman, P. (2017), "The Landscape of Education 'Reform' in Chicago: Neoliberalism Meets a Grassroots Movement." *Education Policy Analysis Archives*, 25 (54): 1–26.

Lipman, P. (2020), "School Closing: Racial Capitalism, State Violence and Resistance." In E. Mayorga, U. Aggarwal, and B. Picower, eds., *What's Race Got to Do with It? How Current School Reform Policy Maintains Racial and Economic Inequality*, 2nd ed. New York: Peter Lang. 129–48.

Lipsitz, G. (2006), *The Possessive Investment in Whiteness: How White People Profit from Identity Politics*. Philadelphia, PA: Temple University Press.

Lipsitz, G. (2019), "The Sounds of Silence: How Race Neutrality Preserves White Supremacy." In K. W. Crenshaw, L. C. Harris, D. M. HoSang, and G. Lipsitz, eds., *Seeing Race Again: Countering Colorblindness across the Disciplines*. Oakland, CA: University of California Press. 23–51.

Lopez, G. R. (2003), "The (Racially Neutral) Politics of Education: A Critical race Theory Perspective." *Educational Administration Quarterly*, 39 (1): 68–94.

Lopez, I. (2006), *White by Law: The Legal Construction of Race*. New York: New York University Press.

Lough, C. (2020), "Black Pupils Warn of N-Word Abuse in UK Private Schools." *Times Educational Supplement*. June 2.

Love, B. (2004), "Brown Plus 50 Counter-Storytelling: A Critical Race Theory Analysis of the Majoritarian Achievement Gap Story." *Equity and Excellence in Education*, 37: 227–46.
Love, B. (2019a), *We Want to Do More than Survive: Abolitionist Teaching and the Pursuit of Educational Freedom*. Boston, MA: Beacon Press.
Love, B. (2019b), "Keynote Speech." Teachers 4 Social Justice Conference. October 12, 2019.
Luna, C., and C. L. Turner (2001), "The Impact of the MCAS: Teachers Talk about High-Stakes Testing." *English Journal*, 91 (1): 79–87.
Luxemburg, R. (2004), "The Historical Conditions of Accumulation, from *The Accumulation of Capital*." In P. Hudis and K. B. Anderson, eds., *The Rosa Luxemburg Reader*. New York: Monthly Review Press. 32–70.
Luxemburg, R. (2010), *Socialism or Barbarism: Selected Writings*. H. Scott and P. LeBlanc, eds. London: Pluto Press.
Lynn, D. (2016), "Claudia Jones' Feminist Vision of Emancipation." *Black Perspectives*. African American Intellectual History Society. September 8. Available online: https://www.aaihs.org/claudia-jones-feminist-vision-of-emancipation/#fn-10690-7.
Lynn, M., and A. D. Dixson, eds. (2013), *Handbook of Critical Race Theory in Education*. New York: Routledge.
Madhubuti, H. R. (1974), "The Latest Purge: The Attack on Black Nationalism and Pan-Afrikanism by the New Left, the Sons and Daughters of the Old Left." *Black Scholar*, 6 (1): 43–56.
Mahler, A. G. (2018), *From the Tricontinental to the Global South: Race, Radicalism, and Transnational Solidarity*. Durham, NC: Duke University Press.
Mahon, R., and S. McBride, eds. (2009), *The OECD and Transnational Governance*. Vancouver: UBC Press.
Mahoney, M. R. (2000), "Constructing Solidarity: Interest and White Workers." *University of Pennsylvania Journal of Labor and Employment Law*, 2: 747–71.
Mahoney, M. R. (2003), "Class and Status in American Law: Race, Interest, and the Anti-Transformation Cases." *South Carolina Law Review*, 76 (4): 799–892.
Mahoney, M. R. (2009), "What's Left of Solidarity? Reflections on Law, Race, and Labor History." *Buffalo Law Review*, 57: 1515–96.
Maisuria, A. (2010), "Ten Years of New Labour Education Policy and Racial Inequality: An Act of Whiteness or Neoliberalism?" In A. Green, ed., *Blair's Educational Legacy: Thirteen Years of New Labour*. New York: Palgrave MacMillan. 171–91.
Maisuria, A. (2012), "A Critical Appraisal of Critical Race Theory (CRT): Limitations and Opportunities." In K. Bhopal and J. Preston, eds., *Intersectionality and "Race" in Education*. New York: Routledge. 76–96.
Maisuria, A. (2014), "The Neo-Liberalisation Policy Agenda and Its Consequences for Education in England: A Focus on Resistance Now and Possibilities for the Future." *Policy Futures in Education*, 12 (2): 286–96. https://doi.org/10.2304/pfie.2014.12.2.286
Maisuria, A. (2018), *Class Consciousness and Education in Sweden: A Marxist Analysis of Revolution in a Social Democracy*. London: Routledge.
Maisuria, A., ed. (2022a), *Encyclopaedia of Marxism and Education*. Leiden: Brill.
Maisuria, A. (2022b), "Navigating the Relational Character of Social Class for Capitalism in the Academy." In I. Burnell, ed., *The Lives of Working Class Academics: Getting Ideas Above Your Station*. Bingley: Emerald Publishing. 1–15.
Maisuria, A. (2022c), "Neoliberalism and Revolution." In A. Maisuria, ed., *Encyclopaedia of Marxism and Education*. Leiden: Brill. 483–500.

Maisuria, A., and D. Beach (2017), "Ethnography and Education." In *Oxford Research Encyclopaedia of Education*. Oxford University Press. Available online: https://oxfordre.com/education/view/10.1093/acrefore/9780190264093.001.0001/acrefore-9780190264093-e-100

Mandel, E. ([1978] 2016), *From Stalinism to Eurocommunism: The Bitter Fruits of "Socialism in One Country."* Chicago: Haymarket Books.

Mandela, N. (1965), *No Easy Walk to Freedom: Articles, Speeches, and Trial Addresses of Nelson Mandela*. New York: Basic.

Mantler, G. (2011), "Black, Brown, and Poor: Civil Rights and the Making of the Chicano Movement." In B. D. Behnken, ed., *The Struggle in Black and Brown: African American and Mexican American Relations during the Civil Rights Era*. Lincoln, NE: University of Nebraska Press. 179–210.

Mao Zedong (1927), "Report on the Investigation of the Peasant Movement in Hunan." Marxists Internet Archive. Available online: https://www.marxists.org/reference/archive/mao/selected-works/volume-1/mswv1_2.htm#s7

Marable, M. (1983a), "The Third Reconstruction: Black Nationalism and Race Relations after the Revolution." In S. R. Shalom, ed., *Socialist Visions*. Boston, MA: South End Press. 101–27.

Marable, M. (1983b), "Response and Self-Critique." In S. R. Shalom, ed., *Socialist Visions*. Boston, MA: South End Press. 138–43.

Marable, M. (1993), "Beyond Racial Identity Politics: Towards a Liberation Theory for Multicultural Democracy." *Race and Class*, 35 (1): 113–30.

Marable, M. (2015), *How Capitalism Underdeveloped Black America: Problems in Race, Political Economy, and Society*, reprint ed. Chicago: Haymarket.

Marable, M., and L. Mullings (1994), "The Divided Mind of Black America: Race, Ideology and Politics in the Post Civil Rights Era." *Race and Class*, 36 (1): 61–72.

Marais, H. (2001), *South Africa: Limits to Change: The Political Economy of Transition*. New York: Zed Books.

Marais, H. (2011), *South Africa Pushed to the Limit: The Political Economy of Change*. London: Zed Books.

Marcuse, H. (1972), *Counterrevolution and Revolt*. Boston, MA: Beacon Press.

Marsh, J. (2011), *Class Dismissed: Why We Cannot Teach or Learn Our Way Out of Inequality*. New York: Monthly Review.

Martin, D. (2011), "Warren Buffett and Corporate School Reformers to Gentrify/Charterize Indianapolis and Other Cities." *Shadowproof*. September 19. Available online: https://shadowproof.com/2011/09/19/warren-buffett-and-corporate-school-reformers-to-gentrify-charterize-indianapolis-and-other-cities

Martin, T. (1976), *Race First: The Ideological and Organizational Struggles of Marcus Garvey and the Universal Negro Improvement Association*. Westport, CT: Greenwood Press.

Marx, K. ([1867] 1976), *Capital*, vol. 1. B. Fowkes, trans. London: Penguin Books.

Marx, K. ([1885] 1978), *Capital*, vol. 2. D. Fernbach, trans. London: Penguin Books.

Marx, K. (1989), *The Civil War in France*, 2nd ed. New York: International Publishers.

Marx, K. (1998), *The German Ideology*. Amherst, NY: Prometheus Books.

Marx, K. ([1847] 1999), "The Poverty of Philosophy." Marxists Internet Archive. Available online: https://www.marxists.org/archive/marx/works/1847/poverty-philosophy/

Marx, K. ([1869] 1999), "Letter to Frederick Engels." Marxists Internet Archive. December 11. Available online: https://www.marxists.org/archive/marx/works/1869/letters/69_12_10-abs.htm

Marx, K., and F. Engels (2008), *The Communist Manifesto*. London: Pluto.
Massey, D. (2011), "Ideology and Economics in the Present Moment." *Soundings*, 48 (11): 29–39.
Massey, D. S., and N. A. Denton (1993), *American Apartheid: Segregation and the Making of the Underclass*. Cambridge, MA: Harvard University Press.
Mathis, W. J., and T. M. Trujillo (2016), *Learning from the Federal Market-Based Reforms*. Charlotte, NC: Information Age.
Matias, C. E. (2015), "Why Do You Make Me Hate Myself?: Re-Teaching Whiteness, Abuse, and Love in Urban Teacher Education." *Teaching Education*, 3: 194–211.
Matsuda, M. (1995), "Looking to the Bottom: Critical Legal studies and Reparations." In K. W. Crenshaw, N. Gotanda, G. Peller, and K. Thomas, eds., *Critical Race Theory: The Key Writings that Formed the Movement*. New York: New Press. 63–79.
Matsuda, M. J., J. C. R. Lawrence III, R. Delgado, and K. W. Crenshaw (1993), *Words That Wound: Critical Race Theory, Assaultive Speech, and the First Amendment*. Boulder, CO: Westview Press.
May, S., and C. S. Sleeter (2010), "Introduction. Critical Multiculturalism: Theory and Praxis." In S. May and C. S. Sleeter, eds., *Critical Multiculturalism: Theory and Praxis*. New York: Routledge. 1–18.
Mayhew, H. (1864), *German Life and Manners as Seen in Saxony at the Present Day: With an Account of Village life—Town Life—Fashionable Life—Married Life—School and University Life, &c., of Germany at the Present*. London: W. H. Allen.
Mayhew, H. ([1861] 2008), *London Labour and the London Poor*. Hertfordshire: Wordsworth Editions.
Mayorga, E., U. Aggarwal, and B. Picower (2020), "Introduction to the Second Edition." In E. Mayorga, U. Aggarwal, and B. Picower, eds., *What's Race Got to Do with It? How Current School Reform Policy Maintains Racial and Economic Inequality*, 2nd ed. New York: Peter Lang. 1–12.
Mbembe, A. (2013), "Necropolitics." *Public Culture*, 15 (1): 11–40.
McClintock, A. (1995), *Imperial Leather: Race, Gender, and Sexuality in the Colonial Contest*. New York: Routledge.
McGrath, E. (1983), "Education: To Stem the Tide of Mediocrity." *Time*. May 9.
McHenry, I. (2008), "Why the Obamas Chose Sidwell: The Anti-Elitist View." *The Provident Friend*. December. Available online: http://providencefriends.org/Resources/Newsletter/2008/PFM_2008_12_Newsletter.pdf
McIntosh, P. (1997), "White Privilege and Male Privilege: A Personal Account of Coming to See Correspondences through Work in Women's Studies." In R. Delgado and J. Stefancic, eds., *Critical White Studies: Looking behind the Mirror*. Philadelphia, PA: Temple University Press. 291–9.
McKay, C. L. (2010), "Community Education and Critical Race Praxis: The Power of Voice." *Educational Foundations*, 24 (1–2): 25–38.
McLaren, P., and N. Jaramillo (2003), "Critical Pedagogy, Latino/a Education, and the Politics of Class Struggle." *Cultural Studies/Critical Methodologies*, 6 (1): 73–93.
McLaren, P., Z. Leonardo, and R. L. Allen (2000), "Epistemologies of Whiteness: Transforming and Transgressing Pedagogical Knowledge." In R. Mahalingam and C. McCarthy, eds., *Multicultural Curriculum: New Directions for Social Theory, Practice, and Policy*. New York: Routledge. 108–23.
McNally, D. (2006), *Another World Is Possible: Globalization and Anti-Capitalism*, 2nd ed. Winnipeg: Arbeiter Ring Publishing.

Meer, N. (2013), "Semantics, Scales and Solidarities in the Study of Anti-Semitism and Islamophobia." *Ethnic and Racial Studies*, 36 (3): 500–15.
Meer, N. (2014), "Revisiting the Crossroads: Returning to The Empire Strikes Back." *Ethnic and Racial Studies*, 37 (10): 1793–801.
Meghji, A. (2020), "Towards a Theoretical Synergy: Critical Race Theory and Decolonial Thought in Trumpamerica and Brexit Britain." *Current Sociology*. November 16. 1–18.
Meghji, A. (2021), "Just what is Critical Race Theory, and what is it doing in British Sociology? From 'Britcrit' to the Racialized Social System Approach." *British Journal of Sociology*, 72 (2): 347–59.
Meghji, A. (2022), *The Racialized Social System: Critical Race Theory as Social Theory*. Cambridge: Polity.
Mehta, J. (2015), *The Allure of Order: High Hopes, Dashed Expectations, and the Troubled Quest to Remake American Schooling*. Oxford: Oxford University Press.
Meredith, M. (1998), *Nelson Mandela: A Biography*. New York: St. Martin's Press.
Meredith, M. (2010), *Mandela: A Biography*. New York: PublicAffairs.
Mertler, C. (2011), "'Teachers' Perceptions of the Influence of *No Child Left Behind* on Classroom Practices." *Current Issues in Education*, 13 (3). Available online: https://cie.asu.edu/ojs/index.php/cieatasu/article/download/392/105
Mészáros, I. (1995), *Beyond Capital*. New York: Monthly Review Press.
Metcalf, S. (2002), "The New Education Law Is a Victory for Bush—and for His Corporate Allies." *Nation*. January 10.
Metzl, J. M. (2020), *Dying of Whiteness: How the Politics of Racial Resentment Is Killing America's Heartland*. New York: Basic Books.
Meyer, G. D., and A. Benavot, eds. (2013), *PISA, Power, and Policy: The Emergence of Global Education Governance*. Oxford: Symposium.
Meyerson, G. (2000), "Rethinking Black Marxism: Reflections on Cedric Robinson and Others." *Cultural Logic*, 6: 1–48.
Mignolo, W. D. (2007), "Delinking." *Cultural Studies*, 21 (2–3): 449–514.
Mignolo, W. D. (2018), "The Decolonial Option." In W. D. Mignolo and C. E. Walsh, eds., *On Decoloniality: Concepts, Analytics, Praxis*. Durham, NC: Duke University Press. 105–226.
Mignolo, W. D. (2020), "The Politics of Decolonial Investigation." *Talk for Theory from the Margins*. November 18. Available online: http://theoryfromthemargins.com/archives-wdm.html
Mignolo, W. D., and C. Walsh (2018), *On Decoloniality: Concepts, Analytics, Praxis*. Durham, NC: Duke University Press.
Miles, R. (1982), *Racism and Migrant Labor*. New York: Routledge and Kegan Paul.
Miles, R. (1989), *Racism*. London: Routledge.
Miles, R. (1993), *Racism after Race Relations*. London: Routledge.
Miles, R., and M. Brown (2003), *Racism*, 2nd ed. New York: Routledge.
Miliband, R. (1989), *Divided Societies: Class Struggle in Contemporary Capitalism*. New York: Oxford University Press.
Milios. J. (2000), "Social Classes in Classical and Marxist Political Economy." *American Journal of Economics and Sociology*, 59 (2): 283–302.
Miller, S., L. R. Wherry, and B. Mazumder (2021), "Estimated Mortality Increases during the COVID-19 Pandemic by Socioeconomic Status, Race, and Ethnicity." *Health Affairs*, 40 (8): 1252–60.
Mills, C. W. (1997), *The Racial Contract*. New York: Cornell University Press.
Mills, C. W. (1999), "European Spectres." *Journal of Ethics*, 3 (2): 133–55.
Mills, C. W. (2000), *The Sociological Imagination*. Oxford: Oxford University Press.

Mills, C. W. (2015), "Global White Ignorance." In M. Gross and L. McGoey, eds., *Routledge International Handbook of Ignorance Studies*. New York: Routledge. 217–27.
Mojab, S., ed. (2015), *Marxism and Feminism*. London: Zed Books.
Mojab, S., and S. Carpenter (2019), "Marxism, Feminism, and 'Intersectionality'." *Journal of Labor and Society*, 22 (2): 275–82.
Molteno, F. (1990), "The Historical Foundations of the Schooling of Black South Africans." In P. Kallaway, ed., *Apartheid and Education: The Education of Black South Africans*. Johannesburg: Raven Press. 45–107.
Montagu, M. F. A. (1952), *Man's Most Dangerous Myth: The Fallacy of Race*. New York: Harper & Brothers.
Moreton, B. (2009), *To Serve God and Wal-Mart: The Making of Christian Free Enterprise*. Cambridge, MA: Harvard University Press.
Morgan, E. S. (1975), *American Slavery, American Freedom*. New York: W. W. Norton.
Morrin, K. J. (2018), "Tensions in Teaching Character: How the 'Entrepreneurial Character' Is Reproduced, 'Refused' and Negotiated in an English academy School." *Sociological Research Online*, 23 (2): 459–76.
Morrison, A. (2020), "Pressley and Warren Call for Racial Data in Coronavirus Testing." WBUR. March 30. Available online: https://www.wbur.org/news/2020/03/30/pressley-warren-race-data-coronavirus-testing
Moss, K. (2003), *The Color of Class: Poor Whites and the Paradox of Privilege*. Philadelphia, PA: University of Pennsylvania Press.
Motala, E., and S. Vally (2010), "'Race,' Class and Education in Post-Apartheid South Africa." In D. Kelsh, D. Hill, and S. Macrine, eds., *Class in Education: Knowledge, Pedagogy, Subjectivity*. London: Routledge. 87–107.
Murakami, K. (2021), "Would Cancelling Student Debt Promote Racial Equity?" *Inside Higher Education*. February 23.
Murakawa, N. (2014), *The First Civil Right: How Liberals Built Prison America*. New York: Oxford.
Murse, T. (2020), "Why Donald Trump's Companies Went Bankrupt." *ThoughtCo*. December 31. Available online: https://www.thoughtco.com/donald-trump-business-bankruptcies-4152019
Mzala (1985), "The Freedom Charter and Its Relevance Today." In *African National Congress, Selected Writings on the Freedom Charter, 1955–1985*. London: Sechaba Publications. 78–101.
Nace, T. (2003), *Gangs of America: The Rise of Corporate Power and the Disabling of Democracy*. San Francisco, CA: Berrett-Koehler.
National Commission on Asian American and Pacific Islander Research in Education (2008), "Asian Americans and Pacific Islanders; Facts, Not Fiction: Setting the Record Straight." CARE. Available online: http://care.gseis.ucla.edu/wp-content/uploads/2015/08/2008_CARE_Report.pdf
National Commission on Excellence in Education (1983), *A Nation at Risk: The Imperative for Educational Reform*. Washington: U.S. Department of Education. Available online: https://eric.ed.gov/?id=ED226006
National Council on Teacher Quality (2015), *2015 State Teacher Policy Yearbook: National Summary*. Washington: NCTQ. Available online: https://www.nctq.org/publications/2015-State-Teacher-Policy-Yearbook
National Nurses United (2020), "National Nurses Statement on George Floyd and National Policing Practices." May 28. Available online: https://www.nationalnursesunited.org/press/national-nurses-statement-george-floyd-and-national-policing-practices

NCES (National Center for Education Statistics) (2016), *Digest of Education Statistics 2015*, 51st ed. Available online: https://nces.ed.gov/pubs2016/2016014.pdf (accessed April 17, 2022).

NCES (National Center for Education Statistics) (2017), "Public Charter School Enrollment." March. Available online: https://nces.ed.gov/programs/coe/pdf/coe_cgb.pdf

National Governors Association (2015), *Expanding Student Success: A Primer on Competency-Based Education from Kindergarten through Higher Education*. Washington, DC: NGA. Available online: https://files.eric.ed.gov/fulltext/ED570497.pdf

National Union of Teachers (2016), *The Mismeasurement of Learning: How Tests Are Damaging Children and Primary Education*. London: NUT. Available online: https://reclaimingschools.files.wordpress.com/2016/11/mismeasurement.pdf

Nayak, A. (2006), "After Race: Ethnography, Race and Post-Race Theory." *Ethnic and Racial Studies*, 29 (3): 411–30.

Neilson, D. (2017), "Re-Situating Capital Vol. 1 beyond Althusser's Epistemological Break: Towards Second-Generation Neo-Marxism." *Continental Thought and Theory*, 1 (4): 231–53.

Ngin, C., and R. D. Torres (2001), "Racialized Metropolis: Theorizing Asian American and Latino Identities and Ethnicities in Southern California." In M. Lopez-Garza and D. R. Diaz, eds., *Asian and Latino Immigrants in a Restructuring Economy*. Stanford, CA: Stanford University Press. 368–90.

Nichols, J. (2011), "ALEC Exposed: Rigging Elections." *Nation*. July 12.

Nkrumah, K. (1971), *Neo-Colonialism: The Last Stage of Imperialism*. Bedford: Panaf.

Norval, A. J. (1994), "The 'Boerewors Curtain' and the 'Metropole': Twenty Years of Southern African Studies." *South African Historical Journal*, 31 (1): 198–204.

NYC Coalition for Educational Justice (2019), "Chronically Absent: The Exclusion of People of Color from NYC Elementary School Curricula." Available online: http://www.nyccej.org/wp-content/uploads/2019/02/reportCEJ-Chronically-Absent-FINAL.pdf

Nyerere, J. K. (1963), "A United States of Africa." *Journal of Modern African Studies*, 1 (1): 1–6.

Oakes, J. (1984), *Keeping Track: How Schools Structure Inequality*. New Haven, CT: Yale University Press.

Oakes, J. (1992), "Can Tracking Research Inform Practice? Technical, Normative, and Political Considerations." *Educational Researcher*, 21 (4): 12–21.

Oakes, J., and A. S. Wells (1998), "Detracking for High Student Achievement." *Educational Leadership*, 55 (6): 38–41.

OECD (2006), *Boosting Jobs and Incomes*. Paris: OECD. Available online: https://www.oecd.org/els/emp/boostingjobsandincomestheoecdjobsstrategy.htm

OECD (2010), "Improving Schools: Strategies for Action in Mexico." Paris: OECD. Available online: https://www.oecd-ilibrary.org/education/improving-schools_9789264087040-en

Ogunrotifa, A. B. (2022), "Between Racialization and White Supremacy: Another Marxist Response to Sean Walton." *Open Journal of Social Sciences*, 10 (2): 240–57.

Olson, J. (2004), *The Abolition of White Democracy*. Minneapolis, MN: University of Minnesota Press.

Omi, M., and H. Winant (1994), *Racial Formation in the United States: From the 1960s to the 1990s*, 2nd ed. New York: Routledge.

Omi, M., and H. Winant (2015), *Racial Formation in the United States*, 3rd ed. New York: Routledge.
Orfield, G., J. Ee, E. Frankenberg, and G. Siegel-Hawley (2016), *Brown at 62: School Segregation by Race, Poverty and State*. May 16. Los Angeles, CA: Civil Rights Project.
Oxfam International (2021), "5 Shocking Facts about Extreme Global Inequality and How to Even it Up." Available online: https://www.oxfam.org/en/5-shocking-facts-about-extreme-global-inequality-and-how-even-it
Oxfam International (2017), "Just 8 Men Own Same Wealth as Half the World." Available online: https://www.oxfam.org/en/press-releases/just-8-men-own-same-wealth-half-world
Panitch, L., and G. Albo, eds. (2015), *The Politics of the Right: Socialist Register 2016*. New York: Monthly Review Press.
Panitch, L., and S. Gindin (2012), *The Making of Global Capitalism: The Political Economy of American Empire*. New York: Verso.
Parenti, M. (1995), *Against Empire*. San Francisco, CA: City Lights Books.
Parker, A., J. Dawsey, M. Viser, and M. Scherer (2020), "How Trump's Erratic Behavior and Failure on Coronavirus Doomed His Reelection." *Washington Post*. November 7.
Parsons, C. (2016), "Ethnicity, Gender, Deprivation and Low Educational Attainment in England: Political Arithmetic, Ideological Stances and the Deficient Society." *Education, Citizenship and Social Justice*, 11 (2): 160–83. DOI:10.1177/1746197916648282.
Parsons, C., and T. Thompson (2017), "Ethnicity, Disadvantage and Other Variables in the Analysis of Birmingham Longitudinal School Attainment Datasets." *Educational Review*, 69 (5): 577–99.
Patel, N., and H. Keval (2018), "Fifty Ways to Leave your Racism." *The Journal of Critical Psychology, Counselling and Psychotherapy*, 18 (2): 61–79.
Patnaik, U., and P. Patnaik (2021), *Capital and Imperialism: Theory, History, and the Present*. New York: New York University Press.
Peet, R. (2007), *Geography of Power: Making Global Economic Policy*. New York: Zed Books.
Peet, R. (2009), *Unholy Trinity: The IMF, World Bank and WTO*, 2nd ed. New York: Zed Books.
Pérez, L. E. (2010), "Enrique Dussel's Etica de la Liberation, US Women of Color Decolonizing Practices, and Coalitionary Politics amidst Difference." *Qui Parle: Critical Humanities and Social Sciences*, 18 (2): 121–46.
Perlstein, L. (2007), *Tested: One American School Struggles to Make the Grade*. New York: Holt.
Perry, B. L., B. Aronson, and B. A. Pescosolido (2021), "Pandemic Precarity: COVID-19 is Exposing and Exacerbating Inequalities in the American Heartland." *Proceedings of the National Academy of Sciences of the United States of America*, 118 (8). Available online: https://www.pnas.org/doi/full/10.1073/pnas.2020685118
Peters, J. W., J. Becker, and J. H. Davis (2017), "Trump Rescinds Rules on Bathrooms for Transgender Students." *New York Times*. February 22.
Pew Research Center (2016), *On Views of Race and Inequality, Blacks and Whites Are World Apart*. Washington: Pew. Available online: http://www.pewsocialtrends.org/2016/06/27/on-views-of-race-and-inequality-blacks-and-whites-are-worlds-apart
Phillips-Fein, K. (2009), *Invisible Hands: The Making of the Conservative Movement from the New Deal to Reagan*. New York: Norton.
Phoenix, A. (1991), *Young Mothers?* Cambridge: Polity Press.

Picca, L. H., and J. Feagin (2007), *Two-Faced Racism: Whites in the Backstage and Frontstage*. New York: Routledge.

Picower, B. (2012), "Teacher Activism: Enacting a Vision for Social Justice." *Equity and Excellence in Education*, 45 (4): 561–74.

Picower, B., and E. Mayorga, eds. (2015a), *What's Race Got to Do with It: How Current School Reform Policy Maintains Racial and Economic Inequality*. New York: Peter Lang.

Picower, B., and E. Mayorga (2015b), "Introduction." In B. Picower and E. Mayorga, eds., *What's Race Got to Do with It: How Current School Reform Policy Maintains Racial and Economic Inequality*. New York: Peter Lang. 1–20.

Piketty, T. (2014), *Capital in the Twenty-First Century*. A. Goldhammer, trans. Cambridge, MA: Harvard University Press.

Planas, R. (2016), "California Passes Game-Changing Ethnic Studies Bill." *Huffington Post*. September 15.

Plaut, V. C., K. M. Thomas, K. Hurd, and C. A. Romano (2018), "Do Color Blindness and Multiculturalism Remedy or Foster Discrimination and Racism?" *Association for Psychological Science (APS)*, 27 (3): 200–6.

Pour-Khorshid, F. (2018), "Cultivating Sacred Spaces: A Racial Affinity Group Approach to Support Critical Educators of Color." *Teaching Education*, 29 (4): 318–29.

Powell, L. F. (1971), "Attack on American Free Enterprise System." August 23. Powell Archives, Washington and Lee University. Available online: https://lawdigitalcommons.bc.edu/cgi/viewcontent.cgi?article=1078&context=darter_materials

Prashad, V. (2007), *The Darker Nations*. New York: The New Press.

Pratt, M. (1992), *Imperial Eyes: Travel Writing and Transculturation*. New York: Routledge.

Prempeh, E. O. K. (2008), "The Anticapitalism Movement and African Resistance to Neoliberal Globalization." In J. Mensah, ed., *Neoliberalism and Globalization in Africa: Contestations from the Embattled Continent*. New York: Palgrave Macmillan. 55–69.

Preston, J. (2010), "Concrete and Abstract Racial Domination." *Power and Education*, 2 (2): 115–25. https://doi.org/10.2304/power.2010.2.2.115

Pulido, L. (2017), "Geographies of Race and Ethnicity II: Environmental Racism, Racial Capitalism and State-Sanctioned Violence." *Progress in Human Geography*, 41 (4): 524–33.

Quijano, A. (2000a), "Colonialidad del Poder, Eurocentrismo y América Latina." In E. Lander, ed., *Colonialidad del Saber, Eurocentrismo y Ciencias Sociales*. Buenos Aires: CLACSO-UNESCO. 201–46.

Quijano, A. (2000b), "¡Qué tal Raza! Revista del CESLA." *International Latin American Studies Review*, 1: 192–200.

Quijano, A. (2000c), "Coloniality of Power and Eurocentrism in Latin America." *International Sociology*, 15 (2): 215–32.

Quijano, A. (2007), "Coloniality and Modernity/Rationality." *Cultural Studies*, 21 (2–3): 168–78.

Quinn, B. (2011), "David Starkey Claims 'the Whites have Become Black'." *Guardian*. August 13. Available online https://www.theguardian.com/uk/2011/aug/13/david-starkey-claims-whites-black

Rafalow, M. H. (2020), *Digital Divisions: How Schools Create Inequality in the Tech Era*. Chicago: University of Chicago Press.

Rampell, C. (2011), "Many with New College Degrees Find the Job Market Humbling." *New York Times*. May 18.

Ransby, B. (2003), *Ella Baker and the Black Freedom Movement: A Radical Democratic Vision*. Chapel Hill, NC: University of North Carolina Press.

Ratcliff, A. J. (2013), "The Radical Evolution of Du Boisian Pan-Africanism." *Journal of Pan African Studies*, 5 (9): 151–70.
Ravitch, D. (1990), "Diversity and Democracy: Multicultural Education in America." *American Educator*, 14 (1): 16–20, 46–68.
Ravitch, D. (2010), *The Death and Life of the Great American School System: How Testing and Choice Are Undermining Education*. New York: Basic Books.
Ravitch, D. (2013), *Reign of Error: The Hoax of the Privatization Movement and the Danger to America's Public Schools*. New York: Knopf.
Ravitch, D. (2016), "The Attack on Public Education in California." *Diane Ravitch's Blog*. June 8. Available online: https://dianeravitch.net/2016/06/08/the-attack-on-public-education-in-california
Reay, D. (2013), "Social Mobility, a Panacea for Austere Times: Tales of Emperors, Frogs, and Tadpoles." *British Journal of Sociology of Education*, 34 (5–6): 660–77.
Reay, D., G. Crozier, and D. James (2011), *White Middle Class Identities and Urban Schooling*. Basingstoke: Palgrave Macmillan.
Reay, D., S. Hollingworth, K. Williams, G. Crozier, F. Jamieson, D. James, and P. Beedell (2007), "'A Darker Shade of Pale?' Whiteness, the Middle Classes and Multi-Ethnic Inner City Schooling." *Sociology*, 41 (6): 1041–60.
Reed, A., Jr. (2016), "How Racial Disparity Does Not Help Make Sense of Patterns of Police Violence." *Nonsite.org*. September 16. Available online: https://nonsite.org/editorial/how-racial-disparity-does-not-help-make-sense-of-patterns-of-police-violence
Reed, A., Jr. (2020), "Disparity Ideology, Coronavirus, and the Danger of the Return of Racial Medicine." *Common Dreams*. April 4.
Reed, A., Jr., and M. Chowkwanyun (2012), "Race, Class, Crisis: The Discourse of Racial Disparity and Its Analytical Discontents." *Socialist Register*, 48 (September 24): 149–75.
Reed, T. F. (2020), *Toward Freedom: The Case against Race Reductionism*. London: Verso.
Reimers, F., and L. Tiburcio (1993), *Education, Adjustment and Reconstruction: Options for Change*. Paris: UNESCO. Available online: https://unesdoc.unesco.org/ark:/48223/pf0000184253
Reuss, A. (2013), "Capitalist Crisis and Capitalist Reaction: The Profit Squeeze, the Business Roundtable, and the Capitalist Class Mobilization of the 1970s." PhD diss. University of Massachusetts Amherst.
Reynolds, T. (2005), *Caribbean Mothers: Identity and Experience in the U.K*. London: Tufnell Press.
Rhoads, E. J. M. (2002), "'White Labor' vs. 'Coolie Labor': The 'Chinese Question' in Pennsylvania in the 1870s." *Journal of American Ethnic History*, 21 (2): 3–32. http://www.jstor.org/stable/27502811
Rhodes, J. H. (2012), *An Education in Politics: The Origins and Evolution of No Child Left Behind*. Ithaca, NY: Cornell University Press.
Richardson, R. (1992), "Race Policies and Programmes under Attack: Two Case Studies for the 1990s." In D. Gill, B. Mayor, and M. Blair, eds., *Racism and Education: Structures and Strategies*. London: Sage Publications. 134–50.
Riddell, J. (2011), *Toward the United Front: Proceedings of the Fourth Congress of the Communist International, 1922*. Leiden: Brill Publishers.
Riep, C., and M. Machacek (2016), *Schooling the Poor Profitably: The Innovations and Deprivations of Bridge International Academies in Uganda*. September. Brussels: Education International. Available online: https://www.ei-ie.org/en/item/25704

:schooling-the-poor-profitably-the-innovations-and-deprivations-of-bridge
-international-academies-in-uganda

Rios-Rojas, A. (2020), "Pedagogies of the Broken-Hearted: Notes on a Pedagogy of Breakage, Women of Color Feminist Decolonial Movidas, and Armed Love in the Classroom/Academy." *Frontiers: A Journal of Women Studies*, 41 (1): 161–78.

Rizga, K. (2017), "Betsy DeVos Wants to Use America's Schools to Build 'God's Kingdom.'" *Mother Jones*. January 17.

Robinson, C. J. (2019), *On Racial Capitalism, Black Internationalism, and Cultures of Resistance*. London: Pluto Press.

Robinson, C. J. (2000), *Black Marxism: The Making of the Black Radical Tradition*. Durham, NC: University of North Carolina Press.

Robinson, W. I. (2014), *Global Capitalism and the Crisis of Humanity*. New York: Cambridge University Press.

Rodney, W. (1983), *How Europe Underdeveloped Africa*. Harare: Zimbabwe Publishing House.

Roediger, D. (2006), "The Retreat from Race and Class." *Analytical Monthly Review*. Special Issue on Class, Exploitation, Consciousness, and Struggle: 38–48.

Roediger, D. (2007), *The Wages of Whiteness: Race and the Making of the American Working Class*, rev. ed. New York: Verso.

Roediger, D. (2017), *Class, Race, and Marxism*. New York: Verso.

Rollock, N. (2012), "The Invisibility of Race: Intersectional Reflections on the Liminal Space of Alterity." *Race Ethnicity and Education*, 15 (1). Available online: https://www.tandfonline.com/doi/abs/10.1080/13613324.2012.638864

Rollock, N. (2014), "Race, Class and the 'Harmony of Dispositions.'" *Sociology*, 48 (3): 445–51.

Roman, L. G. (2015), "Making and Moving Publics: Stuart Hall's Projects, Maximal Selves and Education." *Discourse: Studies in the Cultural Politics of Education*, 36 (2): 200–26.

Runciman, C. (2017), "South African Protesters Echo a Global Cry: Democracy Isn't Making People's Lives Better." *The Conversation*. May 18. https://theconversation.com/south-african-protesters-echo-a-global-cry-democracy-isnt-making-peoples-lives-better-77639

Rust, E. (1999), *No Turning Back: A Progress Report on the Business Roundtable Education Initiative*. Washington: Business Roundtable.

Rustin, B. (1966), "'Black Power' and Coalition Politics." *Commentary*. September 1. 35–40.

Ryan, H. (2016), *Educational Justice: Teaching and Organizing against the Corporate Juggernaut*. New York: Monthly Review.

Saad-Filho, A., and A. Boito (2015), "Brazil: The Failure of the PT and the Rise of the 'New Right.'" In L. Panitch and G. Albo, eds., *The Politics of the Right: Socialist Register 2016*. London: Merlin Press. 213–30.

Sahlberg, P. (2012), "How GERM Is Infecting Schools around the World." *Washington Post*. June 29.

Sahlberg, P. (2016), "The Global Educational Reform Movement and Its Impact on Schooling." In K. Mundy, A. Green, B. Lingard, and A. Verger, eds., *The Handbook of Global Education Policy*. New York: Wiley-Blackwell. 128–44.

Said, E. (1978), *Orientalism*. New York: Pantheon Books.

Sale, K. (1973), *SDS: The Rise and Development of the Students for a Democratic Society*. New York: Vintage.

Saltman, K. J. (2009), "The Rise of Venture Philanthropy and the Ongoing Neoliberal Assault on Public Education: The Case of the Eli and Edythe Broad Foundation." *Workplace*, 16: 53–72.

Saltman, K. J., and A. J. Means, eds. (2019), *The Wiley Handbook of Global Educational Reform*. Hoboken, NJ: Wiley-Blackwell.
Sandel, M. J. (2020), *The Tyranny of Merit*. London: Bloomsbury.
San Juan, E., Jr. (1992), *Racial Formations/Critical Transformations*. Atlantic Heights, NJ: Humanities Press International.
Sankara, T. (1985), "The 'Political Orientation' of Burkina Faso." *Review of African Political Economy*, 12 (32): 48–55.
Santelices, M. V., and M. Wilson (2010), "Unfair Treatment? The Case of Freedle, the SAT, and the Standardization Approach to Differential Item Functioning." *Harvard Educational Review*, 80 (1): 106–33.
Saul, J. S. (1986), "South Africa: The Question of Strategy." *New Left Review*, 160: 3–22.
Saul, J. S. (2002), "Identifying Class, Classifying Difference." In L. Panitch and C. Leys, eds., *Fighting Identities: Race, Religion and Ethno-Nationalism: Socialist Register 2003*. London: Merlin Press. 347–74.
Saul, J. S. (2006), *Development After Globalisation: Theory and Practice for the Embattled South in a New Imperial Age*. London: Zed Books.
Saul, J. S., and P. Bond (2014), *South Africa—The Present as History: From Mrs. Ples to Mandela and Marikana*. Rochester, NY: James Currey.
Saul, S., and K. Taylor (2017), "Betsy DeVos Reverses Obama-era Policy on Campus Sexual Assault Investigations." *New York Times*. September 22.
Savage, M., F. Devine, N. Cunningham, M. Taylor, Y. Li, J. Hjelbrekke, B. Le Roux, S. Friedman, and A. Miles (2013), "A New Model of Social Class? Findings from the BBC's Great British Class Survey Experiment." *Sociology*, 47 (2): 219–50.
Sayer, A. (2010), "Reductionism in Social Science." In R. E. Lee, ed., *Questioning Nineteenth-Century Assumptions about Knowledge*, vol. II. Albany, NY: SUNY Press. 5–39.
Scatamburlo-D'Annibale, V., and P. McLaren (2005), "Class Dismissed? Historical Materialism and the Politics of 'Difference'." In Z. Leonardo, ed. *Critical Pedagogy and Race*. Malden, MA: Blackwell. 141–57.
Schlesinger, A. M., Jr. (1992), *The Disuniting of America*. New York: Norton.
Schneider, M. K. (2014), *A Chronicle of Echoes: Who's Who in the Implosion of American Public Education*. Charlotte, NC: Information Age.
SchoolDash (n.d.), Magna Academy. Available online: https://www.schooldash.com/school/139711 (accessed April 17, 2022).
Schram, S. F., J. Soss, and R. C. Fording (2003), *Race and the Politics of Welfare Reform*. Ann Arbor, MI: University of Michigan Press.
Seccombe, A. (2019), "Ready to Do Battle." *Business Day*. October 4.
Seidman, G. W. (1993), "Facing the New International Context of Development." In J. Brecher, J. B. Childs, and J. Cutler, eds., *Global Visions: Beyond the New World Order*. Boston, MA: South End Press. 175–89.
Seidman, G. W. (1994), *Manufacturing Militance: Workers' Movements in Brazil and South Africa, 1970–1985*. Berkeley, CA: University of California Press.
Seidman, G. W. (2007), *Beyond the Boycott: Labor Rights, Human Rights, and Transnational Activism*. New York: Russell Sage Foundation.
Serwer, A. (2020), "Birtherism of a Nation." *The Atlantic*. May 13. Available online: https://www.theatlantic.com/ideas/archive/2020/05/birtherism-and-trump/610978/
Shalom, S. R., ed. (1983), *Socialist Visions*. Boston, MA: South End Press.
Shapiro, T. (2004), *The Hidden Cost of Being African American: How Wealth Perpetuates Inequality*. Oxford: Oxford University Press.

Sharkey, J. (2020), "Educators Too Must Work to Upend the Roots of Racial Violence." Chicago Teachers Union. June 1. Available online: https://www.ctulocal1.org/posts/educators-too-must-work-to-upend-the-roots-of-racial-violence/

Shawki, A. (2006), *Black Liberation and Socialism*. Chicago: Haymarket.

Singer J. N., A. J. Weems, and J. R. Garner (2017), "Fraternal Twins: Critical Race Theory and Systemic Racism Theory as Analytic and Activist Tools for College Sport Reform." In B. Hawkins, A. Carter-Francique, and J. Cooper, eds., *Critical Race Theory: Black Athletic Sporting Experiences in the United States*. New York: Palgrave Macmillan. 11–55.

Singer, S. (2015), "Standardized Tests Every Day: The Competency Based Education Scam." *Gadfly on the Wall*. November 30. Available online: https://gadflyonthewallblog.com/2015/11/30/standardized-tests-every-day-the-competency-based-education-scam/

Sirota, D. (2013), "Getting Rich Off of Schoolchildren." *Salon*. March 11.

Sivanandan, A. (1982), *A Different Hunger: Writings on Black Resistance*. London: Pluto.

Sivanandan, A. (1985), "RAT and the Degradation of Black Struggle." *Race and Class*, 26 (1): 1–33.

Skeggs, B. (1997), *Formations of Class and Gender: Becoming Respectable*. London: Sage.

Skeggs, B. (2004), *Class, Self, Culture*. London: Routledge.

Slaughter, J. (2015), "Mexican Teachers Resist Their Own Brand of 'Education Reform.'" *Labor Notes*. February 17.

Sleeter, C. E. (1995), "Teaching Whites about Racism." In R. J. Martin, ed., *Practicing What We Teach: Confronting Diversity in Teacher Education*. Albany, NY: State University of New York Press. 117–30.

Sleeter, C. E. (2012), "Confronting the Marginalization of Culturally Responsive Pedagogy." *Urban Education*, 47 (3): 562–84.

Sleeter, C. E., and J. Owuor (2011), "Research on the Impact of Teacher Preparation to Teach Diverse Students: The Research We Have and the Research We Need." *Action in Teacher Education*, 33 (5–6): 524–36.

Smith, C. (2021), "Operation Varsity Blues: The College Admissions Scandal." Netflix. March 17.

Smith, D. (2012), "Lonmin Emails Paint ANC Elder as a Born-Again Robber Baron." *Guardian*. October 24.

Smith, E., and R. Reeves (2020), "SAT Math Score Mirror and Maintain Racial Inequity." Brookings Institution. Available online: https://www.brookings.edu/blog/up-front/2020/12/01/sat-math-scores-mirror-and-maintain-racial-inequity/

Smith, J. J., and D. Stovall (2008), "'Coming Home' to New Homes and New Schools: Critical Race Theory and the New Politics of Containment." *Journal of Education Policy*, 23 (2): 135–52.

Smith, S., and K. Ellis (2017), "Shackled Legacy: History Shows Slavery Helped Build Many U.S. Colleges and Universities." *American Public Media*. September 4. Available online: https://www.apmreports.org/episode/2017/09/04/shackled-legacy

Solomon, A., and K. Rankin (2019), *How We Fight White Supremacy*. New York: Bold Type Books.

Solomos, J., and L. Back (1996), *Racism and Society*. Basingstoke: Macmillan.

Solórzano, D. G., and A. Ornelas (2004), "A Critical Race Analysis of Latina/o and African American Advanced Placement Enrolment in Public High Schools." *High School Journal*, 87 (3): 15–26.

Solórzano, D. G., and T. J. Yosso (2001), "Critical Race and LatCrit Theory and Method: Counter-Storytelling." *International Journal of Qualitative Studies in Education*, 14 (4): 471–95.

South African Congress Alliance (1955), *Freedom Charter*. Johannesburg: African National Congress. Available online: http://www.anc.org.za/content/freedom-charter (accessed April 2022).

Southall, R., and E. Webster (2010), "Unions and Parties in South Africa: COSATU and the ANC in the Wake of Polokwane." In B. Beckman, S. Buhlungu, and L. M. Sachikonye, eds., *Trade Unions and Party Politics: Labour Movements in Africa*. Cape Town: HSRC Press. 131–66.

Spreen, C. A., and S. Vally (2006), "Education Rights, Education Policy and Inequality in South Africa." *International Journal of Educational Development*, 26, no. 4 (July): 352–62.

Spring, J. (2016), *Deculturalization and the Struggle for Equality: A Brief History of the Education of Dominated Cultures in the United States*. New York: Routledge.

Stalin, J. ([1924] 2000), "The October Revolution and the Tactics of the Russian Communists." Marxists Internet Archive. Available online: https://www.marxists.org/reference/archive/stalin/works/1924/12.htm

Stanfield, J. B. (2012), *The Fortune at the Bottom of the Pyramid in Education*. March. Newcastle upon Tyne, England: E.G. West Centre, Newcastle University. Available online: https://egwestcentre.files.wordpress.com/2013/05/fortune-at-the-bottom-of-the-pyramid-in-education.pdf

Stedman-Jones, G. (1971), *Outcast London: A Study in the Relationship between Classes in Victorian Society*. Oxford: Clarendon Press.

Stoler, A. (1995), *Race and the Education of Desire: Foucault's History of Sexuality and the Colonial Order of Things*. Durham, NC: Duke University Press.

Stoler, A. (2002), *Carnal Knowledge and Imperial Power: Race and the Intimate in Colonial Rule*. Berkeley, CA: University of California Press.

Stovall, D. (2006), "Forging Community in Race and Class: Critical Race Theory and the Quest for Social Justice in Education." *Race Ethnicity and Education*, 9 (3): 243–59.

Stovall, D. (2015), "Mayoral Control: Reform, Whiteness, and Critical Race Analysis of Neoliberal Educational Policy." In B. Picower and E. Mayorga, eds., *What's Race Got to Do with It? How Current School Reform Policy Maintains Racial and Economic Inequality*. New York: Peter Lang. 45–58.

Stovall, D., M. Lynn, L. Danley, and D. Martin (2009), "Introduction: Critical Race Praxis in Education." *Race, Ethnicity and Education*, 12 (2): 131–2.

Strauss, V. (2010), "The Irony Behind Obama's Sidwell/D.C. Schools Remarks." *Washington Post*. September 28.

Strauss, V. (2016), "New Book: Obama's Education Department and Gates Foundation Were Closer Than You Thought." *Washington Post*. August 25.

Sturgis, C. (2015), *Implementing Competency Education in K–12 systems: Insights from Local Leaders*. Vienna, VA: INACOL. Available online: https://aurora-institute.org/cw_post/introducing-implementing-competency-education-in-k-12-systems-insights-from-local-leaders/

Sullivan, P. (2020), "Private Schools Hold New Attractions for Rich Parents." *New York Times*. October 9.

Sullivan, S. (2014), *Good White People: The Problem with Middle-Class White Anti-Racism*. Albany, NY: SUNY Press.

Symcox, L. (2002), *Whose History? The Struggle for National Standards in American Classrooms*. New York: Teachers College Press.

Tan, J. P., E. Jimenez, and G. Psacharopoulos (1986), *Financing Education in Developing Countries: An Exploration of Policy Options*. Washington: World Bank.

Task Force on Education for Economic Growth (1983), *Action for Excellence: A Comprehensive Plan to Improve Our Nation's Schools*. June. Denver: Education Commission of the States.

Tate, G. (2011), "Top 10 Reasons Why So Few Black Folk Appear Down to Occupy Wall Street." *Village Voice*. October 19.

Tate, W. F. (1997), "Critical Race Theory and Education: History, Theory, and Implications." *Review of Research in Education*, 22: 195–247.

Taylor, A., V. Pacini-Ketchabaw, S. de Finney, and M. Blaise (2016), "Inheriting the Ecological Legacies of Settler Colonialism." *Environmental Humanities*, 7 (1): 129–32.

Taylor, E. (2009), "The Foundations of Critical Race Theory in Education: An Introduction." In E. Taylor, D. Gillborn, and G. Ladson-Billings, eds., *Foundations of Critical Race Theory in Education*. New York: Routledge. 1–16.

Taylor, E., D. Gillborn, and G. Ladson-Billings, eds. (2009), *Foundations of Critical Race Theory in Education*. New York: Routledge.

Taylor, G., L. Shepard, F. Kinner, and J. Rosenthal (2003), *A Survey of Teachers' Perspectives on High-Stakes Testing in Colorado: What Gets Taught, What Gets Lost*. Boulder: CRESST/CREDE/University of Colorado. Available online: http://cresst.org/publications/cresst-publication-2960

Taylor, K. (2016), *From #Blacklivesmatter to Black Liberation*. Chicago: Haymarket.

Teitelbaum, M. S. (2014), "Is the U.S. Losing the Tech Race?" *Los Angeles Times*. April 20.

Thatcher, M. (1975), "Let Our Children Grow Tall." Speech to the Institute of Socio-Economic Studies. September, 15. Margaret Thatcher Foundation. Available online: https://www.margaretthatcher.org/document/102769

Thatcher, M. (1987), "No Such Thing as Society." Interview for *Women's Own Magazine*. September 23. Margaret Thatcher Foundation. Available online: https://www.margaretthatcher.org/document/106689

Thompson, D. (2016), "Who Are Donald Trump's Supporters, Really?" *Atlantic*. March 1.

Tierney, W. (1993), *Building Communities of Difference: Higher Education in the Twenty-First Century*. Westport, CT: Bergin & Garvey.

Tilsley, A. (2017), "Subtracting Schools from Communities." March 23. Washington: Urban Institute. Available online: https://www.urban.org/features/subtracting-schools-communities

Tingle, R. (2017), "Kim Nil-FUN: Strict Headteacher Is Likened to North Korean Dictator after Advertising for a 'Director of Isolations and Detentions' at His School's New 'Behaviour Correction Unit.'" *Daily Mail*. June 21.

Tomlinson, S. (2008), *Race and Education Policy and Politics in Britain*. New York: Open UP-McGraw-Hill.

Tomlinson, S. (2019), *Education and Race from Empire to Brexit*. Bristol: Policy Press.

Tompkins-Stange, M. E. (2016), *Policy Patrons: Philanthropy, Education Reform, and the Politics of Influence*. Cambridge, MA: Harvard Education Press.

Torres, C. A. (2012), "Critical Social Theory: A Portrait." *Ethics and Education*, 7 (2): 115–24.

Toscano, A. (2007), "Neo-Marxism." In G. Ritzer, ed., *The Blackwell Encyclopedia of Sociology*. Hoboken, NJ: Wiley-Blackwell. 3178–80.

Trades Union Congress (2014), *Education Not for Sale: A TUC Research Report*. March. London: TUC. Available online: https://www.tuc.org.uk/sites/default/files/Education_Not_For_Sale_Repor_Report.pdf

Trotsky, L. ([1930] 2008), *The History of the Russian Revolution*. Chicago: Haymarket Books.

Tulsa Historical Society and Museum (2021), "1921 Tulsa Race Massacre." Tulsa Historical Society and Museum. Available online: https://www.tulsahistory.org/exhibit/1921-tulsa-race-massacre/
Tweedie, N. (2012), "Downhills Primary School Takes on Michael Gove." *Telegraph*. January 17.
Tyler, I. (2008), "Chav Mum Chav Scum." *Feminist Media Studies*, 8 (1): 17–34.
Tyler, I. (2013), *Revolting Subjects: Social Abjection and Resistance in Neoliberal Britain*. London: Zed Books.
Umi, Ahjamu (2019), "China in Africa: A Critical Assessment." *Hood Communist*. Available online: https://hoodcommunist.org/2019/11/21/a-critical-assessment-of-china-in-africa/
United Nations (2022), "Two Years on, COVID-19 Pandemic 'far from over.'" *UN News*. March 9. Available online: https://news.un.org/en/story/2022/03/1113632
United Nations Educational Scientific and Cultural Organisation (1952), *The Race Concept—Results of an Inquiry*. Paris. UNESCO. Available online: https://unesdoc.unesco.org/ark:/48223/pf0000073351
United States Bureau of the Census (2017), "Historical Poverty Tables: People and Families, 1959 to 2016, Table 3." Available online: https://www.census.gov/data/tables/time-series/demo/income-poverty/historical-poverty-people.html
University of Chicago Laboratory Schools (2013), *Kindergarten Program of Study 2013–2014*. Chicago: Laboratory Schools. Available online: https://www.ucls.uchicago.edu/program/nursery-school-kindergarten
Useem, M. (1984), *The Inner Circle: Large Corporations and the Rise of Business Political Activity in the U.S. and U.K.* New York: Oxford University Press.
Valenzuela, A., ed. (2005), *Leaving Children Behind: How "Texas-style" Accountability Fails Latino Youth*. Albany, NY: State University of New York Press.
Valluvan, S., and V. S. Kalra (2019), "Racial Nationalisms: Brexit, Borders and Little Englander Contradictions." *Ethnic and Racial Studies*, 42 (14): 2393–412.
Vally, S. (1998), "Inequality in Education? Revisiting the Provisioning, Funding and Governance of Schooling." *Quarterly Review of Education and Training in South Africa*, 5 (4).
Vally, S. (2018), "The Privatisation of Schooling in South Africa." In S. Kenneth and M. Alex, eds., *Handbook of Global Educational Reform*. Hoboken, NJ: Wiley-Blackwell.
Vally, S., and E. Motala (2014), *Education, Economy and Society*. Pretoria: Unisa Press.
Vally, S., and E. Motala (2017), "Troubling 'Race' as a Category of Explanation in Social Science Research and Analysis." *South African Review of Education (SARE)*, 23 (2): 1–22.
Vasquez Heilig, J. (2012), "Why Do Hedge Funds Adore Charters?" *Cloaking Inequity*. October 23. Available online: https://cloakinginequity.com/2012/10/23/why-do-hedge-funds-adore-charters/ (accessed April 17, 2022).
Virdee, S. (2010), "Racism, Class, and the Dialectics of Social Transformation." In J. Solomos and P. Hill Collins, eds., *The SAGE Handbook of Race and Ethnic Studies*. London: Sage. 135–65.
Virdee, S. (2014), *Racism, Class, and the Racialized Outsider*. London: Bloomsbury.
Virdee, S. (2015), "Opening a Dialogue on Race, Class and National Belonging." *Ethnic and Racial Studies*, 38 (13): 2259–66.
Virdee, S. (2017a), "Race, Class, and Roediger's Open Marxism." *Salvage*. October 25. Available online: http://salvage.zone/online-exclusive/race-class-and-roedigers-open-marxism

Virdee, S. (2017b), "The Second Sight of Racialised Outsiders in the Imperialist Core." *Third World Quarterly*, 38 (11): 2396–410.
Virdee, S. (2019), "Racialized Capitalism: An Account of Its Contested Origins and Consolidation." *The Sociological Review*, 67 (1): 3–27.
Wacquant, L. (2008), *Urban Outcasts: A Comparative Study of Advanced Marginality*. Cambridge: Polity.
Walker, V. S. (1996), *Their Highest Potential: An African American School Community in the Segregated South*. Chapel Hill, NC: University of North Carolina Press.
Wallerstein, I. (2013), "Structural Crisis, or Why Capitalists May No Longer Find Capitalism Rewarding." In I. Wallerstein, R. Collins, M. Mann, G. Derlugian, and C. Calhoun, eds., *Does Capitalism Have a Future?*. Oxford and New York: Oxford University Press. 9–35.
Walton, S. (2020), "Why the Critical Race Theory Concept of 'White Supremacy' Should Not Be Dismissed by Neo-Marxists: Lessons from Contemporary Black Radicalism." *Power and Education*, 12 (1): 78–94.
Warmington, P. (2020), "Critical Race Theory in England: Impact and Opposition." *Identities*, 27 (1): 1–23.
Warren, Bill (1980), *Imperialism: Pioneer of Capitalism*. London: Verso.
Waterhouse, B. C. (2014), *Lobbying America: The Politics of Business from Nixon to NAFTA*. Princeton, NJ: Princeton University Press.
Watkins, W. H. (2001), *The White Architects of Black Education: Ideology and Power in America, 1865–1954*. New York: Teachers College Press.
Weatherford, J. (1988), *Indian Givers*. New York: Ballantine Books.
Webber, J. R. (2010), "Neostructuralism, Neoliberalism, and Latin America's Resurgent Left." *Historical Materialism*, 18 (3): 208–29.
Webber, J. R. (2015), "E. P. Thompson's Romantic Marxism." *Jacobin*. July 24. Available online: https://www.jacobinmag.com/2015/07/making-english-working-class-luddites-romanticism
Welner, K. G., P. H. Hinchey, and A. Molnar, eds. (2010), *Think Tank Research Quality: Lessons for Policy Makers, the Media, and the Public*. Charlotte, NC: Information Age.
Wen, Jiabao (2007), "Our Historical Tasks at the Primary Stage of Socialism and Several Issues Concerning China's Foreign Policy." Embassy of the People's Republic of China in Uganda. Available online: https://www.mfa.gov.cn/ce/ceug//eng/xwdt/t302141.htm
West, A., and E. Bailey (2013), "The Development of the Academies Programme: 'Privatising' School-Based Education in England 1986–2013." *British Journal of Educational Studies*, 61 (20): 137–59.
West, C. (2018), "Toward a Socialist Theory of Racism." *Democratic Socialists of America*. July. Available online: https://www.dsausa.org/files/2018/07/Toward_a_Socialist_Theory_of_Racism.pdf
White House Office of the Press (2010), "President Obama Calls for New Steps to Prepare America's Children for Success in College and Careers." News Release. February 22. Available online: https://obamawhitehouse.archives.gov/realitycheck/the-press-office/president-obama-calls-new-steps-prepare-america-s-children-success-college-and-care
White, T. (2015), "Charter Schools: Demystifying Whiteness in a Market of 'No Excuses' Corporate-Styled Charter Schools." In B. Picower and E. Mayorga, eds., *What's Race Got to Do with It: How Current School Reform Policy Maintains Racial and Economic Inequality*. New York: Peter Lang. 121–45.

Whitman, D. (2008), *Sweating the Small Stuff: Inner-City Schools and the New Paternalism*. Washington: Thomas B. Fordham Institute.
Wilkerson, I. (2020), *Caste: The Origins of Our Discontents*. New York: Random House.
Williams, C. (1974), *The Destruction of Black Civilization: Great Issues of a Race from 4500 B.C. to 2000 A.D.* Chicago: Third World Press.
Williams, E. (1944), *Capitalism and Slavery*. Chapel Hill, NC: University of North Carolina Press.
Williams, D. A. (1983), "Can the Schools Be Saved?" *Newsweek*. May 9. 50–8.
Willis, K. (2017), "'This is Us' Stirs Debate about Transracial Adoption." *Atlanta Black Star*. November 8.
Wilson, W. J. (1997), *When Work Disappears: The World of the New Urban Poor*. New York: Knopf.
Wilson, W. J. (2009), *More Than Just Race: Being Black and Poor in the Inner City*. New York: Norton.
Wilson, W. J. (2011), "The Declining Significance of Race: Revisited & Revised." *Dædalus, The Journal of the American Academy of Arts & Sciences*, 140 (2): 55–69.
Wilson, W. J. ([1980] 2012), *The Declining Significance of Race: Blacks and Changing American Institutions*, 3rd ed. Chicago: The University of Chicago Press.
Winant, H. (2001), *The World Is a Ghetto: Race and Democracy Since World War II*. New York: Basic Books.
Winant, H. (2004), *The New Politics of Race: Globalism, Difference, Justice*. Minneapolis, MN: University of Minnesota Press.
Winant, H., and G. Seidman (2001), "South Africa: When the System Has Fallen." In H. Winant, *The World Is a Ghetto: Race and Democracy Since World War II*. New York: Basic Books. 177–217.
Wing, A. (2003), *Critical Race Feminism: A Reader*. New York: New York University Press.
Winter, C., C. Heath-Kelly, A. Kaleem, and C. Mills (2021), "A Moral Education? British Values, Colour-Blindness, and Preventing Terrorism." *Critical Social Policy*, 42 (1): 85–106.
Wise, A. (2020), "Democrats Blame Trump Rhetoric for Michigan Governor Kidnapping Plot." NPR. October 8.
Wise, T. (2005), *White Like Me: Reflections on Race from a Privileged Son*. Brooklyn, NY: Soft Skull Press.
Wolf, E. (1983), *Europe and the People Without History*. Berkeley, CA: University of California Press.
Wood, E. M. (1994), "Identity Crisis." *In These Times*. June 13. 28–9.
Wood, E. M. (1995), *Democracy against Capitalism: Renewing Historical Materialism*. New York: Cambridge University Press.
Wood, E. M. (1998), *The Retreat from Class: A New "True" Socialism*, 2nd ed. New York: Verso.
Woodward, R. (2009), "Towards Complex Multilateralism? Civil Society and the OECD." In R. Mahon and S. McBride, eds., *The OECD and Transnational Governance*. Seattle: University of Washington Press. 77–95.
World Bank (1988), *Education in Sub-Saharan Africa: Policies for Adjustment, Revitalization, and Expansion*. Washington: World Bank. Available online: http://documents.worldbank.org/curated/en/816101468009945118/pdf/multi-page.pdf
World Economic Forum (2022), "The Global Education Crisis is Even Worse than We Thought: Here's What Needs to Happen." Available online: https://www.weforum.org/agenda/2022/01/global-education-crisis-children-students-covid19/

Wright, J., R. W. Whitaker II, M. Khalifa, and F. Briscoe (2018), "The Color of Neoliberal Reform: A Critical Race Policy Analysis of School District Takeovers in Michigan." *Urban Education*, 55 (3): 1–24.

Wright, R. (1957), *White Man, Listen!* Garden City, NY: Anchor Books.

Wrigley, T. (2019), "The Problem of Reductionism in Educational Theory: Complexity, Causality, Values." *Power and Education*, 11 (2): 145–62.

Yamamoto, E. K. (1997), "Critical Race Praxis: Race Theory and Political Lawyering Practice in Post-Civil Rights America." *Michigan Law Review*, 95 (4): 821–900.

Yancy, G., ed. (2004), *What White Looks Like: African-American Philosophers on the Whiteness Question*. New York: Routledge.

Yancy, G. (2018), *Backlash: What Happens When We Talk Honestly about Race in America*. Lanham, MD: Rowman and Littlefield.

Ydesen, C., and K. E. Andreasen (2020), "Historical Roots of the Global Testing Culture in Education." *Nordic Studies in Education*, 40 (2): 149–66.

Yeshitela, O. (2014), *An Uneasy Equilibrium: The African Revolution Versus Parasitic Capitalism*. St. Petersburg, FL: Burning Spear Publications.

Yosso, T. (2005), "Whose Culture has Capital? A Critical Race Theory Discussion of Community Cultural Wealth." *Race Ethnicity and Education*, 8 (1): 69–91.

Young, I. M. (1990), *Justice and the Politics of Difference*. Princeton, NJ: Princeton University Press.

Young, I. M. ([1990] 2005), "Five Faces of Oppression." In A. E. Cudd and R. O. Andreasen, eds., *Feminist Theory: A Philosophical Anthology*. Hoboken, NJ: Blackwell. 91–104.

Yuval-Davis, N. (2012), "Dialogical Epistemology—An Intersectional Resistance to the 'Oppression Olympics.'" *Gender and Society*, 26 (1): 46–54.

Zavala, M. (2018), *Raza Struggle and the Movement for Ethnic Studies: Decolonial Pedagogies, Literacies and Methodologies*. New York: Peter Lang.

Contributors

Vonzell Agosto is Professor of Curriculum Studies in the Educational Leadership and Policy Studies program at the University of South Florida, United States. Her research explores issues of structural oppression in the work and products associated with curriculum, leadership, mentoring, and social categories of experience such as racism, sexism, and ableism. Her work has been published in *Educational Researcher, Review of Research in Education, Journal of School Leadership,* and the *International Journal of Qualitative Studies in Education.*

Margarita Ines Berta-Ávila is a union organizer with the California Faculty Association (CFA), United States, and currently holds the following positions: Capital Chapter President, CFA Vice President of Chapter Presidents—North, and Bargaining Team Member. In addition, Margarita is a professor in the College of Education at Sacramento State University, United States.

Stephen Brookfield has been involved in the field of education since 1970. He has worked in England, Canada, and the United States, teaching and consulting in a variety of adult, community, organizational, and higher education settings. His overall project is to help people learn to think critically about the dominant ideologies they have internalized and how these can be challenged. His most recent book is *Teaching Race: How to Help Students Unmask and Challenge Racism.*

Tiger Chan is a graduate student in the department of sociology at the University of Cambridge, UK. Her current research focuses on the social production of "mixed race," DNA testing for ancestry and the political management of "mixed" people.

Antonia Darder is Professor Emerita at Loyola Marymount University, United States, where she held the Leavey Chair in Ethics and Moral Leadership. Author of seminal publications in the field, including *Culture and Power in the Classroom, Reinventing Paulo Freire: A Pedagogy of Love, After Race: Racism after Multiculturalism,* and *Decolonizing Interpretative Research,* her work in critical pedagogy, cultural studies, and Latino studies spans nearly four decades.

Noah De Lissovoy is Professor of Cultural Studies in Education at the University of Texas at Austin, United States. His research centers on emancipatory approaches to curriculum, cultural studies, and philosophy, with a focus on the intersecting effects of race, class, and capital. He is the author of *Capitalism, Pedagogy, and the Politics of Being, Education and Emancipation in the Neoliberal Era,* and *Power, Crisis, and Education for Liberation,* and co-author of *Toward a New Common School Movement.*

Nicholas D. Hartlep is Robert Charles Billings Endowed Chair in Education at Berea College, United States, where he chairs the Department of Education Studies. His book *The Neoliberal Agenda and the Student Debt Crisis in U.S. Higher Education*, with Lucille L. T. Eckrich and Brandon O. Hensley (2017), was named an Outstanding Book by the Society of Professors of Education.

Cleveland Hayes is Professor of Education Foundations at Indiana University School of Education, United States. He teaches education foundations to elementary education students and the doctoral program in Critical Race Theory in the Urban Education. He is the co-author (with N. D. Hartlep) of *Unhooking from Whiteness: Resisting the Esprit de Corps*.

Shirin Housee is Senior Lecturer in Sociology at the University of Wolverhampton, UK. Her research focuses on classroom interaction, engagement, student voice, and anti-racist curriculum. Her book *Speaking Out against Racism in the University Space* is testimony to her ongoing passion for student voice and anti-racism.

Pranav Jani is Associate Professor of English and director of Asian American Studies at the Ohio State University, United States, and is affiliated with the South Asian Studies Initiative and the departments of African American & African Studies, Comparative Studies, and Near Eastern Languages & Culture. The author of *Decentering Rushdie: Cosmopolitanism and the Indian Novel in English* (2010) and publications focused on ethnic studies, Marxism, racialization, postcolonial, and anti-colonial thought, he has also been a long-time organizer and activist.

Christy Kulz is a research fellow at the Technical University Berlin, Germany. Her research monograph *Factories for Learning: Producing Raced and Classed Inequality in the Neoliberal Academy School* was published by Manchester University Press and won the Society for Educational Studies' first place book prize.

Kevin D. Lam is Associate Professor at Drake University, United States. His research and teaching focuses on Asian American youth violence, critical theory of racism, critical pedagogy, urban education, and political economy. He is the author of *Youth Gangs, Racism, and Schooling: Vietnamese American Youth in a Postcolonial Context* (2015).

Alpesh Maisuria is Associate Professor of Education Policy in Critical Education, University of the West of England, Bristol, UK. He is the joint deputy editor of the *Journal for Critical Education Policy Studies (JCEPS)*. He is also the co-convener for *Marxism and Education: Renewing Dialogues (MERD)*, a long-standing seminar series. He is co-editor of the *Encyclopedia of Marxism and Education*.

Adam Martinez is a doctoral student in the Cultural Studies in Education program at the University of Texas at Austin, Texas. His academic interests are in *filosofía de* *la liberación*, interaction ritual theory, Marxism, decolonial possibilities, and critical ethnography. He is currently editing a special journal issue on Enrique Dussel's *Política de la Liberación* for the Texas Education Review, which brings together scholars from across the Americas.

Cheryl E. Matias is a full professor and director of Secondary Teacher Education at the University of Kentucky, United States. Her research focuses on race and ethnic studies in education with a theoretical focus on critical race theory, critical whiteness studies, critical pedagogy, and feminism of color. Among her numerous publications, she is the author of *Pedagogies for Deconstructing Race and Gender*.

Ali Meghji is Assistant Professor of Sociology. His research and teaching focuses on social inequalities, bridging the epistemological and methodological divergences between critical race theory and decolonial thought. He is the author of *The Racialized Social System* (2021) and *Decolonizing Sociology* (2020) and the forthcoming book, *Race, Decoloniality and World Crisis*.

Nicholas Ozment is an independent scholar in southern Minnesota, where he taught English at Winona State University, United States, from 2002 to 2010. For the last decade he has served as Rochester's premier tour guide to the history of the city and the world-renowned Mayo Clinic.

Ericka Roland (she/her) is Assistant Professor in the Educational Leadership and Policy Studies Department at the University of Texas at Arlington, United States, whose research interests include leadership development, criticality, equity in higher education, mentoring, and critical methodologies. Her research has appeared in journals such as *Review of Research in Education* and the *Journal of Diversity in Higher Education*.

Howard Ryan is a doctoral student in Sociology at West Virginia University, United States. He has a background in teaching and labor organizing and is the author of *Educational Justice: Teaching and Organizing against the Corporate Juggernaut*.

Christine E. Sleeter is Professor Emerita in the College of Education at California State University Monterey Bay, United States. Past president of the National Association for Multicultural Education and past vice president of the American Educational Research Association, her research focuses on anti-racist multicultural education, ethnic studies, and teacher education. Her most recent books include *Transformative Ethnic Studies in Schools* (with M. Zavala) and *Family History in Black and White* (a novel).

Rodolfo D. Torres is Professor Emeritus of Urban Planning and Public Policy at the University of California, Irvine, United States. He has published widely on theories of the state, racism, to Marxist urban theory and Mexican American labor and politics. He is co-author of *After Race: Race after Multiculturalism* and *Race Defaced: Paradigms of Pessimism, Politics of Possibility*.

Salim Vally is Director of the Centre for Education Rights and Transformation, the South African National Research Foundation's research chair in community, adult and workers' education based at the Faculty of Education, University of Johannesburg, South Africa, and a visiting professor at the Nelson Mandela University (NMU), South Africa. His latest co-edited book is *The University and Social Justice: Struggles across the Globe* (2020).

Index

Abdullah, M.   184
academies   37, 119–20, 121 n.12, 122 n.13, 217
Academies Act (2010)   37
accountability   138
Action for Excellence: A Comprehensive Plan to Improve Our Nation's Schools   22
Adapted Education reform movement   175–6
Adonis, Lord   147
Advanced Placement (AP) courses   215
African American Baseline Essays (Oregon)   185
African Americans   xvii–xviii, 34, 54–5, 95, 129
African National Congress (ANC)   45–50, 82
African National Congress Youth League   45
African nationalism   45
Africans   208
After Race: Racism after Multiculturalism (Darder and Torres)   39, 91, 126
Aggarwal, U.   138
Aguilar, Delia   5–6, 189
Aid to Families with Dependent Children (AFDC)   125
Alexander, Claire   193
Alexander, Neville   39, 48, 82–4, 90 n.1, 94
Alfaro, C.   141
Allen, Ricky Lee   7, 33
Allen, Theodore   34
Amalgamated Transit Union   71
American Legislative Exchange Council (ALEC)   19, 21, 26
Anne Casey Foundation   25
Another World Is Possible (McNally)   41
anti-apartheid movement   45
anti-Asian racism   80

anti-colonial nationalism   78
anti-Muslim racism; *see* Islamophobia
anti-racism   34, 40, 142–5, 200–1
   in education   142–5, 195–6
   teacher mobilization, race-based approach to   142–5
anti-racist   xx
apartheid education   85–7
"April Theses" (Lenin)   76
Arteaga, N.   136
Ashe, S. D.   127–8
Asian Americans   71, 80, 124–6, 128–9
Au, Wayne   13–16
austerity   30
Ayers, R.   142
Ayers, W.   142

Badenoch, Kemi   195
Bagdikian, Ben   23–4
Baggett, H. C.   139–40
Baldwin, James   168
Ball, S.   153, 155
BAME academics   197–8
Banaji, Jairus   76
Bantu Society   46
Baran, Paul A.   172
Barra, Mary   26
Bartolomé, L.   141
Beal, Jennifer   5
Bell, Derrick   191, 196
Bell, Terrel   20
Bennett, L. A., Jr.   164
Bergerson, A. A.   166
Bernstein, B.   183
Bhaskar, Roy   114
Bhattacharya, Tithi   89
Biko, Steve   88
Bilge, Sirma   6
binaries
   gender   221
   of white/non-white   217–18
Black   206–16; *see also* race; racism

cultural politics 64, 148
education, politics of 64 (see also school/educational reforms)
feminism 5, 69, 196–9
inferiority 209
nationalism 4–7
as one's property 61
oppression 54, 70
in OWS movement 54
politics 5, 64–5
radical tradition 5, 163, 188, 197
schools 85–7
unemployment 54
Black, Indigenous, People of Color (BIPOC) xvii, 208
Black Consciousness Movement (BCM) 85, 88
Black Lives Matter movement 70–1, 102, 161, 174, 195
Black Marxism: The Making of the Black Radical Tradition (Robinson) 5, 90 n.1, 188
Black nationalism 187
Blackness 206
Black papers 155
Black/white dichotomy 71
Black-white poverty gap 33–4, 63
Black women 80
Black working-class women 73
Blair, Tony 117, 119, 155
Blaisdell, B. 141
Bloom, Elizabeth 9–10
Boeing 9
Bohrer, Ashley 77
Bolshevik revolutionaries (1917) 76–7
Bond, Patrick 26, 39
Bonilla-Silva, E. 192–3
Bonnett, A. 149–50
Booth, William 149
bosses, revolt of 20–2
Bourdieu, P. 189–90, 213
Brantlinger, Ellen 10
Brent program 35–6
Brewer, Jan 37
Bridge International Academies 28
Bridge model 28
brief constructed responses (BCRs) 16–17
Britain
  class in context of 148–58

colonies 149
culture in twenty-first-century 155–8
neoliberal educational reforms 147–58
race, historic formation of 148–58
racial whiteness 149
state-organized education in 153
urban slums 149
women, working-class 150–1
working class 149–51
Broad, Eli 9
Brown, Jerry 37
Brown, Malcolm 39, 94
Bude, U. 175
Business Coalition for Education Reform (BCER) 25–6
Business Coalition for Excellence in Education 26
Business Leader's Guide to Setting Academic Standards (Business Roundtable) 25
Business Roundtable (BRT) 19, 21–2, 24–5
Butler, Rab 154

Cabral, Amilcar 88, 187–8
Cabrera, N. L. 199
California Faculty Association (CFA) 142–3
Cameron, David 38
capitalism xviii, xx, 5–7, 11, 59, 74–8, 96–7, 104–5, 108–11, 118, 138
  anti-democratic aims of 93
  cast and 180–1
  exploitation of workers 74
  heterogeneity 77
  industrial 74–6
  organization of 107–8
  racial 57, 91–2, 180–1
  relationship to labor 128
  roots of 178–80
  social inequities in 56
  in South Africa 83
  in United States 207–8
  violence in 104, 107–8
capitalist exploitation 189–90
Carbado, Devon 4
Cardoso, M. 175
caste
  and capitalism 179–80
  roots of 178–80

centrist capital   36
Chamber of Commerce   21–2
charter school   9
chattel slaves   208
chavs   157–8
Chibber, Vivek   70–1
Chinese Communist Party   75
Chomsky, Noam   208
Chowkwanyun, M.   92
Christianity   179
Christian National Education   85
Christie, P.   85
Civil Rights movement   64, 183–4
class   xvii–xviii, 3–4, 14, 38–51, 130, 186–9, 193
  arguments, limits of   166
  Blackness   206
  in British context   148–58
  in capital system   105–7
  in critical race analysis of education   54–65
  cultural significance of   156
  and education   210–12
  equivalence   11, 129–30
  interpretation of school reform   18–38
  intersectionality through   5
  in ISO   71–3
  for political analysis   41
  politics   89–90, 129–31
  primacy   6, 69–70, 78, 94
  vs. race   218–20
  reductionism   71, 87–90
  relations   95–6
  retreat from   4–6, 92–4
  revolutionary   76–7
  social   41, 55, 57, 59, 82, 86–7, 93, 192, 211
  in South Africa   45–51, 82–90
  unstable categories   150–2
Class, Race, and Marxism (Roediger)   39
class-conflict model   41
ClassCrits   11
class-primacist   40–1
CLS; *see* critical legal studies
CMP; *see* colonial matrix of power
Cohen, Cathy   64
Cole, Mike   56–8, 62, 186
Colin, Scipio, Jr. III   xvii–xviii
Collective Bargaining Agreement (CBA)   144

Collins, C.   85
Collins, Patricia Hill   6
colonial matrix of power (CMP)   179
colonization   73, 96, 179–81
color-blind racism   8, 12, 71, 140, 165–6
Color Line and the Assembly Line: Managing Race in the Ford Empire, The (Esch)   39
Combahee River Collective   5, 80
Commercial Club of Chicago   32
Common Core   9, 19, 25
communism   7
Communist Party of India (Marxist)   75
Community Cultural Wealth (CCW)   140
competency-based education and training (CBET)   29–30
Confederation of British Industry   19
Confederation of European Business   19
Congress of South African Trade Unions (COSATU)   47–8
conservative ideological web   34–6
CoreCivic   144
Covid-19 pandemic   92, 97–8, 160–1, 212–13
  teachers role during   212–13
  US public schools in   160–1, 212–14
Crenshaw, Kimberlé   6, 8, 73, 190–1
critical legal studies (CLS)   59, 190–3
critical race feminism (CRF)   196–9
critical race theory (CRT)   4–5, 7–8, 12, 54–65, 159–68, 186–9, 190–2, 195, 218–19; *see also* race; racism
  class-related priorities for   62–5
  of education   54–65
  and feminism   196–9
  identity-based politics   58
  Marxian critique of   56–9
  response to Marxian critics   59–62
  scholars   55
  underlaboring   114–16
  on White supremacy   58, 159–68
Critical Realism   114–16, 120 n.2, 121 n.6
critical social theories   169–70
  cycling through and combining   173–4
  identity politics   173–4
  power   173

with Frankfurt School   173–4
terms of engagement   171–3
torus of global education reformulations   174–6
CRT; *see* critical race theory
cultural citizenship   58–9
cultural racism   151–2
cultures   109–10
curriculum   182–5, 202

Daley, Richard   32
Darder, Antonia   4, 12, 39, 56–9, 199
Davis, Angela   88, 189–90
Dawson, Michael   64
decolonial/decoloniality   104–5, 184
Delgado, Richard   59–60, 62–5, 196
Dell   9
Democracy against Capitalism (Wood)   93
DeVos, Betsy   9
diversity   75
Dixson, A. D.   61, 196
Docksai, Ronald   35
Domhoff, William   32
"Double Jeopardy: To Be Black and Female" (Beal)   5
Douglass, Frederick   209
Dreamfields Academy, England   155–6
DREIC   121 n.7
Du Bois, W. E. B.   74, 165, 167, 187–8, 193
Dunn, A. H.   139–40
Dussel, Enrique   110
Dying of Whiteness (Metzl)   165

economic justice   64–5
economic reforms   27–8
economics education   21–2
edu-business   19
education   104, 110–11
 anti-racism in   142–5, 195–6
 Black cultural politics of   64
 capitalist   108
 civil rights   36–7
 and class analysis   210–12
 critical race analysis of   54–65
 market principles for   97
 Marxian critique in   56
 multicultural   140

neoliberal   108
panacea for problems of culture   153–5
reforms in   3–4, 85–7, 92, 100–2, 119–20, 130, 138, 147, 206 (*see also* school reform)
social justice project in   62
social justice transformation   142–5
in South Africa   82–90
in UK   147–58
unionism   142–5
US   100–1
white supremacy in   59–60
educational exchanges   201–2
Educational Justice: Teaching and Organizing against the Corporate Juggernaut (Ryan)   3
education management organizations (EMOs)   119
Education Reform Act (1988)   31, 36, 154
edu-profits   9, 152–3
Ehrenreich, Barbara   14
Ehrenreich, John   14
Elias, Sean   11
Elise, Sharon   143
Emery, Kathy   24
ending oppression   40
engagement, terms of   171–3
Engels, F.   149, 181
England   37–8
 education policy   7–8, 37–8
 school privatization   37–8
 school reforms   37–8
 vs. US charter schools   38
English education policy   7–8
Englishness   151
equality   40
Esch, Elizabeth   39
ethnicity   55
Ethnic Studies movement   184
eugenics movement   113
European American Collaborative Challenging Whiteness   xix–xx
European Being   109
European imperialism   33
evasion, politics of   137–9
Every Student Succeeds Act (2015)   29
experiential knowledge, value of   166

exploitation   xviii, 74, 95-6, 100
exteriority   109-10
Exxon Mobil   9

Fabricant, Michael   9
Fay, B.   170-1
Feagin, Joe   4, 11, 40
female teachers   42-3
Fine, Michelle   9
Fire This Time: The Watts Uprising and the 1960s (Horne)   39
Fisher, A. N.   213
Floyd, George   71, 161
freedom   56
Freedom 2000   22
Freedom Charter (1955)   46
"free from class" analytical paradigms   86
Freeman, Richard   15
Free Schools   119
Freire, Paulo   88
Friedman, Milton   21
funding   124

G7   26
Galeano, E.   180-2
Gane, N.   158
Gardner, David   20
Gates, Bill   9, 28
gender   6, 55, 130, 213
  equivalence   11, 129-30
  inequality   87
  issues   87
genealogy   125-6
GEO Group   144
Gillborn, David   7-8, 13, 18, 59, 62, 65
Gilmore, Ruth Wilson   189, 213
Gilroy, Paul   193
global education reform   169-77
global education reform movement (GERM)   3, 87, 169, 174-6
globalization   33
global white ignorance   165
Goodman, D.   100
Gorlewski, Julie   17
Gove, Michael   147
Gramsci, Antonio   10
grand/totalizing nature theory   6-8, 147
  CRT   7

primacy   6-8
race-based frameworks   6-7
Graves, J. L., Jr.   100
Great War   75
Growth, Employment, and Redistribution (GEAR) strategy   83
growth coalitions   32
Guevara, Che   88

Hall, Stuart   64, 151, 171, 188, 193
Hampton-Tuskegee model   175
Harris, Cheryl   60-1, 162
Harvard   210
Harvey, David   21
Hatcher, Richard   31
Hayek, Friedrich   21
health disparities   92
Heritage Foundation   21
herrenvolk ethics   167
herrschaftskritisch   172
heterosexism   96
Hewlett   9
higher education racism, classroom strategy for   200-1
higher education reform   174-5
high-stakes testing   14-16
Hill, Dave   31, 56, 118, 186
Hill-Brownsville, Ocean   184
Hira, Ron   30
Hirji, Karim   89
Historically Black Colleges and Universities (HBCUs)   175-6
Ho Chi Minh   88
homo economicus   117
Horne, Gerald   39
How Capitalism Underdeveloped Black America (Marable)   39
How Europe Underdeveloped Africa (Rodney)   87
human capital theory   83, 90 n.2
Hunt, Ida Gibbs   188
Hyland, Terry   29-30

"Identifying Class, Classifying Difference" (Saul)   87-8
identity politics   55, 58-9, 61, 89-90, 125-6, 173-4
Iglesias, Elizabeth   64-5
imperialism   33, 75

impoverishment xviii
In Darkest England and the Way Out
 (Booth) 149
individualism 157
industrial capitalism 73–6
inequalities 135–6
injustice of meritocracy 166
institutionalized racism 139
intellectual genealogy 125–6
International Finance Corporation 28
internationalism 78–9
International Monetary Fund
 (IMF) 26–7, 33
International Socialist Organization
 (ISO) 69–70
 class in 71–3
 race in 71–3
intersectionality 4–6, 55, 57–8, 74, 127, 189–90
 class and 57
 critique of 63
 schematic for understanding
  importance of 207–8
 social inequality and 6
Invention of the White Race, The
 (Allen) 34
Islam 201
Islamophobia 62, 96, 201–4
ISO; *see* International Socialist
 Organization

Jackson, George 88
James, C. L. R. 79–80, 87, 88
Jim Crow laws 209
Jones, Claudia 74, 79–80, 193
Juan, E. San, Jr. 184
justice 40

Kandel, Isaac L. 175
Kasrils, Ronnie 48–9
*Keeping Track: How Schools Structure
 Inequality* (Oakes) 215
Kelley, R. D. G. 89–90
Kendi, I. X. xx
King, Martin Luther, Jr. 5
Kliebard, H. M. 183
Knowledge Is Power Program
 (KIPP) 31
Kohli, R. 136, 139–40

labor 189–90
labor migration 128–9
Ladson-Billings, Gloria 41, 60, 198, 201
language 55
Lembede, Anton 45–6
Lenin, V. I. 75
Leonardo, Zeus 11–13, 164
Levine, Marc 30
liberalism 96
liberation 109–10
Lindner, K. 171–2
linked fate 64
Linnaeus, Carl 112
Lipman, Pauline 32, 138
Lipsitz, George 8
living labor 109
Locke, John 114
London Labour and the London Poor
 (Mayhew) 149
Love, Bettina 138, 141, 159
Luna, Catherine 17

Machacek, Mark 28
McGeever, B. 127–8
McGraw-Hill publishing company 30
Machel, Samora 88
McNair, John 188
McNally, David 41
Madhubuti, Haki R. 7, 187
Maisuria, Alpesh 32, 118, 130
Major, John 117
Making Schools Work report
 (2011) 27
Malcolm X 5
Mandate for Leadership 35
Mandela, Nelson 45–7
Maoism 77
Marable, Manning 11, 39, 182
marginalization 138
Marx, K. 40, 45, 66 n.2
 critique in education 56
 critique of critical race theory 56–9
 CRT response to critics of 59–62
 historiography 75
Marxism xviii, 4–5, 12, 39–40, 45, 69–80, 127, 169, 171–2
 as class-only framework 6–7, 41–2, 92–3
 for educational phenomena 171–3

industrial capitalism, emergence
  of   74-6
nationalism   78-9
and racial theory   12, 39
revolutionary class   76-7
as Western European totalizing
  theory   181-2
workers, exploitation of   74
Maryland BRT (MBRT)   24-5
Massachusetts Comprehensive Assessment
  System (MCAS)   17-18
Matias, Cheryl E.   140
Matsuda, Mari   7
May, Shannon   28, 140
Mayhew, Henry   149
Mayorga, Edwin   10, 13, 138
Mazumder, B.   213
Mbembe, Achille   213
media, role of   23-6
Mehta, Jal   20
meritocracy   129
  ideology of   214
  injustice of   166
Metzl, Charles   165, 167
Mignolo, W. D.   179-80, 184
Miles, Robert   39, 94, 98, 126-8, 131
Miller, S.   213
Mills, Charles   3, 158, 165
Moreton, Bethany   22
multicultural education   140
multiculturalism   140
multicultural teacher education   41, 43
Munro, Richard   24
Muslim identity   201
myths, racialized   138

Nader, Ralph   21
Naidoo, Jay   47
naïve realism   121 n.8
National Association of Manufacturers
  (NAM)   21-2
National Commission on Excellence in
  Education (NCEE)   20
National Council on Teacher Quality   26
National Curriculum   31
National Governors Association   25
nationalism   78-9
National Labor Relations Act   121 n.12
National Nurses United   71

Nation at Risk, A   22-3
Naturalization and Immigration Act
  (1965)   128
Neilson, D.   172
neoliberal education   108
neoliberal educational solutions   97
neoliberalism   33-4, 107-9, 118, 152-3
neoliberal reform   147-58
neo-Marxism   172-3
Nevárez, A.   136, 139
New Politics of Race, The (Winant)   51
new social movements   5, 187
Ngin, C.   126
Nkrumah, Kwame   187
No Child Left Behind Act of 2001
  (NCLB)   12-13, 30
nothingness   109-10
Nyerere, Julius   187

Obama, Barack   9, 37, 159-60
Occupy Wall Street (OWS)
  movement   54
OECD; *see* Organization for Economic
  Cooperation and Development
Omi, Michael   4
Operation Varsity Blues (Smith)   216
oppressions   6, 54, 56, 85, 138, 169-70
*Ordinary Country: Issues in the
  Transition from Apartheid to
  Democracy in South Africa, An*
  (Alexander)   39
Organization for Economic Cooperation
  and Development (OECD)   19,
  26, 28-30
Ornelas, A.   215
otherness   109
Overeducated American, The
  (Freeman)   15
Oxfam International   92

Padmore, George   188
Pan-Africanism   4-7, 187-8
Parenti, M.   93
Parsons, Carl   186
Pearson Education   28
pensions   144
people of color   59-60, 63-4, 129, 165,
  213
Perlstein, Linda   16

personalized learning   29
Peterson, Elizabeth   xvii–xviii
Phillips-Fein, Kim   21
Picower, Bree   10, 13, 138
Pizarro, M.   139
POC Caucus   72
political genealogy   125–6
politics
  Black   5, 64–5
  of Black education   64
  of busing   99
  class   89–90, 129–31
  of evasion   137–9
  identity   55, 58–9, 61, 89–90, 125–6, 173–4
Pontiac High School   16–17
positivism   114, 120 n.4, 121 n.9
poverty   xix, 92, 109–10, 149–50
Powell, Enoch   150–1
Powell, Lewis   21, 33
power   173
power relations   95
predominantly white institutions (PWIs)   210
primacy   6–8
prison system   108
privatization   3, 8–10, 27–32, 37–8, 48, 86–7, 108, 119–22, 126, 142, 183
professional/managerial class   14
Program for International Student Assessment (PISA)   28–9
project of liberation   109–10
proletarianization   108
proletariat   xviii
Proud Boys   161
public consciousness   182–5
public schools   10, 26, 38, 140, 154, 212–13
Pulido, L.   171

Quijano, A.   106, 109, 179

race   xvii–xix, 6, 38–51, 112–18, 120 n.1, 130, 193; *see also* critical race theory
  biological basis of   112–13
  Blackness   206
  in British context   148–50
  capitalism   11, 83–6, 88, 90 n.1, 109–10

  and capitalist differences   36–7
  in capital system   105–7
  versus class   218–20
  cultural contamination   150–2
  in educational practice/reforms   99
  equivalence   11, 129–30
  as floating signifier   199
  health disparities and   92
  idea *versus* concept   127–8
  interpretation of school reform   9–13
  in ISO   71–3
  Marxist challenge to   91–103
  poverty and   92
  primacy   4–8, 78
  racism and   98–100
  reductionism   87–90
  relations   93, 98–9, 127, 129
  school reform and   3–4, 32–8, 119–20, 130, 169–70, 182–5, 206
  social construction of   56, 113–14
  social relations and   96–8
  in South Africa   45–51
  state of mind   166–7
  unequal opportunity   209–10
  unstable categories   150–2
"Race, Class, and the Hidden Aims of School Reform" (Ryan)   69
Race, Whiteness, and Education (Leonardo)   12
race-based theory   4–6, 9–13, 127, 186–7; *see also* critical race theory
race-class debate   x–xii, 32–3
racial achievement gap   15
racial capitalism   11, 39–40, 83–6, 88, 90 n.1, 171–2, 180–1
racial domination   164–5; *see also* white supremacy
racial formation theory   4
racial identity   xviii, 55, 58–9, 61, 63
racial inequity   32–3
racial injustice   64
racialization
  capitalism and   124–5
  Marxist understanding of   126–9
  process of   130
racial liberalism   167
racial literacy   141
racial oppression   xvii–xviii, 6, 54, 56, 85, 138

racial spaces   65
racism   xix–xx, 34, 57, 70–1, 108; see also
    critical race theory
    and capitalism   57
    in classroom   138
    color-blind   8, 12, 71, 165–6
    CRT/F   196–9
    cultural   151–2
    as endemic   7, 165
    higher education   200–1
    Islamophobic   62, 201–4
    Marxian theory of   39–42, 57
    materiality of   94–8
    nature of   100
    as oppressive practice   56
    political economy of   128–9
    race and   98–100
    rationalization   137
    structural   11
    and white interests   43–4, 158–68
Racism (Brown)   39
Racism, Class and the Racialized Outsider
    (Virdee)   39
*Racism and Education: Coincidence or
    Conspiracy?* (Gillborn)   7–8
Racism not Race (Graves and
    Goodman)   100
Ramaphosa, Cyril   50
Reay, D.   156
reductionism   172
Reed, Adolph, Jr.   70–1, 92, 103
religion   109–10
Renaissance 2010   32
resistance   100
"Rethinking Black Marxism: Reflections
    on Cedric Robinson and
    Others" (Meyerson)   93–4
revolt of bosses   20–2
revolutionary class   76–7
Richardson, Robin   35–6
Riep, Curtis   28
Robinson, Cedric   5, 39–40, 90 n.1, 93,
    180–1
Robinson, Joan   172
Rodney, Walter   87, 88
Roediger, David   11, 39, 51, 148
Rollock, N.   148
Rousseau, C. K.   61, 196
Rust, Edward   25

Ryan, Howard   69–70, 73, 82, 91, 97,
    104, 112–13, 118–19, 121 n.12,
    125–6, 130, 147, 186–93, 206–7
Ryan, M. K.   213

Said, Edward   75
Saklatvala, Shapurji   188
Salberg, Pasi   174
Sankara, Thomas   187
SASM; *see* South African Students
    Movement
SASO; *see* South African Students
    Organization
Saul, John   39, 45
school/educational reforms   3–4, 32–8,
    119–20, 130, 169–70, 182–5,
    206
    Adapted Education reform
        movement   175–6
    aims of   19
    by asking   10
    beneficiaries   10
    capitalist aims   32–8
    class-based interpretation of   18–38
        capitalist aims   32–8
        neoliberal   26–30
        organized business   20–6
        race   32–8
        theorizing organized business
            sector   30–2
    in colonized countries   175
    conservative ideological web   34–6
    curriculum   182–5
    donors for   9
    edu-business in   19
    English   7–8, 147–58
    as expression of neoliberal
        ideology   9–10
    grand theory regarding   158
    and hidden aims   8–9, 147–8
    insights from England   37–8
    meritocratic ideology   18
    movement   8–9, 19–32
    nature of   10
    neoliberal, as global movement   26–30
        OECD   28–30
        World Bank   27–8
    organized business sector in   20–6
        growth coalitions   32

media, role of 23–6
revolt of bosses 20–2
Task Force on Education for
   Economic Growth 22–3
theorizing 30–2
philanthropic sector in 19
public consciousness and 182–5
purpose of 13
race-based interpretation of 9–18, 32–8
   and capitalist differences 36–7
   test-driven curriculum 16–18
   testing, beneficiaries from 14–16
   white supremacy 13–14
research as humanity 220–1
test-driven 7, 9, 14–16
torus of global 174–6
and whites 13–15
schooling 104
Seaborg, Glenn 20
Seeing Race Again: Countering Colorblindness across the Disciplines (Crenshaw) 8
segregation 209
Seidman, Gay 49–51
self-determination 78–9
seriousness 114
sexism 96
Sharkey, Jesse 71
Shrontz, Frank 25
Sirota, David 9
Sisulu, Walter 45
Sivanandan, Ambalavaner 148, 188
slave labor 180
slavery 73
Sleeter, Christine 41–2, 140–1, 147
Smith, Janet 65
social change 38–51
social class 41, 55, 57, 59, 82, 86–7, 93, 192, 211
   Black people 64
   CRT's engagement of 60–1
   people of color 65
   primacy of 112–13, 120
   in schools 172
   underlaboring 116–18
   warfare 96
social identity 57
social inequities 6, 56, 96

socialism 39–40, 47
Socialist Visions (Shalom) 39–40
social justice 75
   transformation 142–5
   unionism 142–3
social oppression 73
societal oppression 92
Solomon, J. 183
Solomos, J. 155
Solórzano, D. G. 159, 215
Sondel, B. 139–40
South Africa 73, 82–90
   anti-apartheid movement 45
   apartheid education system in 85–6
   capitalism in 83
   class in 45–51, 82–90
   conflicting interpretations 49–51
   education system in 82–90
   GERM in 87
   post-apartheid education system in 86
   post-apartheid era 48–9
   race in 45–51, 82–90
   racial capitalism 82–3, 88, 90 n.1
South African Communist Party (SACP) 47, 78
South African Congress of Trade Unions (SACTU) 47–8
South African Students Movement (SASM) 88
South African Students Organization (SASO) 87
South Africa-The Present as History (Saul and Bond) 39
spirit murdering 138
Stalin, Joseph 47
standardization 138
Standardized Assessment Tests (SATs) 31
Stanfield, James 28
Stanley, Henry Morton 149
Starkey, David 157–8
Stefancic, J. 196
Steiner-Khamsi, G. 175
STEM education 30
Stoler, A. 149–50
Stovall, David 59–62, 65
stratification 41–2
Students in Free Enterprise (SIFE) 22
Sullivan, S. xx

Sweezy, Paul M.   172
Sydnor, Eugene   21
Systemic Racism: A Theory of Oppression (Feagin)   40
systemic racism theory   4

Tambo, Oliver   45
Task Force on Education for Economic Growth   22–4
Tate, Greg   54–5, 60
Tatum, Beverly Daniel   41
teacher mobilization, race-based approach to   136–46
  anti-racism   142–5
  future teachers, impact of preparation on   139–42
  politics of evasion   137–9
  social justice transformation   142–5
  unionism   142–5
teachers   41–3
  of color   135–8, 140–2, 145
  education programs   140–1
  and facilitator   202–4
  role during Covid-19 pandemic   212–13
  unionism   142–5
  white   141–2
Teitelbaum, Michael   30
terms of engagement   171–3
test-driven curriculum   16–18
test-driven school reform   7, 9
testimonios   145
Thatcher, Margaret   8, 118–19, 151–3
Thatcherism   151
Thompson, E. P.   117
Thompson, Trevor   186
Time, Inc.   23–4
Tomlinson, S.   153–4
Toombs, Charles   144–5
Torres, Rodolfo   4, 12, 39, 56–9, 126, 199
torus   170
totality   109–10
Trade Unions and the Labour Relations (Consolidation) Act 1992   121 n.12
Trotsky, Leon   77
Trump, Donald   159–60
Turner, Cara Livingston   17
Tyler, I.   191

underlaboring
  CRT   114–16
  social class   116–18
unionism   142–5
United Kingdom   97–8; *see also* Britain
United States   97–8, 159–61
  anti-racist movements in   189
  Black Lives Matter movement in   161
  capitalism in   207–8
  caste system   178–9
  charter schools   38
  class arguments, limits of   166
  color blindness, countering of   165–6
  Covid-19 pandemic in   160–1, 213–14
  critical legal studies in   59, 190–3
  critical race theory in   4–5, 7–8, 12, 54–65, 159–68, 186–9, 190–2
  education in   100–1
  experiential knowledge, value of   166
  Hampton-Tuskegee model   175
  injustice of meritocracy   166
  president election in   160–1
  racism endemic in   165
  White problem in   163–5
  white racial frame in   162–3
  white supremacy in   161
unseriousness   114
US Chamber of Commerce   19

Victorian middle classes   150
violation, logic of   107–9
violence   104, 107–8, 138, 161, 163–5, 168, 180, 202
  anti-colonial theories of   107–8
Virdee, Satnam   11, 39, 70–1, 96, 150, 158, 193

Wacquant, L.   191
wage of whiteness   33–4
Wallerstein, I.   97
Walmart   22
Walton family   9
Warmington, P.   197–8
Waterhouse, Benjamin   22
Weatherford, J.   180
Webber, J. R.   116–17
Weber, Max   118
Wehr, Kevin   144

West, Cornell 71
What's Race Got to Do with It? (Picower and Mayorga) 10
Wherry, L. R. 213
white capital 33
whiteness 12, 60–1, 109, 114–15, 126–7, 157, 159–68
white problem 163–5
white racial frame 34, 157, 162–3
white racial knowledge 163–5
white supremacy xviii–xx, 7, 11, 59–61, 70–1, 108, 126–7, 199
   CRT on 58–61, 159–68
   in education 59–60
   epistemology of 114–15
   globalization of 33
   race-based interpretation 4, 12–13, 137
   social policies of National Party 85
   as systemic phenomena xx
   violence and 163–5
Wilkerson, I. 178–9, 182
Williams, Eric 187

Wilson, W. J. 212, 215
Winant, Howard 4, 49–50
Winfrey, Oprah 11–12
Wolf, Eric 76
Women, Culture, & Politics (Davis) 189–90
Women's Education Equity program 35
Wood, Ellen Meiksins 6, 95, 116, 129
workers exploitation 74
working class 8, 11, 13–18, 25, 31, 33–4, 39–45, 48–9, 58, 77, 149–50
World Bank 19, 26–8, 33
World Is a Ghetto, The (Winant) 49
World Trade Organization 26
xenoracism 62

Xicana/person of color 136

Yancy, George xix
Yosso, T. J. 159

Zavala, M. 137–8
Zedong, Mao 77
Zuckerburg, Mark 28

www.ingramcontent.com/pod-product-compliance
Ingram Content Group UK Ltd.
Pitfield, Milton Keynes, MK11 3LW, UK
UKHW021905220326
469204UK00008B/191